CRITICAL SURVEY OF LONG FICTION

Spanish Novelists

Editor

Carl Rollyson
Baruch College, City University of New York

SALEM PRESS
Ipswich, Massachusetts • Hackensack, New Jersey

Cover photo:
Miguel de Cervantes (© Stefano Bianchetti/Corbis)

Copyright © 2012, by Salem Press, A Division of EBSCO Publishing, Inc.
All rights in this book are reserved. No part of this work may be used or reproduced in any manner whatsoever or transmitted in any form or by any means, electronic or mechanical, including photocopy, recording, or any information storage and retrieval system, without written permission from the copyright owner. For information, contact the publisher, EBSCO Publishing, 10 Estes Street, Ipswich, MA 01938.

978-1-4298-3698-2

CONTENTS

Contributors iv

Spanish Long Fiction 1
Leopoldo Alas 27
Pío Baroja 39
Juan Benet 49
Vicente Blasco Ibáñez 60
Camilo José Cela 73
Miguel de Cervantes 87
Miguel Delibes 98
José María Gironella 107
Emilia Pardo Bazán 114
Ramón Pérez de Ayala 128
Benito Pérez Galdós 142
Ramón José Sender 165
Miguel de Unamuno y Jugo 175
Juan Valera 186
Ramón María del Valle-Inclán 203

Bibliography 217
Glossary of Literary Terms 220
Guide to Online Resources 232
Category Index 237
Subject Index 239

CONTRIBUTORS

Cynthia A. Bily
Adrian, Michigan

David K. Herzberger
Original Contributor

Barbara L. Hussey
Original Contributor

Alfred W. Jensen
Original Contributor

Charles L. King
Original Contributor

Grove Koger
Boise State University

Rebecca Kuzins
Pasadena, California

Carol S. Maier
Original Contributor

Charles E. May
California State University, Long Beach

Laurence W. Mazzeno
Alvernia College

Jeremy T. Medina
Original Contributor

Harold K. Moon
Original Contributor

Janet Pérez
Original Contributor

Jack Shreve
Original Contributor

Armand E. Singer
Original Contributor

Gilbert Smith
North Carolina State University

David Allen White
Original Contributor

SPANISH LONG FICTION

The prose form that eventually came to be called the novel has always been the least precisely defined of literary genres. For that reason, it is difficult to assign a beginning to the history of the novel in Spanish literature. Most of the prose of the Middle Ages and much of that written during the eighteenth century does not fit very well into the category of long fiction of which the nineteenth century realistic novel is the synthesis. Poetry could be defined—at least until the advent of the experimental poetry of the twentieth century—as a literary form in which the language is ordered through rhyme and meter, and drama is identified by the fact that it is intended for live presentation on a stage. The characteristics that make a work of prose "novelistic," however, have eluded most attempts at precise identification.

The history of the novel in Spain is the history of a form that is constantly new, or "novel." The shape of that history is determined to some extent by a concern for the purpose of the novel, which is really a concern for the effect of the novel on the reader. Throughout the development of long fiction in Spain, as in many other Western cultures, reading for pleasure was considered an idle and potentially dangerous pursuit and reading for edification an admirable pastime. The novel was subjected to a process of more or less subtle censorship by the official institutions of society, which tended to make it justify itself as something other than pure entertainment, as something useful. This social phenomenon is most obvious in the case of the masterpiece of Spanish fiction, Miguel de Cervantes' *Don Quixote de la Mancha* (1605, 1615), but it is manifest even in the earliest extant imaginative prose writing in Spain, the exemplum literature of the thirteenth century.

EARLY DIDACTIC FICTION

The first examples of exemplum prose fiction—probably translations or adaptations of Arabic works—include *Calila e Dimna* (c. 1251; *Calila and Dimna*) and the *Libro de los engaños e los asayamientos de las mujeres* (c. 1253; *Book of Women's Wiles and Deceits*, 1882). The propagation of these early didactic works was facilitated by the increase in the manufacturing of paper in Spain during the thirteenth century and the invention of eyeglasses toward the end of it. This exemplum literature belongs to the tradition of short fiction because of its form—collections of brief prose pieces, each serving as an example of appropriate or inappropriate social conduct—but it presages some of the characteristics of the longer prose forms that eventually evolved into the novelistic form of the seventeenth century and after. As the titles of some of these collections indicate—the anonymous *Libro del consejo e de los consejeros* (early 1200's; book of advice and advisers) and the *Libro de los exemplos del Conde Lucanor y de Patronio* (1328-1335; *Count Lucanor: Or, The Fifty Pleasant Stories of Patronio*, 1868) of Juan Manuel (1282-1348)—the exempla are linked together by a fictional device involving the relationship of central characters: usually an older, wiser counselor who tells the stories to a naïve, inexperienced person for whom the counselor is in some way responsible. Although the "short stories" that form the text may be unrelated to one another, they are unified by the presence and concerns of the teacher and the student.

The collections of exemplary literature were important antecedents of the novel in that the history of long fiction is replete with examples of a great diversity of experience portrayed in a single work, synthesized into a unified narrative through some point of reference, such as one character, locale, or theme. The obviously didactic intent, which often seems to be only a necessary justification for the "idle pleasure" of reading ingenious, sometimes satiric stories, is another characteristic that the novel inherited from medieval prose literature. The tendency toward a more imaginative fictional representation was evident throughout the fourteenth and early fifteenth centuries, culminating in *El Arcipreste de Talavera*, commonly known as *El corbacho* (1498, written 1438; first three parts as *Little Sermons on Sin*, 1959), of Alfonso Martínez de Toledo (1398-c. 1482), who held the position of archpriest of Talavera, and in the work of Diego de San Pedro, a late fifteenth century writer about whom almost nothing is known. His sentimental novels of courtly love, which include the *Tratado de amores de Arnalte y Lucinda* (c. 1481; *Arnalte and Lucenda: A Certayne Treatye Most Wyttely Devysed Orygynally Written in the Spaynysshe*, 1543) and the *Cárcel de amor* (1492; *The Castell of Love*, c. 1549), were precursors of the pastoral and chivalric fiction of the sixteenth century.

CHIVALRIC AND PASTORAL ROMANCES

The advent of a long fictional form that resembled in some ways the modern novel occurred only after the invention of movable type in the late fifteenth century. Although there are two significant examples of adventure fiction in the early 1300's—the *Libro del caballero Zifar* (book of the knight Zifar) and the *Gran conquista de Ultramar* (the great overseas conquest)—the sixteenth century was the first period of extensive dissemination of long prose works. Some of this fiction was from the late fifteenth century, but the large, diverse audience that was the prerequisite for the development of the modern novel did not exist until the advent of printing made books accessible to less than wealthy readers.

The most popular works of fiction were, unquestionably, the romances of chivalry. The primary source of the Spanish version of the Arthurian legend was *Amadís de Gaula* (*Amadis of Gaul*, partial translation, 1567, 1803), originally in Portuguese and widely circulated in manuscript during the fourteenth century, then revised about 1492 by Garci Rodriguez de Montalvo (c. 1480-c. 1550), who published it in 1508. It was so popular that it had been reprinted thirty times by 1587. In the sixteenth century, there appeared a total of twelve books about Amadis and his descendants, including Montalvo's *Las sergas de Esplandián* (c. 1510; *The Sergas of Esplandián*, 1664), *Amadís de Grecia* (sixteenth century; *Amadis of Greece*, 1694), *Lisuarte de Grecia* (1514; *Lisuarte of Greece*, 1652) by Feliciano de Silva (c. 1492-1558), *Palmerín de Oliva* (1511; *Palmerín d'Oliva*, 1588), and *Primaleón* (1512; *Primaleon of Greece*, 1595-1596). The great popularity of the romances of chivalry is evident in the records of the number published and the frequent attempts by the government to ban their publication. The histories of the perfect knights and the rigid codes of honor and courtly love were evidently out of touch with the actual experiences of the readers but surely embodied some important aspiration or truth for the sixteenth century. The romances of chivalry presented an ideal world of absolutes that surely seemed to be more manageable than the vagaries of actual everyday experience.

The pastoral romances, which achieved a popularity almost equal to that of the romances of chivalry, presented an equally ideal world, one based on the Neoplatonic concept of cosmic love as the controlling force of the universe. The reflection of this universal love in the chaste relationship of perfect lovers and the vicissitudes of those who love unwisely dominated novels such as *Los siete libros de la Diana* (c. 1559; *The Seven Books of Diana*, 1596), by Jorge de Montemayor (1520-1561), and *Primera parte de Diana enamorada* (1564; *First Part of Enamored Diana*, 1598), by Gaspar Gil Polo (c. 1519-1585). The pastoral novels were not only representations of shepherds stricken by love but also somewhat polemical as they expounded various humanistic theories about the nature and effects of true love. Miguel de Cervantes (1547-1616) contributed to the genre with *La Galatea* (1585; *Galatea: A Pastoral Romance*, 1833) and continued until his death to promise that he would produce a second part of this successful story. The first two novels of the most important and prolific dramatist of the time, Lope de Vega y Carpio (1562-1635), were in the pastoral mode: *La Arcadia* (1598) and *Los pastores de Belén* (1612; the shepherds of Bethlehem).

Chivalric and pastoral fiction represented an evasion of reality, in that their portrayal of experience was based on an idealized concept of the world. Their appeal was in part a result of the fact that, even though they were not what could be called realistic, they did deal in some way with the real concerns of the reading public—honor, love, and suffering—and in part because those concerns were portrayed in the exotic contexts of heroic exploits and peaceful, bucolic settings. Even more exotic was the subject matter of the Byzantine novel, which often took the form of a Moorish novel and experienced a period of popularity in the sixteenth century. The most successful was the anonymous *Historia de Abindarráez y Xarifa*, more commonly known as the *Historia del Abencerraje y la hermosa Jarifa* (three versions, in 1561, 1562, and 1565; history of the Abencerraje and the beautiful Jarifa) or simply the *Abencerraje*, which narrates a story of love and chivalry in the context of Christian-Moorish conflicts along the Andalusian frontier during the retaking of Spain from the Moors. Another significant example of this genre was the widely read historical novel by Ginés Pérez de Hita (c. 1544-c. 1619), *Las guerras civiles de Granada* (1619, written 1595-1597; *The Civil Wars of Granada*, 1803).

La Celestina and the picaresque

Throughout the sixteenth century, the development of long fiction took two directions. Paralleling the novelistic prose that portrayed the world in the idealistic terms of the chivalric, pastoral, and Byzantine modes was a type of fiction more firmly based on the truth of sixteenth century experience. The earliest example is one of the masterpieces of Spanish literature, first published anonymously in 1499 as the *Comedia de Calisto y Melibea* (comedy of Calisto and Melibea). It reappeared several years later in a series of expanded versions titled *Tragicomedia de Calisto y Melibea* (1502; *Celestina*, 1631), in which there was textual evidence that the author of at least the major part of the work was Fernando de Rojas (c. 1465-1541). The printers of the novel changed the title to *La Celestina* because of the popularity of the main character, an earthy old woman who uses her skills of witchcraft to further her professional reputation as a go-between. It is a story of the passionate love of Calisto and Melibea, doomed to failure by the circumstances of their birth. Some critics have called *La Celestina* the first novel in Spanish, because it portrayed characters from all social classes in a more realistic manner than did the romances, which tended to idealize and perfect the world that they created.

La Celestina became a very popular work, and the name of the old witch, Celestina, entered the lexicon of Spanish as the generic term for a go-between or pimp. Throughout the sixteenth century, there were imitations of *La Celestina* and examples of prose fiction influenced by Rojas's work that presented a fairly realistic portrayal of certain baser aspects of sixteenth century life. A surprisingly frank and erotic account of the life of a prostitute appeared in the *Retrato de la lozana andaluza* (1528; *Portrait of Lozana, the Lusty Andalusian Woman*, 1987), by Francisco Delicado (c. 1480-c. 1534), a priest who published in the following year a treatise on a supposed cure for syphilis, a disease from which he himself suffered.

The sixteenth century work of fiction that had perhaps the greatest impact on the development of the European novel was *La vida de Lazarillo de Tormes y de sus fortunas y adversidades*, published anonymously in 1554 and translated into English as *The Pleasant Historie of Lazarillo de Tormes* (1576; commonly known as *Lazarillo de Tormes*). His work was the first example of what later was called the picaresque novel, the fictional biography (or often, as in this case, autobiography) of a parasitic delinquent. Lazaro, the picaro who narrates his own story, rises above his miserable surroundings by serving a series of masters, using all of his cunning and wit to survive in a cruel society. As he changes from a child to an adult, he accumulates the experience of sustained contact with a deceptive world and becomes as cynical and dishonest as the people who have exploited and mistreated him. *Lazarillo de Tormes* is extraordinary for its brutal satire and comic narrative, particularly in the context of the prevailing literary vogue of heroic chivalric adventures, courtly conduct, and pastoral love.

Lazarillo de Tormes continued the tradition of social realism established by *La Celestina*, and part of that realistic portrayal of society was its consideration of the nature of honor—whether it is something intrinsic or something acquired through conduct. In the later manifestations of the picaresque genre, the theme of honor became more important and often was related to the more specific question of *limpieza de sangre* (purity of blood), a concern central to the plot of *La Celestina*. Particularly after the expulsion or forced conversion of the Jews in 1492 and the Muslims in 1502, purity of blood became a significant question. To be a *converso* (convert, or New Christian) was to be a second-class citizen, barred from positions of public prominence and respect and often harassed and mistreated. Because of the implication that, if honor was inherited and dependent on the purity of Christian blood, a *converso* was not honorable, the theme of intrinsic or acquired honor represented an actual, socially conditioned anxiety of the time.

The concern over discovery of questionable ancestry and the pursuit of recognition of one's honor pervades the satiric exposure of society's hypocrisy that emerges from the texts of the picaresque novel. *La vida y hechos del pícaro Guzmán de Alfarache* (part 1, 1599, part 2, 1604; *The Rogue: Or, The Life of Guzman de Alfarache*, 1622; also known as *The Life and Adventures of Guzman d'Alfarache: Or, The Spanish Rogue*; best known as *Guzmán de Alfarache*), by Mateo Alemán (1547-c. 1614), is the fictional autobiography of a reformed delinquent who, because he has established himself as a respectable citizen, can moralize about Original Sin and redemption as he narrates his devilish escapades. Significant examples of the picaresque novel with innovative variations appeared well into the seventeenth century. The *Libro de entretenimiento de la pícara Justina* (1605; *The Life of Justina, the Country Jilt*, 1707) of Francisco López de Úbeda (died 1620) uses the picaresque form as a thinly veiled satire of the Spanish court. *La hija de Celestina* (1612; *The Hypocrites*, 1657), by Alonso Jerónimo de Salas Barbadillo (1581-1635), was primarily an exploitation of the genre, an entertainment without the moralizing overtones.

In 1618, Vicente Espinel (1550-1624) published a pseudo-picaresque novel, the *Relaciones de la vida del escudero Marcos de Obregón* (*The History of the Life of the Squire Marcos de Obregón*, 1816), which tells the episodic adventures not of a delinquent, but of a respectable man. In the *Segunda parte de la vida de Lazarillo de Tormes, sacada de las crónicas antiguas de Toledo* (1620; *The Pursuit of the Historie of Lazarillo de Tormes*, 1622), Juan de Luna (c. 1590-c. 1650) used the picaresque genre as an attack on the clergy and the Inquisition. The most enduring of the genre, after *The Pursuit of the Historie of Lazarillo de Tormes*, was the *Historia de la vida del Buscón llamado don Pablos* (1626; *The Life and Adventures of Buscón, the Witty Spaniard*, 1657), written by one of the most extraordinary poets of the seventeenth century, Francisco Gómez de Quevedo y Villegas (1580-1645). The history of Don Pablos, a disadvantaged young man who longs to be a gentleman, is an example of the picaresque returning to the witty, humorous narrative of grotesque brutality that characterized *Lazarillo de Tormes*. There is an implicit didacticism in the constant punishment that Don Pablos suffers for trying to move from his lower social class to the more respectable station of the nobility. The tradition of the picaresque novel is, in fact, a continuation of the tradition of the early didactic prose, the exemplum literature of the thirteenth century, another manifestation of the tendency to justify literature as something other than pure entertainment or art.

The motifs of satire and social criticism of the picaresque novel were also evident in other forms of fiction during the sixteenth and seventeenth centuries. *El crotalón* was a satiric dialogue in the style of Lucian (second century C.E.), written and circulated in 1553 (though not published until 1871), which bore the pseudonym Christóphoro Gnósopho and has been attributed to the Erasmian writer Cristóbal de Villalón (c. 1500-1558). Quevedo published a series of *Sueños* (1607-1622; *The Visions of Dom Francisco de Quevedo Villega*, 1667), witty, conceit-filled satires of social types in the form of extravagant hallucinations, and Baltasar Gracián (1601-1658) created a monumental allegorical narrative of prudence, optimism, and pessimistic disenchantment with the world in *El criticón* (1651-1657; *The Critick*, 1681). *El diablo cojuelo* (1641; the lame devil, published in English as *Le Diable Boiteux: Or, The Devil upon Two Sticks*, 1741) of Luis Vélez de Guevara (1579-1644) was an extensive panorama of Spanish society, as were the less successful but more satiric works of the prolific novelist Francisco Santos (c. 1617-c. 1697), which include *Día y noche de Madrid* (1663; day and night in Madrid) and *El arca de Noé y campana de Belilla* (1697; Noah's ark and Belilla's bell). In 1632, Lope de Vega y Carpio produced *La Dorotea* (the story of Dorotea), an autobiographical novel in dialogue influenced by the realistic portrayal of characters in *La Celestina* that deals with the illusions and disillusionment of love and the emptiness of a life restricted to the pursuit of sensual pleasures.

MIGUEL DE CERVANTES

The life of Cervantes fell in the two centuries of the Spanish Golden Age, the sixteenth and seventeenth. The publication of his monumental *Don Quixote de la Mancha* was a culmination of the previous trends of prose fiction in Spanish and a point of departure for the novelistic works not only of the remaining years of the Golden Age but also of the prose literature of the eighteenth century. Examples of all the significant forms of fiction that had developed by 1600 are found in Cervantes' writing. His *Galatea* is a pastoral romance. The picaresque as well as reflections of the early didactic tales appear in the collection of his short novels, the *Novelas ejemplares* (1613; *Exemplary Novels*, 1846), while *Los trabajos de Persiles y Sigismunda* (1617; *The Travels of Persiles and Sigismunda: A Northern History*, 1619) is a Byzantine novel. The chivalric tradition is the foundation of *Don Quixote de la Mancha*, but this vast panorama of Spanish life and literary tradition contains interpolated, self-contained stories that represent all of these styles of literature. *Don Quixote de la Mancha*, in fact, is a work of fictional literature that deals directly with fictional literature and its relationship to real, historical experience. It is a culmination of the tendency to regard literature as serving some motive other than pleasurable entertainment, yet it is as much a satire of that tendency as a restatement of the conviction that literature does—and perhaps should—influence its audience in an edifying manner.

The emphasis on literature and its audience is clear in the basic presuppositions of the history of Don Quixote—that his insanity is the result of reading too many chivalric romances and that his assuming the role of a knight errant is the result of his interpreting the romances as history rather than fiction. The episodes with moralizing commentary of Don Quixote and his squire Sancho Panza are reminiscent of the early exemplum literature but are rendered ironic by the insanity of the counselor and the shifting of roles of the knight and the squire as teacher and student. This vast and complex novel seems to be concentrated on a theme of the fickleness of human perception, but it is in fact an exploration of the nature of reality and the various illusions to which humans succumb in the course of their ambitious quest for respectability, honor, or mere survival.

The history of Don Quixote is, above all, the narrative of a continual process of experiencing the world as it really is, a slow disintegration of idealistic visions, both optimistic and pessimistic, of the world. *Don Quixote de la Mancha* is unquestionably what it has been called by numerous critics, the first modern novel. The astounding diversity of motifs and perspectives present in the narrative signify a radical departure from all the previous forms of prose fiction. While the pastoral, the chivalric, the picaresque, the Byzantine, and the sentimental novel begin with presuppositions or postulates about the nature of reality and are developed, for the most part, according to those a priori convictions, Cervantes' novel is an exploratory text that develops independent of any fixed notion about the nature of reality or the strictures of a particular literary genre.

Although *Don Quixote de la Mancha* has often been described as a satire of the romances of chivalry, it is more accurate to interpret the novel as a satire of the tendency to regard an idealistic concept of reality as a valid model for human conduct. Don Quixote believes that the codes and rituals of chivalry are viable in his historical reality. The humorous satire of the text derives from the futility of transferring that fictional vision to his real experience. In his prologues and his novel, Cervantes creates characters who proclaim that *Don Quixote de la Mancha* was written with the intent of destroying the influence of the romances of chivalry. Throughout the seventeenth and eighteenth centuries, that claim of authorial intent was repeated in hundreds of critiques, imitations, and adaptations of Cervantes' novel. It is more likely that the popularity of the literature of chivalry and the fact that there were many nobles who actually performed chivalric rituals as a form of entertaining, idle pastime provided Cervantes with a theme that would be at once ridiculous and credible, and provide an incomparable opportunity to develop the dichotomy of appearance and reality that forms the unifying concept of his novel. As he proclaimed the efficacious intent of his work, Cervantes was also exploiting the commonplace notion of the potentially pernicious effect of idle reading and participating in the tendency to justify literary art by its usefulness.

Because of the widespread success of *Don Quixote de la Mancha*, there were many imitations. One of the most interesting and significant cases occurred before Cervantes had completed the second part, which was published in 1615. In 1614, someone published the *Segundo tomo del ingenioso hidalgo Don Quixote de la Mancha* (*A Continuation of the Comical History of the Most Ingenious Knight, Don Quixote de la Mancha*, 1705) under the pseudonym Alonso Fernández de Avellaneda. Most critics have judged this spurious second part, commonly referred to as the "false Quixote," to be inferior to Cervantes' work and to be a ridiculous, unimaginative attempt at Cervantine satire. Understandably, Cervantes was furious and even included a critique of the false Quixote in his own second part.

The Eighteenth Century

Although *Don Quixote de la Mancha* had considerable influence in the seventeenth century, the most significant manifestations of the impact of Cervantes' work on Spanish literature appeared during the Enlightenment, along with evidence of the influence of Quevedo and Gracián. That these three writers were emulated during the eighteenth century is understandable, for it was the supreme age of social criticism and the last great attempt in European culture to renovate society according to rational principles. It was a time of supreme optimism, in which intellectuals were convinced that, through judgment, insight, and good taste, a perfect world could be established. Thus, Quevedo and Gracián, as social satirists, were appealing enough to be imitated by Diego de Torres Villarroel (1693-1770) in his satiric fantasy of life in Madrid, the *Visiones y visitas de Torres con Don Francisco de Quevedo por la corte* (1727-1728; visions and visits of Torres with Don Francisco de Quevedo in the court). Cervantes was also attractive as the writer who, according to the generally accepted critical judgment of the century, had single-handedly driven out a contemporary social evil, the romances of chivalry.

Many writers prefaced their works with comments about Cervantes' accomplishment and the promise that they would do the same—eradicate some flaw of society through a judicious satire. The most notable examples were Francisco de Isla (1703-1781) and José Cadalso (1741-1782). Isla's voluminous *Historia del famoso predicador Fray Gerundio de Campazas, Alias Zotes* (part 1, 1758, part 2, 1770; *The History of the Famous Preacher Friar Gerund de Campazas, Alias Zotes*, 1772) is a satiric attack on the extravagant preachers of the day, whose sermons were so filled with ingenious conceits and convoluted language that no one understood much of what they said. Cadalso's major work was the *Cartas marruecas* (1789; Moroccan letters), a collection of letters exchanged among a young Moor living in a Christian household in Spain, his Moorish mentor in Morocco, and the Christian host. The epistolary work has no significant evidence of Cervantine influence, but Cadalso's preface compares his attempt to improve society through social criticism to Cervantes' intent.

There is a paucity of significant eighteenth century Spanish novels, for the Spanish Enlightenment was primarily an age of the essay, didactic poetry, and exemplary drama. The most interesting form of prose literature was a hybrid form, a type of essayistic prose work that made use of novelistic devices such as the portrayal of imaginary characters who represented more or less obviously real people or fictional characters from the Spanish literary tradition. It was an age of polemics, and much of the "essayistic fiction" was pointedly didactic and argumentative, often witty and ingenious in its direct attacks on certain individuals. Most of the major writers of the second half of the century engaged in the literary exchanges, though most did so through poetry or short prose pieces. The two most significant examples of works that can be termed novelistic in the context of the literary values of the period are *Los literatos en cuaresma* (1773; writers during Lent), by the poet and fabulist Tomás de Iriarte (1750-1791), and *Los gramáticos: Historia chinesca* (c. 1783; the grammarians: a Chinese history), a fierce attack on Iriarte and his entire family, by Juan Pablo Forner (1756-1797).

Of the more traditional novelists, the notable examples were Pedro de Montengón y Paret (1745-1824), who wrote sentimental historical novels, and José Mor de Fuentes (1762-1848), whose epistolary novel *El cariño perfecto: O, Los amores de Alfonso y Serafina* (c. 1795; perfect affection, or the love of Alfonso and Serafina) continued the Renaissance literary tradition of praise of country life and scorn of the court.

Romanticism and *Costumbrismo*

During the early years of the nineteenth century, few novels were published in Spain; in part, this was a consequence of a particularly strong expression of the recurring idea that prose fiction is immoral and detrimental to its readers. Indeed, the government attempted, with some success, to suppress the publication of novels. In spite of an official ban on translated fiction, a Valencia publishing house began in 1816 to publish a collection of novels that introduced foreign novelists to the ever-growing Spanish reading public.

The Romantic influences prevalent during the 1820's and 1830's resulted in a spate of historical novels, some written by the outstanding literary figures of the Spanish Romantic movement. The dramatist Francisco Martínez de la Rosa (1787-1862) published his historical novel *Doña Isabel de Solís, Reyna de Granada* in parts from 1837 to 1846. One of the finest Romantic poets, José de Espronceda (1808-1842), developed the typical Romantic themes of spiritual vacuity and despair over the failure of love in *Sancho Saldaña* (1834). Mariano José de Larra (1809-1837), the satiric essayist whose suicide and funeral rallied the Romantic writers to a proclamation of unity against a disapproving Establishment, published *El doncel de don Enrique el doliente* (1834; the squire of Sir Henry the Sufferer). The best of the historical novels appeared several years after a strong ideological reaction to Romanticism had set in. *El Señor de Bembibre* (1844; *The Mystery of Bierzo Valley: A Tale of the Knights Templars*, 1938), by Enrique Gil y Carrasco (1815-1846), is unusual because of its strong evocation of a regional Leonese setting and its development of the conflict between traditional values and the Romantic despair that results from a loss of faith in the moral, religious, and intellectual beliefs that formed those values. There were also hundreds of historical novels published by lesser-known writers such as Wenceslao Ayguals de Izco (1801-1873), Francisco Navarro Villoslada (1818-1895), and Manuel Fernández y González (1821-1888), who, in spite of their popularity, never gained the attention of literary scholarship.

Particularly popular during the Romantic period and the remainder of the nineteenth century were the *novelas por entregas*, or *folletines*, serialized novels that appeared either in magazines or in separate installments that were sold a chapter at a time. The most striking feature of early nineteenth century historical fiction and the serial novels was the apparent indifference to a careful, convincing portrayal of physical reality; this is the feature that also distinguished this fiction from the literary tradition of works such as *La Celestina*, *Lazarillo de Tormes*, and *Don Quixote de la Mancha*, as well as from post-1850 fiction. More in the tradition of fiction based on preconceived notions about the nature of reality and experience—the tradition of the pastoral and the chivalric romance—the nineteenth century historical novel did not contribute significantly to the development of the novel as an artistic form until the advent of the most notable novelist of the century, Benito Pérez Galdós (1843-1920).

A major influence on the novel at midcentury was the importation of the French novels of Eugène Sue (1804-1857), six of which were translated and published in 1844 alone. Sue's novels inspired in Spanish writers an interest in a different type of historical novel, one that dealt with recent events and propagated social and political ideas. Significant examples were Ayguals's *María: O, La hija de un jornalero* (1845-1846; Mary, or the daughter of a day laborer) and *Misterios de las sectas secretas: O, El francmasón proscrito* (1847-1852; mysteries of secret sects, or the proscribed Freemason) by José M. Riera y Comas (1827-1858).

The more careful observation of recent historical reality evident in these novels had a parallel in another type of fiction that pervaded the middle years of the century—the *costumbrista* literature. The popular *costumbrista* sketches portrayed specific "authentic" aspects of everyday life in Spain in precise detail and often with a nostalgic attitude toward the quaint, typical customs that were disappearing with the advance of the modern world. The *costumbrista* tradition influenced two important novelists who began publishing in the mid-nineteenth century, Fernán Caballero (pseudonym of Cecilia Böhl von Faber, 1796-1877) and Pedro Antonio de Alarcón (1833-1891). Fernán Caballero is an unusual case in the history of Spanish fiction. Usually credited with preparing the way for the important realistic novelists of the second half of the century, she wrote her novels in German or French and had them translated for publication by her agent. She was best known for *La gaviota* (1849; *The Sea-Gull: Or, The Lost Beauty*, 1867), which is typical of all of her novels, moralizing and somewhat sentimental, superficially descriptive in the tradition of the *costumbrista* sketches.

Alarcón was an aggressive proponent of the conservative Catholic point of view. Except for his delightful, whimsical *El sombrero de tres picos* (1874; *The Three-Cornered Hat*, 1886), which inspired the ballet by the Spanish composer Manuel de Falla (1876-1946) and is reminiscent of the exemplum literature of the Middle Ages and the *Exemplary Novels* of Cervantes, his novels are rather severely ideological. *El final de Norma* (1855, wr. 1850; *Brunhilde: Or, The Last Act of Norma*, 1891), *El escándalo* (1875; *The*

Scandal, 1945), and *El niño de la bola* (1880; *The Child of the Ball*, 1892; also known as *The Infant with the Globe*, 1959) are attacks on irreligion, immorality, and the liberal ideas that were prevalent during Alarcón's career. *La pródiga* (1882; *True to Her Oath: A Tale of Love and Misfortune*, 1899) is a more interesting novel; it narrates the story of a woman's illicit sexual behavior and suicide, stimulated by an idealized Romantic attitude toward love.

Realism

The triumph of the nineteenth century "liberal" movement in Spain, the September Revolution of 1868, which dethroned the Bourbon monarchy and led to the establishment of the short-lived republic in 1873, was a turning point in the history of the novel. The aspirations, problems, and anxieties of Spanish society were, rather suddenly, appropriate material for narrative fiction, and the decade of the 1870's was fertile ground for the thesis novel, a type of fiction in which the theme seems to unduly determine the structure, characterization, and plot development. It was also the decade of intense interest in the idealism of the German philosopher Karl Christian Friedrich Krause (1781-1832). The intellectual movement appropriately called Krausism, which emphasized a harmony of the spiritual and the rational and stressed principles of liberal education, led to the establishment in 1876 of the Institución Libre de la Enseñanza (Free Institute of Teaching) by Francisco Giner de los Ríos (1839-1915), a disciple of the Spanish intellectual leader Julian Sanz del Río (1814-1869), who was in turn a student and disciple of Krause. Krausism had a considerable, if temporally limited, effect on the novelists of the period, such as Juan Valera (1824-1905) and Pérez Galdós, whose novel *El amigo Manso* (1882; *Our Friend Manso*, 1987) is a disenchanted portrayal of a Krausist professor. During the 1870's, Pérez Galdós established himself as a significant novelist with the thesis novels that would bring him extensive recognition as an enemy of religious and social intolerance—*Doña Perfecta* (1876; English translation, 1880), *Gloria* (1876-1877; English translation, 1879), and *La familia de León Roch* (1878; *The Family of León Roch*, 1888).

In contrast to Pérez Galdós's liberalism, which was moderate but impressive for its contrast to prevailing social attitudes, the regional novels of José María de Pereda (1833-1906), published during the 1870's, are characterized by a reinforcement of traditional values and institutions, as in *Los hombres de pro* (1872; the supporters), *El buey suelto* (1877; the freed ox), and *Don Gonzalo González de la Gonzalera* (1878). Pereda went on to write the most widely read novelistic accounts of provincial life in Spain, characterized by a *costumbrista* nostalgia and idealism about rural society—*El sabor de la tierruca* (1881; the smell of the land), *Sotileza* (1884; English translation, 1959), and *Peñas arriba* (1895; atop the mountain). Pereda's fiction had an enormous appeal for its own kind of exoticism, the life of the simple country people, but his lack of detached, objective narrative rendered his fiction less significant to the development of the dominant trend of nineteenth century fiction—realism—in spite of the astounding wealth of descriptive details in his novels.

A more significant novelist was Juan Valera (1824-1905), who began his career with *Pepita Jiménez* (1874; *Pepita Ximenez*, 1886), an elegant, refined, and subtle work that in less judicious hands would have been a blatant thesis novel. His later works, which include *Las ilusiones del doctor Faustino* (1875; *The Illusions of Doctor Faustino*, 2008), *Doña Luz* (1879; English translation, 2002), *Juanita la larga* (1896; English translation, 2006), and *Genio y figura* (1897; spirit and form), presented idealized studies of the difficulties of love and the emotional frustrations resulting from the conflict between worldliness and spirituality.

The other novelist of the time who, with Valera, Alarcón, and Pérez Galdós—for *Pepita Ximenez*, *The Three-Cornered Hat*, and *Doña Perfecta*—gained considerable recognition in Europe and the United States was Armando Palacio Valdés (1853-1938). The less familiar novels of Palacio Valdés were more significant to the development of nineteenth century fiction than the immensely popular *Marta y María* (1883; *The Marquis of Peñalta*, 1886), *José* (1885; English translation, 1901), and *La hermana San Sulpicio* (1889; *Sister Saint Sulpice*, 1890). *La espuma* (1891; *The Froth*, 1891) and *La fé* (1892; *Faith*, 1892) are innovative novels of social and religious protest with fantastic elements that imply political symbolism.

The most significant novelists of the century were, unquestionably, Emilia Pardo Bazán (1851-1921), Clarín (pseudonym of Leopoldo Alas, 1852-1901), and Benito Pérez Galdós. Pérez Galdós was the literary giant of the century, for the quantity and sustained quality of his fiction, while Clarín's reputation and importance as a major novelist rested on a single, monumental work, *La regenta* (1884; English translation, 1984). Although Emilia Pardo Bazán produced many novels that were widely read and continues to gain the somewhat qualified respect of literary scholarship, she was most influential for her activities as a literary critic and her rather outrageous public image. A robust woman who smoked cigars in public and alienated many with her feminist ideas and outspoken manner, Pardo Bazán was the first writer in Spain to publish commentaries on French naturalism—*La cuestión palpitante* (1883; the burning question)—and was instrumental in creating widespread interest in the nineteenth century Russian novelists. While she praised the literary talent of Émile Zola (1840-1902), she condemned the impersonal, scientific observation characteristic of his naturalistic fiction. She proposed instead a balance of naturalistic and idealistic fictional motifs, a sort of hybrid ideological approach that was the perspective, if not the theory, of the realists.

Pardo Bazán's pronouncements were considered rather scandalous, and her novels were equally offensive to the conservative establishment. *La tribuna* (1883; *The Tribune of the People*, 1999) portrays the struggles of a young woman caught in the unpleasantries of urban working-class life. *Los pazos de Ulloa* (1886; *The Son of the Bondwoman*, 1908; also known as *The House of Ulloa*, 1992) and *La madre naturaleza* (1887; mother nature), her best-known novels, are somewhat idealized portraits of lusty, earthy conflicts between the idle aristocracy and the greedy, rural working class. The themes of sometimes illicit sexual behavior and class conflicts dominate *Insolación* (1889; *Midsummer Madness*, 1907) and *Morriña* (1889; *Morriña: Homesickness*, 1891), but in the later novels, such as *La quimera* (1905; the chimera) and *La sirena negra* (1908; the black siren), Pardo Bazán's perspective shifted to one of more conservative and religious ideology.

The career of Clarín was also established primarily through his activities as a literary critic, but his personality was more serene and his public image more that of an intellectual, humanistic spokesman for the liberal consciousness. Except for his elegant and moving narrative *Su único hijo* (1890; *His Only Son*, 1970), Clarín's only novel was *La regenta*, a vast panorama of life in a provincial capital developed around the interior conflict of Ana Ozores, a young woman married to a much older man and tempted by her sexual attraction to her priest and the local playboy. Clarín's judicious and subtly satiric portrait of the manners and mores of Spanish society is rivaled in excellence and perceptivity only by the *novelas contemporáneas* of Pérez Galdós.

Benito Pérez Galdós

Since the death of Pérez Galdós in 1920, the general reading public of Spain has been more familiar with his historical novels, the *Episodios nacionales* (1873-1912; national episodes), than with his realistic novels of contemporary urban society, the *novelas españolas contemporáneas* (contemporary Spanish novels), although these have always received more serious attention from scholars. The forty-six *episodios* form a fictionalized history of Spain's recent past, from the Battle of Trafalgar in 1805 to the Restoration of the Bourbon monarchy in 1874. While these are historical novels, they are somewhat unusual in that all the principal characters are fictional personages whose lives are intertwined with historical figures and events to a greater or lesser degree, depending on the particular novel. Throughout the *episodios*, which Pérez Galdós published at the amazing rate of from one to five per year from 1873 to 1879 and again from 1898 to 1912, the recent past is revealed as primarily a struggle between two opposing ideologies, the traditional Carlist point of view and the progressive, liberal ideas that led to the revolution of 1868 and the establishment of the First Republic in 1873. In contrast to the development of the historical novel in Spain and elsewhere, Pérez Galdós's *episodios* are very much a part of the realistic fictional mode that dominated the second half of the nineteenth century. While they are somewhat more ideologically directed than the *novelas españolas contemporáneas*, they lack the nostalgic idealization of the past evident in most historical fiction before Pérez Galdós.

After the thesis novels of the 1870's, which usually are referred to as Pérez Galdós's *novelas de la primera época* (novels of the first period), the novelistic development of Pérez Galdós changed dramatically. With *La desheredada* (1881; *The Disinherited Lady*, 1957), Pérez Galdós began what eventually became an all-encompassing portrait of urban middle-class life in Madrid. The twenty-eighth novel, *Casandra* (1905), is usually considered the end of the series, because Pérez Galdós's last two novels—*El caballero encantado*

(1909; the enchanted knight) and *La razón de la sinrazón* (1915; the reason of non-reason)—are markedly different and so peculiar that they are often disregarded as unfortunate postscripts to a remarkable career.

Pérez Galdós was known for his liberal tendencies, as indicated by the title of the first biography published in English, H. Chonon Berkowitz's *Benito Pérez Galdós: Spanish Liberal Crusader* (1948). The label of liberal, however, must be understood in the context of the last decades of the nineteenth century. Pérez Galdós's novels are not primarily political, and they certainly are not radical in their treatment of middle-class society. They are, rather, fairly objective representations of the established institutions of urban Spain and the amazing variety of human experience that one might expect in such a diversified society. The censure of morally aberrant behavior that is evident in the work of many novelists of the century is replaced by a sympathetic understanding in novels such as *Tormento* (1884; *Torment*, 1952), *Ángel Guerra* (1890-1891), and *Tristana* (1892; English translation, 1961), which was the source of a 1970 film version by the Spanish director Luis Buñuel, who also made a film version of Pérez Galdós's *Nazarín* (1895; the Nazarene) in 1958. In novel after novel, Pérez Galdós exposed with masterfully subtle irony the hypocrisies and foibles of the middle class.

Whether he was portraying the unfortunate plight of a mediocre bureaucrat fired from his job with only months to go before acquiring a retirement pension in *Miau* (1888; English translation, 1963) or the excruciating task of a pretentious housewife trying to solve the riddle of bourgeois society—how to get away with spending ten times what one earns—in *La de Bringas* (1884; *The Spendthrifts*, 1951), Pérez Galdós maintained a congenial and benevolent narrative voice. Through his consummate ability to give the impression that his narrative is more objective than it in fact is, Pérez Galdós creates characters who reveal themselves as they really are. The variety and complexity of their aspirations, of their admirable spirit or deplorable lack of it, of their naïveté or cynical wisdom are evident in all of Pérez Galdós's contemporary novels, but more so in his two longest works, *Fortunata y Jacinta* (1886-1887; *Fortunata and Jacinta: Two Stories of Married Women*, 1973) and the Torquemada cycle (published in English translation as *Torquemada* in 1986)—*Torquemada en la hoguera* (1889; *Torquemada in the Flames*, 1956), *Torquemada en la cruz* (1893; *Torquemada's Cross*, 1973), *Torquemada en el purgatorio* (1894; Torquemada in purgatory), and *Torquemada y San Pedro* (1895; Torquemada and Saint Peter). The epic history of Fortunata, an earthy, uneducated young woman from the slums of Madrid, and Jacinta, a respectable, middle-class woman, both in love with the same errant playboy, is one of the most extraordinary novels of the European realist tradition. The story of Francisco Torquemada, a moneylender of questionable social origin who establishes himself as a prominent member of the new upper middle class through his financial dexterity and his marriage to an impoverished aristocrat, is in some ways the most important fictional work of Pérez Galdós. At no other point did he explore so thoroughly the essence of the nineteenth century social phenomenon of the dependence of respectability on the acquisition of material wealth. It is significant that Pérez Galdós dominated the development of the realistic novel in the last decades of the nineteenth century, for he created a vast body of fiction that exemplifies all that the realistic tradition in fiction has, in retrospect, been judged to represent—an artistic creation through which the varied truths of nineteenth century urban existence are revealed.

Generation of '98

At the beginning of the twentieth century, several nineteenth century novelists, such as Pérez Galdós, Pardo Bazán, and Palacio Valdés, were still active, and there were others whose principal work retained the tone and the concerns of the late nineteenth century. Vicente Blasco Ibáñez (1867-1928), after the enormous success of naturalistic novels such as *La barraca* (1898; *The Cabin*, 1917) and *Cañas y barro* (1902; *Reeds and Mud*, 1928), turned to the anti-German wartime novels that became popular in Spain and abroad—*Los cuatro jinetes del Apocalipsis* (1916; *The Four Horsemen of the Apocalypse*, 1918) and *Mare Nostrum* (1918; English translation, 1919). The ultraconservative Catholic novelist Ricardo León (1877-1943) continued the tradition of the thesis novel with *Casta de hidalgos* (1908; *A Son of the Hidalgos*, 1921) and *El amore de los amores* (1917; *The Wisdom of Sorrow*, 1951), and Concha Espina de la Serna (1877-1955) published *La esfinge maragata* (1914; *Mariflor*, 1924) and *El metal de los muertos* (1920; the metal of the dead), novels characterized by an unusual combination of subjective sentimentality and social protest in response to the deplorable conditions of the life of the working classes.

While these and other novelists cultivated a wide reading public, the prose fiction that is recognized as of extraordinary importance was produced by another group of writers, many of whom formed a sort of informal literary alliance that came to be called the Generation of '98. These novelists, poets, dramatists, and essayists held two things in common—their attempts at innovation in their literary work and a concern for the regeneration of Spain after the humiliating defeat suffered in the Spanish-American War in 1898. The second of these concerns—the quest for a rebirth through a spiritual awakening and an affirmation of authentic, individual values—was the subject of much essayistic and journalistic writing, and it passed into the fiction of the period, usually as a subtle ideological base rather than as an overt expression. A concurrent movement in Spanish American literature that cultivated a conscious aestheticism through radical innovations in prose and poetry, *Modernismo*, was related to the artistic concerns of the writers of the Generation of '98 and had considerable influence on their search for innovative expressive forms.

Certain novelists of the period, such as Miguel de Unamuno y Jugo (1864-1936), Pío Baroja (1872-1956), Azorín (pseudonym of José Martínez Ruiz, 1873-1967), and Ramón Pérez de Ayala (1880-1962), were clearly participants in the ideological and artistic Generation of '98, according to the three following prerequisites aptly defined by the British Hispanist Donald L. Shaw:

participation in a personal quest for renewed ideals and beliefs; interpretation of the problem of Spain in related terms, i.e., as a problem of mentality, rather than as political or economic and social; and acceptance of the role of creative writing primarily as an instrument for the examination of these problems.

The other major novelist of the time, Ramón María del Valle-Inclán (1866-1936), seemed disinterested in the "Spanish problem," although the satiric observation of Spanish society in many of his works indicates that his interest was greater than suggested by the lack of direct, soul-searching statements that characterize the novels, plays, poems, and essays of other writers of the Generation of '98. Valle-Inclán's interest was primarily aesthetic, however, and his first important novels, the four exotic *Sonatas*—*Sonata de primavera* (1904; spring sonata), *Sonata de estío* (1903; summer sonata), *Sonata de otoño* (1902; autumn sonata), and *Sonata de invierno* (1905; winter sonata), which were published together in English as *The Pleasant Memoirs of the Marquis de Bradomín: Four Sonatas* (1924)—show a marked influence of *Modernismo* in their apparent indifference to questions of morality and their emphasis on the development of pure aesthetic artifice. Valle-Inclán's later novels, notably *Tirano Banderas: Novela de tierra caliente* (1926; *The Tyrant: A Novel of Warm Lands*, 1929) and *El ruedo ibérico* (1927-1958; the Iberian arena)—*La corte de los milagros* (1927; the court of miracles), *Viva mi dueño* (1928; long live my master), and *Baza de espadas* (serialized 1932, published 1958; spade trick)—present a bitter censure of all levels of Spanish society, both rural and urban, through an aesthetic distortion achieved by a systematic deformation of the characters and the milieu. This type of fictional narrative, which Valle-Inclán called earlier in his career the *esperpento* (distorted mirage), anticipated the *tremendismo* of the post-Spanish Civil War novel initiated by Camilo José Cela (1916-2002).

Azorín, who adopted his pseudonym from the name of the protagonist of his early novel *La voluntad* (1902; the will), was obsessed for a short period with the problem of the struggle between thought and action, a major preoccupation of the Generation of '98. *La voluntad* develops the alternatives of acceptance of nihilism or resignation to the Nietzschean doctrine of eternal recurrence. The anguish of *La voluntad* became a quiet resignation mixed with nostalgia for the past in *Antonio Azorín* (1903) and *Las confesiones de un pequeño filósofo* (1904; confessions of a little philosopher). In later novels, such as *Don Juan* (1922; English translation, 1923) and *Doña Ines* (1925), the emphasis remained on a frustrated resignation in the face of time and its destructive power. The last novels of Azorín, written after 1927, were experimental departures from the traditions of realism, but they are generally regarded by critics as being more ambitious than successful.

The most astounding novelist of the early twentieth century, for the sheer volume of his work if not for its artistic accomplishment, was Pío Baroja, whose more than fifty novels form a fictional document of modern Spanish society equaled only by the novels of Pérez Galdós. Baroja is indeed a curious case. From 1901, the year of his first significant novel,

La casa de Aizgorri (the house of Aizgorri), to his last novels in the 1950's, his novelistic technique and the ideological bases of his work remained essentially unchanged. The style is simple, direct, and unadorned by the aesthetic mannerisms that characterize at least some of the work of almost every major twentieth century novelist. The ideological vision is clear throughout his work, and on it is founded his early trilogy *La lucha por la vida* (1904; *The Struggle for Life*, 1922-1924)—*La busca* (1904; *The Quest*, 1922), *Mala hierba* (1904; *Weeds*, 1923), and *Aurora roja* (1904; *Red Dawn*, 1924). Life is a struggle for survival, and only the fittest survive through the only remedy that exists for the inevitable *abulia*, or lack of will—individual action, action without aim, finality, or social implications of any kind. Any hint of meaning in life, any emotion—love, for example—is simply a *mentira vital* (vital lie) that enables the individual to bear the truth of the lack of meaning in the world. The intellect destroys illusions, as Sacha realizes in *El mundo es ansí* (1912; the world is thus), and action is the only alternative to the paralysis of the will that leads to the disillusionment and suicide of Andrés Hurtado in *El árbol de la ciencia* (1911; *The Tree of Knowledge*, 1928).

Baroja wrote what at first seems to be a variety of fiction—adventure novels, historical novels, biographical and autobiographical fiction—but his approach scarcely changed as he moved from one to the other. Some are dominated by narrated action, and some are made up almost entirely of conversations in which his characters reveal their own manifestations of the conflict of the intellect and the emotions. Baroja's strongest trait is his ability to evoke a sense of the physical atmosphere through a careful choice of details. It is perhaps not surprising that Baroja had many admirers, including Cela, who asserted that the entire twentieth century Spanish novel stems from Baroja, and Ernest Hemingway (1899-1961), who declined the invitation to serve as a pallbearer at Baroja's funeral, claiming to be unworthy of the honor.

The truly monumental figure of the Generation of '98 was Miguel de Unamuno y Jugo, essayist, poet, dramatist, philosopher, philologist, and novelist. Partly because of the enormous prestige that he had acquired by the first years of the twentieth century, he was unofficially designated as the father of the Generation of '98. After his first attempt at fiction, *Paz en la guerra* (1897; *Peace in War*, 1983), his novels represented an extraordinary break with the realist tradition of the nineteenth century and embodied the spiritual and ontological anguish that characterized much of the work of the early twentieth century Spanish writers, as well as the existentialist writings of French authors such as Jean-Paul Sartre (1905-1980) and Albert Camus (1913-1960). The scene in *Niebla* (1914; *Mist*, 1929) in which the despairing hero Augusto Pérez confronts the author Unamuno and asserts his independence from him is frequently cited as an important precursor of the techniques of the Italian playwright Luigi Pirandello (1867-1936). This scene is equaled in its fantastic and ridiculous but serious implications only by the novel's prologue, written by another character in the novel, Víctor Goti, who calls Unamuno a liar, and by the epilogue, written by Augusto Pérez's dog.

This "game of fiction," as Unamuno's narrative tricks have been called, has serious existentialist implications that Unamuno continued to explore in *Abel Sánchez: Una historia de pasión* (1917; *Abel Sánchez*, 1947), a fascinating version of the Cain and Abel story. It is a complex history of ontological envy, developed through a simple, straightforward narrative interspersed with fragments of Joaquín's (Cain's) confessional journal and a suggestion that the entire story is a novelistic text written by Abel's son. Unamuno further questioned existence and its relationship to fictional characters in the strange, autobiographical *Cómo se hace una novela* (1927; *How to Make a Novel*, 1976) and *La novela de don Sandalio, jugador de ajedrez* (1930; the novel of Don Sandalio, chess player). Unamuno's last novel, which is in a sense a fictionalization of *Del sentimiento trágico de la vida en los hombres y en los pueblos* (1913; *The Tragic Sense of Life in Men and Peoples*, 1921), his famous treatise on the conflict of faith and reason, was *San Manuel Bueno, mártir* (1931; *Saint Manuel Bueno, Martyr*, 1956). Again Unamuno plays with fiction in a Cervantine fashion, as the novel, which is the confessional memoir of a young woman who suspects that her priest does not believe in eternal life, turns out to be a manuscript found by a fictionalized Unamuno who claims to have only edited it for publication. Unamuno's fiction was a radical departure from the realist tradition, for at almost no point did it attempt to objectively portray contemporary historical reality. It did, however, transform the novel into what it would be throughout much of the twentieth century, a means of investigating and reflecting on the question of human existence.

Ramón Pérez de Ayala, like Unamuno, began his career with a novel in the realist tradition, *Troteras y danzaderas* (1913; trotting and dancing around), and then began to experiment with more innovative narrative devices. His *Prometeo, Luz de domingo, La caída de los Limones: Tres novelas poemáticas de la vida española* (1916; *Prometheus, Sunday Sunlight, The Fall of the House of Limón: Three Poematic Novels of Spanish Life*, 1920) are not poetic in the usual sense, but grotesque, brutal distortions of the literary legends of Prometheus and Odysseus (*Prometheus*), of the daughters of the Spanish epic hero El Cid (*Sunday Sunlight*), and of the Spanish conquistadores (*The Fall of the House of Limón*). *La pata de la raposa* (1912; *The Fox's Paw*, 1924), *Belarmino y Apolonio* (1921; *Belarmino and Apolonio*, 1931, 1990) and, to a lesser extent, the 1923 novel published in two parts, *Luna de miel, luna de hiel* and *Los trabajos de Urbano y Simona* (published together in English translation as *Honeymoon, Bittermoon*, 1972), create complex situations of varied perspectives on single realities. The two final novels of Pérez de Ayala, published in 1926, *Tigre Juan* and *El curandero de su honra* (combined in English translation as *Tiger Juan*, 1933), are generally considered to be his finest accomplishments. As a restatement in Freudian terms of the story of Don Juan and the theme of honor and sexual fidelity so pervasive during the Golden Age, these novels are further manifestations of Pérez de Ayala's penchant for creating fiction from the legends and classics of early Spanish literature.

Three other novelists, contemporaries of the writers of the Generation of '98 but lacking achievements as substantial as those of Unamuno, Baroja, and Azorín, were Gabriel Miró (1879-1949), Ramón Gómez de la Serna (1888-1963), and Benjamín Jarnés (1888-1949). Miró's reputation among literary scholars has grown over the years, but his refined aestheticism and his refusal to turn his novels into topical studies of the "Spanish problem" limited the popular appeal of his work in the early part of the twentieth century. Much of his prose work consisted of collections of short pieces, and his novelistic production was limited to four penetrating psychological novels about the complexities of human behavior, *Las cerezas del cementerio* (1910; the cherries of the cemetery), *El abuelo del rey* (1915; the king's grandfather), *Nuestro Padre San Daniel* (1921; *Our Father San Daniel*, 1930), and *El obispo leproso* (1926; *The Leper Bishop,* 2008), in which Miró evoked the experience of provincial life in Spain in an elegant narrative style.

Gómez de la Serna, quite in contrast to Miró, created for himself a significant reputation as the creator of the *greguería*, a form of epigrammatic statement made up of witty, surprising, and often trivial metaphors. Some of his novels, such as *El doctor inverosímil* (1914; the unbelievable doctor), seem to be little more than collections of *greguerías*, and only his novel about the relationship of the game of fiction to human existence, *El novelista* (1923; the novelist), is of particular interest. Eight of his novellas were published in English translation under the title *Eight Novellas* in 2005. Jarnés was a much more substantial novelist, with an ideological perspective that recalls Unamuno and an elegant, elaborately cultivated style similar to Miró's. There is much introspective concern in his texts for the creative act of narrative observation and for the meaning of existence. Jarnés's unconventional narrative techniques in novels such as *Locura y muerte de nadie* (1929; madness and death of a nobody) and *Teoría del zumbel* (1930; theory of the top-string) made his work too esoteric for a general audience. His later work—*Lo rojo y lo azul: Homenaje a Stendhal* (1932; the red and the blue: homage to Stendhal) and *Venus dinámica* (1943; dynamic Venus)—is more conventional, with a more traditional approach to plot and characterization.

The Civil War and the Franco era

The Spanish Civil War (1936-1939), a bloody conflict between the conservative Nationalists and the liberal Republican forces that led to the establishment of the dictatorship of Francisco Franco (1892-1975), had an extraordinary effect on the history of the twentieth century Spanish novel. Many of the outstanding literary figures went into exile and produced their most important novels in countries other than Spain. Also, the war experience became the material with which the novel dealt, in much the same way that the social malaise resulting from the disaster of 1898 had become the subject matter for novels in the early part of the century.

The two novelists who established themselves most successfully as representatives of postwar fiction are Camilo José Cela (1916-2002) and Juan Goytisolo (born 1931). Cela's *La familia de Pascual Duarte* (1942; *The Family of Pascual Duarte*, 1946, 1964) initiated the literary vogue of *tremendismo*, a pessimistic cultivation of the shocking, grotesque aspects of human experience. A later novel, *La colmena* (1951; *The Hive*, 1953), portrays the wretchedness of life in postwar Madrid through multiple narrative perspectives. Goytisolo's early novels, *Juego de manos* (1954; *The Young Assassins*, 1959) and *Fiestas* (1958; English translation, 1960), attacked the repression and psychological deprivation of Franco's Spain in a conventional narrative style typical of social realism. His principal contribution to the innovative postwar novel is his trilogy of exile—*Señas de identidad* (1966; *Marks of Identity*, 1969), *Reinvindicación del conde Don Julián* (1970; *Count Julian*, 1974), and *Juan sin tierra* (1975; *John the Landless*, 1975). The first of the trilogy is a fictionalized autobiographical account of the exile's return to Barcelona that makes use of diverse narrative techniques and multiple points of view but remains a rather conventional novel for its time. The second and third novels of the trilogy, however, are bitter, grotesque experimental narratives that attempt to convey an overwhelming repulsion and an obsession with the destruction of every traditional value of society. Over the course of his career, Goytisolo has published more than two dozen works of fiction. His later novels include *La saga de los Marx* (1993; *The Marx Family Saga*, 1999) and *Carajicomedia: De Fray Bugeo Montesino y otros pája de vario plumaje y pluma* (2000; *A Cock-Eyed Comedy: Starring Friar Bugeo Montesino and Other Faeries of Motley Feather and Fortune*, 2002).

Other postwar novelists experimented with narrative techniques, conveying an equally pessimistic view of Spanish society in a less shocking way than Goytisolo. *El Jarama* (1956; *The One Day of the Week*, 1962), by Rafael Sánchez Ferlosio (born 1927), and *Tiempo de silencio* (1962; *Time of Silence*, 1964), by Luis Martín-Santos (1924-1964), are portraits of Spanish society that are made up of fragmented, anecdotal mosaics, examples of a kind of social realist subject matter transformed through experimental narrative devices.

Luis Goytisolo (born 1935), the brother of Juan Goytisolo, first attracted critical attention with *Las afueras* (1958; the suburbs), a novel that portrays postwar Catalonia in terms of the contradictory forces at work in the economic and class structures of society. Gonzálo Torrente Ballester (1910-1999), a professor of history and literature and well-known drama critic, produced an impressive series of successful novels beginning with *El señor llega* (1957; the master comes), many of which are unusual narratives about the process of novelistic invention. For his most ambitious and successful work, *La saga/fuga de J. B.* (1972; the legend/flight of J. B.), Torrente Ballester won the coveted Crítica Prize, only one of many literary awards that he received during his career.

José María Gironella (1917-2003) and Miguel Delibes (born 1920), two novelists who remained in Spain during and after the wartime experience, represent two very different trends in fiction. Gironella's epic war trilogy—*Los cipreses creen en Dios* (1953; *The Cypresses Believe in God*, 1955), *Un millón de muertos* (1961; *One Million Dead*, 1963), and *Ha estallado la paz* (1966; *Peace After War*, 1969)—is among the most widely read accounts of the Spanish Civil War. Delibes is a less popular novelist, but he is respected for his elegant style, his sympathetic portrayal of the simple, natural life of the country, and the gradual evolution of his work. *El camino* (1950; *The Path*, 1961) is a charming story of rural society. *Mi idolatrado hijo Sisí* (1953; my beloved son Sisí) is a cynical but delicate satire of middle-class aspirations. *Cinco horas con Mario* (1966; *Five Hours with Mario*, 1988) is an experiment in interior monologue, and *Parábola del náufrago* (1969; *The Hedge*, 1983), a technically innovative allegorical fantasy. *El hereje* (1998; *The Heretic*, 2006) is a dense historical novel that is built out of dialogue rather than narrative.

Some of the best postwar fiction was produced by a group of novelists who were adults at the time of the war and remained in exile after 1939. Ramón José Sender (1902-1982), the only one of these to achieve wide recognition, produced a vast amount of fiction beginning with the appearance of his first successful novel, *Imán* (1930; *Earmarked for Hell*, 1934; also known as *Pro Patria*, 1935). Sender's work is characterized by an Unamunian preoccupation with the meaning of human existence. In novels such as *Crónica del alba* (1942-1966, 3 volumes; *Before Noon*, volume 1, 1957) and *La esfera* (1947, 1969; *The Sphere*, 1949), published first in 1939 as *Proverbio de la muerte* (proverb of death) and subsequently published in an expanded version with the new title, he achieved a distinctive fusion of realistic and fantastic techniques.

Antonio Barea (1897-1957), Francisco Ayala (born 1906), and Max Aub (1903-1972), the other exiled novelists of considerable significance, did not match the volume of work that Sender produced, nor did they enjoy his success. Barea's *La forja de un rebelde* (1941-1944; *The Forging of a Rebel*, 1941-1946) is a fictionalized autobiographical memoir of the prewar and war years in Spain. Ayala, a prolific novelist as well as a short-story writer, created a brutal, cruel portrait of life in a fictional Spanish American republic in *Muertes de perro* (1958; *Death as a Way of Life*, 1964) and its sequel, *El fondo del vaso* (1962; the bottom of the glass). Ayala's *El jardín de las delicias* (1971; the garden of delights), the source of the 1970 film by the Spanish director Carlos Saura (born 1932), is a dazzling display of novelistic art, a mosaic of references to the painting by Hieronymus Bosch (1450-1516) that forms the narrative of the psychic suffering of a twentieth century industrialist left paralyzed after an automobile accident.

The most esoteric of these novelists was the avant-garde writer Max Aub. His cycle of novels about the war experience, *El laberinto mágico* (1943-1968; the magic labyrinth), is a complex tapestry of fragmented characterizations and conversations that together form an interpretation and analysis of the psychological manifestations of wartime experience. Aub's most unusual work is *Jusep Torres Campalans* (1958; English translation, 1962), a painstakingly detailed biography of a fictitious artist and friend of Picasso. As if following the tradition of Unamuno, Aub evoked through this "biography" questions of the relationship between art and life.

During the late 1940's and the 1950's, a new generation of novelists began to emerge who were dedicated to a neorealist fictional mode as a means of exploring the nature of the human condition, particularly as it is manifested in a repressive society. Ignacio Aldecoa (1925-1969), author of *El fulgor y la sangre* (1954; lightning and blood), was an active stimulus to this revival of the novel through his journalistic criticism and his association with other writers such as Sánchez Ferlosio, Jesús Fernández Santos (1926-1988), Juan Goytisolo, José Luis Castillo Puche (1919-2004), and Carmen Martín Gaite (1925-2000).

A striking feature of the period after the Spanish Civil War was the unusual number of women who established themselves as successful novelists. In 1944, Carmen Laforet (1921-2004) won the prestigious Nadal Prize for her neorealist novel of tedium and repression, *Nada* (English translation, 1958). The prominence achieved by Laforet, Martín Gaite, Dolores Medio (1911-1996), and Ana María Matute (born 1926), whose *Primera memoria* (1960; *School of the Sun*, 1963) also was awarded the Nadal Prize, is a significant phenomenon, given the disadvantaged position of women during the Franco era. Of these writers, Martín Gaite has received the most lasting and serious attention from critics for works such as *El balneario* (1954; the spa), *Ritmo lento* (1963; slow rhythm), and *El cuarto de atrás* (1978; *The Back Room*, 1983), *La reina de las nieves* (1994; *The Farewell Angel*, 1999), and *Lo raro es vivir* (1996; *Living's the Strange Thing*, 2004).

While this group of women novelists enjoyed considerable success, the Spanish novel of the 1970's and 1980's was dominated by men, particularly Juan Goytisolo, Juan Marsé (born 1933), and Juan Benet (1927-1993)—the novelist who, according to some critics, established the new direction in fiction evident in Goytisolo's *Count Julian* and in Delibes's *The Hedge*. Benet's trilogy consisting of *Volverás a Región* (1967; *Return to Región*, 1985), *Una meditación* (1970; *A Meditation*, 1982), and *Una tumba* (1971; a tomb) is the complete antithesis of the realist tradition of Pérez Galdós and the neorealist tradition of the postwar novel. The narrative style is so difficult that the work seems almost unintelligible at first, though the identity of the characters and the details of the plot begin to emerge toward the end of the first novel through various techniques that reveal the text as an exaggerated evocation of memory. Marsé's first success was *Últimas tardes con Teresa* (1966; last afternoons with Teresa), a kind of "suburban" novel characterized by a blend of psychological and objective realism. The irony of Marsé's tone, however, limits the novel's tendency toward social realism. Marsé also attracted considerable critical attention for *Si te dicen que caí* (1973; *The Fallen*, 1976), a narrative of ambiguous accounts of the war years woven into the details of social existence in postwar Spain, and for *El embrujo de Shanghai* (1993; *Shanghai Nights*, 2006) and *Rabos de lagartija* (2000; *Lizard Tails*, 2003). He won the Cervantes Prize in 2008.

As the dictatorship ended with the death of Francisco Franco in 1975, the Spanish novel gradually ceased to be a discourse concentrated on a response to the circumstances of life under the existing totalitarian regime. It became, rather, primarily a consideration of the various forces at work in society as the post-Franco struggle for power began to take shape.

The Novel after Franco

The Spanish novel from 1950 to the end of the Franco regime in 1975 was dominated by two significantly different trends that have characterized the novel throughout its history. The neorealist mode is a continuation of the attempt of prose fiction to create an aesthetic experience that parallels the varied experiences of historical, "real" human existence. The other trend, represented by the diverse textual experimentation of the more innovative novelists such as Juan Goytisolo and Benet, represents the attempt to portray the authentic nature of human experience more effectively through a nontraditional narrative.

These two tendencies in prose fiction continued to be apparent in the novel after 1975, but there is evidence of a preference for a less complex narrative style. One of the manifestations of this trend is the emergence of a significant number of novelists working in the genre of detective or crime fiction. The first novel of Eduardo Mendoza (born 1943), *La verdad sobre el caso Savolta* (1975; *The Truth About the Savolta Case*, 1992), is an example of the genre, as are many of the novels of Lourdes Ortiz (born 1943), Benet's *El aire de un crimen* (1980; scent of a crime), and *Visión del ahogado* (1977; a drowned man's vision), by Juan José Millás (born 1946). Manuel Vázquez Montalbán (1939-2003) cultivated the genre with a series of novels about his fictional hero Pepe Carvalho, a bodyguard for U.S. president John F. Kennedy turned detective. Among his many novels of this type, all characterized by a perverse sense of humor unusual in the Spanish fiction of the period, are *Yo maté a Kennedy* (1972; I killed Kennedy), *Los mares del sur* (1979; *Southern Seas*, 1986), and *El delantero centro fue asesinado al atardecer* (1988; *Offside*, 1996).

Many of the novelists who established themselves before and during the Franco era continued to publish in the period after 1975. Cela's *Mazurka para dos muertos* (1983; polka for two dead people) and Delibes's *Los santos inocentes* (1981; the innocent saints) are evidence of the continued vitality of the older writers. Cela won the Nobel Prize in Literature in 1989, "for a rich and intensive prose, which with restrained compassion forms a challenging vision of man's vulnerability." The principal novelists of the 1960's and 1970's, such as Juan and Luis Goytisolo, Benet, Marsé, and Martín Gaite, continued to enjoy considerable success and enhanced their reputations as significant figures in the history of the Spanish novel.

In the last decade of the twentieth century and the beginning of the twenty-first, decisive changes were occurring in the novel, not so much in terms of narrative form as in ideology. After the end of the Franco era, the principal discourse of the novel gradually ceased to be a dialogue with the social forms that thrived under the totalitarian regime. It became instead a response to the emerging ideological factions of the new democratic society. The younger novelists, such as Lourdes Ortiz, Rosa Montero (born 1951), Antonio Muñoz Molina (born 1956), Esther Tusquets (born 1936), and Terenci Moix (1943-2003), produced numerous novels that explore the influences of popular culture and the various conflicting ideologies (sexist, fascist, communist, capitalist) that shaped Spanish society in the late twentieth century. Muñoz Molina, who resides in the United States, set *Beltenebros* (1989; *Prince of Shadows*, 1993) in post-Civil War Madrid. After he moved to New York, several of his works were published in English translation, including *Beatus ille* (1986; *A Manuscript of Ashes*, 2008), set near the end of Franco's dictatorship; *El invierno en Lisboa* (1987; *Winter in Lisbon*, 1999), about a jazz pianist; *Sefarad* (2001; *Sepharad*, 2003), whose narrator is a man in Madrid nostalgic for the village in which he grew up; and *En ausencia de Blanca* (1999; *In Her Absence*, 2006), about a Spanish civil servant.

Tusquets is a leading feminist voice in Spanish fiction, and her work is marked by powerful images of female and lesbian sexuality. *El mismo mar de todos los veranos* (1978; *The Same Sea as Every Summer*, 1990), the first novel in a trilogy, was one of the first Spanish lesbian novels. The protagonist in *Para no volver* (1985; *Never to Return*, 1999) is a straight middle-aged woman undergoing psychoanalysis. In *Con la miel en los labios* (1997; with honey on the lips), Tusquets depicts the struggles of student activists and lesbians during the last years of Franco's rule. Catalan writer Moix, a self-educated anarchist, published eleven novels, most of them criticizing oppression under Franco, especially as experienced by gay men. His works have sold millions of copies in Spain, but he has remained virtually unknown outside the country. His best-known works include *No digas que fue un sueño* (1986; say not that it was a dream) and *El amargo don de la belleza* (1996; the bitter gift of beauty).

From its beginning, Spanish prose fiction has portrayed the circumstances of human existence in terms of the surrounding reality and the predominant ideological perspectives of the period in which it was created. The novelistic narrative of the late twentieth century period was characterized by considerations of issues that were suppressed either by official governmental actions or by societal taboos during the earlier years of the century. The novel of this era posed questions about concepts of gender, homosexuality, psychoanalysis, and the dominant power structures of society, questions that often were presented in terms of the conflict between the prevailing ideologies of Francoist Spain and those gaining prominence in the Spain of the new democracy. Prose fiction continues to be marked by the opposing tendencies that have characterized the genre from its beginning, the struggle between realist representation and various experimental, innovative modes of portraying the world. In its diversity of form and its singularity of purpose—the representation of human experience—the complex genre of linguistic and literary art that is the novel in Spain is heir to the tradition of Cervantes.

Gilbert Smith
Updated by Cynthia A. Bily

BIBLIOGRAPHY

Charnon-Deutsch, Lou. *Gender and Representation: Women in Spanish Realist Fiction*. Philadelphia: J. Benjamins, 1990. Significant study addresses the sexual polarization of nineteenth century Spanish society and the patriarchal values and ideologies of gender inscribed in the fictional discourses of the major novelists, including José María de Pereda, Juan Valera, Clarín, and Benito Pérez Galdós.

Close, Anthony. *The Romantic Approach to Don Quixote*. New York: Cambridge University Press, 1978. Critical overview that had considerable repercussions in Hispanic studies. Presents a general discussion of the Romantic interpretation of *Don Quixote de la Mancha*, from the time of the Romantic movement through the realist period, the Generation of '98, and twentieth century criticism.

Dunn, Peter N. *Spanish Picaresque Fiction: A New Literary History*. Ithaca, N.Y.: Cornell University Press, 1993. Significant work by a prominent Hispanist presents a study of the reading public and the cultural implications of the picaresque form of fiction.

Gies, David Thatcher. *The Cambridge History of Spanish Literature*. New York: Cambridge University Press, 2004. Comprehensive history of Spanish literature covers the years from the early Middle Ages to the early twenty-first century. Includes a chronology of Spanish history, literature, and art.

Gold, Hazel. *The Reframing of Realism: Galdós and the Discourses of the Nineteenth Century Novel*. Durham, N.C.: Duke University Press, 1993. Effective study examines the novels of Pérez Galdós from the perspective of narrative frame theory. Discusses his work in the context of the nineteenth century novel.

Johnson, Carroll B. *Don Quixote: The Quest for Modern Fiction*. Boston: Twayne, 1990. Provides a general introduction to the historical context of Cervantes' novel and the characteristics of the book-reading public of the seventeenth century.

Landeira, Ricardo. *The Modern Spanish Novel, 1898-1936*. Boston: Twayne, 1985. Introductory study covers the period from the Generation of '98 to the beginning of the Spanish Civil War in 1936, including discussion of the works of Vicente Blasco Ibáñez, Miguel de Unamuno y Jugo, Pío Baroja, Ramón María del Valle-Inclán, and Ramón Pérez de Ayala.

Moss, Joyce. *Spanish and Portuguese Literatures and Their Times: The Iberian Peninsula*. Detroit, Mich.: Gale Group, 2002. Analyzes fifty works in about ten pages each, tracing the connections between the works and the political and social contexts in which they were written.

Sánchez Conejero, Cristina, ed. *Spanishness in the Spanish Novel and Cinema of the Twentieth-Twenty-first Century*. Newcastle, England: Cambridge Scholars, 2007. Collection of essays focuses on authors—including Manuel Rico, Juan Goytisolo, and lesser-known writers—whose works explore the meanings of Spanish and Iberian identity.

Schumm, Sandra J. *Reflection in Sequence: Novels by Spanish Women, 1944-1988*. London: Associated University Press, 1999. Examines seven novels whose protagonists struggle for self-realization in a restrictive Spanish society.

Solé-Leris, Amadeu. *The Spanish Pastoral Novel*. Boston: Twayne, 1980. Provides a general introduction to the pastoral novel and the literary tradition of which it is a product, with considerations of the novels of Montemayor, Gil Polo, and Cervantes.

Thomas, Gareth. *The Novel of the Spanish Civil War, 1936-1975*. New York: Cambridge University Press, 1990. Discusses the portrayal of the Spanish Civil War and the conditions of exile in the novels of José María Gironella, Max Aub, Francisco Ayala, Antonio Barea, Castillo Puche, and Ana María Matute. Presents interesting considerations of the propagandistic Republican novel and the process of myth creation in Nationalist fiction.

Turner, Harriet, and Adelaida López de Martinez, eds. *The Cambridge Companion to the Spanish Novel: From 1600 to the Present*. New York: Cambridge University Press, 2003. Collection of essays by a variety of scholars covers the development of the Spanish novel from Cervantes to the modern novelists. Includes a chronology and a bibliography.

LEOPOLDO ALAS

Born: Zamora, Spain; April 25, 1852
Died: Oviedo, Spain; June 13, 1901
Also known as: Leopoldo Enrique García Alas y Ureña; Clarín

PRINCIPAL LONG FICTION
La regenta, 1884 (2 volumes; English translation, 1984)
Su único hijo, 1890 (*His Only Son*, 1970)

OTHER LITERARY FORMS

In addition to two major novels, Leopoldo Alas (AHL-ahs) published more than eighty short stories or novelettes, including "Pipá," "Doña Berta" (English translation), "El sombreto del señor cura," "¡Adiós, Cordera!" (English translation), "Dos sabios," and "Zurrita." Many of these pieces have been collected and republished under such titles as *Cuentos morales* (1896, 1973), *¡Adiós, Cordera! y otros cuentos* (1944), *Cuentos de Clarín* (1954), and *Cuentos escogidos* (1964). Alas's collections of literary and political essays include *El derecho y la moralidad* (doctoral thesis, 1878), *Solos de Clarín* (1881, 1971), *La literatura en 1881* (1882; with Armando Palacio Valdés), *Nueva campaña, 1885-1886* (1887), *Mezclilla* (1889), *Ensayos y revistas* (1892), *Palique* (1893, 1973), and *Galdós* (1912). His only attempt at theater is the play *Teresa* (pr., pb. 1895). An important general compilation of Alas's work is that of Juan Antonio Cabezas, *Obras selectas* (1947, 1966), which includes both of the major novels, twenty-five short stories, and thirty-seven articles.

ACHIEVEMENTS

Leopoldo Alas, frequently known by his pseudonym Clarín, is considered one of the four or five most important figures of nineteenth century Spanish realism, along with Benito Pérez Galdós, Emilia Pardo Bazán, Juan Valera, and José María de Pereda. While Alas was recognized early in his literary career for the excellence of his short stories and for the biting criticism of his essays, he was, like Stendhal, generally misunderstood by his own generation. His fame now rests primarily on his two major and lengthy works, particularly *La regenta*, considered by many critics as the second greatest novel in the Spanish language, after Miguel de Cervantes' *Don Quixote de la Mancha* (1605, 1615). Since the centennial celebration of Alas's birth in 1952, studies of his best short stories and of *His Only Son* have finally brought about a relatively balanced view of his artistic achievements.

Alas was one of the most prolific and certainly one of the most feared of all literary critics in Spain during the second half of the nineteenth century. By the end of his life, he could lash out mercilessly at a mistake in grammar by some aspiring writer or politician and, by a single stroke of the pen, destroy that person's career. With respect to literary ideology, his essays call, above all, for a realism based on exactness of observation and psychological depth, within a moral framework. Alas also was one of the few to insist that his contemporaries inform themselves of literary developments taking place north of the Pyrenees.

Biography

Leopoldo Enrique García Alas y Ureña, the third son of a local civil governor, was born on April 25, 1852, in Zamora, a town some 250 kilometers (155 miles) northwest of Madrid, Spain. At the age of seven, he was sent to the Jesuit *colegio* of San Marcos in León, where he spent several happy months despite the fact that his blond hair, short and slight stature, and myopic vision set him apart somewhat from his schoolmates. It was there that he began to develop both the sentimentality and the sense of moral discipline that were to become so evident in his later thought and writing.

The following summer, Alas and his family moved to the northern city of Oviedo, where he was to spend the rest of his life and which was to be the setting for his masterpiece *La regenta*. While working for his *bachillerato*, he continued to develop an extremely competitive spirit, as he strove to compensate for physical weaknesses by a precocious and inquiring mind. During his fourth year of study, Alas and his classmates were profoundly moved by the revolution of General Juan Prim and its aftermath, and it was during this period that Alas began to contemplate the complexities of social justice and the disillusionments that arise when idealized hopes are dashed by the harsh realities of political life.

At age twenty, Alas was in Madrid, preparing for his doctorate and feeling nervous, melancholy, and increasingly homesick for his native Asturias. A naturally critical temperament and a stubborn reluctance to embrace philosophical or literary fads delayed his acceptance of Sanz del Río's Krausism and the naturalistic approach being preached by Émile Zola, but, as with his subsequent ideological views, once these ideas were accepted, Alas was to defend them with sincerity and passion.

At age twenty-three, Alas began publishing articles in Madrid-based journals, and in October, 1875, he adopted the pseudonym Clarín. The name was chosen perhaps in lighthearted recognition of Pedro Calderón de la Barca's famous gracioso in *La vida es sueño* (1635; *Life Is a Dream*, 1830) or perhaps because of the musical tradition of the time, by which an orchestra might pause to allow for a clear, often moving solo by the clarion, or *clarín*. Alas's barbs soon produced many enemies, and it was not long before he found himself forced to change sidewalks to avoid confrontations; he took to target shooting and fencing lessons in preparation for some inevitable duels.

One immediate result of Alas's critical pen came when the minister of public instruction, one of the figures whom the young writer had derided in print, rejected him for the *cátedra*, or professorship, of political economy at the University of Madrid, despite the youth's having clearly surpassed his competitors in the *oposiciones*. This experience was a bitter lesson in social and political realities, one that would be reflected in the biting satire of *La regenta* and in some of the short stories.

Two years of happiness followed, however, as Alas fell in love with and married Onofre García Argüelles and was awarded two *cátedras*, first in Zaragoza and then, in 1883, at the University of Oviedo. There followed a period of intense writing, with little sleep and but a few mouthfuls of food a day. A feverish creative effort produced the second volume within six months, despite the severe emotional impact of his father's death. Not surprisingly, Alas's health began to fail. Increasingly disillusioned with society, he continued to produce articles exposing truths few wanted to hear. In some areas, his power became immense, as illustrated by the firing of a public official because of Alas's anger at the official's mispronunciation of a single word.

During the summer of 1892, while secluded in his beloved country retreat at Guimarán, Alas suffered a severe mental crisis, but he soon recovered with the rediscovery of the sentimentality and religious contentment of his youth. This change became evident immediately afterward in some of his short stories, particularly "Cambio de luz" and, later, those in *Cuentos morales*. Alas's long resistance to proper medical care finally caught up with him, however, and, overcome by intestinal tuberculosis, he died on June 13, 1901.

Analysis

The realistic novel in Spain arose out of a particular set of historical circumstances and from diverse streams of intellectual growth. These included social and economic factors (the rise of a middle-class, materialistic society, the Revolution of 1868, and the underlying political, religious, and economic corruption of the Restoration period) and scientific influences (positivism, Darwinism, and the Industrial Revolution). They also included philosophical currents (the eighteenth century position that truth can be discovered through the senses and, later, the influence of Krausism), and, most particularly, such literary developments as the influence of and reaction against Romanticism, currents from France (the realism of Honoré de Balzac, Gustave Flaubert, and Stendhal, and Zola's naturalism), and the rediscovery of Cervantine and traditional Spanish realism.

The Spanish realistic novel, particularly as exemplified by Alas, revealed some points of emphasis that differed from the French: a stronger continuity of thought and feeling with previous Romantic tendencies, a more pronounced stress on spiritual and religious matters, a regionalist framework (such as Alas's focus on Asturias and Oviedo), and the constant presence of the Cervantine influence. The last characteristic included the special use of character and authorial perspectives that expose the ambiguity and complexity of reality, a distinctive brand of literary irony, and devices that produce the effect of character autonomy.

Within this general framework, Alas's linguistic refinements and extremely subjective point of view deviated from the slightly more objective approach of many of his own

Spanish contemporaries. Furthermore, while all realistic writers were critical of their environment, Alas, more than most, failed to camouflage his didactic stance. His realism, rather, is to be found in the solidity and extraordinary depth of his major psychological studies, his powers of observation and the resulting exactness of detail, and his intricate play of character-author perspectives. Like most of the major novelists of the second half of the nineteenth century in Spain, Alas evolved somewhat in his later years away from the realistic-naturalistic focus toward a more "idealistic" inspiration. Leo Tolstoy, rather than Balzac or Zola, became the most significant foreign influence during this period. The Asturian writer came to abandon, to an extent, his preoccupation with aesthetic theory and literary novelty in the search for a more transcendent, spiritual, often symbolic approach.

LA REGENTA

La regenta, Alas's first and greatest novel, stands as one of the supreme achievements of nineteenth century realism in Spain and the rest of Europe. In it, one can see a reawakening in the Iberian Peninsula of what György Lukács called the "novel of romantic disillusionment." Certainly, it is one of the most powerful creations of modern psychological realism. In *La regenta*, all of Alas's literary theories were put into effect: A strong, ideological tone and theme provided a framework for exploring psychological motivations; the actualities of contemporary Spanish society are portrayed; and the smallest of details contributes to artistic ends. The work reflects the author's conception of art as an *ancha ventana abierta* (wide-open window), in which Alas the critic could search for justice, Alas the educator could search for truth, and Alas the artist could search for beauty.

The book is many things in one: an autobiography (in its reflection of the author's own personality, culture, ideology, and actual experiences); a regional novel (to the extent that its setting, called Vetusta, is the city of Oviedo); a treatise on national traits, both historical and contemporary; and the greatest of all Spanish "naturalistic" creations. (One must add, immediately, that none of the major realistic novelists in Spain subscribed totally to Zola's concept of philosophical determinism or to full descriptive treatment of grotesque or crude realities.)

Despite the novel's length and complexity, the basic threads of the action can be summarized in a few sentences. In broadest terms, the plot traces the process by which the heroine, Ana Ozores, is drawn into an adulterous relationship with an aristocratic Don Juan, Alvaro Mesía. Conflict arises from Ana's physical attraction to Alvaro, which battles against idealistic, spiritual impulses nurtured by her confessor, Don Fermín de Pas, and natural inclination versus conjugal duty. The rest of the plot is a study of these figures and the behavior of literally hundreds of other characters who inhabit a city plagued by political corruption and social and moral degeneration. Ana's vacillations—the very basis for the action as well as the novel's style and structure—dramatize the need for love, both in the form of human companionship and in what Sherman Eoff has called "a personal and sympathetic relationship with Deity."

Alas's tone, his approach to his characters, and his setting are not "realistically" neutral. The author's own feelings range through sarcasm, criticism, displeasure, hatred, sympathy, derision, and open, light humor. Just as evident, if not as pertinent to the work's artistry, however, are Alas's ideological, utilitarian themes; his condemnation of indifference, narrowness, provincialism, ignorance, pedantry, moral degradation, religious hypocrisy, and political corruption; and his dissection of a city in which, as Michael Nimetz puts it, "sex and religion occupy the same shrine and neutralize each other in the process," thus producing a state of general frustration.

Alas's irony is present everywhere. The many types and variations of ironic comment range from those that are primarily linguistic ("Vetusta, la muy noble y leal ciudad . . . hacía la digestión del cocido y de la olla podrida") to those directed toward characterization, as in descriptions of such minor characters as Don Saturnino; those related to manners or customs of the general population, as in the description of the casino library, where the books are "de más sólida enseñanza" but where "la llave de aquel departamento se había perdido"; and those that present purer, more open humor (as in Don Víctor's reenactments of Calderonian honor plays).

The implied author's actual position—that is, his presence as it relates to the action—can best be described in the words of Frank Durand.

> Alas believed the author (as opposed to a character within the novel) to be best qualified to interpret a character's thoughts, actions, and motivations. . . . Because Alas knows all, the reader not only sees characters through the author's eyes but, entering their consciousness, sees reality through the eyes of the characters themselves. Thus the author's omniscient point of view carries within itself, so to speak, narrower individual points of view. The resultant multiple perspectives serve to delineate the different characters as well as to develop the major themes and the main action of the novel.

At times the author himself is clearly speaking. At other moments, the reader is projected into the thoughts and feelings of the major characters. The judicious combination of these two points of view allows for an extensive as well as an intensive view of the characters and the city, and serves also to maintain a high level of interest throughout an extremely lengthy narrative.

With respect to language, realism is enhanced by the following elements: the inclusion of extremely exact detail, a frequent appeal to the senses, vivid imagery designed to highlight the animal nature of the city and its inhabitants, and a nearly constant sense of theatrical immediacy. Some stylistic traits, however, reveal the author's conscious attempt to draw attention to language itself and thus to rise above realism: the use of reiteration, frequent "extremist" tendencies (antithetical expressions, hyperboles, paradoxes), and authorial allusions (usually ironic) to art or literature.

Much of Alas's realism depends on the creation of what might be called a total atmospheric reality. With the exception of Pèrez Galdós's *Fortunata y Jacinta* (1886-1887;

Fortunata and Jacinta: Two Stories of Married Women, 1973), *La regenta* captures the urban social and physical milieu more completely than any single Spanish work of the nineteenth century. Few modern readers would deny that the novel is too long. The outcome of Ana's story is powerful, however, precisely because the process preceding it goes on for so long. The background descriptions are, at the least, needed for an understanding of the external pressures and the heaviness of the material world that contribute to the denouement. The atmosphere of Vetusta (Oviedo) is in itself a major antagonist in the novel. Above all, the novel's descriptions contribute to the author's central goal: character study, the attempt to reveal the psychological complexity that positivistic naturalism had reduced to a series of systematized formulas. While the secondary figures are meant to represent types, Ana Ozores and Don Fermín de Pas are remarkably real and autonomous.

Several significant methods are used to achieve this depth. Alas reveals his characters from multiple perspectives: To the reader, the characters appear as what they are, what they think they are, and what others think they are. Frequently, actual mirrors are used to dramatize this complex play of perspectives. All the major characters are actors. The reader, also engulfed in so many points of view, tends also to confuse illusion and reality. The result is a sense of the characters' distance and autonomy from authorial control, a Cervantine appearance of verisimilitude. The use of purposeful contrasts and parallels among the major and minor figures—such as de Pas's spiritual motivations versus Alvaro's licentious intentions, Don Víctor's preoccupations versus Ana's troubles, Obdulia versus Visitación, Camoirán or Cayetano versus Mourelo—constitutes another means of making the characters more vivid and more plausible.

Alas traces, carefully and logically, the historical and environmental origins and the subsequent development of Ana's predicament: her need for love and her yearning for a child. The factors presented include the lack of a mother's presence, the frequent absence of her father, the cruelty of her nurse Doña Camila, a frightening night when she is stranded alone on a boat with her childhood playmate, the later treatment she receives from an indifferent father, the hypocrisy and cruelty of her aunts, her escape through a marriage without love, the depressive atmosphere of Vetusta, the plots of Visitación and Alvaro to effect her downfall, and the advice of Don Fermín. Her turn to religion (in the person of her confessor, Don Fermín), of course, thwarts even further her psychological, sexual, and maternal cravings. Ana is an individualistic creation, neither all good nor all evil. An inherent vanity, for example, offsets the purity of her intentions. Nevertheless, she also offers a mixture of traits and perspectives that is definitely representative of the Spanish people: a quixotic "madness," masochistic tendencies, mystical inclinations, the need for love and approval, a strong sense of pride and individuality, and, above all, a romantic, idealistic nature.

The author seems to have had even closer affinity to the personality and aspirations of the other main character. Although Don Fermín's flaws occasionally suggest a symbolic role of evil incarnate (vanity, hypocrisy, cruelty, desire for power), he is, nevertheless, a completely convincing, individualized figure. Conflicting desires for power and for escape from the vulgar existence of Vetusta create many of his frustrations. Dominated from childhood by an overpowering, ambitious mother and lacking, like Ana, the love and affection that go with a normal upbringing, he sees the regenta as a threefold means of achieving his own mental stability and satisfaction: He can help another human being by offering spiritual assistance; he can satisfy his need to dominate; and, unconsciously, he can find sexual release. Ironically, the last two impulses, his desire for conquest and his passion, lead him to forget the wisest means of approach. The first motivation, of course, reveals that he is not entirely evil. In essence, he is an ambiguous creation.

La regenta is thus fundamentally the story of two individuals who are frustrated by their environment and by the absence of love; each is trapped within a social role (wife, priest), and each sees in the other a chance for salvation. Both exemplify vividly the metaphysical conflict between a single perceiving consciousness and the social environment, between aspiration and realization, between illusion and reality—warring factors that constitute the basis of Alas's realism as well as the approach of the Spanish realistic movement in general.

The other characters function mainly in relation to these two figures and exemplify type portraiture: Alvaro as a cowardly and calculating Don Juan, the symbol of *poder laico*; Doña Paula (see María Remedios in Pèrez Galdós's *Doña Perfecta*, 1876; English translation, 1880) typifying the forces of avarice and tyranny; the maid Petra as the marvelous embodiment of what one critic calls "suspicacia y socarronería de personaje de clase popular . . . muy español"; and so on.

Alas's artistry is revealed in many ways that surpass the usual limits of nineteenth century realistic delineation. His use of symbolism (for example, the banquet scene in the casino, which ironically parallels Leonardo da Vinci's depiction of the Last Supper) and meticulous structural planning demonstrate clearly the depth of his originality. With respect to the latter element, such critics as J. I. Ferreras and Durand have analyzed in detail the complicated network of parallels and calculated contrasts, the elements of a "circular" nature and the complex system of flashbacks that constitute the novel's narrative construction.

Contrary to the opinion of many critics, *La regenta* is not a simple example of Zolaesque naturalism. Ana's personality and her downfall are not the direct result of the moral laxity around her; they stem, rather, from her reactions against the city. Her adultery is a kind of triumph of love, possible only after twenty-eight chapters of careful, convincing preparation. The final *desenlace* (conclusion) is brought about by fortuitous circumstances (Petra's actions). Alas is saying that the pressures of the environment are strong and, in fact, may cause changes in a person's life. Yet the instances of free will in *La regenta*, along with the moments of humorous satire mentioned above, illustrate the author's rejection of Zola's sweeping pessimism and the maintenance of a more traditionally Spanish point of view.

In *La regenta*, Alas demonstrates most clearly his own particular version of the Spanish realistic formula. His utilitarian approach, his highly subjective irony and satire, his deliberate artistry in manipulating language—these and other elements reflect the author's conscious rejection of strictly realistic writing. In his usually explicit statement of themes, he departed from the norm of his Spanish contemporaries, yet his attention to exactness and detail, the numerous variations on authorial and character perspective, and the profundity of the novel's psychological studies reveal a true attempt to achieve a complete or total transcription of genuine human conflicts and aspirations.

HIS ONLY SON

If *La regenta* is characterized by the ridicule of provincial customs through carefully detailed description, *His Only Son* reduces society to its most dominating, abstract features: The precise delineation of physical settings and realistic conflicts is replaced by an operatic universe of melodramatic contrivances and the invisible, inner elements of psychological reverie. *His Only Son* is a novel of transition, reflecting the decline of naturalism and the competing influence of various fin de siècle trends: Idealistic, symbolic, and decadent elements combine with a distinctly modern flavor, a purposeful ambiguity that forces the reader to participate more actively in the interpretation of events. Masculine and feminine roles are confused or reversed, the plot exhibits surprising turns of direction, and a more "authentic," alienated protagonist anticipates the problematic hero of the *generación del 98*, or Generation of '98. Its first readers saw the novel as a Zolaesque study of eroticism and physiological needs, and its emphasis on psychology over externality and its very subjective comic vein reveal a distinct divergence from naturalistic practices.

Critics have been particularly perplexed by the work's ambiguity (the time and setting are indefinite, the question of the hero's paternity is left unresolved, and so on), not realizing until years later that Alas was attempting a very Cervantine statement concerning the relativism and lack of clarity of everyday reality. The plot line itself is simple and, in fact, almost insignificant. In a poor, provincial town, Bonifacio Reyes (Bonis), of a family in decline, marries the despotic Emma Valcárcel but soon becomes the lover of Serafina Gorgheggi, a member of an opera company. Emma, amid an atmosphere of corruption and abulia and provoked by the entrance into her house of the Italian singers, becomes involved in an affair with the baritone Minghetti. Eventually, Bonis's main preoccupation turns from the romantic fantasies of his *tertulia* to a fanatic belief in the importance of the family, seeing in the birth of a son ("su único hijo," a phrase from the Apostles' Creed laden with symbolic ramifications) a means of self-redemption.

In the church where the child's baptism is to take place, Serafina avenges her lover's change of heart by claiming that the father is actually Minghetti. As the novel closes, Bonis denies this and quixotically insists that the child is his. The reader is struck by the similarity to the closing of *La regenta* (the protagonist is in a church and, in each case, tormented by rejection), but Bonis's case is more pathetic than tragic. He has been misled by the private cult of the family and fatherhood, not by any kind of Christian mysticism or belief in dogma. If Ana's end demonstrates the double failure of love and an exalted religiosity, the protagonist's downfall here is one of both the romantic ideal and of "la religión del hogar."

Like the characters of *La regenta*, the figures here attempt to project fiction on reality (the *Don Juan Tenorio* play in the first novel, the world of opera here), and in both works a chorus of gossip and *murmuración* provides the ironic backdrop. In *His Only Son*, however, the characters are archetypal, skeletal abstractions, often presented through hyperbolic caricature, in consonance with exaggerated, theatrical melodrama. This is evident in such scenes as Bonis and Serafina's lovemaking, Emma and Bonis's marital crises, and Emma's hysteria and fears of miscarriage. Gone are the positive-negative tensions of *La regenta*, replaced by a general world of resentment in which, by a few relatively simple strokes, Alas constructs a society of degenerate romantics, a few ridiculous human beings, sometimes grossly deformed and almost always repugnant. The author's irony remains, but a more ambiguous perspective forces the reader to look for essences, not explanations.

The six secondary figures are nonindividualistic representatives of but a few social traits, usually within a dualistic framework: Don Juan Nepomuceno hides carnal desire by a romantic facade; Korner is a "spiritual" dreamer but also a materialistic glutton; Mochi and Minghetti use personal attraction for economic gain; and Marta hides her sensuality, ego, and greed by an appearance of idealism. Serafina is even more systematically presented as a dual figure: beautiful and ugly, the angel and the devil, the voluptuous temptress and the serene madonna, romantic and sensuous, loving and materialistic. She is the embodiment of the conflict between good and evil, and evil triumphs in the end. Her English-Italian background and even her name reinforce this aspect of duality: "Serafina," meaning celestial seraph; her family name "Gorgheggi," broken down to "gorgo," meaning vortex or abyss, and "gorgone," the mythological Gorgon, suggesting the Medusan female. The secondary characters all use an "attractive" front to win over others, while a real, negative side leads them to exploit those around them.

Bonis is the clearest example of psychological duality in the novel, alternatively ridiculous and moving, comic and sad, indecisive and creative, in need of erotic excitement yet searching for peace. He vacillates between romantic fantasy and bourgeois needs (symbolized by his flute and slippers, respectively), both of which represent ways to escape reality. The disintegration of his personality is the result of his inability to reconcile these two forces. Bonis feels hatred for the materialistic world, yet in fact he is a typical *burgués* (bourgeois). The key to his personality (and, indeed, to the whole novel) is the ambivalence inherent in his description as a *soñador sonoliento*. Alas himself is not sure whether to like or hate his protagonist's delicate, dreaming, gentle nature, whether to identify and commiserate with him or to poke fun at him.

From a broader viewpoint, Bonis is a caricature of nineteenth century Romanticism in crisis. He is the archetypal figure of the nonhero who wants to be a hero. Alienated both from society and from himself, he sees the exploration of his own identity—in the form of an inner journey to the past and to his father's nature—as a heroic venture. In comparison with Ana, however, there is no heroism in his victimization; his conflict is more with self than with others, and there is no wall of misunderstanding between him and society, as in *La regenta*. In contrast to Ana, he shows no initiative, no capacity to try to rise above his vulgar surroundings. In *His Only Son*, the importance of the will is seen either in its misdirection (Emma) or in its nonexistence (Bonis). The only vestige of the hero's grandeur is the protagonist's readiness to sacrifice himself for his son's future.

Bonis's attraction to Serafina stems in part from a romantic attachment to the memories of his mother. Eroticism and filial love are combined and linked with nostalgia for the past. At times, one feels that he uses his love for the mother figure as a way to repress his sensuality. Then, as the novel progresses and Bonis sees a heavenly "Annunciation" of his future son's birth in Serafina's song (chapter 12), he concludes that divine coincidence has brought about the revelation of Emma's pregnancy on the same day that he breaks with Serafina. His longing for a child subsequently develops to the point of a religious cult, where fatherhood and motherhood join in him as a kind of *sacerdote*, or priest: Like God, he will offer "his only son" as a benefit for all humankind. In this thought, and in the notion that the earth is ruled by paternal Providence, he seems to find the security he needs and the moral support or atonement for his past conduct. Romantic raptures thus give way to fatherly love as the focus of ideality; at the same time, his longing for a son represents his need for another *yo* (or "I"), for a new beginning.

Emma ("Emma," perhaps a reminder of the twisted views of Gustave Flaubert's Emma Bovary; "Valcárcel," "val" or valley, as in an open sewer; and "carcel," imprisonment for Bonis) is basically a type character, a study in diabolical deformation that anticipates some of Ramón María del Valle-Inclán's depictions a few decades later. She is the epitome of the decadent *fuerza maléfica*, a malevolent force: perverse, spoiled, capricious, morbidly sensual, neurotic, and unnatural in her rejection of motherhood. Bonis and Alas think of her in terms of archetypal epithets: a Fury, witch, dragon, vampire; the proverbial femme fatale, as opposed to Serafina, who comes to represent angelic maternalism.

The reader is thus thrown into a world of characters exhibiting surprising traits: The man is more feminine than the aggressive, nonmaternal woman; his lover comes to personify domesticity and his wife to represent perverse eroticism; Emma finds her own lover when she learns of Bonis's relationship with Serafina, rather than resigning herself to her fate, as would other nineteenth century female characters. The unpredictable nature of human reality set forth in the novel is one of the work's many modern attributes.

Thematically, *His Only Son* is not particularly original, presenting a somewhat traditional, ironic exposure of the failings of idealized concepts and dogmas, when a simplified or falsified viewpoint clashes with the true complexity of reality. Rather than making a direct attack on pseudo-Romanticism per se, Alas is deriding the maintenance of any form of belief determined by other than spontaneous, internal motives. There are, he says, no exterior, abstract, or secondhand formulas for life. Reality cannot be reduced to either matter or mind but, rather, is characterized by the vacillation between the physiological and the spiritual. Other ideas in the novel—the need to face oneself rather than attempt to escape, the possible exaltation of family roots, an attack against a life oriented toward physical pleasure—are corollaries of the central theme. All of these concepts, finally, are seen in the context of personal and universal values rather than a framework of national or societal decay, as is the case in *La regenta*.

Alas's novelistic production can be viewed as a reflection of the disillusionments and frustrations of his own life and of his critical stance toward society. His two major novels have much in common—psychological depth, authorial irony, and explicit thematic statement—but the passage from *La regenta* to *His Only Son* reveals a number of significant developments in technique and characterization. These differences, in turn, relate to the change from a period in which realistic and naturalistic elements were dominant to one in which the influences of symbolism, decadence, and idealistic spirituality are more evident.

Alas's initial preoccupation with the problems of Spanish society places him clearly in a literary line that runs from Francisco de Quevedo y Villegas (1580-1645) to Mariano José de Larra (1809-1837) and, later, to the Generation of '98. He was among the very few writers of his time who were able to utilize much of Spain's literary heritage, particularly Cervantine elements, while still anticipating a number of twentieth century techniques.

Jeremy T. Medina

OTHER MAJOR WORKS

SHORT FICTION: *Pipá*, 1886; *Doña Berta, Cuervo, Superchería*, 1892; *Cuentos morales*, 1896, 1973; *El señor y lo demás, son cuentos*, 1900; *¡Adiós, Cordera! y otros cuentos*, 1944; *Cuentos de Clarín*, 1954; *Cuentos escogidos*, 1964; *Superchería, Cuervo, Doña Berta*, 1970; *El gallo de Sócrates, y otros cuentos*, 1973; *Ten Tales*, 2000.

PLAY: *Teresa*, pr., pb. 1895.

NONFICTION: *El derecho y la moralidad*, 1878 (doctoral thesis); *Solos de Clarín*, 1881, 1971; *La literatura en 1881*, 1882 (with Armando Palacio Valdés); *Sermón perdido*, 1885; *Cánovas y su tiempo*, 1887; *Nueva campaña, 1885-1886*, 1887; *Mezclilla*, 1889; *Rafael Calvo y el teatro español*, 1890; *Ensayos y revistas*, 1892; *Palique*, 1893, 1973; *Crítica popular*, 1896; *Siglo pasado*, 1901; *Galdós*, 1912; *Doctor Sutilis*, 1916; *Páginas escogidas*, 1917; *Epistolario de Menéndez y Pelayo y Leopoldo Alas*, 1941; *Leopoldo Alas: Teoría y crítica de la novela española*, 1972; *Preludios de 'Clarín,'* 1972; *Obra olvidada*, 1973.

MISCELLANEOUS: *Obras selectas*, 1947, 1966.

Bibliography

DuPont, Denise. *Realism as Resistance: Romanticism and Authorship in Galdós, Clarín, and Baroja*. Lewisburg, Pa.: Bucknell University Press, 2006. Explores the boundaries between realism and Romanticism in novels by three Spanish authors: Alas's *La regenta*, Benito Pérez Galdós's first series of *Episodios nacionales*, and Pío Baroja's *The Struggle for Life*. All three novels feature quixotic characters who act as authors, a theme DuPont traces to the influence of Spanish writer Miguel de Cervantes.

Franz, Thomas R. *Valera in Dialogue = In Dialogue with Valera: A Novelist's Work in Conversation with That of His Contemporaries and Successors*. New York: Peter Lang, 2000. Chronicles the debate among Alas and his contemporaries Juan Valera and Benito Pérez Galdós over the aesthetics of Spanish realist fiction, and how this debate influenced Alas's successors, namely Miguel de Unamuno y Jugo and Ramón María del Valle-Inclán.

Gilfoil, Anne W. "Disease as a Dis/Organizing Principle in Nineteenth-Century Spain: Benito Pérez Galdós, Leopoldo Alas, and Emilia Pardo Bazán." In *Science, Literature, and Film in the Hispanic World*, edited by Jerry Hoeg and Kevin S. Larsen. New York: Palgrave Macmillan, 2006. Gilfoil's essay and the others in this book chart the relationship between literature and science in Hispanic literature and culture by analyzing Spanish-language literature and films.

Goode, Stephen. "Return of a Nineteenth-Century Classic." *Washington Times*, February 18, 2007. Goode expresses his praise for *La regenta*, arguing that the novel is "surprisingly modern" and that its "well-rendered interior monologues, carried on in the minds" of its characters "lift this book out of the late Victorian era when it made its appearance, and make it feel truly at home today."

Medina, Jeremy T. *Spanish Realism: The Theory and Practice of a Concept in the Nineteenth Century*. Potomac, Md.: José Porrúa Turanzas, 1979. Medina analyzes works by Alas and other nineteenth century Spanish authors, discussing how and why these works exemplified the realistic literature of that time and place.

Sinclair, Alison. *Dislocations of Desire: Gender, Identity, and Strategy in "La regenta."* Chapel Hill: University of North Carolina, Department of Romance Languages, 1998. Sinclair takes a psychoanalytical approach to Alas's novel, examining how the narration and text of *La regenta* are similar to the workings of the human psyche.

Valis, Noel. "Death and the Child in *Su único hijo*." *Hispanic Review* 70, no. 2 (Spring, 2002). An analysis of Alas's novel *His Only Child*, focusing on the chimerical son, who is the object of protagonist Bonifacio Reyes's desire and obsession.

PÍO BAROJA

Born: San Sebastián, Spain; December 28, 1872
Died: Madrid, Spain; October 30, 1956
Also known as: Pío Baroja y Nessi

PRINCIPAL LONG FICTION
La casa de Aizgorri, 1900
Aventuras, inventos y mixtificaciones de Silvestre Paradox, 1901
Camino de perfección, 1902 (*Road to Perfection*, 2008)
El mayorazgo de Labraz, 1903 (*The Lord of Labraz*, 1926)
Aurora roja, 1904 (*Red Dawn*, 1924)
La busca, 1904 (*The Quest*, 1922)
Mala hierba, 1904 (*Weeds*, 1923)
La lucha por la vida, 1904 (collective title for previous 3 novels; *The Struggle for Life*, 1922-1924)
La feria de los discretos, 1905 (*The City of the Discreet*, 1917)
Paradox, rey, 1906 (*Paradox, King*, 1931)
La ciudad de la niebla, 1909
Zalacaín el aventurero, 1909 (*Zalacaín the Adventurer*, 1997)
César o nada, 1910 (*Caesar or Nothing*, 1919)
El árbol de la ciencia, 1911 (*The Tree of Knowledge*, 1928)
Las inquietudes de Shanti Andía, 1911 (*The Restlessness of Shanti Andía, and Other Writings*, 1959)
El mundo es ansí, 1912 (English translation, 1970)
Memorias de un hombre de acción, 1913-1935 (22 volumes)
La sensualidad pervertida, 1920
La leyenda de Juan de Alzate, 1922 (*The Legend of Juan de Alzate*, 1959)
El cura de Monleón, 1936

OTHER LITERARY FORMS

Pío Baroja (bah-ROH-hah) wrote short stories, essays, memoirs, and verse in addition to his many novels. Some of his novels are written in dialogue; in fact, Anthony Kerrigan presents *The Legend of Juan de Alzate* as a play in his introduction to *The Restlessness of Shanti Andía, and Other Writings*. Among Baroja's last books are his seven volumes of *Memorias* (1955), in which he availed himself of whole sections lifted from his fiction, which is, in turn, often autobiographical.

Baroja's first book was a collection of short stories, *Vidas sombrías* (1900; somber lives), which demonstrated a sympathetic tenderness for his characters that would diminish as his literary career advanced. Some of the stories are very short slice-of-life vignettes, and others concern the supernatural, such as "El trasgo" (the goblin) and "Medium." Some explore the psychology of women: "Agueda" treats the romantic stirrings in the mind of a disabled girl in the manner of Tennessee Williams's *The Glass Menagerie* (1944), and "Lo desconocido" ("The Unknown") probes the sudden and temporary urge of a bourgeois woman, traveling on a train with her husband, to flee the confines of the coach into the fascination of the night beyond. Others of these early stories contain the nuclei of future novels, such as "Un justo" (a just man), which prefigures *El cura de Monleón* and "Los panaderos" (the bakers), which anticipates the trilogy *The Struggle for Life*.

Baroja's second collection of short stories, *Idilios vascos* (1901-1902; Basque idylls), includes "Elizabide el vagabundo" (the love story of a vagabond), remarkable for its happy ending; a thirty-eight-year-old bachelor returns to Spain from Uruguay, falls in love, and to his surprise, finds that his love is reciprocated.

Baroja's essays do not differ substantially from his novels in view of the fact that he never hesitates to pack his novels with his own opinions. Baroja is not noted for the depth of his philosophical thinking, and he failed to assimilate with genuine understanding much of the material that he cites from the great philosophers.

In the book-length essay *Ciudades de Italia* (1949; cities of Italy), Baroja expresses his fear that the work will be a *chapuza* (botch-job) because he is not an art lover, a good tourist, or an aesthete. Art, as Baroja had told his readers years before, is child's play in comparison to the serious business of philosophy. Neither is he a lover of Italy; although he would have preferred to visit the United States or Germany, he chose Italy because it was cheaper to visit.

El tablado de Arlequín (1901; harlequinade) is an ongoing diatribe against Spaniards for their abulia. *Juventud, egolatría* (1917; *Youth and Egolatry*, 1920) summarizes the author's views on politics, religion, sex, morality, literature, and a host of other topics; the volume also contains a brief study of three of his ancestral clans—the Goñis, the Zornozas, and the Alzates, the humorous tone of which cannot disguise the pride Baroja takes in the contemplation of his own lineage.

Nuevo tablado de Arlequín (1917; new harlequinade) contains a brief history of Baroja's native Basque village, Vera del Bidasoa, and a long apologia for the German cause in World War I. *Vitrina pintoresca* (1935; picturesque showcase) treats a potpourri of topics ranging from the Jesuits, the Jews, and the Masons to the rivers of Spain, haunted houses, and the demons of carnival.

Baroja's attempts at poetry appear in *Canciones del suburbio* (1944; songs from the outskirts), published at the end of his career, not without the author's misgivings. This book is scarcely to be judged by the standards of serious poetry but is valuable inasmuch as it sheds light on Baroja the person. Indeed, Camilo José Cela considers the poems the best single book through which to become acquainted with their author.

Achievements

Gerald Brenan dubbed Pío Baroja the greatest of Spanish novelists, second only to Benito Pèrez Galdós. Pedro Salinas called the gallery of Baroja's characters "perhaps the richest" of Spanish literature. In 1972, G. G. Brown wrote that Baroja's influence on the modern Spanish novel has been greater than that of all of his contemporaries put together, and added that although non-Spanish readers may find this "puzzling," Baroja's popularity in Spain is an "indisputable fact." Brown's aside is clearly directed at those English-language critics who have been cool in their appraisal of Baroja's art.

Critic Gregorio Marañon attributed to Baroja a major role in forging a social conscience in the middle-class Spanish youth of his generation. Marañon characterized the books of Baroja's Madrid trilogy, *The Struggle for Life*, as three breaches in the wall of self-absorption that blinded the Spanish bourgeoisie to the misery amid which the majority of their compatriots lived. Although the *generación del 98*, or Generation of '98, counted among its numbers figures more intellectual than Baroja, he is the only one of them to have a significant following. Cela declared that the entire post-Civil War novel springs from his works and decried the fact that Baroja was not awarded the Nobel Prize. Indeed, the influence of Baroja is to be found in subsequent novels by such authors as Cela, Juan Antonio Zunzunegui, Miguel Delibes, José María Gironella, Ignacio Aldecoa, and Luis Martín-Santos.

Baroja stands apart from the nineteenth century realistic novelists who strived to arrange the elements of their fiction into interpretive patterns from which their readers could glean transcendent meaning. Through the example of his fiction, which chronicles the random inconsequentiality of his characters' lives, Baroja can therefore be credited, as Brown observes, with an attempt to reform what for thirty centuries has been seen as one of the principal functions of art—to organize experience into meaningful patterns.

Among American authors who profited from reading Baroja are John Dos Passos and Ernest Hemingway. Dos Passos, who wrote about Baroja in *Rosinante to the Road Again* (1922), was especially influenced by Baroja's anarchic tendencies, at least until the time of his disenchantment with the political Left in the later 1930's and, like Baroja, he wrote many of his novels in trilogies. Hemingway, who cherished Baroja's commitment to narrative brevity, paid homage to the Basque octogenarian at his deathbed; in his personal correspondence he deplored the fact that publisher Alfred Knopf had "dropped" Baroja when he did not sell well in the United States.

Although Baroja encouraged the myth of his simple and unappreciated bohemian existence, this is not quite the case. At the time of his death, he left behind the not unimpressive sum of 750,000 pesetas, and in 1934, he was elected to the Royal Spanish Academy.

Biography

Pío Baroja y Nessi was the third son of Serafín Baroja y Zornoza (1840-1915) and Carmen Nessi y Goñi (1849-1935). The young Baroja was extremely knowledgeable about his ancestry and careful to note that he was seven-eighths Basque and one-eighth Italian; his mother's surname, Nessi, was of Italian origin. His father was a mining engineer with a literary bent who was more concerned with what his friends thought of him than with the esteem of his family. An older brother, Ricardo Baroja (1871-1953), a painter and inventor, also was a writer. In 1879, the senior Baroja took his family to live in Madrid, then they moved to Pamplona; in 1886, they moved once again to Madrid.

Although not an exceptional student, Baroja entered the School of Medicine in Madrid at the age of fifteen and by 1891 completed his medical studies in Valencia. Two years later, he completed his thesis and obtained a position as practitioner in the Basque village of Cestona. The pettiness of small-town life and the suffering and the poverty that he was forced to witness daily disgusted him, and he decided to abandon his medical career. What he did not abandon, however, was the medical knowledge he had acquired; his novels are peopled with a host of doctors, and his dialogue bristles with the names and exploits of the heroes of medicine and physiology.

Baroja returned to Madrid to help his brother manage the family bakery, which allowed him to become familiar with the lower social orders of Madrid, a subject that would provide material for some twenty novels of his own creation. His venture into business was not successful, and it has been suggested that Baroja's hostility toward socialism may stem from his difficulties while running the bakery with the unions to which his employees belonged.

In 1898, Spain suffered the fiasco of the Spanish-American War, and in its soul-searching wake was born the Generation of '98. Although he is generally considered to have been a member of this group, Baroja himself denied any such affiliation: He scorned the artistic artifice of Ramón María del Valle-Inclán, disagreed with José Ortega y Gasset regarding the purpose of the novel, and resented the self-importance of Miguel de Unamuno y Jugo. Toward the popular novelist Vicente Blasco Ibáñez he harbored a deep loathing.

In 1899, Baroja made his first visit to Paris, and by 1900, when he published his first book, he was writing for such periodicals as *El país*, *El imparcial*, and *Revista nueva*. After purchasing a home in his native Basque village of Vera del Bidasoa in 1912, he divided his time between there and his home in Madrid, which he shared with his mother. He never married but had a number of liaisons that proved unsatisfactory. Although he grudgingly gave his support to Francisco Franco as the lesser of two evils at the outbreak of the Spanish Civil War, he left Spain voluntarily for Paris in the summer of 1936 and did not return until 1940.

During Baroja's final days, Ernest Hemingway, who had recently won the Nobel Prize, paid Baroja a visit. He brought with him a pair of socks and a bottle of his favorite whiskey, and told Baroja that the prize rightfully belonged to him. *Time* magazine, in October, 1956, recorded Baroja's succinct but unfortunately apocryphal reaction to such lavish praise: "Caramba." The less romantic truth is that in his arteriosclerotic haze, Baroja could do no more than respond to this tribute with an uncomprehending stare.

Analysis

Near the end of his life, Pío Baroja listed those historical personalities who had sustained his interest the longest: the naturalist Charles Darwin; the chemist Louis Pasteur; the physiologist Claude Bernard; the philosophers Friedrich Nietzsche, Arthur Schopenhauer, and Immanuel Kant; and the poets Lord Byron, Giacomo Leopardi, and Gustavo Adolfo Bécquer. His writing was permanently influenced by such French and Spanish serial writers as Xavier de Montepin and Manuel Fernández y González and by the Spanish picaresque novel. He admired Charles Dickens but not William Makepeace Thackeray, Stendhal but not Gustave Flaubert, Paul Verlaine but not Marcel Proust, and Giacomo Leopardi but not Alessandro Manzoni. Despairing of the world's capacity to produce writers of the highest caliber continually (his motto was "Nothing new under the sun"), he declared that the likes of Fyodor Dostoevski and Leo Tolstoy would not be seen again.

Baroja was as misanthropic and pessimistic as his mentor Schopenhauer and, also like the German philosopher, has been characterized as a misogynist. Baroja's references to the ignorance, greed, and superficiality of Spanish women are legion, yet his misogyny seems to be an ancillary property of his all-embracing misanthropy rather than an independent prejudice. Baroja's pessimism is reflected in his diction—in the frequent appearance of such words as *imbécil*, *estúpido*, and *absurdo*, as well as a bevy of more colorful words such as *energúmeno* (madman) and *gaznápiro* (simpleton). One of his favorite words for everything is *farsante* (farcical).

Baroja boasted that he used no word in his novels that was not appropriate in conversation, yet this does not preclude experimentation with unusual words that caught his fancy, for example, *cachupinada* (entertainment) and *zaquizamí* (garret). His love of the colorful is evident in the phrase he used to characterize himself—*pajarraco del individualismo* (big, ugly bird of individualism). Despite Baroja's commitment to the colloquial mode, he generally avoided slang unless it was for the purpose of local color in dialogue. In *The Struggle for Life* trilogy especially, his dialogue is strewn with italicized vocabulary peculiar to the low life of Madrid, for example, *aluspiar* (to stalk), *diñar* (to die), *jamar* (to eat). The practice of italicizing the vocabulary of the low life would be accepted and used even more by his follower Juan Antonio Zunzunegui, who came to occupy Baroja's vacant chair in the Royal Spanish Academy.

Baroja had an ear for pronunciation as well. When he returned to the Basque country after several years in Madrid as a child, he was ridiculed for his Madrilenian accent, and, on occasion, he notes this accent in his characters. He also had a penchant for decorating his prose with the lyrics of traditional songs not only in Basque but also in the other peninsular dialects; even in his essay on Italy, lyrics in the Italian dialects are cited. Indeed, refrains and simple repetitions for musical effects are typical of all of his prose.

Contemptuous of stylistic preciosity, he defended his right as a novelist to be terse and even ungrammatical. Because he avoided grammatical convolutions so consistently, his works are easier reading than many other Spanish classics and are, therefore, very popular in introductory literature courses wherever in the world that Spanish is taught.

Long non-Spanish names that point to the incontestable Basque origin of the characters that they denote are frequent in Baroja's novels. His fascination with anthropology is obvious in his abundant use of ethnological designations (for example, *samnita*, the name of a pre-Roman tribe of southern Italy, is used generally as "stalwart" in *Lord of Labraz*) and in his sweeping generalizations about race (for example, Sacha in *El mundo es ansí* observing that there is not a significant difference between northern and southern Spaniards, as there is among Italians). Baroja's use of the novel as a forum to hold forth on just about anything brings about many allusions to figures from the past, not only political leaders and writers but also physiologists, philosophers, painters, and anthropologists, who are more often German, French, or Italian than Spanish.

Baroja's sensitivity to the suffering in life and his abhorrence of human cruelty and hypocrisy made him a severe judge of the human condition. He hated religion, which he believed is a dangerous illusion foisted on Europeans by the Semites. His novel *El cura de Monleón*, which deals with a Basque priest's loss of faith, is unfortunately unsuccessful because Baroja, as an unbeliever, simply could not understand the depth of emotion such a loss of faith would entail for a priest. God is conceived as *patoso*, a bungler who, if he exists at all, is to be found in the scientific laboratory. Just as fiercely, Baroja abhorred the laws of the state, and his novel *Red Dawn* explores the world of anarchy and anarchists. Like the author himself, the protagonist of *Red Dawn*, Juan Alcazán, is a humanitarian, rather than a doctrinal, anarchist; Baroja himself never dared to act on any of the anarchistic tendencies that he felt.

All Baroja's novels contain adventure, and if his adventuresome characters do not overcome the obstacles with which they are confronted, it is because they lose faith in life and fall victim to abulia. César Moncada, for example, in *Caesar or Nothing*, tries to imitate Cesare Borgia, but his Machiavellian goals fail in the face of his innate pessimism. At the age of seventy, Baroja said that he still felt, as he had at the age of fifteen, a distant enthusiasm for adventure without really believing in it.

Baroja's fiction embraces a wide geographic purview. Some novels portray the Basque provinces of Spain, whose countryside he considered the purest and most authentic in Europe, isolated from the cement-and-cinema falsity of contemporary "civilization." Some portray the low life of Madrid (for example, *The Struggle for Life*), others have the Carlist Wars as a backdrop (for example, *Zalacaín el aventurero* and the Aviraneta series), and Andalusia is represented with originality in *The City of the Discreet*. Still others take place outside Spain (for example, *La ciudad de la niebla*, that is, London) or have as protagonists characters who are not Spanish (for example, Sacha Savarof, a Russian medical student who is observed in France, Switzerland, Italy, Russia, and Spain in *El mundo es ansí*).

Paradox, King

Paradox, King, a novel almost exclusively in dialogue, is one of Baroja's most highly acclaimed creations. Written in two weeks, it is a masterful combination of satire and fantasy, of misanthropy and humor. The restless Silvestre Paradox, a poverty-stricken inventor, joins an expedition to Africa organized to establish a Jewish colony, and is accompanied by a colorful group of naturalists, soldiers, and adventurers. The ship that takes them to Africa is wrecked in a storm and the survivors are taken captive in Bu-Tata, capital of the kingdom of Uganga. Once the captives conciliate the initially hostile natives, Paradox is proclaimed King, and the group institutes a European form of government that emphasizes complete freedom and dispenses with laws, schools, and teachers. At length, the French feel obliged to intervene; they bring "civilization" to Africa in the form of tuberculosis, alcoholism, and prostitution. The hospital fills up with epidemic victims, and Princess Mahu is driven to dancing nude in a nightclub.

Baroja uses the peculiarities of his characters to satirize his own aversions. There is, for example, the overbearing feminist Miss Pich, who insists that Socrates, William Shakespeare, and King David were women; her "fate" is to be raped by savages. The cynicism of *Paradox, King* concerning the lack of commitment among educators, theologians, and scientists, and the notion that humans can never escape the evils of civilization, even in a utopia, are totally in keeping with the fundamentals of Baroja's thinking.

The Tree of Knowledge

Like *Paradox, King*, Baroja's other masterpiece, *The Tree of Knowledge*, which the author believed was his best philosophical novel, emphasizes dialogue. The novel also contains the author's most successfully drawn protagonist, Andrés Hurtado, a sad and sensitive man whose pastimes, reading, attitudes, and sympathies closely parallel Baroja's own. Hurtado goes to Madrid to study medicine and is soon disillusioned by the inadequacy of his professors and the coldness of the hospital staff. Neither does his family afford him any relief from his pessimism, since he is incompatible with his father; he adores his little brother, Luisito, but the child soon dies of tuberculosis.

Once he becomes a doctor, Hurtado accepts a post in an isolated village, where he observes the same crassness and inhumanity as he had observed in the city. When he returns to Madrid, as he must, he meets Lulu, a woman of humble origins, and they marry. Hurtado considers himself unfit for fatherhood and knows that Lulu is not robust, but she becomes pregnant in defiance of biological probability. Just when marriage seems to have saved Hurtado from despair, Lulu dies, and Hurtado, refusing to confront an intolerable reality, decides to commit suicide.

Zalacaín el aventurero

Another popular novel, regarded by Baroja as one of his best, is *Zalacaín el aventurero*. Instinctively rather than intellectually philosophical in the manner of Hurtado, Zalacaín emerges as a hero unfettered by convention who tests his destiny. An orphan, Zalacaín comes under the influence of his cynical old uncle, Tellagorri, who comes to appreciate Zalacaín when he sees evidence of the boy's pluckiness. Zalacaín grows up to be successful in all of his endeavors, in war, in his career as a smuggler, and with women. At length, he dies in a dispute instigated by his wealthy brother-in-law, Carlos Ohando, who is resentful of Zalacaín for earning the love of his sister Catalina. The hero's violent death is consistent with the romantic conception of the novel, and the three roses laid on his grave by Linda, Rosita, and Catalina further suggest the hero of a romantic ballad.

THE RESTLESSNESS OF SHANTI ANDÍA

Baroja's early novel *The Restlessness of Shanti Andía*, belatedly translated into English some five decades after its original publication, is a complicated tale of maritime adventure that takes place in the idyllic Basque fishing village of Lúzaro. Shanti is torn by his loyalty to the Basque countryside and to the sea and is, as Beatrice Patt observes, a collector of adventures lived by others. He idolizes his dead uncle, Juan de Aguirre, a sea captain whose mysterious voyages made him a village myth. Much of the novel is taken up by Shanti's attempts to unravel his uncle's past, which involves tales of piracy, mutiny, buried treasure, and the slave trade. As pessimistic as Andrés Hurtado, Shanti comes across as a passive observer before the action-filled drama of someone else's heroics, a drama that he himself must narrate.

Although Baroja's dissatisfaction with human, and especially Spanish, society is everywhere evident in his fiction, the fast pace of his narrative and the lyric description that provides a background of poetry and almost druidic awe before the phenomena of nature keep his novels from being morbid. Those who dislike Baroja have chosen to emphasize his nonconformist and anarchistic nature, his melancholy, and the illogic of some of his pet arguments, while his admirers have chosen to emphasize the author's gentle nature hidden behind a defensive mask of sarcasm, a pose that he himself delighted in keeping alive. Nevertheless, there is little in his nearly one hundred books that escaped the severity of his uncompromising judgment against the false world of convention and complacency that engulfs the lives of most people and seals them off forever from compassion.

Jack Shreve

OTHER MAJOR WORKS

SHORT FICTION: *Vidas sombrías*, 1900; *Idilios vascos*, 1901-1902.

POETRY: *Canciones del suburbio*, 1944.

NONFICTION: *El tablado de Arlequín*, 1901; *Juventud, egolatría*, 1917 (*Youth and Egolatry*, 1920); *Nuevo tablado de Arlequín*, 1917; *La caverna del humorismo*, 1919; *Momentum catastrophicum*, 1919; *Divagaciones apasionadas*, 1924; *Entretenimientos*, 1927; *Aviraneta: O, La vida de un conspirador*, 1931; *Vitrina pintoresca*, 1935; *Pequeños ensayos*, 1943; *Ciudades de Italia*, 1949; *La obsesión del misterio*, 1952; *Memorias*, 1955 (7 volumes).

MISCELLANEOUS: *Obras completas*, 1946-1951 (8 volumes).

BIBLIOGRAPHY

Barrow, Leo L. *Negation in Baroja: A Key to His Novelistic Creativity*. Tucson: University of Arizona Press, 1971. Explores the novelist's technique of "creating by destroying" as a rebellion against conventional Western values. Discusses the style, dialogue, atmosphere, characterization, and landscape in his novels to explain how Baroja uses fiction to express his philosophical, political, and social attitudes.

Devlin, John. *Spanish Anticlericalism: A Study in Modern Alienation*. New York: Las Americas, 1966. Links Baroja with other prorepublican writers whose works exhibit strong anticlerical bias. Locates the source of his disdain for religion in the agnosticism that underlies his novels.

DuPont, Denise. *Realism as Resistance: Romanticism and Authorship in Galdós, Clarín, and Baroja*. Lewisburg, Pa.: Bucknell University Press, 2006. Explores the boundaries between realism and Romanticism in novels by three Spanish authors: Baroja's *The Struggle for Life*, Leopoldo Alas's *La regenta*, and Benito Pérez Galdós's first series of *Episodios nacionales*. All three novels feature quixotic characters who act as authors, which DuPont traces to the influence of an earlier Spanish author—Miguel de Cervantes.

Landeira, Ricardo. *The Modern Spanish Novel, 1898-1936*. Boston: Twayne, 1985. A chapter on Baroja surveys the novelist's achievement and discusses *Paradox, King* and the other novels in the trilogy dealing with "The Fantastic Life." Considers the novel the bitterest of the three in attacking social ills.

Murphy, Katharine. *Re-Reading Pío Baroja and English Literature*. New York: Peter Lang, 2004. Murphy points out the many structural similarities between Baroja's early fiction and the novels of his contemporaries in England and Ireland, most notably Joseph Conrad, Thomas Hardy, E. M. Forster, and James Joyce. Her examination focuses on how Baroja and the English-language authors treat human consciousness, the identity and role of the artist, European landscapes, and questions of form, genre, and representation.

_____. "Subjective Vision in *El árbol de la ciencia* and *Jude the Obscure*." *Bulletin of Spanish Studies* 79, no. 2/3 (March, 2002): 331-353. Murphy compares Baroja's novel to Hardy's *Jude the Obscure*, examining how both novels use a single-consciousness technique that reflects the modernist interest in subjective experience. She also finds similarities between the two novels' creation of characters who cannot be explained by the reader or the author.

Patt, Beatrice P. *Pío Baroja*. New York: Twayne, 1971. Excellent introduction to the writer and his works. Briefly discusses Baroja's attitudes toward the church and state. Reviews Baroja's use of extended dialogue in *Paradox, King*; points out how it permits him to introduce personal prejudices into a work he considered "half-fantasy, half-satirical poem."

Reid, John T. *Modern Spain and Liberalism*. Stanford, Calif.: Stanford University Press, 1937. Extensive study of Baroja's novels as documents chronicling the social and political climate in his country. Claims the novelist intends that his works serve as statements of the principles of liberalism that counter the fascist tendencies of his homeland.

Turner, Harriet, and Adelaida López de Martínez, eds. *The Cambridge Companion to the Spanish Novel: From 1600 to the Present*. New York: Cambridge University Press, 2003. Essays trace the development of the Spanish novel, including Baroja's *The Tree of Knowledge, El mundo es ansí*, and other novels. Situates him within the broader context of Spanish literature.

JUAN BENET

Born: Madrid, Spain; October 7, 1927
Died: Madrid, Spain; January, 1993
Also known as: Juan Benet Goitia

PRINCIPAL LONG FICTION
Volverás a Región, 1967 (*Return to Región*, 1985)
Una meditación, 1970 (*A Meditation*, 1982)
Una tumba, 1971 (novella)
Un viaje de invierno, 1972
La otra casa de Mazón, 1973
En el estado, 1977
Del pozo y del Numa: Un ensayo y una leyenda, 1978 (novella)
El aire de un crimen, 1980
Saúl ante Samuel, 1980
En la penumbra, 1983 (novella)
Herrumbrosas lanzas, I-VI, 1983
El caballero de Sajonia, 1991 (novella)

OTHER LITERARY FORMS

Although best known for his novels, Juan Benet (buh-NEHT) gained recognition as a superb essayist and short-story writer as well. His essays range in scope from music to linguistics, but his most perceptive writings are those on literary theory: *La inspiración y el estilo* (1965), *Puerta de tierra* (1970), *El ángel del Señor abandona a Tobías* (1976), and *La moviola de Eurípides* (1982). Above all, Benet articulates a literary posture that underscores the importance of style and enigma in the creation of fiction.

Benet's short stories have been collected in several volumes, including *Nunca llegarás a nada* (1961), *Cinco narraciones y dos fábulas* (1972), *Sub rosa* (1973), and *Trece fábulas y media* (1981). For the most part, the stories parallel his longer fiction in style and theme, though they are often more playful in tone. Benet also wrote four plays—*Max* (pb. 1953), *Agonía confutans* (1969), *Anastas: O, El origen de la constitución* (pb. 1970), and *Un caso de conciencia* (1970)—but none was performed during his lifetime with either critical or commercial success.

ACHIEVEMENTS

Juan Benet can perhaps be regarded most accurately as a novelist's novelist (or a critic's novelist) who wrote difficult works for a minority public. Indeed, his fiction rarely permits even the most experienced reader to feel at ease. After finishing a Benet work, one is left with the disquieting thought that one has missed the point or that there are many more points than one could possibly imagine—or, worse yet, that there is no point at all. Benet challenges his readers to rethink critical traditions that demand decisive meanings or that wrest from analysis unresolved ambiguities. His is a pluralistic fiction, a narrative of ideas forged with a style at once intricate and dense.

Despite the professed irritation of many critics with the difficult nature of his fiction, Benet gained recognition as one of Spain's most distinguished contemporary writers. He was one of the first novelists of the post-World War II era to break with neorealism in Spain and to offer a more subjective and experimental fiction in its place. Since 1969, when *A Meditation* was awarded the prestigious Premio Biblioteca Breve, Benet became one of the most prolific writers of his time. He continued to garner literary prizes (including the important Premio de la Crítica for *Herrumbrosas lanzas, I-VI*) and was invited to lecture throughout Western Europe and the United States. Perhaps more important, he began to have a profound influence on younger writers seeking new directions for the Spanish novel. Benet's fiction served as an imposing symbol of innovation and change in postwar Spain, and the unique vision that he brought to his craft propelled him to the forefront of his profession even as he remained aloof from the literary and critical establishment.

Biography

Juan Benet was born Juan Benet Goitia in Madrid on October 7, 1927, to Tomas Benet and Teresa Goitia. Benet was one of those extraordinary individuals who successfully cultivated his talents in two often conflicting pursuits: the scientific rigor of modern engineering and the aesthetic demands of creative writing. He was an avid reader in his youth and came to know intimately such master novelists as Stendhal, Gustave Flaubert, Fyodor Dostoevski, and Miguel de Cervantes. By the age of twenty, he was a regular participant in the literary *tertulias* of novelist Pío Baroja, one of the few modern Spanish writers whom Benet admired. He did not discover his true literary mentor (and his desire to be a writer), however, until 1947, when in a bookstore in Madrid he stumbled upon the work of William Faulkner. Faulkner's influence on Benet was decisive, and much of Benet's stylistic complexity, as well as his tragic vision of time and history, is rooted in Faulkner's mythical Yoknapatawpha County and the decadent American South that Faulkner meticulously created.

Benet graduated from the School of Engineering in Madrid in 1954 and served as a civil engineer and contractor throughout the Iberian Peninsula. Much of his early work, however, was centered in the northwestern provinces of León and Asturias, where he constructed roads and dams for the Spanish government. Isolated in the mountains for long periods of time, with only his work crew as company, Benet read classical philosophy and wrote fragments of fiction that would later appear in his novels. In 1963, while supervising construction of a dam on the Porma River, he began to revise a manuscript titled "El guarda," which four years later would become his first published novel, *Return to Región*. Over the next decade Benet successfully balanced his career as an engineer with his newly won fame as a novelist. His stature as an author continued to grow not only in Spain but also elsewhere in Europe and in the Americas.

In the last part of his life he devoted nearly all of his time to writing, even though he insisted in 1967, shortly after the publication of *Return to Región*, that he was an author only by avocation. Thus, Benet's engineering past must be viewed as crucial to his development as a novelist. His work in remote areas of Spain not only afforded him time to think and write but also presented him with the physical and psychological ambience for his mythical Región, the fictional setting for nearly all of his long fiction and microcosm of postwar Spain.

Analysis

Juan Benet falls chronologically into the group of writers commonly known as the Generation of '50. The realistic orientation and engagé approach to literature espoused by these writers (including Jesús Fernández Santos, Juan Goytisolo, Luis Goytisolo, and Rafael Sánchez Ferlosio) became the predominant literary force in Spain for nearly three decades following the Spanish Civil War (1936-1939). For the most part, novelists of this period defined their task as the verbal reproduction of a familiar reality, the shared world of reader and writer. The most important Spanish fiction written during the 1950's and early 1960's thus portrays everyday events in conventional novelistic forms.

Despite Benet's chronological affiliation with the writers of this period, he represents a direct antithesis to their fundamental literary canons. Indeed, his negative assessment of neorealistic fiction and his emphasis on style and enigma made him one of the most original Spanish writers of the twentieth century. His first collection of short stories, *Nunca llegarás a nada*, clearly transgresses the canons of social realism and foreshadows the tone, style, and thematic concerns that Benet develops more intensely in his long fiction. Rather than record the observable in his narrative, Benet seeks instead to probe beneath the surface of reality and explore what he terms "the zone of shadows." The abstruse and often inaccessible fiction that results has set Benet radically apart from the neorealism of the early postwar period as well as from the more experimental writing of the 1970's.

With the exception of *En el estado*, Benet set all of his novels in Región, a mythical region created in the fashion of Faulkner's Yoknapatawpha County or Gabriel García Márquez's Macondo. This private narrative world stands as the most explicit symbol of the ruin and despair that form the central motif of Benet's fiction. First created in 1961 in the short story "Baalbac, una mancha," Región did not achieve full realization until *Return to Región*, in which its geographic and enigmatic peculiarities are presented in detail. From one point of view, Región is the aggregate of characters, events, and social themes that, in Benet's view, constitute twentieth century Spanish society. More important than the social background, however, is the enigmatic reality of Región itself, portrayed by Benet on varying levels of complexity. On one hand, he depicts Región and the surrounding area with scientific precision. In fact, Región is described in such detail that the captivated reader searches to locate it on a map of Spain. Its flora and fauna, its landscape, and even its geological formation are portrayed with equal exactness of description, thus creating a reality that appears both authentic and identifiable in the physical world outside the text.

Benet establishes the real in Región in order to undermine it, however—to place in doubt its correspondence with the everyday world of observable reality. For the most part, he achieves this not explicitly, through use of the supernatural, but more subtly, by means of conflicting descriptions and recurrent suggestions of the unreal. In the first place, he portrays Región in a full state of decadence, surrounded by hostile landscapes and immersed in a threatening temperate zone. The entire area is a massive labyrinth of streams, valleys, forests, and deserts that have a life and meaning of their own. Throughout his fiction, but most forcefully in *Return to Región*, Benet constructs an ambience in which he underscores the extreme and contrasting elements of the physical environment: desert/luxuriant vegetation; heat/cold; mountain/valley; rivers/dried-up streams; life/death. Nature serves to deter outsiders (known as intruders) from entering Región, and the unwary visitor often falls victim to the hostility of the area, never to be seen or heard from again.

Within the hostile physical world of Región, Benet creates a complementary reality characterized by the enigmatic and the inexplicable. For example, mysterious wildflowers grow only on the soil of tombs; strange sounds and lights terrify travelers at night; a mythical woodsman, Numa, guards the forest of Mantua and kills with a single shot any intruder who crosses its boundaries. On a rational level, Benet explains neither the origins nor the ultimate consequences of these and a host of similar elements that constitute the world of Región. They inhere in the murky area beneath the surface of reality and frequently defy logical explanation.

RETURN TO REGIÓN

Nearly all of Benet's long fiction is cast in a similar stylistic and thematic mold. Both the consistency and the complexity of his fiction can be shown most succinctly through a discussion of the Región trilogy, *Return to Región*, *A Meditation*, and *Un viaje de invierno*. Although the latter two works were published without delay and received immediate attention from critics, *Return to Región*, first novel of a then unknown writer, was sold to Ediciones Destino only after a long process of submissions and rejections. Symptomatic of the Spanish literary scene of the time, one of Benet's rejection letters assured him that because his novel lacked dialogue the public would not read it. *Return to Región* is now considered one of the most important Spanish novels of the postwar era.

What traditionally has been called plot does not exist in *Return to Región*. Instead, the novel consists of a complex framework of third-person narration and pseudodialogues between the two principal characters, Doctor Sebastián and Marré Gamallo. Daniel Sebastián is an aging doctor who has been living in solitude for nearly a quarter of a century in Región, with little else to do but drink, remember, and care for a child driven insane by the absence of his mother. One evening he is visited by a woman, Marré Gamallo, and throughout the night the two characters carry on a soliloquy-like dialogue in which they evoke their pasts and examine their destinies. During the Spanish Civil War, the woman was the lover of Sebastián's godson, Luis I. Timoner, and this love represented for her the only happiness in her lifetime. She has returned to Región in search of the fulfillment that she lost when Luis fled into the mountains near the end of the war. For his part, Doctor Sebastián awakens the phantasmagorical events of his past and remembers in particular his unfulfilled passion for María Timoner, Luis's mother. Through the memories of Sebastián and his visitor, and with the additional comments of the third-person narrator, the reader is able to reconstruct the fragmented history of the ruination of Región and its habitants.

Much of the narrative of *Return to Región* is devoted to the creation of a milieu that became the cornerstone of Benet's fiction: the pervasive desolation of Región. Within this atmosphere, the threatening physical reality of the area not only stands as a striking tableau of ruin but also permeates the inhabitants through a process of antipathetic osmosis: A direct relationship exists between the geographic location, climatic conditions, and physical ruin of the town and the spiritual malaise of Región's inhabitants. The moral dilapidation of Doctor Sebastián, for example, resembles the condition of his decaying house, and María Timoner is compared to the withered leaves of the black poplar trees. Both characters are submerged in the hellish atmosphere of the moribund province, with scant hope for redemption.

Like many twentieth century writers, Benet deliberately fragments his narratives into puzzlelike structures that do not yield their meaning to a passive reader. Although the chronological duration of *Return to Región* is only one night, the psychological time spans nearly four decades, from 1925 to an unspecified present during the 1960's. Hence the temporal focus continually shifts, and time periods are fused so that the past is felt not as distinct from the present but as included in it and permeating it. Benet achieves this linkage primarily through the uncertain crucible of memory. During the course of their conversation, Dr. Sebastián and Marré Gamallo recapture a complex past that is patently destructive and capable of overwhelming any sense of hope in the present or future. In essence, the two characters possess a past that "was not." That is to say, there exists little from their previous lives that can be remembered in a positive sense. They resemble the characters in Faulkner's *The Sound and the Fury* (1929), to whom nothing can happen because everything has already happened. As one of the children in Faulkner's novel declares: "I am not is, I am was." The elusive present and nonexistent future thus stand helpless before the past, which engenders stagnation and despair rather than growth and fulfillment. Benet's novel affirms the destructive power of time at every turn of the page, and his characters regress toward a past that exists only to remind them that they are condemned to a life of nothingness.

Throughout his numerous theoretical essays on literature, Benet argues that style is the central component of fiction. Once a writer has developed a highly personal and fluid style, he or she is able to transcend the purely informational aspects of the novel—plot, setting, characters—and produce work of more lasting value. For Benet, the world was an enigma that he sought to penetrate and subsequently portray in his fiction. On one level, therefore, language serves as a means of discovery: The more developed a writer's style, the more perceptive will be the discovery. It is important to point out, however, that for Benet discovery was merely a prerequisite of creation. The writer does not merely represent what he or she perceives but rather invents a singular fictional reality through the skillful use of language. Style therefore serves as an enabling device that reifies imagination and affords new ways of knowing the world.

Benet's style is perhaps best described as labyrinthine. His sentences are frequently the length of a full page or more and include parentheses, parentheses within parentheses, and subordinate clauses that unite to form a syntactical webwork. Benet's style is, in fact, a persistent maze of obstacles replete with complex obtrusions, delays, ambiguous interpolations, and confusions. When used by the third-person narrator of *Return to Región*, the baroque sentences increase the enigmatic nature of the particular reality at hand. The narrator eschews words and linguistic structures that portray a world imitative of our own; hence, everything associated with what he says becomes part of a rarefied atmosphere aimed at precluding complete and rational understanding. A similar method defines the nature of the characters. Essentially stylized creations, their dialogue is the antithesis of realistic speech patterns. The conversation of Doctor Sebastián and Marré Gamallo, for example, is indistinguishable from the discourse of the narrator. The reader thus grows confused as one narrative voice blends into another and is lost amid the complicated labyrinth of words. Much of Benet's style and technique, it seems, is part of a deliberate plan to withhold meaning from the reader. As a result, the world of Región remains ambiguous and mysterious within the language that creates and sustains its very existence.

A MEDITATION

A Meditation, Benet's second novel, displays many of the stylistic and philosophical traits evident in *Return to Región* but represents a more ambitious undertaking than the earlier work. Written in the first person, *A Meditation* is precisely what the title suggests: a meditation on the past that covers a time span of nearly fifty years, from 1920 to the late 1960's. Although the novel is composed of an artistically manipulated structure rather than a loosely formed stream of consciousness, the events and characters that are presented do not appear in a specific chronological arrangement. Instead, the unnamed narrator evokes a succession of fragmented memories that frequently remain vague and incomplete. The novel consists of one long paragraph, a feature that Benet stressed by submitting it to the publishers on a long, unbroken roll of paper rather than in the normal fashion of sequentially typed pages. The linear, uncut nature of the manuscript, however, by no means resembles the internal structure and content of the novel. In the manner of

Marcel Proust and Faulkner, Benet's nameless narrator scrutinizes the past in an attempt to recover and understand the nature of his family, friends, and previous existence in the vicinity of Región.

The traditional use of plot, which in *Return to Región* is reduced to a minimum, regains significance in *A Meditation*. There is no dramatic development and subsequent denouement, however, and the sequence of events in the novel could easily be rearranged. As the narrator's mind wanders through the past, certain incidents and characters are summoned into consciousness and placed in view of the reader. No single event or character, however, is presented in its entirety during a specific moment in the novel. Instead, Benet creates a maze of interpenetrating segments that represent the narrator's voluntary and involuntary memory and the desire for a "remembrance of things past."

Benet's treatment of time and memory in *A Meditation* clearly resembles the temporal concerns evident in *Return to Región*. In both novels, time plays an integral part in the psychological and physical ruin of Región and its inhabitants and serves as a point of departure for philosophical speculation. In *A Meditation*, however, the reflections on time by the first-person narrator are actually reflections on the writing of the novel itself. Since the narrative consists of the recollection and subsequent expression of past events, any kind of temporal speculation must necessarily reflect on the construction of the work. Time and recollection, which form the intrinsic essence of the novel, thus play equal roles in both its form and its content.

While memory provides the means for examining or recovering the past, the whole notion of time—past, present, future—embodies a fundamental thematic preoccupation of *A Meditation*. In addition to its role in the structure of the narrative, which consists of the continual amassing of fragmented memories, time is treated concretely in the form of Cayetano Corral's clock and in abstraction by means of the narrator's numerous digressions. The mysterious clock, which has been in Cayetano's possession for several years, does not run. Although he has worked on the clock since he gained possession of it, he is less concerned with repairing its mechanical parts than with understanding its function: the making of time. He fails in his efforts because, as the entire novel aims to show, time is not measured by the rhythmic pulsating of the clock but by the mechanism of the human psyche. In all of Benet's fiction, time becomes above all that which destroys: The past is an absence that creates a void for the present as well as the future. Although the first-person narrator of *A Meditation* indeed evokes past events, and in the process creates a self as a product of that past, the novel affirms the way in which Benet's characters do not grow and change through time in a positive sense but rather remain stagnant within the ruin that they inevitably embody.

Benet's style in *A Meditation* is similar to that of *Return to Región* but more complex. In some respects, the novel resembles Marcel Proust's *À la recherche du temps perdu* (1913-1927; *Remembrance of Things Past*, 1922-1931), especially in narrative structure and technique. The influence of Faulkner, however, remains predominant in Benet's complex use of language. Like the American author, Benet frequently amasses words in a manner that has caused some critics to charge him with prolixity. Many of Benet's sentences cover several pages, and it becomes a difficult task to remain attentive to the assorted ideas contained in one of the narrator's thought patterns. On the other hand, Benet's peripatetic style is crucial to the content and structure of the novel and to the complicated way in which he formulates his meditation. Benet's sentences are perhaps best defined as saturated solutions: Images and topics are juxtaposed through the transcendent life of the mind, which continually explores obscure and enigmatic elements of reality.

One of the recurrent stylistic features of Benet's fiction, and one particularly important in *A Meditation*, is the presentation of contradictory suggestions within a single context. Just as William Faulkner employs oxymoronic or near-oxymoronic terms in many of his novels, so Benet utilizes contradictory statements to keep his narratives in a state of flux or suspension, thus inspiring uncertainty and confusion in the reader. The oxymoronic descriptions that Benet employs in *A Meditation* are constructed by the simultaneous suggestions of disparate or contrasting elements and therefore create a sharp polarity or tension. Both objects and characters are portrayed in this fashion and form part of the essential paradox of the novel. On one hand, Benet achieves a kind of order and coherence by virtue of the clear and sharp antitheses that the contrasts involve. On the other hand, however, such descriptions create disorder and incoherence by virtue of their qualities of irresolution and contradiction. Hence, the reality of *A Meditation*, evoked through the uncertain authority of memory and conveyed by the uninhibited flow of language, is the enigmatic domain of the human psyche.

UN VIAJE DE INVIERNO

Many critics consider *Un viaje de invierno* (a winter journey), the final novel of the Región trilogy, to be Benet's most abstruse piece of fiction. Once again, the reader must penetrate a world created by marathon sentences, a complex framework of recurring images, an ambiguous temporal structure, and an interrelated series of events that remain essentially unexplained in terms of motivation and ultimate resolution. Although *Un viaje de invierno* represents Benet's maximum effort to eliminate plot as an integral part of the novel, most of the narrative revolves around the uncertain configuration of a fiesta. Demetria holds the affair each year, ostensibly to honor the return of her daughter Coré, who annually spends six months away from Región; the novel begins with the writing and mailing of the invitations and ends with a vague description of the party. Any attempt, however, to comprehend the complex reasons for holding the celebration or to untangle the temporal confusion that surrounds the event encounters intransigent opposition. Demetria is unable to determine the number of guests she has invited, and she does not know how many attend, as she has never been to the party herself. Coré does not appear in the narrative, and the party is painted in such mysterious, rarefied tones that one is only able to guess at its implied meaning: for Demetria, an opportunity to exercise her will; for the guests, an ephemeral mitigation of their loneliness and a flight from the pain of daily life.

Arturo, the other principal figure of the novel, works as Demetria's servant. He has apparently (although we do not know for certain) worked as a handyman at other homes in the area, and each change of job brings him closer to the source of the Torce River. Arturo himself knows little about his past, except that for nearly all of his life he has labored on the farms along the Torce valley and has slowly journeyed up the river. It is a "winter's journey," as the title of the novel indicates, one that seems to lead him inescapably toward death, yet the impetus for the journey is shrouded in mystery and borders on the magical. Arturo's future was determined early in his youth when one evening he listened to a waltz (*el vals K*) in the music conservatory where his mother worked as a cleaning woman. In the same way that Doctor Sebastián in *Return to Región* is condemned to suffer in Región after reading his future on the telegraph wheel, Arturo is destined to seek meaning in life at the head of the Torce River. The meaning that he seeks, of course, is correlated with death, toward which he inevitably and mysteriously journeys. This fatalistic destiny represents the future of nearly all of Benet's characters and inheres in the atmosphere of ruin and anguish that pervades his fiction.

As in his first two novels, Benet's style in *Un viaje de invierno* creates an uneasy and portentous mood. His style in the latter work, however, seems based on a more studied attempt to avoid translating sensation into perception. A cognitive knowledge of something, be it of a character, an object, or a particular ambience, is of secondary importance to the pure consciousness of it. In this sense, Benet can be viewed as an idealist: Because one's consciousness seizes nothing but manifestations, reality is illusory. Indeed, when reading *Un viaje de invierno*, the reader senses that he or she is before the dream of reality instead of reality itself. For example, neither Coré nor Amat (Demetria's absent husband) ever appears as a concrete being in the novel; rather, both exist only as manifestations of Demetria's nostalgic memory. Demetria herself, whose existence is never seriously doubted, embodies Benet's predilection for the intangible and the ethereal. She is known to the inhabitants of Región by more than one name (Demetria, Nemesia, Obscura), and Benet never ascribes concrete physical characteristics to her. Her hand, for example, is *impalpable*, and she speaks words that sound without resonance. Her voice has no pitch or tone, and when she touches Arturo, he senses, yet does not feel, her hands. In short, Benet's method of portraying Demetria and the other figures of the novel points to the notion that we can discern only the image of something and not the thing itself.

The ethereal essence of his characters, however, in no way alleviates their existential despair. As in his previous novels, this despair in large part stems from the oppressive power of time. One is never aware in *Un viaje de invierno* of a pure present, and a specific past is not very often exclusively defined. In fact, Benet seems purposely to create a timeless vision of reality in which past and present are interfused to form a vague series of occurrences that defy order and reason. This notion of temporal uncertainty bears directly on the title of the novel as well as one of its central motifs: the journey. Nearly all of the characters set out on journeys—to Central Europe, to the Torce River, to town, and so on. In one fashion or another, however, all of the trips revolve around the fiesta. Because the party cannot be located in time by any of the characters, it becomes clear that they undertake their journeys in order to exist in a temporal vacuum where past, present, and future do not possess any reality.

Like the characters in the earlier novels of the trilogy, however, the characters of *Un viaje de invierno* are trapped by the past, even as time moves forward and passes them by. If life consists of a continuation of the past into an ever-growing and expanding present, then the characters of *Un viaje de invierno* can have no hope for the future. Their lives are defined by a temporal vortex in which being is divorced from the linear progression of time. Although the fiesta represents for the characters an opportunity to grasp Martin Heidegger's "silent strength of the possible," they are ensnared by stagnation, where meaning remains elusive. This is the ultimate message of Benet's fiction, one that is affirmed even as he conceals it in the contradictory and enigmatic world of Región.

David K. Herzberger

Other major works

SHORT FICTION: *Nunca llegarás a nada*, 1961; *Cinco narraciones y dos fábulas*, 1972; *Sub rosa*, 1973; *Cuentos completos*, 1977; *Trece fábulas y media*, 1981; *Una tumba, y otros relatos*, 1981.

PLAYS: *Max*, pb. 1953; *Agonía confutans*, pb. 1969; *Teatro*, 1970 (includes *Anastas: O, El origen de la constitución*, *Agonía confutans*, and *Un caso de conciencia*).

NONFICTION: *La inspiración y el estilo*, 1965; *Puerta de tierra*, 1970; *El ángel del Señor abandona a Tobías*, 1976; *En ciernes*, 1976; *¿Qué fue la guerra civil?*, 1976; *La moviola de Eurípides*, 1982; *Artículos, 1962-1977*, 1983; *Sobre la incertidumbre*, 1983; *Cartografía personal*, 1997; *La sombra de la guerra*, 1999.

TRANSLATION: *A este lado del Paraiso*, 1968 (of F. Scott Fitzgerald's novel *This Side of Paradise*).

Bibliography

Cabrera, Vincente. *Juan Benet*. Boston: Twayne, 1984. Good introductory study examines Benet's works as a whole, including his novels.

Compitello, Malcolm Alan. *Ordering the Evidence: "Volverás a Región" and Civil War Fiction*. Barcelona: Puvill Libros, 1983. Illuminates the historical aspects of *Return to Región* in terms of the Spanish Civil War.

Ferrán, Ofelia. *Working Through Memory: Writing and Remembrance in Contemporary Spanish Narrative*. Lewisburg, Pa.: Bucknell University Press, 2007. Benet's novels are among those analyzed in a study of Spanish literature published from the 1960's through the 1990's. Demonstrates how these novels explore present memory as a way for Spaniards to recover from the traumatic and repressive past of the Spanish Civil War and the regime of Francisco Franco.

Herzberger, David K. *The Novelistic World of Juan Benet*. Clear Creek, Ind.: American Hispanist, 1976. Analyzes Benet's novels by examining them in the light of the author's own theories.

Manteiga, Roberto C., David K. Herzberger, and Malcolm Alan Compitello, eds. *Critical Approaches to the Writings of Juan Benet*. Hanover, N.H.: University Press of New England, 1984. Collection of critical essays on Benet's work includes a foreword in which the author explains his works in an international context.

Margenot, John B., III. "Character Questing in Juan Benet's *Volverás a Región*." *Modern Language Studies* 19, no. 3 (Summer, 1989): 52-62. Analyzes the novel in terms of a mythical quest by its characters, focusing on the characters' physical movement to Región as well as their psychological exploration through time and memory.

_____, ed. *Juan Benet: A Critical Reappraisal of His Fiction*. West Cornwall, Conn.: Locust Hill Press, 1997. Collection of essays aims to reevaluate Benet's work from the perspective of the late twentieth century. Includes bibliographical references and index.

Rodríguez, Joe. "Reason, Desire, and Language: Reading Juan Benet's Trilogy as a Relational Totality." *Bulletin of Spanish Studies* 83, no. 2 (March, 2006): 241-263. Focuses on three of Benet's novels—*Return to Región, A Meditation*, and *Un viaje de invierno*—describing their narrative techniques and their relationships to one another.

Turner, Harriet, and Adelaida López de Martínez, eds. *The Cambridge Companion to the Spanish Novel: From 1600 to the Present*. New York: Cambridge University Press, 2003. Collection of essays tracing the development of the Spanish novel includes a discussion of Benet's novels *Return to Región, A Meditation*, and *Saúl ante Samuel*, among others.

Walkowiak, Marzena M. *A Study of the Narrative Structure of "Una meditación" by Juan Benet*. Lewiston, N.Y.: Edwin Mellen Press, 2000. In-depth study of *A Meditation* explains the novel's complex world by exploring its narrative structure and plot, the role of its characters, the narrator's point of view, and its treatment of time and space. Places the book within the context of post-World War II political and literary developments within Spain.

VICENTE BLASCO IBÁÑEZ

Born: Valencia, Spain; January 29, 1867
Died: Menton, France; January 28, 1928

PRINCIPAL LONG FICTION
  Arroz y tartana, 1894 (*The Three Roses*, 1932)
  Flor de mayo, 1895 (*The Mayflower: A Tale of the Valencian Seashore*, 1921)
  La barraca, 1898 (*The Cabin*, 1917; also known as *The Holding*, 1993)
  Entre naranjos, 1900 (*The Torrent*, 1921)
  Sónnica la cortesana, 1901 (*Sonnica*, 1912)
  Cañas y barro, 1902 (*Reeds and Mud*, 1928)
  Los muertos mandan, 1902 (*The Dead Command*, 1919)
  La catedral, 1903 (*The Shadow of the Cathedral*, 1909)
  El intruso, 1904 (*The Intruder*, 1928)
  La bodega, 1905 (*The Fruit of the Vine*, 1919)
  La horda, 1905 (*The Mob*, 1927)
  La maja desnuda, 1906 (*Woman Triumphant*, 1920)
  La voluntad de vivir, 1907
  Sangre y arena, 1908 (*The Blood of the Arena*, 1911; better known as *Blood and Sand*, 1913)
  Luna Benamor, 1909 (includes short stories; English translation, 1919)
  Los Argonautas, 1914
  Los cuatro jinetes del Apocalipsis, 1916 (*The Four Horsemen of the Apocalypse*, 1918)
  Mare Nostrum, 1918 (English translation, 1919)
  Los enemigos de la mujer, 1919 (*The Enemies of Women*, 1920)
  El paraíso de las mujeres, 1922 (*The Paradise of Women*, 1922)
  La tierra de todos, 1922 (*The Temptress*, 1923)
  La reina Calafia, 1923 (*Queen Calafia*, 1924)
  El papa del mar, 1925 (*The Pope of the Sea: An Historic Medley*, 1927)
  A los pies de Venus, 1926 (*The Borgias: Or, At the Feet of Venus*, 1930)
  En busca del Gran Kan, 1929 (*Unknown Lands: The Story of Columbus*, 1929)
  El Caballero de la Virgen, 1929 (*The Knight of the Virgin*, 1930)
  El fantasma de las alas de oro, 1930 (*The Phantom with Wings of Gold*, 1931)

OTHER LITERARY FORMS

In addition to his novels, Vicente Blasco Ibáñez (BLAHS-koh ee-BAHN-yays) wrote early romances, including such works as the novella *El conde Garci-Fernández* (1928), *¡Por la patria! (Romeu el guerrillero)* (1888), *La araña negra* (1928; a collection of short fiction), and *¡Viva la república!* (1893-1894). Blasco Ibáñez later repudiated these early romances as unworthy of preservation. Blasco Ibáñez also wrote short stories and novelettes, including *Fantasías, leyendas, y tradiciones* (1887), *El adiós a Schubert* (1888; stories of a distinctly romantic nature and quite different from the author's mature pieces), and, later *Cuentos valencianos* (1896), *La condenada* (1899), *El préstamo de la difunta* (1921), *Novelas de la costa azul* (1924), and *Novelas de amor y de muerte* (1927). His nonfiction includes *Historia de la revolución española, 1808-1874* (1890-1892), *París: Impresiones de un emigrado* (1893), *En el país del arte* (1896; *In the Land of Art*, 1923), *Oriente* (1907), *Argentina y sus grandezas* (1910), the thirteen-volume *Historia de la guerra europea de 1914* (1914-1919), *El militarismo mejicano* (1920; *Mexico in Revolution*, 1920), the three-volume *La vuelta al mundo de un novelista* (1924-1925; *A Novelist's Tour of the World*, 1926); *Una nación secuestrada: Alfonso XIII desenmascarado* (1924; *Alfonso XIII Unmasked: The Military Terror in Spain*, 1924), *Lo que será la república española: Al país y al ejército* (1925), *Estudios literarios* (1933), and *Discursos literarios* (1966); and one play, *El juez* (pb. 1894). Translations of many of Blasco Ibáñez's short stories have been collected in *The Last Lion, and Other Tales* (1919) and *The Old Woman of the Movies, and Other Stories* (1925).

Achievements

Vicente Blasco Ibáñez is probably the most widely read Spanish novelist, both in Spain and abroad, except for Miguel de Cervantes. Certainly he was one of the most prolific writers his country ever produced (his collected works run to forty volumes) a result of his extraordinarily dynamic and energetic nature and of his determination to show both the positive and the negative aspects of Spain to his countrymen and to the world.

Blasco Ibáñez has not received a balanced judgment from literary critics. Most have offered exaggerated praise or scorn for his works or have ignored him altogether. For many years, many Spanish critics denied the value of his novels because they rejected his radical political ideas, they envied his financial success, or they held a low opinion of his literary origins. (Blasco Ibáñez did not participate in some of the stylistic renovations of the *generación del 98*, or the Generation of '98, adhering instead to many of the realistic-naturalistic practices of the nineteenth century, thought by many to be out of date.) While Blasco Ibáñez's attacks on the Spanish political scene and eventual millionaire status led to ostracism by his Spanish contemporaries, such English-speaking critics as William Dean Howells, Havelock Ellis, Walter Starkie, Gerald Brenan, A. Grove Day, and Edgar Knowlson, Jr., offered a fairer perspective.

Certainly there are significant defects in some of Blasco Ibáñez's works. Without question, his early Valencian novels represent his greatest achievement, revealing a powerful double legacy that cannot be ignored: a pictorial, concrete, at times poetic style of strength and beauty, and a striking portrayal of human action. Later in his career, as Blasco Ibáñez strayed farther and farther from the format and the setting he knew best, the aesthetic value of his novels declined dramatically. While a definitive study of his total literary production remains to be done, analyses of individual novels have at least offered glimpses into the genuine artistry of his best works.

Biography

Vicente Blasco Ibáñez was born in a room over a corner grocery in Valencia on January 29, 1867. From his parents, he inherited the vigor of the Aragonese peasants, and from an impoverished childhood, he gained the spirit of struggle and defiance. During his early years, the lad of sturdy build, brown eyes, and curly hair could be seen more often walking the beach of nearby Cabañal or talking to fishermen and sailors than sitting at his desk in school. By the age of fourteen, he had written a cloak-and-dagger novel, by age fifteen had published a short story in the Valencian dialect, and by age sixteen had run away from the University of Valencia to Madrid. There, while doing secretarial work for the aging writer Manuel Fernández y González, he gained the inspiration for his first series of lengthy writings—a dozen romances that he later repudiated. By age seventeen, he had published a poem advocating chopping off all the crowned heads of Europe, starting with Spain.

The death of Alfonso XII in 1885 marked the young writer's start as republican conspirator and frequent political prisoner. After completing his law degree in 1888 and his first forced exile in France (brought on by increasingly anticlerical speeches), Blasco Ibáñez married his cousin, María Blasco del Cacho, who was to endure his tempestuous nature and stormy career. They had five children before their separation immediately prior to the outbreak of World War I. On November 12, 1894, Blasco Ibáñez released the first issue of *El pueblo*, a journal that he was to run virtually single-handedly and in which many of his best works would appear in serial form. It was into this enterprise that he poured all of his energy and stamina, as well as the entirety of his parents' inheritance.

Blasco Ibáñez proved to be a born leader of crowds, self-assured, fluent in his oratory, with a booming voice whose warmth quickly dispelled any first impression of coldness that might have been caused by his pointed beard, his mustache, and his aquiline nose. As time passed, he grew to be increasingly impulsive and impatient to eliminate the stupidity, ignorance, and laziness around him. Antireligious in a city venerated as the repository of the Holy Grail, and republican in a region noted for its conservative monarchism, he never avoided the chance for an iconoclastic stance.

Nevertheless, his election as the Valencian representative for the journal *Las cortes* in 1898 was the first of many. To his growing political fame was added an international literary reputation with the French translation of *The Cabin* in 1901. In 1904, he abandoned his home at La Malvarrosa on the Valencian shore to take up residence in Madrid and other Spanish cities.

The year 1909 found Blasco Ibáñez making two trips to Argentina, first to give lectures and subsequently to supervise the development of some new settlements. There he remained, fighting harsh climates and jungle dangers, until economic difficulties led him back to Europe immediately prior to World War I. Shortly afterward, he launched into a campaign to help the Allies, in the form of *Historia de la guerra europea de 1914*, speeches throughout neutral Spain, and several novels, of which *The Four Horsemen of the Apocalypse* had the greatest political and financial impact. When unexpected wealth poured in from this work's reprints, translations, and film rights, he moved to the French Riviera, where most of his last novels were written.

By 1925, Blasco Ibáñez had undertaken a triumphant tour of the United States, composing lengthy travel literature based on a six-month luxury-liner trip around the world, when he received news of the death of his wife. Within months, he married the daughter of a well-known Chilean general and soon thereafter, in failing health, retired to his Riviera home to churn out his final writings. The night before his sixty-first birthday, weakened by pneumonia, diabetes, and overwork, he died uttering the words "my garden, my garden," a reflection of his ardent desire to have his Menton garden resemble those of his beloved Valencia. In his will, he bequeathed his home to "all the writers of the world" and insisted that he not be buried in a nonrepublican Spain. On October 29, 1933, two years after the proclamation of the Second Republic, his body was moved to Valencia amid the impassioned eulogies of those who had scorned him years before. More than forty-seven years later, as renovations were undertaken on the Blasco Ibáñez home at La Malvarrosa, the first international symposium on Don Vicente's works was held, and a determination to rectify the critical neglect of his work was voiced.

Blasco Ibáñez was a man of action first and a writer second. His works bear a profound and constant autobiographical stamp—the mark of a rebel, a revolutionary journalist, a colonizer, a sailor, a fighter for the cause of peasants, fishermen, and slum dwellers, and an exile who attacked his government yet remained loyal to Spanish traditions, as reflected in his tireless efforts to glorify his country's imperial past and to combat the anti-Spanish legend. It is with at least some justification that he is remembered by many of his countrymen more for his life than for his writings.

ANALYSIS

Following Vicente Blasco Ibáñez's first romances, five phases can be distinguished in the course of his prolific career. Into the first fall his Valencian works, from *The Three Roses* (which he considered his first novel) through *Reeds and Mud* and including two collections of stories, *Cuentos valencianos* and *La condenada*. Within this group, three works can be considered the novelist's masterpieces: *The Mayflower*, *The Cabin*, and *Reeds and Mud*. Second are his novels of social protest, written between 1903 and 1905 and dealing with the Catholic Church (*The Shadow of the Cathedral*, set in Toledo, and *The Intruder*, set in the Basque provinces) or with the exploitation of workers in vineyards and in large cities (*The Fruit of the Vine* and *The Mob*, set in Jérez de la Frontera and Madrid, respectively). "Art," the author explains, "should not be simply a mere manifestation of beauty. Art should be on the side of the needy defending forcefully those who are hungry for justice." Nevertheless, interminable didactic monologues, long ideological question-and-answer dialectics, and overtly symbolic characterization lessen the aesthetic worth of these works.

The third phase comprises psychological novels in which the author stresses character development within specific settings: *Woman Triumphant* (Madrid), *La voluntad de vivir* (the aristocracy of Madrid and Paris), *Blood and Sand* (bullfighting in Seville and Madrid), *The Dead Command* (Balearic Islands), and *Luna Benamor* (Gibraltar). While some of these works are admirable for their characterization and for their descriptions of landscape and local customs, they are clearly inferior to the Valencian writings. Fourth are cosmopolitan and war novels, including *Los Argonautas* (a detailed account of a transatlantic journey, envisioned as the first in a series of works dealing with Latin America) and several novels written to defend the Allied cause: *The Four Horsemen of the Apocalypse, Mare Nostrum, The Enemies of Women, The Temptress,* and *Queen Calafia*. These novels proved to be as popular as they were lacking in artistic merit. Finally, Blasco Ibáñez's fifth phase includes historical novels of Spanish glorification, ranging from the account of Pope Benedict XIII's life to the voyages of Columbus and a love story set in Monte Carlo.

In some ways, Blasco Ibáñez is a transitional figure between the age of the realistic novel (1870-1900) and the Generation of '98. Works such as *The Fruit of the Vine* and *The Mob* demonstrate his participation in the ninety-eighters' preoccupation with Spanish social issues, and most of his works, particularly in his early periods, reveal the extraordinary sensitivity to landscape that Pío Baroja's generation would display. Blasco Ibáñez's regionalistic *costumbrismo* and use of descriptive detail are techniques that relate him to the earlier generation of Benito Pérez Galdós and José María de Pereda.

It was Blasco Ibáñez who introduced the *pueblo*, rather than the middle class, as a frequent source for the novel's protagonist, a character who struggles heroically against his environment and his own animal instincts. A convincing narrative action of sharp contrasts; a pictorial, concrete, sensual, often impressionistic realism of strength and beauty; and an admirable tightness and unity of plot are the features that set the Valencian novels apart as his most accomplished works.

Blasco Ibáñez was not a contemplative man, and his themes, while relevant and often powerful, are not complex or subtle. His modes of characterization, his third phase notwithstanding, are a far cry from the probing, individualizing approach of most of the late nineteenth century realists. His figures lack depth, are often excessively masculine and melodramatic, and seldom rise above mere types. They can be divided into two classes: good and bad. These opposites are inevitably caught up in an eternal struggle with each other or with nature. There are few inner battles of conscience, few motivations aside from those of glory, power, sexual gratification, or mere survival. Nevertheless, Blasco Ibáñez's main type—the man of action, passion, animal instinct, and rebellion—is a graphic and powerful creation, made convincing by the sheer force of his portrayal, if not by any unique identity.

Batiste (*The Cabin*), Retor (*The Mayflower*), Toni (*Reeds and Mud*), and, in later novels, Sánchez Morueta (*The Intruder*), Gallardo (*Blood and Sand*), Centauro (*The Four Horsemen of the Apocalypse*), Ferragut (*Mare Nostrum*), and Renovales (*Woman Triumphant*) are such characters, presented in deliberate (albeit artificial) contrast to their opposites; these are weak and lazy types, such as Tonet (*The Mayflower*) and the other Tonet (*Reeds and Mud*). Blasco Ibáñez's women are also one-sided—oppressed and overworked domestics, conventional society figures, or women of action and conquest. The last group would include Dolores (*The Mayflower*), Neleta (*Reeds and Mud*), Leonora (*The Torrent*), Doña Sol (*Blood and Sand*), and la Marquesita (*The Fruit of the Vine*). Finally, one should note that, even if Blasco Ibáñez did not create great characters, he was able to succeed in capturing dramatically the heterogeneity of the masses. Pimentò of *The Cabin*, who represents the people of the region around the Valencian *huerta*, is one striking example of this skillful portrayal.

Although Blasco Ibáñez has often been referred to as the Spanish Zola, he rejected the naturalists' pseudoscientific, analytical approach and emphasis on crude detail, came to mitigate the impression of fatalistic determinism through his admiration of humankind's will to fight and a suggestion of optimism, and, finally, often presented a lighter, less objective, and more poetic tone than is the norm in Émile Zola's novels. Nevertheless, there are many moments in Blasco Ibáñez's work when a strong measure of pessimism and philosophical determinism or the use of unpleasant language and description demonstrate the influence of French naturalism.

Finally, one should not forget that Blasco Ibáñez produced some of the finest Spanish short stories of the modern era. One has only to look at the moving portrait of the protagonist of "Dimoni" to realize the author's skill in this genre. John B. Dalbor, the major critic to have undertaken detailed studies of these pieces, believes that many of the stories are in fact superior to the author's novels and that the very best of these stories are to be found in the collections *Cuentos valencianos*, *La condenada*, and *El préstamo de la difunta*. In the Valencian novels, Blasco Ibáñez's descriptive power—tumultuous, exuberant, dramatic, and exact—is most evident, a talent that sprang from keen observation and an uncanny ability to improvise.

THE MAYFLOWER

These virtues are evident in Blasco Ibáñez's second novel, *The Mayflower*, set in the fishing village of Cabañal; the descriptions of regional scenes and customs and many of the characters are typically drawn from observation at first hand. The plot concerns the struggles of the poor fishermen of the Valencia area. Pascualet, called "El Retor" because of his benign clerical appearance, works and saves so that some day he can afford his own boat and free himself from the demands of another captain. His spendthrift brother, Tonet, is lazy and hates manual labor. When their father is killed at sea, their mother, Tona, cleverly converts her husband's boat into a beach tavern, where she earns a meager but adequate living for the family. El Retor goes to sea as an apprentice, but Tonet turns to drink and women until he leaves for service in the navy. By this time, a child, Roseta, has been born of Tona's affair with a passing *carabinero*. When Tonet returns to find that his brother has married the seductive Dolores, he soon agrees to marry Rosario, who has waited for him for many years. Soon Tonet renews (unbeknown to El Retor) his previous youthful encounters with Dolores, and battles between the sisters-in-law increase in frequency and intensity, despite the attempts at reconciliation managed by the ancient village matriarch, Tía Picores. A boy born to El Retor and Dolores is actually Tonet's child.

After years of hard work and saving, and after a tense smuggling adventure that results in a considerable profit, El Retor is able to arrange for the building of the finest vessel ever seen in the village, named *Flor de Mayo* after the brand of tobacco that had been smuggled into Spain on the earlier trip. Prior to the ship's second sailing, Rosario reveals to El Retor that for years his brother has had an affair with Dolores and that his son is really Tonet's offspring. After a night of shock and humiliation and after refusing for the moment to avenge the affront by his brother, El Retor sets sail in one of the worst storms to afflict the coast of Cabañal. In a suspenseful and tumultuous final chapter, El Retor confronts his brother on board the *Flor de Mayo*, extracts a confession from him, and then refuses to give him the boat's single life jacket. Instead, he puts it on the boy and tosses him overboard. The lad is thrown upon the rocks, and the ship is ripped apart by the fury of the wind. Dolores and Rosario, watching the action from the shore, mourn their loss, and old Tía Picores shouts a final condemnation of the people of Valencia, who are ultimately responsible for the deaths the women have witnessed.

Blasco Ibáñez's viewpoint is usually one of relative neutrality and omniscience, and, as is the case with other Valencian novels, he frequently transports the reader through the minds of the various characters. Some subjective authorial control, however, is evident in the progressively dominant tone of fatalism, the use of situational irony, and moments of open humor.

The style is natural and spontaneous, at times distinctly colloquial. The reader is most impressed by the fresh, graphic, highly sensuous descriptive passages, lyric moments in which a vivid plasticity and an appeal to the senses predominate. Indeed, it seems logical that Blasco Ibáñez dedicated the novel to his childhood friend Joaquín Sorolla, the artist whose vivid transcription and dazzling colors are reflected in the novelist's prose. The reader is immersed in descriptions of Cabañal and of the sea. One can envision the dawn after a night of rain, hear the distant whistle of the first trains leaving Valencia, and smell the wet earth of the village streets and the strong odors (presented in naturalistic fashion) of the local fish market. Animal images abound, and the leitmotifs of human bestiality and the human-sea relationship are the two main elements around which the novel's symbolism is constructed. (The sea itself, for example, represents the inexorable force of destiny.)

The characters are generally flat, since Blasco Ibáñez's frequent suggestion of naturalistic predestination precludes any substantial psychological development. Rather, the author was more interested in description and in constructing a rapid, suspenseful plot line for the daily readers of *El pueblo*, in which the work first appeared. Tonet is pleasure-loving, unrepentant, lazy, and self-centered. His brother El Retor is the first of Blasco Ibáñez's strong heroes, trustworthy, naïve, hardworking, and stubborn. In the last two chapters, an introspective glimpse into his musings is of a kind almost unique among the Valencian novels; a long interior monologue suggestive of Miguel de Unamuno y Jugo's later portraits of inner conflict and uncertainty reveals that, if it were not for the pressures of time and the force of his own tumultuous nature, Blasco Ibáñez might have created psychological portraits of considerable depth. Finally, of some importance is the way in which the author develops the entire *pueblo* as a kind of mass character, accustomed to the hell of life's struggle and to the constant challenge of death.

The central thematic statement of the novel concerns humankind's futile fight against the bestiality of human instincts and the powerful forces of nature. Secondary themes include a condemnation of excessive pride, a parody of religious rituals, and criticism of the villagers' exploitation by the people of Valencia.

The novel's structure is built around two main lines of action: El Retor's attempts to escape from poverty and the adulterous relationship between Tonet and Dolores. As in a number of the later Valencian works, the plot follows a regular, unified pattern: several expository chapters, consisting of an episodic introduction and two chapters of retrospective background; after that, the main action develops as a rectilinear, basically causal progression, within which the main costumbristic "digressions" become integral parts of the whole (the market scene, the Good Friday procession, the smuggling expedition, and the blessing of the boats). The unity of *The Mayflower*, like that of the other novels of the period, derives above all from the fact that Blasco Ibáñez wrote with a clear goal: to capture a people and a region. The powerful descriptions and vigorous, dramatic depiction of the villagers' primitive and difficult existence are the narrative manifestations of this purpose and represent those aspects of the work that are of greatest value.

THE CABIN

Blasco Ibáñez's third Valencian novel, *The Cabin*, was his first universally acclaimed masterpiece. It developed as the final version of a short story that he composed while hiding from the police during four days in 1895. The plot is extremely simple, lacking any kind of secondary complication and moving without distraction toward the final tragedy. In the village of Alboraya, in the *huerta* region north of Valencia, Tío Barret is evicted by a usurious landlord, whom Barret then kills in a burst of anger. For ten years, the villagers prevent anyone from working the land, as revenge for Barret's fate and as a warning to other landowners against mistreatment of the *huertanos*. Nevertheless, Batiste and his family arrive to restore the property and its shack. Pimentô, the village bully and loafer and a local warden for the rationing of irrigation use, causes Batiste to lose his water rights.

Meanwhile, other members of the family suffer: The daughter Roseta's romance with the butcher's apprentice is destroyed, and the three boys must fight their way home from school every day. The youngest son is thrown into a slimy irrigation ditch, which leads to his death. At this point, the villagers seem to repent of their actions and take charge of the funeral. Soon, however, Batiste is lured into a tavern fight with Pimentò, which leads to their shooting each other. On the night Pimentò dies from his wounds, Batiste awakens to find the cabin on fire. As the shack burns, the villagers leave the family to their plight.

The style of *The Cabin* exhibits those attributes already mentioned. Moments of naturalistic delineation and melodramatic animal imagery are perhaps more frequent than in *The Mayflower*, and the color red becomes particularly prominent (linking images of blood, earth, the irrigation water, the fire, the tavern atmosphere, and so on). Batiste (the stoic, hardworking protagonist typical of Blasco Ibáñez's works) and Pimentò (the cowardly incarnation of collective egotism and laziness) are opposite, unidimensional poles of character presentation. The latter figure and the various representatives of the village "chorus" exemplify well the author's powerful glimpses of mass psychology.

Structurally, the novel demonstrates a typical plan: three introductory chapters concerning the arrival of Batiste and then the past tragedy of Tío Barret, four of increasing conflict, and three final chapters in which the boy's funeral suggests a momentary peace and the final disaster is presented. Each of the ten chapters is built tightly into an organic whole, yet each demonstrates a kind of aesthetic autonomy, focusing on a single incident or anecdote. A strict causal line and the careful use of foreshadowing, contrast, and leitmotif add to the impression of structural unity. Finally, cyclical factors are evident, as Barret's story at the start and Batiste's fate at the end are meant to appear similar.

A sense of fatalism and inevitability, similar to that of *The Mayflower*, is created as thematic statements are made in condemnation of the landowners' exploitation and the hypocrisy and pride of the villagers, and in support of the will to struggle for individual liberty and the need to curb one's bestial instincts, to fight against nature and the influence of collective heredity.

The novel, then, is concerned with humankind's courageous attempts to overcome nearly insurmountable obstacles. This struggle is presented on two main levels, one socioeconomic and regional, the other of universal dimensions. Batiste finds work but discovers that he must betray his fellow *huertanos* in breaking the boycott against using forbidden lands. Blasco Ibáñez, however, is ambiguous in his loyalties; one first feels sympathy for the tenant farmers as Tío Barret's eviction is described, only to have one's allegiance shift to a man fighting against the farmer's prejudice and conservatism. The author admires worker solidarity but also respects Batiste's determination to better himself. This confusion, R. A. Cardwell believes, "might be counted the major flaw of the novel." The ending is also ambiguous.

At first glance the ending seems to demonstrate Blasco Ibáñez's pessimism about the power of society and tradition in thwarting individual enterprise, but on a deeper level it may suggest the author's optimism about a person's capacity for courageous struggle and a faint hope for eventual success. This ambiguity, in turn, relates to the universal level of meaning inherent in this and other Valencian novels. Humanity will continue to fight throughout the cyclical pattern of human existence. Blasco Ibáñez's novel thus suggests (albeit subtly) the final stage of the realistic movement of the 1890's, in which the materialistic naturalism of the previous decade gave way to idealistic themes of the need for human understanding and sympathy.

Within the trajectory of the Valencian works themselves, *The Cabin* seems to represent a middle position between the emphasis on socioeconomic concerns of *The Three Roses* and a later emphasis on the way a person acts when confronted by the universal laws of an all-powerful nature. *Reeds and Mud*, with its extraordinary depiction of such natural forces, is the most powerful expression of this subsequent focus.

REEDS AND MUD

While not recognized as such by all the critics, Blasco Ibáñez's last Valencian novel, *Reeds and Mud*, is probably his single greatest literary achievement. "It is the one work," the author confided to his friend Camilo Pitollet, "which holds for me the happiest memories, the one which I composed with the most solidity, the one which I think is the most rounded." The novel is one of the most thorough adaptations by any major Spanish writer of the tenets of French naturalism.

The scene is set between 1890 and 1900 in the swamplike region of the Albufera lake near Valencia, an area known to Blasco Ibáñez's non-Valencian readers for its rice fields and plentiful game birds. The narrative itself is constructed on three levels: first, the story of three generations—the old fisherman Tío Paloma, his hardworking son, Toni, and his rebellious, irresponsible grandson, Tonet; second, the lush, all-pervading atmosphere of the Albufera; and third, a constant, "transcendent" feeling of the power of destiny, the irrevocable pressures of an abstract, deterministic force.

The plot demonstrates the sharp singleness of effect that one generally finds in a short story and traces the love affair between Tonet and Neleta from childhood to disaster, years later. While the lad is away at war, the latter marries a sickly but rich tavern owner, Cañamèl, to escape her impoverished existence. The subsequent illicit love affair between Tonet and Neleta leads to a series of events in which humans are again shown to be defenseless against the destructive forces of nature and animal instinct. Tonet suffers an emotional breakdown. Cañamèl dies after specifying in his will that Neleta cannot retain their property if she remarries or associates in an intimate way with another man. After Neleta gives birth to Tonet's child, she refuses to see her lover openly and orders him to abandon the child in the city across the lake, to escape further suspicion of violating the terms of the will. Instead, fear, remorse, and accidents of fate lead Tonet to throw the infant into the lake. When his dog later discovers the baby's corpse, Tonet seeks escape from life's misery in suicide.

Blasco Ibáñez's skillful shifts in point of view contribute a great deal to the novel's sense of realism. Such shifts frequently reveal a single incident from several different perspectives. Despite the strong measure of objectivity and the relative lack of overt authorial comment, Blasco Ibáñez's humor breaks through now and then as a means of comic relief from the growing tension of the plot line; this is noticeable, for example, in the juvenile enthusiasm of Don Joaquín during a hunting incident and Sangonera's "religious love affair" with the three *pucheros*. Above all, *Reeds and Mud* includes Blasco Ibáñez's most striking descriptive passages, revealing the freshness, the spontaneity, the richness and sensual power that constitute his most significant artistic contribution.

As always with the Valencian novels, no figures are presented in great depth. Each seems to represent dominant passions or vices: laziness (Tonet), drunkenness (Sangonera), avarice (Neleta), the will to work and struggle (Toni), hatred for the changing times (Paloma), and so on. Certainly, all the characters are seen to blend in naturalistic fashion into the landscape around them (although they stand alongside nature rather than being consistently overpowered by it). Tonet is a victim of his own weaknesses: his indifference, his laziness, his hypocrisy, his yearning for adventure, and (under the influence of Neleta) his greed. Caught between the philosophies of his father and grandfather, Tonet is unable to shake off his inertia to make any decision regarding his life. Neleta comes also to represent the force and fecundity of nature. Sangonera, one of Blasco Ibáñez's most memorable types, is at the same time comic and pathetic, a kind of nineteenth century hippie or a modern version of the Golden Age *gracioso*, the comic "servant" who nevertheless is able to utter some very wise convictions. Toni corresponds to Batiste of *The Cabin* and to El Retor of *The Mayflower*, demonstrating the persistence, hard work, self-denial, and undying spirit of struggle that the author so admired.

Thematically, *Reeds and Mud* reveals the fullness of Blasco Ibáñez's acceptance of many tenets of the naturalists' philosophy. The human battle against the bestiality of human instincts and the powerful forces of nature is once again shown to be futile. Precluding an entirely naturalistic interpretation, however, are such factors as the exaltation of Paloma's and Toni's respective kinds of strength, the absence of heredity as a significant force, and a few elements of sheer coincidence in the plot line. (The plot itself does not reveal the strict logic of *The Cabin*; Tonet's suicide, for example, is not really the necessary outcome of causal factors.) Other related but minor thematic concerns again include the condemnation of egotism and envy and a criticism of humankind's drive to accumulate material goods at the expense of nature.

The novel's structure follows Blasco Ibáñez's typical pattern. The main action builds to three peaks, in scenes of adultery, infanticide, and suicide. As usual, a series of techniques is employed to achieve the effect of extraordinary unity: causal links of plot; the skillful integration into the narrative of the main costumbristic scenes (in this case, there are three—the raffle of the best fishing locations, the Fiesta del Niño Jesús, and the hunting expeditions, or *tiradas*); parallels and corresponding incidents; and the skillful use of timing, contrast, and the repetition of leitmotifs. In *Reeds and Mud*, Blasco Ibáñez succeeds most fully in achieving the aim of the Valencian novels: the lifelike rendering (rather than didactic or moralistic evaluation) of a region—its people, its customs, its ambience.

THE FOUR HORSEMEN OF THE APOCALYPSE

Although far inferior artistically to the best of his Valencian novels, Blasco Ibáñez's greatest popular success was *The Four Horsemen of the Apocalypse*. Here the protagonist, Julio Desnoyers, is an elegant young Argentine whose father, a Frenchman, had migrated to Argentina because of the Franco-Prussian War of 1870-1871. After making his fortune in South America, the elder Desnoyers takes his family to Paris. Julio decides to marry Margarita Laurier, a frivolous divorcée, but the outbreak of World War I produces a profound change in the thinking of both. Margarita abandons her interests in fashion and social activities and dedicates herself to the wounded soldiers as a nurse. Julio enlists and sacrifices his life fighting the Germans.

The title derives from the biblical book of Revelation, which describes the four scourges of plague, war, hunger, and death—forces that, the elder Desnoyers prophesies, will walk the earth again. The novel was written as an instrument of propaganda for the Allied cause, and its major weakness is its heavy-handed and exaggerated condemnation not only of the German military establishment but also of the German people and the entirety of German culture. An extraordinarily detailed and vivid account of the Battle of the Marne is the novel's one positive achievement.

Blasco Ibáñez's works are, to say the least, uneven. While his later novels will doubtless continue to be read for years, it is his early masterpieces that earn for him a major place in modern Spanish literature. When adequate studies of his novels are produced and acceptable translations of his best works appear, the world will acknowledge his magnificent descriptions of land and sea and of regional life around Valencia and his powerful portraits of individuals struggling against overwhelming internal and external obstacles.

Jeremy T. Medina

OTHER MAJOR WORKS

SHORT FICTION: *Fantasías, leyendas, y tradiciones*, 1887; *El adiós a Schubert*, 1888; *Cuentos valencianos*, 1896; *La condenada*, 1899; *Luna Benamor*, 1909 (includes the novel of the same title; English translation, 1919); *The Last Lion, and Other Tales*, 1919; *El préstamo de la difunta*, 1921; *Novelas de la costa azul*, 1924; *The Old Woman of the Movies, and Other Stories*, 1925; *Novelas de amor y de muerte*, 1927.

PLAY: *El juez*, pb. 1894.

NONFICTION: *Historia de la revolución española, 1808-1874*, 1890-1892; *París: Impresiones de un emigrado*, 1893; *En el país del arte*, 1896 (*In the Land of Art*, 1923); *Oriente*, 1907; *Argentina y sus grandezas*, 1910; *Historia de la guerra europea de 1914*, 1914-1919 (13 volumes); *El militarismo mejicano*, 1920 (*Mexico in Revolution*, 1920);

Una nación secuestrada: Alfonso XIII desenmascarado, 1924 (*Alfonso XIII Unmasked: The Military Terror in Spain*, 1924); *La vuelta al mundo de un novelista*, 1924-1925 (3 volumes; *A Novelist's Tour of the World*, 1926); *Lo que será la república española: Al país y al ejército*, 1925; *Estudios literarios*, 1933; *Discursos literarios*, 1966.

MISCELLANEOUS: *Obras completas*, 1923-1934 (40 volumes); *Obras completas*, 1964-1965 (3 volumes).

BIBLIOGRAPHY

Anderson, Christopher L. *Primitives, Patriarchy, and the Picaresque in Blasco Ibáñez's "Cañas y barro."* Potomac, Md.: Scripta Humanistica, 1995. Anderson reevaluates the novel *Reeds and Mud*, focusing on the portrayal of its female characters, whom he considers within the context of a male-dominated society.

Anderson, Christopher L., and Paul C. Smith. *Vicente Blasco Ibáñez: An Annotated Bibliography, 1975-2002*. Newark, Del.: Juan de la Cuesta, 2005. Extensively annotated compilation of writings by and about Blasco Ibáñez that updates Paul Smith's *Vicente Blasco Ibáñez: An Annotated Bibliography* (1976), which lists works published between 1882 and 1974.

Day, A. Grove, and Edgar C. Knowlton. *V. Blasco Ibáñez*. New York: Twayne, 1972. Survey of Blasco Ibáñez's life and canon that includes a discussion of his revolutionary influences, cosmopolitan experiences, interest in social protest and human psychology, glorification of Spain, and intense dislike of Germans.

Howells, William Dean. "The Fiction of Blasco Ibáñez." *Harper's* 131 (1915): 956-960. Howells, an American novelist and literary critic, praises Blasco Ibáñez's literary skill.

Medina, Jeremy T. *The Valencian Novels of Vicente Blasco Ibáñez*. Valencia, Spain: Albatros Ediciones, 1984. A study of five novels with themes relating to Valencia: *The Three Roses*, *The Mayflower*, *The Cabin*, *The Torrent*, and *Reeds and Mud*. Medina has written two other studies of Blasco Ibáñez's novels, both published by Albatros Ediciones. These studies are *The "Psychological" Novels of Vicente Blasco Ibáñez* (1990) and *From Sermon to Art: The Thesis Novels of Vicente Blasco Ibáñez* (1998).

Oxford, Jeffrey Thomas. *Vicente Blasco Ibáñez: Color Symbolism in Selected Novels*. New York: Peter Lang, 1997. Analyzes the use of color in some of Blasco Ibáñez's novels, arguing that although he was a naturalist, he often depicted life in a subjectively artificial way that belied the naturalists' attempt to objectively portray reality.

Swain, James O. *Vicente Blasco Ibáñez, General Study: Special Emphasis on Realistic Techniques*. Knoxville: University of Tennessee Press, 1959. A critical study of Blasco Ibáñez's work, with one chapter focusing on the realistic images of war in *The Four Horsemen of the Apocalypse*.

CAMILO JOSÉ CELA

Born: Iria Flavia del Padrón, Spain; May 11, 1916
Died: Madrid, Spain; January 17, 2002
Also known as: Camilo José Cela Trulock

PRINCIPAL LONG FICTION
La familia de Pascual Duarte, 1942 (*The Family of Pascual Duarte*, 1946, 1964)
Pabellón de reposo, 1943 (*Rest Home*, 1961)
Nuevas andanzas y desventuras del Lazarillo de Tormes, 1944
La colmena, 1951 (*The Hive*, 1953)
Mrs. Caldwell habla con su hijo, 1953 (*Mrs. Caldwell Speaks to Her Son*, 1968)
La Catira, 1955
Tobogán de hambrientos, 1962
Vísperas, festividad, y octava de San Camilo del año 1936 en Madrid, 1969 (*San Camilo, 1936: The Eve, Feast, and Octave of St. Camillus of the Year 1936 in Madrid*, 1991)
Oficio de tinieblas, 5, 1973
Mazurka para dos muertos, 1983 (*Mazurka for Two Dead Men*, 1993)
Cristo versus Arizona, 1988 (*Christ Versus Arizona*, 2007)
El asesinato del perdedor, 1994
La cruz de San Andres, 1994
Madera de Boj, 1999 (*Boxwood*, 2002)

OTHER LITERARY FORMS

The novels of Camilo José Cela (SAY-lah) constitute but a fraction of his literary production. He excelled as a short-story writer and author of travel books, having published more than half a dozen volumes in each of these genres. *Esas nubes que pasan* (1945; passing clouds) contains twelve tales previously published in periodicals. It was followed by *El bonito crimen del carabinero y otras invenciones* (1947; the patrolman's nice crime and other inventions), *El gallego y su cuadrilla* (1949; the Galician and his team), *Baraja de invenciones* (1953; deck of inventions), *El molino de viento* (1956; the windmill), *Gavilla de fábulas sin amor* (1962; bag of loveless fables), *Once cuentos de fútbol* (1963; eleven soccer tales), and others.

Cela's early travel books were superior to the later ones, the better ones including *Viaje a la Alcarria* (1948; *Journey to Alcarria*, 1964), *Del Miño al Bidasoa* (1952; from the Miño to the Bidasoa), *Judíos, moros, y cristianos* (1956; Jews, Moors, and Christians), *Primer viaje andaluz* (1959; first Andalusian trip), *Viaje al Pirineo de Lérida* (1965; trip to the Lérida Pyrenees), *Páginas de geografía errabunda* (1965; pages of vagabond geography), and *Viaje a U.S.A.* (1967; trip to the U.S.).

Cela has many volumes of essays to his credit, including *Mesa revuelta* (1945; messy table); *La rueda de los ocios* (1957; wheel of idleness); *Cajón de sastre* (1957; tailor's box); *La obra literaria del pintor Solana* (1958; the literary work of the painter Solana), which was Cela's entrance speech to the Royal Spanish Academy; *Cuatro figuras del '98* (1961), on four writers of the Generation of '98; *Al servicio de algo* (1969; in service to something); *A vueltas con España* (1973; around again with Spain); *Vuelta de hoja* (1981; turning the page); and *El juego de los tres madroños* (1983; the shell game).

Cela's miscellaneous prose works include his unfinished memoirs, *La cucaña* (the cocoon), of which the first volume, *La rosa* (the rose), published in 1959, spans his childhood. Cela also cultivated what he called *apuntes carpetovetónicos* (carpetovetonic sketches), a term alluding to the mountains of central Spain. These brief literary etchings or vignettes—*Historias de España: Los ciegos, los tontos* (1958) and *Los viejos amigos* (1960, 1961)—combine humor, irony, anger, pity, and a bittersweet affection, and portray beggars, the blind, village idiots, prostitutes, and a host of the poor and indigent. His short stories and novellas range from the exquisitely crafted stylistic tour de force, in which popular language or regional dialect is captured in all of its inimitable regional flavor, to the condensed, violent shocker, the prose poem, and the ironic vignette. The itinerant wanderings of the narrator of picaresque novels are updated in his travel books, as Cela adapted the form to covert sociopolitical commentary.

During the 1960's, Cela published several limited-edition works for the collectors' market, some with illustrations by Pablo Picasso and others featuring artistic photography, most of them short on narrative and long on the visual, including *Toreo de salón* (1963; living room bull-fighting), *Las compañías convenientes* (1963; appropriate company), *Garito de hospicianos* (1963; poorhouse inmates), *Izas, rabizas, y colipoterras* (1964; bawds, harlots, and whores), *El ciudadano Iscariote Reclús* (1965; citizen Iscariot Reclus), *La familia del héroe* (1965; the hero's family), and a series of seven *Nuevas escenas matritenses* (1965-1966; new Madrid scenes). His *Obra completa* (complete works) first appeared in 1962 and was finished in 1983.

Achievements

With the death and exile of many writers of previous generations, Spanish literature languished during and after the Spanish Civil War (1936-1939). The first sign of rebirth was Camilo José Cela's novel *The Family of Pascual Duarte*, which sparked a host of imitators and set the pattern for the novel during much of the 1940's, a movement known as *tremendismo*. His next novels were successful, if less imitated, and his fame was assured with *The Hive*, which became the prototype for the social novel of the 1950's and 1960's. It is extremely rare that a Spanish writer is able to live by his or her pen, and Cela managed to do so. He was elected to the prestigious Royal Spanish Academy in 1957 and was appointed independent senator to represent intellectual interests and views by King Juan Carlos in 1978. In 1989, he was awarded the Nobel Prize in Literature. Many of his works have been translated, and for nearly four decades he was considered one of Spain's foremost novelists. Cela was a trendsetter, interesting as an innovator, stylist, and caricaturist but not as a creator of memorable characters or plots.

Biography

Born Camilo José Cela Trulock in 1916, Camilo José Cela occasionally made literature of his life, and many biographies of him contain apocryphal data. Although his mother grew up in Spain, she was a British citizen; his father was a customs official, and the family moved often.

Cela was an indifferent student in religious schools attended the University of Madrid from 1934 to 1936, during which time he published his first poems. In 1936, he dropped out of school to serve on the side of General Francisco Franco and his rebels in the Spanish Civil War. He returned to the university from 1939 to 1943, a period during which he published his first articles and short stories as well as his famous first novel, *The Family of Pascual Duarte*. Although Cela studied law, medicine, and philosophy, he did not complete a degree. His literary knowledge was largely self-taught, the fruit of reading the Spanish classics while recovering from bouts of tuberculosis as a young man. Cela likewise became a serious student of regional Spanish history and folkways and an untiring lexicographer of sexual and scatological speech. Cela married María del Rosario Conde Picavea in 1944; their only child, a son, was born in 1946.

Over the years Cela involved himself in several publishing enterprises, and in 1957 he founded the influential journal *Papeles de Son Armadans*. This was the first Spanish periodical of its kind to circumvent the censorship of the Franco regime, possible in large part because of Cela's having fought on the winning side during the Spanish Civil War. Despite his connections, Cela found it expedient to avoid the political limelight by moving to the Balearic Islands during the 1960's. There he counted among his friends such luminaries as artist Joan Miró and poet Robert Graves. Only after winning the Nobel Prize in 1989 did he return to the Spanish mainland. Cela and his first wife were divorced in 1991, at which time Cela married journalist Marina Castaño.

Analysis

Camilo José Cela had an inimitable way with language, a personal style that is instantly recognizable after minimal acquaintance, thanks to his characteristic handling of the *estribillo* (tag line), alliterative and rhythmic prose, parallelistic constructions, grotesque caricatures with moments of tenderness, unabashed lyricism with ever-present irony, and the incorporation of popular sayings or proverbs, vulgarities, and obscenities in the context of academically correct and proper passages. His art more closely approaches the painter's than the dramatist's, and it is far removed from the adventure novel.

With the exception perhaps of *The Family of Pascual Duarte*, Cela's novels have little action and a preponderance of description and dialogue. As a painter with words, one of whose favorite subjects is language itself, unflaggingly aware of its trivializations and absurdities yet fascinated with nuances, examining and playing with words, Cela produced ironic conversations, incidents, and scenes that often could very well stand alone. This characteristic, usually one of his virtues as a writer, becomes at times a vice, for he tends to repeat himself and also to produce novels in which there is little if any character development, and often no sustained or sequential action—no plot in the traditional sense. The reader whose interest in a piece of fiction is proportional to "what happens" may find Cela's short stories more rewarding than his novels.

Because it inspired many imitations, Cela's first novel, *The Family of Pascual Duarte*, is considered the prototype of a novelistic movement called *tremendismo*, an allusion to its "tremendous" impact upon the reader's sensibilities. *Tremendismo*—a modified naturalism that lacks the scientific pretensions of the French movement, and to which expressionistic ingredients were added—was characterized by depiction of crimes of sometimes shocking violence, a wide range of mental and sexual aberrations, and antiheroic figures. Frequently repulsive, deviant, and nauseating acts, as well as an accumulation of ugly, malformed, and repugnant characters, were portrayed against a backdrop of poverty and social problems. To this naturalistic setting were added expressionistic techniques including stylized distortion and the use of caricature and dehumanization (reduction of characters, or acts, or both, to animalistic levels). *Tremendismo* had links with postwar existentialism in the absurdity of the world portrayed, the concern with problems of guilt and authenticity, and the radical solitariness and uncommunicative nature of its characters. In part, the movement was inspired by the horrors of the Spanish Civil War, providing an outlet for outrage when overt protest was impossible.

Not all of Cela's early novels fit this class: The accumulation of violent and sadistic or irrational crimes that are found in the prototypical first novel disappeared in its successor, *Rest Home*, which is set in a tuberculosis sanatorium, an environment the author had occasion to know well. *Rest Home* uses the diary form, excerpts from the writings of several anonymous patients. The sense of alienation and despair that results from helplessness pervades this novel as the victims battle not only their disease but also the indifference of the world at large and the callousness or cruelty of medical personnel; this insensitivity to death, humanity's cruelty to others, is the "tremendous" element in this otherwise quiet, hopeless, almost paralytic novel. In *The Hive*, it is the overall tone or atmosphere (there is only one crime, an unsolved murder), an atmosphere of defeatism, cynicism, and sordid materialism, that is characteristic of *tremendismo*. Still, although critics continue to talk of *tremendismo* in *The Hive*, it is so modified and attenuated that there is a legitimate question as to whether the world portrayed in the novel can rightly be so described.

The Family of Pascual Duarte

Pascual Duarte, the protagonist and narrative consciousness of *The Family of Pascual Duarte*, is a condemned criminal on death row who has undertaken to write his confession as a sort of penance, at the behest of the prison chaplain. Cela utilizes a model derived from the classic Spanish picaresque novel, clearly perceptible in the early chapters—a technique that undoubtedly served to make the somewhat scabrous material more acceptable to the regime's puritanical but strongly nationalist and traditionalistic censors. The frequent appearances of roads, inns and taverns, squalid settings, and marginal characters all reflect the picaresque tradition, as does the first-person, autobiographical form.

Pascual's home life, with a brutal father who made his money illegally, an alcoholic and altogether beastly mother (clearly patterned on the mother of the prototypical picaro, Lazarillo de Tormes), and a sister who became a teenage prostitute, was an endless round of brawls. Exemplifying the notion that hopeless situations go from bad to worse is his mother's promiscuity and the birth of his half brother, Mario, an imbecile who comes into the world at the same time that Pascual's father, locked in a wardrobe, is dying amid hideous screams after having been bitten by a rabid dog.

Mario never learns to walk or talk but drags himself along the floor like a snake, making whistling noises. He is kicked in the head by his putative father, which results in a festering sore, and finally has an ear and part of his face eaten by a pig as he lies in the street. His brief, unhappy existence comes to an end at the age of seven or eight when he falls into a large stone container of olive oil and drowns. Pascual's grotesquely lyric recollection of the child's one moment of "beauty," with the golden oil clinging to his hair and softening his features and expression, is typical of Cela's art. The burial of Mario (attended only by Pascual and a village girl, Lola, who was attracted to him) is climaxed by Pascual's rape of Lola atop Mario's newly dug grave. It is characteristic of Cela also to combine Eros and Thanatos, sexuality and death: Humanity is viewed as a sensual animal, its reproductive appetite or instincts aroused by the presence of death.

Pascual's name alludes to the Paschal lamb, or Easter sacrifice, and in an author's foreword to a special edition of the novel printed outside Spain for use by English-speaking students of Spanish, Cela spoke of the "pro-rata of guilt" or responsibility that each member of society shares for the crimes committed by one of that society's members, suggesting that persons are products of the society in and by which they are formed and thus, at best, only partially culpable for their acts. Pascual is a product of the dregs of society, whose existence is the result of the worst kind of social injustice, yet he displays no greed or resentment of the easy life of the wealthy; his crimes are usually crimes of passion and, with the exception of the killing of his mother, are not premeditated.

Significantly, Pascual is always morally superior in one or more ways to his victims, suggesting that he is to be viewed as something of a primitive judge and executioner, taking justice into his own hands. His meting out of retribution spares neither person nor beast: He shoots his hunting hound because the dog looked at him the wrong way (interpreted by him as sexual desire or temptation); he knifes his mare (and only transportation) because she had shied, throwing Pascual's pregnant bride and causing her to miscarry; he strangles his first wife in a moment of temporary insanity, upon learning that while he was jailed for knifing a man in a tavern brawl, she had survived by selling herself to El Estirao, the pimp exploiting Pascual's sister; and he later asphyxiates El Estirao when the pimp taunts him. The ax-murder of his mother (who subverted the scruples of his first wife and was ruining his second marriage as well) is one of the bloodiest and most violent passages in contemporary Spanish fiction, yet the reader cannot entirely condemn Pascual.

The novel alternates chapters of violent action with slower, introspective and meditative chapters that not only vary the narrative rhythm but also serve to present the human side of the criminal, who might otherwise appear nothing less than monstrous. They also make it clear that Pascual is completely lacking in social consciousness; his crimes are not politically motivated, nor do they have any connection with revolution in the social sense—a point that is extremely important to the hidden message of the novel as a whole. Although Pascual's autobiographical memoir is abruptly ended by his execution (he had narrated his life only up to the slaying of his mother), it is possible to deduce from evidence elsewhere in the text that he spent some fifteen years in the penitentiary as a result of his conviction for matricide; he was released at a moment immediately prior to the outbreak of the Spanish Civil War that coincided with a brief but bloody social revolution that swept his home province of Badajoz. The reader deduces (for the cause of his execution is nowhere stated) that Pascual has been convicted of the murder of the Count of Torremejía, the major clue being the dedication of his memoirs to the Count, Don Jesús, accompanied by an ambiguous statement that could mean that he killed him, but could also convey the idea of a mercy killing, assuming that he found the Count dying in agony, perhaps having been tortured by terrorists.

A supreme irony inheres in Pascual's having received extremely light sentences—from two to fifteen years—for several previous killings, while he is executed as a common criminal for what might normally have been classed an act of war, because the victim was an aristocrat. Given the totalitarian censorship in force at the time the novel was written, none of this is overtly expressed; it is necessary to have a thorough knowledge of contemporary Spanish history and to be aware of such details as the social revolution in Badajoz, likewise unmentioned in the novel, to be able to interpret the otherwise enigmatic denouement to Pascual's career of violence.

One of the clearest proofs that Cela's major virtue is his style is the fact that, despite competent translations, his works have been relatively ill received by readers of the English-language versions; his style, like poetry, is lost in translation. Too closely bound to colloquial idiom and regional dialect to be fully translatable, Cela's prose must be appreciated in the original. Thus, Pascual Duarte's story is atypical in being able to stand on its own in other cultures, as was confirmed by the success of the 1976 film version, which won a best actor's award at the Cannes International Film Festival for José Luis Gómez. With all of his contradictions, Pascual is Cela's most complex and memorable character; none of his subsequent novels contains characters sufficiently developed to intrigue the reader and sustain his or her interest.

The Family of Pascual Duarte has been compared by critics repeatedly to Albert Camus's *L'étranger* (1942; *The Stranger*) because of proximity in date of appearance and certain other similarities (the antihero and protagonist-narrator of each novel is a condemned killer awaiting execution, one who speaks impassively of his life and exhibits a shocking lack of internalization of society's values). The differences between the two novels are many, however, the most important being that the narrative consciousness of *The Stranger* is an educated and moderately cultured man, guilty of a single, senseless "reflex" crime, and the philosophical dimension of Camus's writing, while not utterly alien to Cela, is so attenuated because of the audience for which the novel was intended that its impact is minimal.

THE HIVE

The Hive, regarded by many critics as Cela's masterpiece, occupied much of the novelist's time between 1945 and 1950. Because it lacks both plot and protagonist, consisting of a series of loosely connected sketches, some have suggested that Cela must have used as his model John Dos Passos's *Manhattan Transfer* (1925); both novels attempt a wide-ranging portrait of urban life. The similarities are relatively superficial, however, and a major difference exists in the treatment of time: *Manhattan Transfer* covers some twenty years, while *The Hive* spans only a few days. The action in *The Hive* takes place during the winter of 1943, and a specific reference is made to the meeting of Winston Churchill, Joseph Stalin, and Franklin D. Roosevelt in November of that year, undoubtedly selected by Cela because it was one of the worst periods for Spain, a time when postwar reconstruction had not begun, wartime shortages had grown worse, and the countries that might have helped Spain were too occupied with World War II to think of the Spanish people's plight.

This background is very significant to the ambience and psychological climate of the novel; characters are either concerned with where their next meal will come from or are involved in the black market and the abuse of the hungry. Many characters are moochers who hang around cafés in the hope of being offered a drink or a meal, or at least a cigarette, while several girls and women are obliged to sell themselves for food, medicine, or small necessities.

In *The Hive*, Cela brings together a number of characters with no more mutual relationship than that which results from being in the same place for a brief time. The common site in part 1 is the café of Doña Rosa. Although the author in one of his many prologues to the successive editions claims that he did nothing but go to the plaza with his camera, "and if the models were ugly, too bad," this suggestion of objective, mimetic technique must not be taken too literally, for large doses of his characteristic exaggeration, dehumanization, and caricature are present, as can be appreciated in the figure of Rosa, one of Cela's most repugnant females.

Exceedingly fat, Rosa smokes, drinks, coughs continually, dotes upon bloody tales of violence and crime, is foulmouthed, and has such a habit of peeling off her face that she is compared to a serpent changing its skin; she has a mustache, beaded with sweat, its hairs like the little black "horns" of a cricket, and spends her days insulting and cheating the customers. There is also a suggestion that she is a lesbian. Much of the negative presentation becomes understandable when one reflects that Doña Rosa is an outspoken advocate of Adolf Hitler: At a time when no criticism of fascism was possible inside Spain, Rosa presents such extreme physical and moral ugliness that her ideological preferences necessarily suffer by association.

Several other recurring motifs of Cela's fiction are apparent in *The Hive*: the division of humanity into the basic categories of victims and victimizers, the obsessive preoccupation with aberrant sexuality, the notion that the bad are many and the good are few (and generally not too bright), the concept that humankind is innately cruel, and the insistent repetition of tag lines and names or nicknames. So frequent and systematic is the use of nicknames and variants of the names of characters that, when combined with the large number of characters and the usual brevity of their appearances, it is next to impossible to determine exactly how many characters there are, as well as to be sure in many cases whether a character is completely new or one previously met and now reappearing under a nickname. Various commentators have placed the total number of characters at 160, but other estimates suggest more than 360. Obviously, with few exceptions, characters are superficially drawn, usually caricatures; only a handful can be said to have any psychological depth.

Each of the novel's six parts is unified by some common denominator (in addition to the time, for there is a certain simultaneity of events in each part or chapter). In the first part, all the characters have some relationship to the café of Doña Rosa, whether as employees, regular customers, or accidental visitors. In the second part, events take place in the street, beginning immediately outside the café as Martín Marco, a ne'er-do-well who serves as a sort of link between various parts and locales, is kicked out for not paying his bill. Some of the customers are followed from the street to their houses, while others are seen in the third part in still another café, where Martín also goes to talk with still more characters (several of whom are under police surveillance and apparently arrested before the novel's end, implicating Martín also).

The next part returns to the street and events late at night after the closing of the cafés, when the wealthy go to after-hours clubs and the poor must use the vacant lots for their furtive encounters. The common denominator of part 5 is eroticism, with a wide range of amorous intrigues (light on sentiment and heavy on sexuality) and views of several houses of ill repute of different economic levels. There is also a recurring theme of loss, as most of the characters lose something (dreams, hope, illusions, virginity). The clearest example is the case of an adolescent girl, an orphan sold by her aunt to an aged pedophile. The sixth part is united by the numerous reawakenings with the new day, some characters in their homes, others in brothels, Doña Rosa in her café before dawn, the homeless gypsy boy beneath the city bridge, some breakfasting and others hungry, part of the city already going to work and a few about to go to bed. The protagonist, if there is one, is collective: the city of Madrid, which is the beehive of the title, with its workers and drones.

Reviewers of the English translation saw *The Hive* as a passable example of the "low-life genre," but if one is sufficiently familiar with the sociopolitical situation of Spain at the time the novel was written, it is possible to extract additional meanings. All of the numerous characters of the novel reappear several times, with the exceptions of Suárez, who is gay, and his lover; the two are accused of complicity in the murder of Suárez's mother, Doña Margot, not on the basis of any evidence but because their sexual identity was not acceptable. The two are taken to police headquarters for interrogation and simply disappear for the remainder of the novel, a case of critique via omission, a not uncommon technique in the rhetoric of silent dissent.

Another interest of the novelist is the invisible links between human beings, who are usually themselves unaware of those links. Thus Matilde, a widowed pensioner and client of Doña Rosa, owns a boardinghouse where Ventura Aguado, lover of Rosa's niece, resides—connections unknown to all concerned, reflecting existential theories of human relationships. A much more elaborate development of this theme occurs in Cela's *Tobogán de hambrientos*, in which each chapter presents a new cast of characters, linked only by one tenuous contact with a single character from the previous chapter. Thus, in chapter 1, an entire family appears; the following chapter may present the family and relatives and friends of the boyfriend of one daughter of the family in the first chapter, and chapter 3 may take up the associates and relatives of the garbage collector of the family of the boyfriend, chapter 4 the boss of the daughter of the garbage collector, and so on, through a certain number of chapters after which the process is reversed and the novelist proceeds in inverse order, through the same groups, back to the point of origin.

While mild in comparison with many of Cela's later works, *The Hive* was daring for its day, and Spanish publishers refused to touch it; it was published in Buenos Aires, Argentina, and smuggled into Spain, selling so well that the government (which levied a profitable tax on several stages of the book business) authorized an expurgated edition, which in turn was soon prohibited and withdrawn from circulation when objectionable points were found—a procedure repeated nine times by 1962. Not only is *The Hive* significant from the standpoint of literary history as a model for the neorealistic "social" novel in Spain during the 1950's and 1960's; it also had considerable import in its day as a manifestation of liberal intellectual opposition to the Franco dictatorship and its policies.

The Hive was a turning point in Cela's development as a novelist, marking a transition from rural to urban settings and from a semitraditional format to open experimentalism and fragmentary structures. Although the novel's transitions from character to character and scene to scene may seem abrupt or arbitrary, they are in fact artfully calculated and serve to make otherwise censurable material more palatable than if it had been presented in its totality, without interruption or suspension.

Mrs. Caldwell Speaks to Her Son

The fragmentary nature of *Mrs. Caldwell Speaks to Her Son* is even more apparent, with more than two hundred brief chapters, in which sequential or connected action is again lacking. The time element is extremely vague and diffuse; the narration is almost totally retrospective but not in any semblance of chronological order. Mrs. Caldwell speaks in the second-person singular (the familiar you, or "thou") to her son Ephraim, sometimes reminiscing, sometimes railing, at other times waxing lyrical (there are even sections that are lyric asides, in the nature of prose poems, such as one quite lengthy piece titled "The Iceberg"). Bit by bit, it becomes apparent to the reader that Mrs. Caldwell's relationship with her son has abnormal undertones, including incest, abuse, sexual or psychological bondage, and possibly crimes involving third parties; subsequently, it is revealed that Ephraim is dead and has been so for many years, drowned in unexplained circumstances in the Aegean Sea. Mrs. Caldwell, the reader realizes, is insane; whether any of the things she recalls actually happened is a matter of conjecture, as is the reality of the ending, for she is supposedly burned to death when she paints flames on the wall of her room in the asylum.

Surrealistic elements are more prominent in *Mrs. Caldwell Speaks to Her Son* than in any of Cela's previously published prose, although they abound in his early book of poetry *Poemas de una adolescencia cruel* (1945), written for the most part during the Spanish Civil War and published in 1945. The surrealistic substratum comes to the surface periodically during the writer's career and is especially evident in the hallucinatory oratorio *María Sabina* (1967), performed in 1970, and in *El solitario*, a series of absurdist and surrealistic sketches published in 1963. It comes to the fore in Cela's long fiction in *San Camilo, 1936*, and in *Oficio de tinieblas, 5*. Readers whose concept of Cela had been based on acquaintance with his best-known novels were surprised and disconcerted by what seemed to be an abrupt about-face on his part, a switch from an objective and essentially realistic manner to extreme subjectivity of focus, with an emphasis upon vanguard experimentalism in *San Camilo, 1936*, and *Oficio de tinieblas, 5*. In fact, both the extended second-person monologue of the former and the extreme discontinuity of the latter are clearly anticipated in *Mrs. Caldwell Speaks to Her Son*.

San Camilo, 1936

San Camilo, 1936, and *The Hive* are comparable in providing panoramic views of Madrid at similar points in Spanish history (1936 and 1942, respectively); in both, historical events are interwoven with everyday concerns. Both novels feature an enormous cast and exhibit a strong awareness of social injustice, poverty, hunger, and exploitation. In both, Cela's characteristic emphasis on sexual themes, abnormality, deviance, and the scatological are prominent, and both encompass only a few days in the life of the capital. Both are essentially plotless, depending upon strict temporal and spatial limitation for unity in place of the structuring function normally exercised by plot; both lack protagonists in the normal sense, although the city of Madrid may play this role. Both novels feature innumerable cuts, abrupt changes of scene, shifts of focus, and an architectonic design, a complex pattern the most visible features of which are repetition and parallelism.

However, *San Camilo, 1936*, is far from being a mere extension or replay of the earlier novel; a most significant difference is the setting in republican Spain, which imparts a sense of freedom, even license, lacking in *The Hive*. The days spanned in *San Camilo, 1936*, are marked by major historical events, immediately preceding and following the outbreak of the Spanish Civil War in July of 1936.

The action of *San Camilo, 1936* begins on Sunday, July 12, 1936, which witnessed the political assassination of Lieutenant Castillo, in reprisal for his part in the killing, three months before, of a cousin of José Antonio Primo de Rivera, founder of the Falange. Revenge for Castillo's killing, a gangster-style execution of conservative opposition leader Calvo Sotelo on July 13, led to a series of riots and was the pretext for the uprising on July 16 of General Franco and several other military leaders, obliging the republican government to distribute arms to the populace on July 18. These events, and the funerals of both victims (July 14), are re-created from the vantage point of several witnesses in the novel, although the underlying reasons are not elucidated and the historical antecedents are not mentioned.

The atmosphere of growing tension and pent-up violence is subliminally reinforced through the novelist's concentration on a series of minor crimes, accidental deaths, actual and attempted political reprisals by both extremes, repetitive motifs of blood and suffering, and an intensifying irrational desire on the part of the narrative consciousness to kill. An impression of neutrality is nevertheless sustained; with three decades of hindsight, the novelist's ire is directed less at those at either extreme of the Spanish political spectrum than at foreign intervention—a significant departure from the usual strongly partisan accounts of the Spanish Civil War.

OFICIO DE TINIEBLAS, 5

Oficio de tinieblas, 5, is a novel only in the loosest sense, a logical extension of Cela's continuing experimentation with the genre; its obsessive preoccupation with Eros and Thanatos, its language and tone are indubitably his. Discontinuous in structure, this work comprises nearly twelve hundred "monads" (numbered paragraphs or subdivisions) abounding in references to farce, concealment, deceit, flight, self-effacement, defeat, inauthenticity, self-elimination, betrayal, prostitution, alienation, and death. Cela's disappointed idealism and his retreat into apparent cynicism are expressed in *San Camilo, 1936*, in the theme of massive prostitution—of the state, the nation, the leaders and lawmakers, the ideologies, the totality of Spanish existence. In *Oficio de tinieblas, 5*, Cela's retreat takes the form of a desire for death and oblivion, counterpointed by an obsessive emphasis on sexual aberration (the novel is saved from being pornographic by learned euphemisms, Latin and medical terminology for sexual organs and activity).

Mazurka for Two Dead Men

The new freedom of Spain's post-Franco era is reflected in *Mazurka for Two Dead Men*, Cela's first novel to be published after Franco's death. Here, Cela continues his exploration of violence, portraying the monotonous brutality of peasant life in his native Galicia with fablelike simplicity. Told by multiple narrators, the novel takes place during the first four decades of the twentieth century and treats the Spanish Civil War as merely the culmination of a long cycle of violence. Any appearance of neutrality has been suspended, however, as the pro-Franco characters are clearly villainous, the prorepublicans heroic. Perhaps more notable are the appearances in the novel of a character named Don Camilo and a family named Cela.

Christ Versus Arizona

In 1954, Cela had been welcomed in Venezuela as a guest of honor and commissioned to write a novel set there. The result was *La Catira*, an ambitious book that nevertheless made clear Cela's lack of interest in sustained narrative. The novel that followed *Mazurka for Two Dead Men* is similarly set outside Spain but makes clear one manner—itself often daunting—in which Cela has overcome this apparent defect. As its title suggests, *Christ Versus Arizona* takes place in the American Southwest. Told through the brutal words of Wendell Liverpool Espana, the novel deals with events in Arizona during the final two decades of the nineteenth century and the first two of the twentieth century. These events include the legendary gunfight at the OK Corral, an event in which Cela expressed much interest and whose site he visited. Espana relates his sordid story of violence and murder in a long monologue without paragraph breaks that clearly reveals his mental state but that makes considerable demands of the reader.

El asesinato del perdedor

El asesinato del perdedor continues Cela's increasingly difficult experimental style and relates the story—if it can be called that—of Mateo Ruecas, who commits suicide while in prison. The novel is not divided into chapters but rather incorporates the seemingly unrelated (if uniformly brutal and vulgar) monologues of a host of unidentified secondary characters. Cela's first novel to be published after he received the Nobel Prize, *El asesinato del perdedor* may well reflect Cela's well-known disdain for authority and "proper" behavior.

Janet Pérez
Updated by Grove Koger

Other major works

SHORT FICTION: *Esas nubes que pasan*, 1945; *El bonito crimen del carabinero y otras invenciones*, 1947; *El gallego y su cuadrilla*, 1949; *Baraja de invenciones*, 1953; *El molino de viento*, 1956; *Nuevo retablo de don Cristobita*, 1957; *Historias de España: Los ciegos, los tontos,* 1958; *Los viejos amigos,* 1960, 1961 (2 volumes); *Gavilla de fábulas sin amor,* 1962; *El solitario,* 1963; *Once cuentos de fútbol,* 1963; *Toreo de salón,* 1963; *Izas, rabizas, y colipoterras,* 1964; *El ciudadano Iscariote Reclús,* 1965; *La familia del héroe,* 1965; *El hombre y el mar,* 1990; *Historias familiares,* 1998.

POETRY: *Poemas de una adolescencia cruel,* 1945 (also known as *Pisando la dudosa luz del día,* 1960); *María Sabina,* 1967; *Cancionero de la Alcarria,* 1987; *Poesía completa,* 1996.

NONFICTION: *Mesa revuelta,* 1945; *Viaje a la Alcarria,* 1948 (*Journey to Alcarria,* 1964); *Del Miño al Bidasoa,* 1952; *Judíos, moros, y cristianos,* 1956; *Cajón de sastre,* 1957; *La rueda de los ocios,* 1957; *La obra literaria del pintor Solana,* 1958; *Primer viaje andaluz,* 1959; *La rosa,* 1959 (volume 1 of *La cucaña,* his unfinished memoirs); *Cuatro figuras del '98,* 1961; *Las compañías convenientes,* 1963; *Garito de hospicianos,* 1963; *Páginas de geografía errabunda,* 1965; *Viaje al Pirineo de Lérida,* 1965; *Viaje a U.S.A.,* 1967; *Al servicio de algo,* 1969; *A vueltas con España,* 1973; *Vuelta de hoja,* 1981; *El juego de los tres madroños,* 1983; *El asno de Buridán,* 1986; *Galicia,* 1990; *Blanquito, peón de Brega,* 1991; *Memorias, entendimientos, y voluntades,* 1993; *El color de la mañana,* 1996.

MISCELLANEOUS: *Obra completa,* 1962-1989; *Nuevas escenas matritenses: Fotografías de Enrique Palazuelo,* 1965-1966.

BIBLIOGRAPHY

Busette, Cedric. *"La Familia de Pascual Duarte" and "El Túnel": Correspondences and Divergencies in the Exercise of Craft.* Lanham, Md.: University Press of America, 1994. Busette compares and contrasts the debut novels of Cela and Ernesto Sábato, analyzing their narrative, language, protagonists, and other aspects of the two novels.

Cela, Camilo José. Interview by Valerie Miles. *Paris Review* 38, no. 139 (Summer, 1996): 124-163. A lengthy interview in which Cela discusses his personal life and career, including his family and academic background, literary training, some of his works, and thoughts on censorship.

Charlebois, Lucile C. *Understanding Camilo José Cela.* Columbia: University of South Carolina Press, 1998. A thorough but difficult study of Cela's progressively difficult novels. Each chapter focuses on one of the novels, beginning with *The Family of Pascual Duarte* through *La cruz de San Andres.* Includes a chronology and a select bibliography.

Henn, David. *C. J. Cela: La Colmena.* 1974. Reprint. London: Grant & Cutler, 1997. An eighty-page brief study of *The Hive,* usually recognized as Cela's masterpiece. Part of the Critical Guides to Spanish Texts series. Includes an updated bibliography.

Hoyle, Alan. *Cela: "La familia de Pascual Duarte."* London: Grant & Cutler, with Tamesis Books, 1994. Another book in the Critical Guides to Spanish Texts series, providing an analysis of Cela's first and best-known novel.

Kerr, Sarah. "Shock Treatment." *The New York Review of Books*, October 8, 1992. A review and article discussing Cela's novels *The Family of Pascual Duarte*, *Journey to Alcarria*, *The Hive*, *Mrs. Caldwell Speaks to Her Son*, and *San Camilo, 1936*.

McPheeters, D. W. *Camilo José Cela*. New York: Twayne, 1969. An accessible, though dated, overview of Cela's work, part of the Twayne World Authors series. Includes a chronology and a useful bibliography of secondary sources.

Mantero, Manual. "Camilo José Cela: The Rejection of the Ordinary." *Georgia Review* 49, no. 1 (Spring, 1995): 246-250. Mantero provides an appreciation of Cela's most representative works, describing the author's use of humor and names, characterization, and refusal to accept the routine or ordinary.

Peréz, Janet. *Camilo José Cela Revisited: The Later Novels*. New York: Twayne, 2000. Peréz updates and expands McPheeters's 1969 overview. Concentrates on Cela's novels. Includes biographical material, an index, and an annotated bibliography for further study.

Turner, Harriet, and Adelaida López de Martínez, eds. *The Cambridge Companion to the Spanish Novel: From 1600 to the Present*. New York: Cambridge University Press, 2003. Cela's work is discussed in several places, particularly in chapter 11, "The Testimonial Novel and the Novel of Memory." Helps to place Cela's work within the broader context of the Spanish novel.

MIGUEL DE CERVANTES

Born: Alcalá de Henares, Spain; September 29, 1547
Died: Madrid, Spain; April 23, 1616
Also known as: Miguel de Cervantes Saavedra

PRINCIPAL LONG FICTION
La Galatea, 1585 (*Galatea: A Pastoral Romance*, 1833)
El ingenioso hidalgo don Quixote de la Mancha, 1605, 1615 (*The History of the Valorous and Wittie Knight-Errant, Don Quixote of the Mancha*, 1612-1620; better known as *Don Quixote de la Mancha*)
Novelas ejemplares, 1613 (*Exemplary Novels*, 1846)
Los trabajos de Persiles y Sigismunda, 1617 (*The Travels of Persiles and Sigismunda: A Northern History*, 1619)

OTHER LITERARY FORMS

Miguel de Cervantes (sur-VAHN-teez) never sought acclaim as a writer of fiction. He longed for the more popular success and financial rewards offered by the stage and hoped to gain a more prestigious literary reputation as a great poet, as evidenced by the time and dedication he committed to his long derivative poem *Viaje del Parnaso* (1614; *The Voyage to Parnassus*, 1870). These ambitions were unrealized. In fact, he admits in the poem of 1614 that heaven never blessed him with the poetic gift. His efforts in the theater did not bring him success at the time but did produce some significant work. Cervantes contributed to the Spanish theater not only by writing plays but also by stirring critical debate. In chapter 48 of the first part of *Don Quixote de la Mancha*, Cervantes attacked the Spanish stage and certain kinds of popular plays. This attack prompted a response from Lope de Vega y Carpio, *Arte nuevo de hacer comedias en este tiempo* (1609; *The New Art of Writing Plays*, 1914) that was the central piece of dramatic theorizing of the Golden Age of Spanish theater. Cervantes also wrote one epic tragedy, *El cerco de Numancia* (wr. 1585, pb. 1784; *The Siege of Numantia*, 1870), a play praised in later centuries by Johann Wolfgang von Goethe, Percy Bysshe Shelley, Friedrich Schlegel, and Arthur Schopenhauer, and he published a collection of eight comedies and eight interludes in 1615. These works were never performed in the author's lifetime. The eight interludes, one-act farces that would have been performed as intermission pieces, are original, dynamic, and highly theatrical. They rank with the finest work in the one-act form by Anton Chekhov, August Strindberg, and Tennessee Williams.

ACHIEVEMENTS

Cervantes belongs to that elite group of supreme literary geniuses that includes Homer, Vergil, Dante, Geoffrey Chaucer, and William Shakespeare. The first to establish his

Miguel de Cervantes
(Library of Congress)

greatness as a writer through the medium of prose fiction, Cervantes is acknowledged as an influential innovator who nurtured the short-story form and, more important, shaped the novel, sending it into the modern world. The list of succeeding masters of the novel who paid homage to Cervantes either through direct praise or imitation is awesome— among them Daniel Defoe, Tobias Smollett, Henry Fielding, Laurence Sterne, Jonathan Swift, Sir Walter Scott, Charles Dickens, Voltaire, Stendhal, Honoré de Balzac, Gustave Flaubert, Victor Hugo, Goethe, Thomas Mann, Ivan Turgenev, Nikolai Gogol, Fyodor Dostoevski, Washington Irving, Herman Melville, Mark Twain, William Faulkner, and Saul Bellow; all of these authors recognized an indebtedness to the Spanish writer who, at the end of a lifetime of failure and disappointment, created the unlikely Knight of La Mancha and sent him out into the Spanish landscape with his equally unlikely squire, Sancho Panza. *Don Quixote de la Mancha* remains Cervantes' greatest gift to the world of literature.

If Cervantes became a giant in world literature by creating his mad knight, he also gave Spanish literature its greatest work. Cervantes' life and career spanned the glory days of

Spain's eminence as a great empire as well as the beginning of its fall from world power. Cervantes re-created this Spain he knew so well in his great work. His love of his native Spain is evident in the generosity of detail with which he created the backdrop of his novel—the inns, the food, the costumes, the dusty roads, the mountains, the rogues, the nobility, the arguments, the laughter. The superb realization of his world set a standard that has guided novelists for centuries; Cervantes' rendering of his native Spain has by extension given us the England of Dickens, the Paris of Balzac, the Russia of Dostoevski.

Cervantes' imaginative depiction of his native land also has influenced subsequent Spanish literature. Most Spanish writers feel an indebtedness to Cervantes and regard his work with awe. Such modern masters of Spanish literature as José Ortega y Gasset and Miguel de Unamuno have written extensive studies and detailed commentaries on his great novel, treating it with a reverence usually reserved for religious writings. Cervantes, in creating Don Quixote, gave Spain its greatest masterpiece, and his figure has loomed majestically over all subsequent Spanish literature.

Cervantes' contributions to the development of the novel form are considerable. In addition to re-creating the texture of daily life in the Spain of his day, he became an innovator in the form of the novel. *Don Quixote de la Mancha* is a strange kind of prose epic, with its singularly odd hero with his visions of virtue and glory riding into a mundane and common world. From the first, Cervantes saw how the richness of the older epic form might be adapted to the new prose form to create a new vision, grand and common, eloquent and humorous, ideal and real, all at once. Cervantes quickly mastered the ability to elevate the common; the greatest of all later novelists have also mastered this unlikely duality—a large ideal vision that must find expression within the confines of a real world, whether that world be the streets of London, an American whaling vessel, or a Russian prison camp.

Cervantes also freed his characters to exist within a more real world and to behave as more realistic human beings. The Don in all of his madness is still rooted in the Spain of his day, and Sancho Panza is the embodiment of a class as well as an attitude toward life. The characters also relate to one another through recognizable conversation. Cervantes made dialogue an integral part of the novel form, allowing his characters to speak their minds with the same freedom with which they travel the roads of Spain. Such conversations have been a part of most novels ever since.

Finally, and perhaps most important, Cervantes bequeathed to humankind a compelling vision of itself—man as committed idealist combined with man as foolish lunatic. Don Quixote rides out of the pages of the novel with a magnetic presence that has fascinated many subsequent artists. Honoré Daumier, Pablo Picasso, and many other painters have put him on canvas; Richard Strauss has placed him in an orchestral tone poem; Jules-Émile-Frédéric Massenet and Manuel de Falla have rendered him on the opera stage; and Tennessee Williams has brought him into American drama. The fascinating figure of the foolish knight continues to command the attentions of other artists. The Don remains a popular figure, too, appearing on the Broadway musical stage and in television commercials. The novel that Cervantes created is second only to the Bible in the number of different languages into which it has been translated, but the appeal of the title character extends beyond literature into the dream life of humankind.

Biography

In the most interesting of the full-length comedies by Miguel de Cervantes published in 1615, *Pedro de Urdemalas*, the title character dreams ambitiously of becoming all the great personages that a man can become: pope, prince, monarch, emperor, master of the world. After a career that is typical of a picaro or any other adventurous Spanish rogue of the time, Pedro finds his wishes realized when he becomes an actor and enters imaginatively into the ranks of the great. In much the same way, Cervantes' great ambitions in life were never realized; the only satisfaction he found was in a world he himself created.

In one sense, Cervantes' greatest adventure was his own life. Born Miguel de Cervantes Saavedra in a small university city not far from Madrid, he traveled constantly with his family in his early years. His father, an impoverished and impractical man who attempted to earn a living as a surgeon, kept the family moving, from Valladolid to Córdoba, from Seville to Madrid. Cervantes learned the life of the road and the diversity of city life in Spain as a youth. In his twenties, he journeyed to Italy, perhaps fleeing from arrest as a result of a duel; there, he entered the service of Cardinal Aquaviva. In 1569, he enlisted in the Spanish army and went to sea. Cervantes was present at the Battle of Lepanto in 1571, serving under the command of Don John of Austria in the famous victory against the Turks. Cervantes rose from his sickbed to join in the battle and was twice wounded, one wound leaving his left hand permanently incapacitated. With his brother, Rodrigo, he embarked for Spain in 1575, but their ship was seized by Turkish pirates, and Cervantes spent five years in captivity as a slave.

Ransomed by monks, Cervantes returned to Spain, but not to glory and acclaim. With his military career at an end because of his paralyzed hand, Cervantes fell into poverty and moved from one failure to another, including an apparently unhappy marriage in 1584. Moving about Spain as in his youth, he again gained an education in the character and behavior of the Spanish lower classes, an education that continued when he was imprisoned twice in Seville, once in 1597 and again in 1602, both times, it is assumed, the result of financial difficulties. Despite a life of bad luck, missed opportunities, and little reward for his talent, Cervantes did achieve a popular success when the first part of *Don Quixote de la Mancha* was published in 1605, although his finances saw only minor improvement. In 1615, the second part of the novel appeared, to challenge the "false" sequels being produced by other writers seeking to capitalize on the book's success. Cervantes died in Madrid in 1616, at peace, having received the Sacraments.

Analysis: Don Quixote de la Mancha

Many critics maintain that the impulse that prompted Miguel de Cervantes to begin his great novel was a satiric one: He desired to satirize chivalric romances. As the elderly Alonso Quixano the Good (if that is his name) pores over the pages of these books in his study, his "brain dries up" and he imagines himself to be the champion who will take up the vanished cause of knight-errantry and wander the world righting wrongs, helping the helpless, defending the cause of justice, all for the greater glory of his lady Dulcinea del Toboso and his God.

As he leaves his village before dawn, clad in rusty armor and riding his broken-down nag, the mad knight becomes Don Quixote de la Mancha. His first foray is brief, and he is brought back home by friends from his native village. Despite the best efforts of his friends and relations, the mad old man embarks on a second journey, this time accompanied by a peasant from his village, Sancho Panza, who becomes the knight's squire. The Don insists on finding adventure everywhere, mistaking windmills for giants, flocks of sheep for attacking armies, puppet shows for real life. His squire provides a voice of down-to-earth reason, but Quixote always insists that vile enchanters have transformed the combatants to embarrass and humiliate him. Don Quixote insists on his vision of the ideal in the face of the cold facts of the world; Sancho Panza maintains his proverbial peasant wisdom in the face of his master's madness.

In their travels and adventures, they encounter life on the roads of Spain. Sometimes they are treated with respect—for example, by "the gentleman in green" who invites them to his home and listens to Quixote with genuine interest—but more often they are ridiculed, as when the Duke and Duchess bring the knight and squire to their estate only for the purpose of mocking them. Finally, a young scholar from Quixote's native village, Sampson Carrasco, defeats the old knight in battle and forces him to return to his home, where he dies peacefully, having renounced his mad visions and lunatic behavior.

Themes

While it is necessary to acknowledge the satiric intent of Cervantes' novel, the rich fictional world of *Don Quixote de la Mancha* utterly transcends its local occasion. On the most personal level, the novel can be viewed as one of the most intimate evaluations of a life ever penned by a great author. When Don Quixote decides to take up the cause of knight-errantry, he opens himself to a life of ridicule and defeat, a life that resembles Cervantes' own life, with its endless reversals of fortune, humiliations, and hopeless struggles. Out of this life of failure and disappointment Cervantes created the "mad knight," but he also added the curious human nobility and the refusal to succumb to despair in the face of defeat that turns Quixote into something more than a comic character or a ridiculous figure to be mocked. Although there are almost no points in the novel where actual incidents from Cervantes' life appear directly or even transformed into fictional disguise, the tone and the spirit, the succession of catastrophes with only occasional moments of slight glory, and the resilience of human nature mark the novel as the most personal work of the author, the one where his singularly difficult life and his profoundly complex emotional responses to that life found form and structure.

If the novel is the record of Cervantes' life, the fiction also records a moment in Spanish national history when fortunes were shifting and tides turning. At the time of Cervantes' birth, Spain's might and glory were at their peak. The wealth from conquests of Mexico and Peru returned to Spain, commerce boomed, and artists recorded the sense of national pride with magnificent energy and power. By the time *Don Quixote de la Mancha* was published, the Spanish Empire was beginning its decline. A series of military disasters, including the defeat of the Spanish Armada by the English and the revolt of Flanders, had shaken the once mighty nation. In the figure of Don Quixote, the greatest of a richly remembered past combines with the hard facts of age, weakness, and declining power. The character embodies a moment of Spanish history and the Spanish people's own sense of vanishing glory in the face of irreversible decline.

Don Quixote de la Mancha also stands as the greatest literary embodiment of the Counter-Reformation. Throughout Europe, the Reformation was moving with the speed of new ideas, changing the religious landscape of country after country. Spain stood proud as a Catholic nation, resisting any changes. Standing alone against the flood of reform sweeping Europe displayed a kind of willed madness, but the nobility and determination of Quixote to fight for his beliefs, no matter what the rest of the world maintained, reflects the strength of the Spanish will at this time. Cervantes was a devout and loyal believer, a supporter of the Church, and Don Quixote may be the greatest fictional Catholic hero, the battered knight of the Counter-Reformation.

The book also represents fictionally the various sides of the Spanish spirit and the Spanish temper. In the divisions and contradictions found between the Knight of the Sad Countenance and his unlikely squire, Sancho Panza, Cervantes paints the two faces of the Spanish soul: The Don is idealistic, sprightly, energetic, and cheerful, even in the face of overwhelming odds, but he is also overbearing, domineering Sancho, who is earthy, servile, and slothful. The two characters seem unlikely companions and yet they form a whole, the one somehow incomplete without the other and linked throughout the book through their dialogues and debates. In drawing master and servant, Cervantes presents the opposing truths of the spirit of his native land.

CHARACTERIZATION

The book can also be seen as a great moment in the development of fiction, the moment when the fictional character was freed into the real world of choice and change. When the gentleman of La Mancha took it into his head to become a knight-errant and travel through the world redressing wrongs and winning eternal glory, the face of fiction permanently changed. Character in fiction became dynamic, unpredictable, and spontaneous. Until that time, character in fiction had existed in service of the story, but now the reality of change and psychological energy and freedom of the will became a permanent hallmark of fiction, as it already was of drama and narrative poetry. The title character's addled wits made the new freedom all the more impressive. The determination of Don Quixote, the impact of his vision on the world, and the world's hard reality as it impinges on the Don make for shifting balances and constant alterations in fortune that are psychologically believable. The shifting balance of friendship, devotion, and perception between the knight and his squire underlines this freedom, as does the power of other characters in the book to affect Don Quixote's fortunes directly: the niece, the housekeeper, the priest, the barber, Sampson Carrasco, the Duke, and the Duchess. There is a fabric of interaction throughout the novel, and characters in the novel change as they encounter new adventures, new people, and new ideas.

One way Cervantes chronicles this interaction is in dialogue. Dialogue had not played a significant or defining role in fiction before *Don Quixote de la Mancha*. As knight and squire ride across the countryside and engage in conversation, dialogue becomes the expression of character, idea, and reality. In the famous episode with windmills early in the first part of the novel (when Quixote views the windmills on the plain and announces that they are giants that he will wipe from the face of the earth, and Sancho innocently replies, "What giants?"), the dialogue not only carries the comedy but also becomes the battleground on which the contrasting visions of life engage one another—to the delight of the reader. The long exchanges between Don Quixote and Sancho Panza provide priceless humor but also convey two different realities that meet, struggle, and explode in volleys of words. In giving his characters authentic voices that carry ideas, Cervantes brought to fiction a new truth that remains a standard of comparison.

THE NARRATOR

Don Quixote de la Mancha is also as modern as the most experimental of later fiction. Throughout the long novel, Cervantes plays with the nature of the narrator, raising constant difficult questions as to who is telling the story and to what purpose. In the riotously funny opening page of the novel, the reader encounters a narrator not only unreliable but also lacking in the basic facts necessary to tell the story. He chooses not to tell the name of the village where his hero lives, and he is not even sure of his hero's name, yet the narrator protests that the narrative must be entirely truthful.

In chapter 9, as Don Quixote is preparing to do battle with the Basque, the narrative stops; the narrator states that the manuscript from which he is culling this story is mutilated and incomplete. Fortunately, some time later in Toledo, he says, he came upon an old Arabic manuscript by Arab historian Cide Hamete Benengeli that continues the adventures. For the remainder of the novel, the narrator claims to be providing a translation of this manuscript—the manuscript and the second narrator, the Arab historian, both lacking authority and credibility. In the second part of the novel, the narrator and the characters themselves are aware of the first part of the novel as well as of a "false Quixote," a spurious second part written by an untalented Spanish writer named Avallaneda who sought to capitalize on the popularity of the first part of *Don Quixote de la Mancha* by publishing his own sequel. The "false Quixote" is on the narrator's mind, the characters' minds, and somehow on the mind of Cide Hamete Benengeli. These shifting perspectives, the multiple narrative voices, the questionable reliability of the narrators, and the "false" second part are all tricks, narrative sleight of hand as complex as anything found in the works of Faulkner, Vladimir Nabokov, or Jorge Luis Borges. In his *Lectures on Don Quixote* (1983), Nabokov oddly makes no reference to Cervantes' narrative games; perhaps the old Spanish master's shadow still loomed too close to the modern novelist.

None of these approaches to the novel, however, appropriate as they may be, can begin to explain fully the work's enduring popularity or the strange manner in which the knight and his squire have ridden out of the pages of a book into the other artistic realms of orchestral music, opera, ballet, and painting, where other artists have presented their visions of Quixote and Sancho. A current deeper and more abiding than biography, history, national temper, or literary landmark flows through the book and makes it speak to all manner of readers in all ages.

Early in the novel, Cervantes begins to dilute his strong satiric intent. The reader can laugh with delight at the inanity of the mad knight but never with the wicked, unalloyed glee that pure satire evokes. The knight begins to loom over the landscape; his madness brushes sense; his ideals demand defense. The reader finds him- or herself early in the novel taking an attitude equivalent to that of the two young women of easy virtue who see Quixote when he arrives at an inn, which he believes to be a castle, on his first foray. Quixote calls them "two beauteous maidens . . . taking air at the gate of the castle," and they fall into helpless laughter, confronted with such a mad vision of themselves as "maidens." In time, however, because of Quixote's insistence on the truth of his vision, they help him out of his armor and set a table for him. They treat him as a knight, not as a mad old fool; he treats them as ladies, and they behave as ladies. The laughter stops, and, for a pure moment, life transforms itself and human beings transcend themselves.

CONTRADICTIONS

This mingling of real chivalry and transcendent ideals with the absurdity of character and mad action creates the tensions in the book as well as its strange melancholy beauty and haunting poignancy. The book is unlike any other ever written. John Berryman has commented on this split between the upheld ideal and the riotously real, observing that the reader "does not know whether to laugh or cry, and does both." This old man with his dried-up brain, with his squire who has no "salt in his brain pan," with his rusty armor, his pathetic steed, and his lunatic vision that changes windmills into giants and flocks of sheep into attacking armies, this crazy old fool becomes a real knight-errant. The true irony of the book and its history is that Don Quixote actually becomes a model for knighthood. He may be a foolish, improbable knight, but with his squire, horse, and armor he has ridden into the popular imagination of the world not only as a ridiculous figure but also as a champion; he is a real knight whose vision may often cloud, who sees what he wants to see, but he is also one who demonstrates real virtue and courage and rises in his rhetoric and daring action to real heights of greatness.

Perhaps Cervantes left a clue as to the odd shift in his intention. The contradictory titles he assigns to his knight suggest this knowledge. The comic, melancholy strain pervades "Knight of the Sad Countenance" in the first part of the novel, and the heroic strain is seen in the second part when the hero acquires the new sobriquet "Knight of the Lions." The first title comes immediately after his adventure with a corpse and is awarded him by his realistic companion, Sancho. Quixote has attacked a funeral procession, seeking to avenge the dead man. Death, however, cannot be overcome; the attempted attack merely disrupts the funeral, and the valiant knight breaks the leg of an attending churchman. The name "Knight of the Sad Countenance" fits Quixote's stance here and through much of the book. Many of the adventures he undertakes are not only misguided but also unwinnable. Quixote may be Christlike, but he is not Christ, and he cannot conquer Death.

The adventure with the lions earns for him his second title and offers the other side of his journey as a knight. Encountering a cage of lions being taken to the king, Quixote becomes determined to fight them. Against all protest, he takes his stand, and the cage is opened. One of the lions stretches, yawns, looks at Quixote, and lies down. Quixote proclaims a great victory and awards himself the name "Knight of the Lions." A delightfully comic episode, the scene can be viewed in two ways—as a nonadventure that the knight claims as a victory or as a genuine moment of triumph as the knight undertakes an outlandish adventure and proves his genuine bravery while the king of beasts realizes the futility of challenging the unswerving old knight. Quixote, by whichever route, emerges as conqueror. Throughout his journeys, he often does emerge victorious, despite his age, despite his illusions, despite his dried-up brain.

When, at the book's close, he is finally defeated and humiliated by Sampson Carrasco and forced to return to his village, the life goes out of him. The knight Don Quixote is replaced, however, on the deathbed by Alonso Quixano the Good. Don Quixote does not die, for the elderly gentleman regains his wits and becomes a new character. Don Quixote cannot die, for he is the creation of pure imagination. Despite the moving and sober conclusion, the reader cannot help but sense that the death scene being played out does not signify the end of Don Quixote. The knight escapes and remains free. He rides out of the novel, with his loyal companion Sancho at his side, into the golden realm of myth. He becomes the model knight he hoped to be. He stands tall with his spirit, his ideals, his rusty armor, and his broken lance as the embodiment of man's best intentions and impossible folly. As Dostoevski so wisely said, when the Lord calls the Last Judgment, man should take with him this book and point to it, for it reveals all of man's deep and fatal mystery, his glory and his sorrow.

David Allen White

OTHER MAJOR WORKS

PLAYS: *El trato de Argel*, pr. 1585 (*The Commerce of Algiers*, 1870); *Ocho comedias y ocho entremeses nuevos*, 1615 (includes *Pedro de Urdemalas* [*Pedro the Artful Dodger*, 1807], *El juez de los divorcios* [*The Divorce Court Judge*, 1919], *Los habladores* [*Two Chatterboxes*, 1930], *La cueva de Salamanca* [*The Cave of Salamanca*, 1933], *La elección de los alcaldes de Daganzo* [*Choosing a Councilman in Daganzo*, 1948], *La guarda cuidadosa* [*The Hawk-Eyed Sentinel*, 1948], *El retablo de las maravillas* [*The Wonder Show*, 1948], *El rufián viudo llamada Trampagos* [*Trampagos the Pimp Who Lost His Moll*, 1948], *El viejo celoso* [*The Jealous Old Husband*, 1948], and *El vizcaíno fingido* [*The Basque Imposter*, 1948]); *El cerco de Numancia*, pb. 1784 (wr. 1585; *Numantia: A Tragedy*, 1870; also known as *The Siege of Numantia*); *The Interludes of Cervantes*, 1948.

POETRY: *Viaje del Parnaso*, 1614 (*The Voyage to Parnassus*, 1870).

BIBLIOGRAPHY

Bloom, Harold, ed. *Cervantes*. New York: Chelsea House, 1987. Collection of essays addresses topics such as the picaresque, the trickster figure, Cervantes' biography and use of language, and his attitude toward realism and the literary tradition. Includes an informative introduction, a chronology, a bibliography, and an index.

_____. *Cervantes's "Don Quixote."* Philadelphia: Chelsea House, 2001. Collection reprints essays about the novel written by well-known authors and critics, including Thomas Mann, Franz Kafka, W. H. Auden, Vladimir Nabokov, and Mark van Doren. Includes an introduction by Bloom, bibliographical references, and index.

Cascardi, Anthony J., ed. *The Cambridge Companion to Cervantes*. New York: Cambridge University Press, 2002. Collection of essays places Cervantes' life and work within historical and social context and discusses Cervantes' relation to the Italian Renaissance and his influence on other writers. An essay titled "*Don Quixote* and the Invention of the Novel" focuses on the well-known work.

Castillo, David R. *(A)wry Views: Anamorphosis, Cervantes, and the Early Picaresque*. West Lafayette, Ind.: Purdue University Press, 2001. Looks at anamorphosis, or visual perception, in the writings of Cervantes and other works of Spanish picaresque literature from the sixteenth and seventeenth centuries. Includes bibliography and index.

Close, A. J. *Cervantes and the Comic Mind of His Age*. New York: Oxford University Press, 2000. Analyzes ideas about comedy and comedic writing in the Spanish Golden Age and describes how Cervantes' works reflected those ideas. Includes bibliography and index.

Durán, Manuel. *Cervantes*. New York: Twayne, 1974. Provides a sound introduction to the author, with chapters on Cervantes' life and his career as a poet, playwright, short-story writer, and novelist. Includes notes, chronology, and annotated bibliography.

Hart, Thomas R. *Cervantes' Exemplary Fictions: A Study of the "Novelas ejemplares."*

Lexington: University Press of Kentucky, 1994. Presents a reading of *Exemplary Novels* within the literary conventions of other popular novels of the seventeenth century, drawing on the literature not only of Spain but also of France, Italy, and England. Argues that novels in that era were meant to elicit readers' surprise or wonder and describes how Cervantes' work attains that goal.

McCrory, Donald P. *No Ordinary Man: The Life and Times of Miguel de Cervantes.* Chester Springs, Pa.: Peter Owen, 2002. Thorough biography is based, in part, on original research and unpublished material. Places Cervantes' life within the context of sixteenth and seventeenth century Spanish history. Includes bibliographical references and index.

Mancing, Howard. *Cervantes' "Don Quixote": A Reference Guide.* Westport, Conn.: Greenwood Press, 2006. An excellent companion for undergraduate students and for general readers. Individual chapters explore themes, criticism, language and style, publishing history, and other topics. Select bibliographies make this an important resource.

Nabokov, Vladimir. *Lectures on "Don Quixote."* Edited by Fredson Bowers. New York: Harcourt Brace Jovanovich, 1983. College lectures by a great twentieth century novelist are divided into portraits of Don Quixote and Sancho Panza, the structure of the novel, the use of cruelty and mystification, the treatment of Dulcinea and death, and commentaries on Cervantes' narrative methods. An appendix contains sample passages from romances of chivalry.

Riley, E. C. *Cervantes's Theory of the Novel.* 1962. Reprint. Newark, Del.: Juan de la Cuesta, 1992. Provides a detailed examination of Cervantes' views on questions of literary practice in terms of traditional issues in poetics, such as art and nature, unity, and purpose and function of literature. Includes bibliography and indexes of names and topics.

Weiger, John G. *The Substance of Cervantes.* London: Cambridge University Press, 1985. Provides valuable insights into Cervantes' craft as a writer by exploring questions such as the relationship of art and reality, the functions of authors and readers, the elusive nature of truth, the dynamics of society, and the significance of the individual and of communication between individuals. Augmented by a bibliography and an index.

Williamson, Edwin, ed. *Cervantes and the Modernists: The Question of Influence.* London: Tamesis, 1994. Collection of essays explores the novelist's impact on such twentieth century writers as Marcel Proust, Thomas Mann, Primo Levi, Carlos Fuentes, and Gabriel García Márquez.

MIGUEL DELIBES

Born: Valladolid, Spain; October 17, 1920
Also known as: Miguel Delibes Setién

PRINCIPAL LONG FICTION
La sombra del ciprés es alargada, 1948
Aún es de día, 1949
El camino, 1950 (*The Path*, 1961)
Mi idolatrado hijo Sisí, 1953
Diario de un cazador, 1955
Diario de un emigrante, 1958
La hoja roja, 1959
Las ratas, 1962 (*Smoke on the Ground*, 1972)
Cinco horas con Mario, 1966 (*Five Hours with Mario*, 1988)
Parábola del náufrago, 1969 (*The Hedge*, 1983)
El príncipe destronado, 1973
Las guerras de nuestros antepasados, 1974 (*The Wars of Our Ancestors*, 1992)
El disputado voto del señor Cayo, 1978
Los santos inocentes, 1981 (novella)
Cartas de amour de un sexagenario voluptuoso, 1983
El tesoro, 1985
377A, Madera de héroe, 1987 (*The Stuff of Heroes*, 1990)
Señora de rojo sobre fondo gris, 1991
Diario de un jubilado, 1995
El hereje, 1998 (*The Heretic*, 2006)

OTHER LITERARY FORMS

Though primarily a novelist, Miguel Delibes (deh-LEE-bays) has published several books of travel impressions, including *Por esos mundos* (1961; round about the world), *Europa, parada, y fonda* (1963; Europe, stops, and inns), *USA y yo* (1966; U.S.A. and I), and *La primavera de Praga* (1968; springtime in Prague); short narratives, including the collections *La partida* (1954; the departure), *Siestas con viento sur* (1957; siestas with a southern breeze), and *La mortaja* (1970; the shroud); and books on hunting and fishing, including *Aventuras, venturas, y desventuras de un cazador a rabo* (1977; adventures, good and bad luck of a small game hunter) and *Mis amigas las truchas* (1977; my trout friends). He also has published miscellaneous books of articles, commentary, and essays, as well as newspaper articles and comments and impressions written in diary form. Asked by the Spanish government to write a tourist guide of Old Castile, Delibes produced *Viejas historias de Castilla la Vieja* (1964; old tales of Old Castile), a work that for its narrative-descriptive passages of lyric force is one of the author's most memorable and revealing books (though it was unacceptable as a travel guide); it is sometimes classified as a novella.

Achievements

Miguel Delibes is without doubt one of Spain's most significant novelists to emerge since the end of the Spanish Civil War in 1939. His first novel, *La sombra del ciprés es alargada*, published by the Barcelona publisher Destino in 1948, won the prestigious Eugenio Nadal Prize in 1947. Though probably his worst novel, it was decisive in influencing him to continue his efforts at writing fiction, efforts that he has realized while working simultaneously for many years as a professor in the School of Commerce in Valladolid and on the editorial staff of the newspaper *El norte de Castilla*, serving as its director from 1958 to 1963.

As a novelist, Delibes's work has been marked by a steady growth and progression in style and content, causing the critics to observe that each new Delibean book is better than the last one. In general, Delibes has progressively moved away from a traditional and detailed realism reminiscent of the nineteenth century to a more poetic and symbolic realism, experimentation in structure and techniques, and a more economical, direct, and unaffected style. However, his direction toward simplicity has been broken somewhat in some later works, such as *Five Hours with Mario* and *The Hedge*, in which his more complex and convoluted syntax serves the purpose of making style reflect content, especially, according to Janet Díaz, the "troubled psychological atmosphere and torment" of the protagonist. Delibes's novels have been widely translated into the leading European languages. Numerous doctoral theses on his work have been completed in American and European universities.

A strong and independent voice in contemporary Spanish fiction, Delibes has adhered to no group or movement inside or outside Spain, though he has absorbed from them whatever he saw as beneficial to his own character and temperament as a man and as a writer. Though neither a regionalist nor a novelist of customs (*costumbrista*) in the traditional sense, he has continued to live in Valladolid and portray what he knows best: the rural people and landscape of Old Castile. In particular, his distinctive use of rural Castilian speech has won high praise; notable also is his creation of rural Castilian atmospheres and characters.

Biography

Born Miguel Delibes Setién on October 17, 1920, into a bourgeois family in Valladolid, a provincial capital in Old Castile, Delibes was reared as a strict Catholic. Though his father was liberal in his views, his mother was very conservative; in his childhood and adolescence, her orientation seemed to dominate; in adult life, his father's Catholic liberalism prevailed. By the time the Spanish Civil War began, the future novelist, though not yet seventeen years old, had graduated from high school. A year later, he joined the Nationalist navy and served on a cruiser patrolling the Cantabrian Coast.

After the war, Delibes, having been refused reenlistment in the navy because of nearsightedness, took specially provided accelerated courses in both law and business, obtaining degrees in both areas in 1941. In 1943, he took an intensive three-month course in journalism in Madrid. In 1945, through competitive examinations (*oposiciones*), he won the chair of mercantile law in the School of Commerce in Valladolid, succeeding his father. Later he changed his subject to the history of culture. In 1946, he married Angeles de Castro. In 1947, he wrote his first novel-manuscript, partly in an attempt to rid himself of his obsession with death—an obsession he had had since childhood. Submitted to the Nadal competition, the manuscript won its prestigious prize, and it appeared in 1948 as *La sombra del ciprés es alargada*.

During the next several years, Delibes worked on the editorial staff of *El norte de Castilla*, Spain's second oldest continuously operating newspaper, and held his professorial post in the School of Commerce while continuing to write novels. His second novel, *Aún es de día*, appeared in 1949; according to Díaz, it resembles his first novel in its "rather ponderous, rhetorical style." Critics generally agree that Delibes found his proper style in his third novel, *The Path*, published in 1950, a work that, unlike his first two novels, almost instantly became an unqualified critical success. In 1955, *Diario de un cazador* was awarded the Miguel de Cervantes Prize. While continuing his increasingly successful career as a novelist and writer of short fiction, Delibes fulfilled his journalistic duties with distinction, rising to be assistant director of *El norte de Castilla* from 1952 until 1958 and director from 1958 until 1963 (when political pressures from the Franco regime forced his resignation).

A Catholic, though liberal in his views, a faithful husband and father of seven children, a passionate lover of nature and an avid fisherman and hunter, Delibes disclaims all pretensions to intellectualism. Gonzalo Sobejano aptly describes Delibes's whole career as a search for authenticity, a search for his own proper path. Delibes has traveled extensively, including in the United States. He has a broad cosmopolitan view and concern for the problems of contemporary humanity, not only for the people of Spain. In 1975, he was admitted to the Royal Spanish Academy, primarily in recognition of his achievements as a novelist.

Analysis

Critics generally divide Miguel Delibes's novels into two periods or types. Written in the first manner are the author's first two novels, *La sombra del ciprés es alargada* and *Aún es de día*, and his fourth novel, *Mi idolatrado hijo Sisí* (my adored son Sisí), published in 1953. With the publication of *The Path* in 1950, his third novel, Delibes inaugurated his second manner, which implied a definite break with his earlier rhetorical, rather sluggish, analytical, and traditionally realistic style. Since 1950, with the exception of his brief reversion to traditional realism in *Mi idolatrado hijo Sisí*, a novel that advances an anti-Malthusian thesis, Delibes has evolved in the direction of freer artistic expression, of what has been called poetic realism (as against his former "analytic realism").

During his second phase, Delibes has experimented freely with new techniques and structures. Plot has all but disappeared and a third-person narrative point of view has been replaced with the author-narrator merging his voice with that of the protagonist to form a central narrative consciousness with a double perspective: that of the narrator and that of the protagonist. Though the two perspectives coalesce, they can be distinguished by the alert reader. Technical and structural innovations made by Delibes are expressive of his continuing search for his own most authentic mode or path of novelization (although he has sometimes been suspected of following current literary vogues in pursuit of critical acclaim). Novels of his second period are generally characterized by a reduction in time and space and by single-minded, simpleminded protagonists; what the works lose in complexity they gain in unity and concentrated force. The action on the primary plane in *The Path* occurs in one night, in *Five Hours with Mario* also in one night, in *The Wars of Our Ancestors* in seven consecutive evenings, and all occur in a single house or room.

In ideology or thematic content, one finds little if any real changes between the author's early and later periods. An intensified anguish over the dangers to humankind's freedom and dignity, inherent in modern technological paternalistic societies, and the growing lack of communication or human solidarity in today's world, however, especially mark some of his more recent novels, notably *Five Hours with Mario* and *The Hedge*. His main motifs, as pointed out by Díaz, remain as constants in his work: the shadow of death, the importance of nature, the life and landscape of rural Old Castile (with its severe socioeconomic problems and abandonment by the Central Spanish Government), a preference for child protagonists (*The Path*, *Smoke on the Ground*, *El príncipe destronado*) or elementary, abnormal, or "primitive" characters (the Rat Hunter in *Smoke on the Ground*, Pacífico Pèrez in *The Wars of Our Ancestors*), and the individual in his difficult relationships with others and with society at large (*The Wars of Our Ancestors*). His more recent novels include biting satire of the Catholic Church's apparent impotence in effecting a genuine spiritual-moral transformation of the Spanish character. Since childhood, Delibes has occasionally suffered from periods of pessimism, a mood that seems to have intensified in his more recent novels.

Pío Baroja and Camilo José Cela appear to be two of the principal influences upon Delibes as a writer of fiction. His irony and his dry, laconic description of gruesome scenes as well as his use of nicknames and repetition of descriptive phrases or tag lines, often ironic, to identify characters (for example, the priest "who was a great saint"), especially recall Cela.

THE PATH

Through the memory flashbacks of Daniel, the eleven-year-old protagonist of *The Path*, on the night before his expected departure—for further schooling in the city—from the Castilian village in which he was born and has lived all of his life, the reader enters into the "world" of the protagonist. In that "world," Daniel's personal life is projected outward toward the collective life of the village; the individual and his society in this work fuse into an artistic unity. Past and present are also interwoven through Daniel's memory flashbacks, though the narrator often intervenes to provide his own perspective on the events and situations being recalled. The narrator interjects without destroying the reader's illusion that the central narrative consciousness is that of the child-protagonist; in fact his added perspective subtly contributes to the narrative's sense of reality or verisimilitude.

Essentially plotless, a series of anecdotes given unity primarily by the protagonist himself—he is telling his personal story—the work simultaneously draws a vivid portrayal of village life in Spain while elaborating upon the author's favorite themes: death, childhood, nature, and neighbor (or humankind's relationship in society). Daniel, enamored of his life as the son of a poor cheesemaker in the village, believes that his "path" or "way" in life should be to remain where he is. His father, however, wants his son to develop his possibilities to the fullest, and to achieve that end he believes that it is imperative that Daniel acquire a higher education than that available in the village. At great sacrifice, Daniel's father is sending him to the city. Through the opposing views of father and son, important differences between Spanish rural and city life become visible, leading some critics to regard the work as in praise of country life and scorn of life in the city; it can be more accurately described as simply an effort to present the realities of each. Though without a double time dimension, *Smoke on the Ground*, published almost twelve years later, bears close thematic and structural resemblance to *The Path*. In the later work, however, the reader is made much more painfully aware of the cultural, moral, and economic deprivation of life in a Castilian village.

FIVE HOURS WITH MARIO

Five Hours with Mario will undoubtedly remain one of Delibes's most perfectly constructed and important novels. When it appeared in 1966, critics almost universally commented on its seemingly radical break from the novelist's former, more conventional patterns. In a recent study, however, Luis Gonzalez del Valle demonstrates that in structure, narrative techniques, and themes, it bears a marked resemblance to *The Path*. In Gonzalez del Valle's opinion, it constitutes a partial return to the earlier work.

The book opens with a full-page reproduction of an announcement of funeral arrangements for Mario Collado, a professor and unsuccessful writer, who died unexpectedly at the age of forty-nine in March of 1966. Though not named, the setting is a provincial Spanish capital strikingly similar to Valladolid. Following the obituary notice is an untitled chapter, followed by twenty-seven numbered chapters and closing with an untitled chapter, a kind of epilogue. In the untitled introductory chapter, Carmen, Mario's widow of Spanish bourgeois mentality, in her mind and in conversation with her close female friend Valen, reviews the day, which began with the discovery of Mario's death, funeral arrangements, visits to express condolences, and so on. It is now midnight, and she prepares to spend the morning hours by her husband's corpse. The rest of the novel, except for its last short chapter, consists of her interior monologue or unilateral dialogue in which she addresses Mario's corpse in the familiar second person (*tú*), reviewing in flashbacks their life together.

In her harsh, spiteful, and uncomprehending criticism of Mario—a post-Vatican II Catholic who championed the cause of social justice—she gives full vent to her frustration. In a free association of ideas, reiterating certain obsessions, she sometimes rants and raves. In the process of accusing her dead husband of what she perceives to be his many shortcomings, however, she reveals herself to the reader as an ignorant, self-centered, addle-headed hypocrite and thus condemns herself. At the same time, by implication she condemns (unconsciously, of course) the middle-class Spanish society whose values she so faithfully mirrors and of which she is a product. In the final chapter, the couple's oldest son, Mario, thinking that he has heard his mother talking aloud to the corpse, enters the room. By what he says, the reader gathers some hope that the wounds of a divided Spain—as represented by Mario and Carmen—may eventually be healed.

The novel constitutes a study of an absolutely incompatible marriage, but it is more than that. On an allegorical level, Mario comes obliquely to represent an open and democratic Spain, post-Vatican II Catholicism, love and human solidarity, and the abolition of social and economic inequities, while his widow represents a closed and traditional Spain, a dogmatic pre-Vatican II Church, the preservation of social classes, and an unauthentic, materialistic mode of living. By presenting Mario as a corpse and making Carmen express concepts acceptable to the Spanish political regime of the time, Delibes adroitly avoided official censorship while at the same time improving the novel's artistic quality, a masterpiece in irony. The author wisely avoided painting Mario as a hero; he is seen as an ineffectual and impractical idealist and as a mediocre writer. In presenting him in human proportions, often ambiguous, the novel gains in artistic power. It has been adapted for the stage, and it enjoyed a long and successful run in Spanish theaters.

THE HEDGE

Reminiscent of Franz Kafka's *Der Verwandlung* (1915; *Metamorphosis*, 1936), Eugène Ionesco's *Le Rhinocéros* (1959; *Rhinoceros*, 1960), and Aldous Huxley's *Brave New World* (1932), *The Hedge* portrays in anguished, nightmarish sequences the slow but certain metamorphosis of Jacinto San José, a symbol of the contemporary human in a technological and increasingly uniform and paternalistic society, into a ram, a sacrificial victim of an all-pervasive collectivity that has extracted from him the last vestiges of his individuality and personhood. Some critics saw in the work a radical new direction, an attempt to join the vanguard in novelistic innovation, especially to emulate the latest in Hispanic novels. In reality, however, *The Hedge*, though a parable rather than a realistic novel, with a setting and atmosphere more European than strictly Spanish, is consonant with the nature of Delibes as a man and as a novelist. It once more demonstrates his profound concern for the dignity and freedom of the individual and his relationship with contemporary society. Its unconventional techniques are in accordance with the author's openness to experimentation and are, as Sobejano has indicated, artistically essential to the work as a whole.

Jacinto, a humble and timid bookkeeper working for the gigantic organization presided over by the rotund Don Abdón, dares one day to ask the meaning of what he is doing, whether he is adding zeros or the letter *O*. His lack of total conformity to the organization thenceforth is suspect and leads to his being sent to a rest home in the country where in helpless isolation he is metamorphosed into a ram, having lost his long, desperate, and tormented battle to preserve his human personality. All is experienced by the reader from *inside* the anguished consciousness of Jacinto, an effect primarily achieved through interior monologues of the protagonist but further reinforced through a series of autodialogues in which Jacinto speaks in second person familiar to his image in the mirror and through the tone and perspective of the narrative sections.

A much noted (and irritating) technique is the use through much of the novel of the verbal designations for punctuation rather than their conventional signs; thus comma, period, semicolon, open parenthesis, close parenthesis, and so on, are all spelled out in the text. The effect on the reader is that of listening to a colorless, impersonal office dictation, which thus heightens the sense of alienation experienced by Jacinto. Much of the book is concerned with the degradation of language (as a parallel to the degradation of man), through which Delibes sought to make form reflect content while at the same time parodying some contemporary novelists who propose the destruction of language as one of their missions.

The Hedge is a mixture of realism and fantasy, appropriate to a parable. It constitutes a powerful metaphor of the plight of contemporary humans in a slowly disintegrating, impersonal society, and in its success in communicating the author's (Jacinto's) deep anguish lies its greatest merit.

The Wars of Our Ancestors

In *The Wars of Our Ancestors*, Delibes employs what Díaz calls a "retrospective-reconstructive technique," a technique by which a whole novelistic world is created indirectly through introspection or conversation during a very short period, a technique employed in *The Path* and in *Five Hours with Mario*. The technique is not at all uncommon, though it has many variations; Ramón José Sender, for example, used it with notable effectiveness in *Mosén Millán* (1953; better known as *Réquiem por un campesino español*; *Requiem for a Spanish Peasant*, 1960). In effect, nothing much happens except introspection and conversation in the present, the primary plane of action, while the major action of the novel is that which is evoked from the past, the secondary plane of action and of time.

The Wars of Our Ancestors opens with an untitled brief introductory section or untitled prologue in which a psychiatrist, the fictitious Dr. Burgueño López, tells of his association with Pacífico Pèrez, a convict in a penal sanatorium, and offers to the reader a faithful transcript of taped conversations he had with Pèrez during seven consecutive evenings, May 21 through May 27, 1961; each conversation makes up a chapter. The book closes with a kind of epilogue (slightly more than a page in length) in which Dr. Burgueño López relates the death of Pacífico Pèrez on September 13, 1969. Before dying, Pèrez gives the psychiatrist permission to publish the transcript of the seven conversations. Through the indirect device of presenting the conversations as taped and transcribed by Dr. Burgueño López, Delibes sought to distance himself as author from the text and to lend to it an illusion of a document placed in the hands of the reader without intermediaries.

The novel is a reconstruction in conversations, guided gently by the psychiatrist, of Pacífico Pèrez's upbringing in a small, poverty-stricken Castilian village and his subsequent life in prison. Pèrez speaks in the language of the Castilian peasant, attesting once again the importance Delibes attaches to this element in his work. The book's title refers to humankind's deep propensity for making war on neighbors. Pacífico was brought up by his great-grandfather, grandfather, and father, each of whom had fought for Spain in a war; they regarded it as inevitable that Pacífico would have "his war" and consequently set about educating him for violence. For great-grandfather Pèrez, it was either "sangra o te sangrarán" ("bleed them or they will bleed you"); Pacífico found this philosophy repugnant and turned inward in deep distress. When the brother of his girlfriend surprises Pacífico half naked with his sister, Pacífico impulsively kills the brother—without fear or hate. Refusing to defend himself in court, he is imprisoned. In prison he finds freedom; he would rather live out of society (or at least on its margin) than pay the terrible price of participation, "bleed them or they will bleed you." The conflict between the individual and society remains unresolved for Delibes, just as it did for Baroja before him. In its despairing tone and atmosphere, *The Wars of Our Ancestors* recalls *The Hedge*. Indeed, with advancing age, the author's pessimism seems to have deepened.

Charles L. King

OTHER MAJOR WORKS

SHORT FICTION: *La partida*, 1954; *Siestas con viento sur*, 1957; *La mortaja*, 1970; *Tres pájaros de cuenta y tres cuentos olvidados*, 2003.

NONFICTION: *Por esos mundos*, 1961; *Europa, parada, y fonda*, 1963; *El libro de la caza menor*, 1964; *Viejas historias de Castilla la Vieja*, 1964; *USA y yo*, 1966; *La primavera de Praga*, 1968; *Vivir al día*, 1968; *S.O.S.*, 1976; *Aventuras, venturas, y desventuras de un cazador a rabo*, 1977; *Mis amigas las truchas*, 1977; *Dos viajes en automóvil: Suecia y Países Bajos*, 1982; *El otro fútbol*, 1982; *La censura de prensa en los años 40, y otros ensayos*, 1985; *Castilla habla*, 1986; *Mi vida al aire libre: Memorias deportivas de un hombre sedentario*, 1989; *Pegar la hebra*, 1990; *El último coto*, 1992; *Conversaciones con Miguel Delibes*, 1993; *He dicho*, 1996; *Correspondencia, 1948-1986*, 2002.

Bibliography

Agawu-Kakraba, Yaw B. *Demythification in the Fiction of Miguel Delibes*. New York: Peter Lang, 1996. Agawu-Kakraba examines several of Delibes's novels, including *Five Hours with Mario, The Stuff of Heroes, The Path, The Hedge*, and *Smoke on the Ground*, to demonstrate how Delibes's fiction criticized the myths of heroism, stoicism, progress, and other elements of Francisco Franco's totalitarian ideology.

Boucher, Teresa Claire. *Existential Authenticity in Three Novels of Spanish Author Miguel Delibes*. Lewiston, N.Y.: Edwin Mellen Press, 2004. Boucher seeks to determine if Delibes has been correctly characterized as a "novelist of authenticity." She analyzes his work in terms of existential philosophy and examines the "existential inauthority" in his novels *Five Hours with Mario, Señora de rojo sobre fondo gris*, and *Cartas de amor con un sexagenario voluptuoso*.

Díaz, Janet W. *Miguel Delibes*. New York: Twayne, 1971. One of the few English-language books about Delibes aimed at the student or general reader. Provides a biography of Delibes and analyses of his works. Includes chronology and bibliography.

Dinverno, Melissa. "Dictating Fictions: Power, Resistance and the Construction of Identity in *Cinco horas con Mario*." *Bulletin of Spanish Studies* 81, no. 1 (January, 2004): 49-76. A study of *Five Hours with Mario*, describing how Delibes's novel charts the fundamental economic, cultural, social, and political changes that were occurring in Spain when the novel was published in 1966.

Meyers, Glenn G. *Miguel Delibes: An Annotated Critical Bibliography*. Lanham, Md.: Scarecrow Press, 1999. Meyers has compiled an extensive annotated bibliography listing literary criticism of Delibes's work. The book also includes a biography tracing Delibes's origins and development as a writer and an analysis of trends in Delibes's criticism.

Schwartz, Ronald. "Delibes and *Parabola del naufrago* (1969)." In *Spain's New Wave Novelists: 1950-1954: Studies in Spanish Realism*. Metuchen, N.J.: Scarecrow Press, 1976. Delibes's novel *The Hedge* is one of the books examined in this study of Spanish realism. The book also includes a chapter defining the characteristics of the "Spanish new wave novel" and another chapter placing these novels in their broader literary and historical context.

JOSÉ MARÍA GIRONELLA

Born: Darnius, Spain; December 31, 1917
Died: Arenys de Mar, near Barcelona, Spain; January 3, 2003
Also known as: José María Gironella Pous

PRINCIPAL LONG FICTION
Un hombre, 1946 (*Where the Soil Was Shallow*, 1957)
La marea, 1949
Los cipreses creen en Dios, 1953 (*The Cypresses Believe in God*, 1955)
Un millón de muertos, 1961 (*One Million Dead*, 1963)
Mujer, levántate y anda, 1962
Ha estallado la paz, 1966 (*Peace After War*, 1969)
Condenados a vivir, 1971
Los hombres lloran solas, 1986
La dud inquietante, 1988
A la sombra de Chopin, 1990
El corazón alberga muchas sombras, 1995
Se hace camino al andar, 1997
El apocalipsis, 2001
Por amor a la verdad, 2003

OTHER LITERARY FORMS

The renown of José María Gironella (hee-roh-NEH-yah) springs from the series of panoramic novels that depict the Spanish Civil War, although the author published in a variety of literary forms. His first work in print was poetry (*Ha llegado el invierno y tú no estás aquí*, 1945), but he quickly abandoned the genre in favor of the novel. *Los fantasmas de mi cerebro* (1959; *Phantoms and Fugitives: Journeys to the Improbable*, 1964; includes translation of *Todos somos fugitivos*) is the documentation in a series of essays of a nervous breakdown. A partial collection of Gironella's short stories appears in *Phantoms and Fugitives*.

Gironella also produced travel books—*Personas, ideas, y mares* (1963; persons, ideas, and seas), *El Japón y su duende* (1964; Japan and her ghosts), and *En Asia se muere bajo las estrellas* (1968; in Asia you die under the stars)—along with essays that outline his personal vision in a wide variety of subjects, newspaper articles, literary analyses, criticism, biographical accounts, interviews, and meditations. *China, lágrima innumerable* (1965; China, countless tears) is an expanded essay accompanied by photographs. *Gritos del mar* (1967; shouts from the sea) collects in one volume various articles previously published in periodicals.

Achievements

José María Gironella has been labeled as a post-Spanish Civil War writer belonging to the realist tradition of nineteenth century literature, a fact that places him in Spain's Generation of '36. His novels represent a rupture in the trend toward introspection and intellectualization that existed prior to the Civil War. Gironella is a serious writer who identifies with the common person, desiring to convey through literature his own experiences in life. One is impressed by his sincerity and flexibility, his awe and optimism as he effects his personal ongoing search for knowledge and willingly shares it. Gironella's major literary success has centered on his personal commitment to explain, through the historical novel, the reality and complexity of the Spanish Civil War (1936-1939); his epic novels *The Cypresses Believe in God* and *One Million Dead*—made both discrete and panoramic through the author's attempt to be objective—have become international best sellers.

Biography

José María Gironella—whose full name was José María Gironella Pous—spent his early life in the northeastern Spanish province of Gerona, the locale of his most successful literature. His childhood desire to enter the priesthood was abandoned primarily because his attitude toward the Catholic Church had failed to crystallize. He worked at various unskilled positions until the eve of the Spanish Civil War, at which time he was employed in the Arús Bank in Gerona. During the war, Gironella served on the side of the Nationalists with a battalion of ski soldiers in the Pyrenees mountains. At the conclusion of the conflict, he returned to Gerona. He had already begun to write, and now he nurtured this desire with a position as a newspaper reporter and contributor of articles to various journals.

In 1946, Gironella married his childhood sweetheart, Magda, and won the coveted Nadal Prize with the publication of his first novel. A year later, Gironella and his wife left Spain illegally and began several years of travel throughout Europe. During this time, he published his second novel, and, in 1951, he suffered a nervous breakdown. Gironella freely wrote about his illness while he sought relief at various clinics. The publication of *The Cypresses Believe in God* brought international recognition, and its sequel, *One Million Dead*, was also well received. These works assured for their creator a place in the literary history of Spain. The novelist returned to a residence in his native country, but until his death in 2003, he traveled extensively throughout the world while continuing to write.

Analysis

According to José María Gironella, the seed for his mammoth enterprise, to create in novel form an explanation of historical events in contemporary Spain, was planted December 30, 1937. Spain was in its second winter of civil war. Gironella was serving as a ski soldier in the Pyrenees along Spain's border with France when he was approached by a French girl from among the many skiers who frequented the area. Tearing a button from Gironella's uniform as a souvenir, the girl quickly darted away on her skis, but not before inquiring as to the ridiculousness of shooting one's brothers. This incident provoked in the young Spaniard a desire to explain to this girl and the entire world what was occurring in his country. Sixteen years later, with the publication of *The Cypresses Believe in God*, Gironella's effort became a reality. This first work of the series covers the pre-Civil War period, from April, 1931, to July, 1936, and won for its author Spain's national prize for literature in 1953. It is considered to be the author's masterpiece.

THE CYPRESSES BELIEVE IN GOD

The Cypresses Believe in God is an ambitious epic written in the realistic tradition; it neither defends nor condemns but rather observes and records, with the attitude that the reader may reach his or her own conclusions relative to the events that are narrated. To afford continuity to the epic, the author has selected one family, the Alvears, and one location, the city of Gerona, in Catalonia, as representative of all Spanish families and places who contribute to the amalgam of the period that incubates the war. The Alvears are thus elevated to a symbolic stature, and Gerona as well becomes a microcosm of the entire country, one in which the reader can view the evolution of those forces that divided Spain into two uncompromising extremes.

Though it is a panoramic work, sociopolitical in intent, *The Cypresses Believe in God* is also the chronicle of a family. Matías Alvear, a Castilian and clerk at the local telegraph office, is married to Carmen Elgazu, a Basque. In the home, there is an atmosphere of mutual respect in spite of the native differences, which are reflected also in the contrasts among the three children. César, given to meditation and spiritual matters, enters the priesthood aided by the urging of his mother. Pilar is sheltered and obedient. Ignacio, a mirror of the author, is both an idealist and a skeptic. He is the protagonist who, like Spain itself, bears the burden of an inner struggle as he searches but continues to doubt during the course of the national conflict. The novel is primarily Ignacio's story, narrating his journey into adulthood and documenting the challenges and growth that are associated with the individual, the family, and the national scene as well.

Upon leaving the seminary, Ignacio determines to experience life as abundantly as possible. He acquires a position at a bank while continuing to work toward a degree in law. Through Ignacio and his association with various individuals, the reader is provided a tour of the culture and institutions of Gerona, the intellectual arguments and positions of all political parties, platforms, and events, in a variety of social environments. Ignacio's cousin, José, representing the voice of the Falange, schools the protagonist in anticlericalism and introduces him into politics. Together, they attend political meetings and discussions. David and Olga Pol allow Ignacio the perspective from the political Left, and they, in turn, instruct Ignacio in their ideology. They escort the protagonist to an overcrowded mental institution and discuss with him the need for social reform. These and other characters serve as representatives of the various social and political points of view.

The fictional episodes of the Alvear family and Ignacio's experiences are interwoven with the historical events surrounding the deterioration of the political crisis. The protagonist becomes romantically involved with the aristocrat Ana María, and while on vacation with his family, he quits school and later returns to the study of law. A schoolmate, Mateo Santos, a leader of the Falange, becomes a major character through his romantic involvement with Pilar. As the threat of war escalates, the Communists, reacting to the execution of a member of the party, set fire to the cypress forests around Gerona. This action is for Ignacio's brother, César, a signal of the potential for a godless Spain, as these stately trees symbolize a belief in the deity (hence the title of the novel). This act of violence brings the Falange into political prominence, and the atrocities escalate on both sides. Ignacio's political commitment remains nebulous, although he has developed feelings for Marta de Soria, a Falangist leader.

The protagonist passes part of his law examinations, but the political situation forces him to postpone the completion of his studies. His friend, Mateo Santos, who has been detained, is freed and goes into hiding. César is detained also and, despite Ignacio's belated attempt to save his brother, is executed for no good reason. This death, although fulfilling César's desire to achieve martyrdom, demonstrates the chaos that accompanies the violence of the period. The novel closes with César's execution, and the reader, who is not subjected to his moralizing, is nevertheless impressed that a senseless action has occurred.

The character of Ignacio is a combination of idealism and hope in conflict with doubt and skepticism. He represents a struggle between reason and emotion and is a symbol of two Spains, the struggle between the progressive and the traditional. Inasmuch as Gironella utilizes the protagonist to effect a composite view of the Spain of that period, the character has been assessed as a transparent window, without depth of character or personal convictions, through which one might view the opinions and intrigues that precipitated the war. Indeed, one of the principal shortcomings of the novel is the protagonist's failure to generate a strong personal commitment to anything. Yet the character is artfully drawn and does represent an active force in the novel.

Ignacio and his creator believe that the individual, through his or her own moral capabilities, will survive over the collective. Each Spaniard will develop a personal interpretation of the war based on his or her own experiences. It is this personal concept, directed toward the future in the hope of creating a more sensitive and searching national conscience, that distinguishes Gironella. In spite of the tragedy of the war, Gironella teaches that each side may retain its personal dignity and yet recognize the courage and honor of the other.

The epic nature of the novel is enhanced by the artistic integration of historical data with fiction. Thus, the sweeping proportions of *The Cypresses Believe in God* do not diminish the reality that the novel is about a family. For Gironella, the family is the basic unit of a successful society, and throughout this novel an accounting is made of each of the Alvears. The novel succeeds on both levels, yet the breadth of the work is extensive at the expense of depth. Historical, economic, and political intricacies, as well as family episodes of minor importance, could have been omitted.

ONE MILLION DEAD

One Million Dead narrates the period from July 30, 1936, to April 1, 1939, and purports to provide a panoramic view of the war years. The author portrays the two factions simultaneously and attempts to be as impartial as possible. Gironella evinces a skill for meticulous documentation and verisimilitude, and, as for the preceding volume, he spent years collecting data, interviewing Spanish and foreign participants and witnesses, and searching archives for pertinent newspapers, photographs, and editorials. His personal participation in the conflict contributes to his insight. The title of this novel is intended to stand for the actual number of those who died in the conflict—slightly less than half a million—as well as those who, possessed by hate, destroyed their own souls.

In this novel, the Alvear family continues to occupy center stage, but the setting broadens to include all parts of Spain. The action begins in the cemetery where César has been killed. Ignacio discovers his brother's body and is haunted by the speculation that he might have been able to save him. The incident ignites a criticism of the war by the protagonist, who, with his family, is neutral as the struggle escalates. Ignacio's present sweetheart, Marta de Soria, a Falange activist, escapes to France. She has a short-lived relationship with an Italian soldier who, like many other characters in this volume, introduces an international thread to the fabric of the conflict. As the war proceeds, Ignacio finally enlists in the Nationalist armies as a medical aide. His travels take him to Barcelona and Madrid, where he works in a hospital for the wounded. He also experiences a journey into the Pyrenees, where he meets a group of Nationalist soldiers in a ski patrol. He is awed by the peace that he finds in these mountains. This and many other incidents in the novel reveal the author's autobiographical stamp on the action of the narrative.

Ignacio's mother adopts a homeless orphan whose parents had been killed at Guernica. As the war draws to a close, the various members of the family are drawn again to Gerona. Mateo de Soria also returns, as does his sister, Marta. Together, the family attends the first public mass to be held in Gerona's cathedral in three years. The novel concludes with a quiet scene in which General Francisco Franco, at work in his office in Nationalist headquarters, is informed by an aide that the war is officially over. Franco simply responds that it is good and, thanking the aide, returns to his work.

This novel is broader in scope than its predecessor. It narrates the war from the point of view of both factions, not simply from a military perspective; it includes sociological, religious, and political intrigues as well. The author remains apart and detached as he analyzes each occurrence without judging. This preference for the external and for objective distance does not serve Gironella well in his portrayal of the inner world of his characters. As a result, the vitality of some of the characters in *The Cypresses Believe in God* is fettered in the sequel. The author isolates himself from individuality, though he makes an effort to portray the distinctive souls of the provinces of Spain and to bless his characters with a unique and personal psychological depth. In each case, the author fails, a victim of his need to discover objectively and explain the significance of the Civil War.

Although *One Million Dead* does not accommodate the empathy that might unlock the interior world of its characters, it is a systematic, organized analysis of the war. *The Cypresses Believe in God* has been termed a novel with historical pretensions, whereas *One Million Dead* has been judged a historical work interlaced with fiction.

The fictional aspect of the novel is further weakened by the author's tendency to stereotype minor characters and to level certain judgments based on their political affiliations. Communists, for example, are generally portrayed as villains in contrast to the noble efforts of the Falangists. Although Gironella insists on impartiality in his portrayal of the historical and political aspect of his novels, there is a tendency to favor the Nationalist platform. His continual reminder of the strength of the family unit as the key to Spain's hope for the future is a constant reiteration of the Nationalist theme. The victorious Falange is spared severe criticism, although it has been argued that Gironella was required to tread with care to avoid possible censorship. As the novel concludes, General Franco is portrayed, without excessive praise or propaganda, as the hope of Spain's future.

PEACE AFTER WAR

Peace After War—a slow-paced and all-too-predictable sequel to *One Million Dead*—treats the period between 1939 and 1941. Its emphasis is on the reconstruction of Spain under Franco, and the author praises the reforms of the Nationalists while portraying an atmosphere of unity and pride. Reform and greater national liberty through changes instituted by the government are emphasized, while resentment against the regime is kept to a minimum. Gironella demonstrates complete acceptance of Franco's policy and places emphasis once again on the fictional aspects of the work. The Alvears are reunited. Ignacio graduates from the University of Barcelona and assumes a life given more to reflection than to action. His sweetheart, Marta de Soria, devotes her attention to politics, while Ignacio renews his affection for his first love, Ana María.

The marriage of Pilar to Mateo Santos assumes a more important position in this novel. Mateo displays a fanatical zeal to sacrifice his life, if necessary, in the fight against Communism. Pilar makes an unsuccessful attempt to dissuade him, but, unable to draw from herself the strength she requires, she withdraws to her family for moral support. Pilar's foil is her cousin, Paz, sensual, alienated from the family because of her leftist politics, but, unlike most of Gironella's protagonists, strong and motivated.

In addition to his Spanish Civil War cycle, Gironella published several other novels, but his reputation ultimately will rest on a single work, *The Cypresses Believe in God*. Although in many respects this novel has dated badly, it retains its historical value as a sweeping portrait of Spain during a crucial period in its history.

Alfred W. Jensen

OTHER MAJOR WORKS

SHORT FICTION: *Todos somos fugitivos*, 1961 (English translation, 1964).

POETRY: *Ha llegado el invierno y tú no estás aquí*, 1945.

NONFICTION: *El novelista ante el mundo*, 1954; *Los fantasmas de mi cerebro*, 1959 (*Phantoms and Fugitives: Journeys to the Improbable*, 1964; includes translation of *Todos somos fugitivos*); *Personas, ideas, y mares*, 1963; *El Japón y su duende*, 1964; *China, lágrima innumerable*, 1965; *Gritos del mar*, 1967; *Conversaciones con don Juan de Borbón*, 1968; *En Asia se muere bajo las estrellas*, 1968; *Cien españoles y Dios*, 1969; *El Mediterraneo es un hombre disfrazado de mar*, 1974; *El escandola de Tierra Santa*, 1977; *Carta a mi padre muerto*, 1978; *Cita en el cementerio*, 1983; *Jerusalén de los Evangelios*, 1989; *Yo, Mahoma*, 1989; *Carta a mi madre muerta*, 1992; *Nuevos 100 españoles y Dios*, 1994.

BIBLIOGRAPHY

Boyle, John F. "True Fiction." *Commonweal* 130, no. 12 (June 20, 2003). Boyle discusses *The Cypresses Believe in God*, praising the novel for its well-conceived story and its ability to give "shape, color, and substance in understanding the Spanish Civil War."

Longyear, R. M. "*The Cypresses Believe in God.*" In *Masterplots: Eighteen Hundred One Plot Stories and Critical Evaluations of the World's Finest Literature*, edited by Frank N. Magill et al. Vol. 3. Pasadena, Calif.: Salem Press, 1996. Gironella's masterpiece, *The Cypresses Believe in God*, is reviewed in this collection of brief but comprehensive critical essays examining the best of world literature.

Schwartz, Ronald. *José María Gironella*. New York: Twayne, 1972. This volume, the only full-length study of Gironella in English, provides a comprehensive account of his achievements and works. Includes a bibliography.

Thomas, Gareth. *The Novel of the Spanish Civil War*. New York: Cambridge University Press, 1990. Gironella's trilogy receives a chapter, and the introductory chapters are valuable in providing a context. The citations from Gironella and his critics are all in the original Spanish or French.

EMILIA PARDO BAZÁN

Born: La Coruña, Spain; September 16, 1851
Died: Madrid, Spain; May 12, 1921

PRINCIPAL LONG FICTION
Pascual López, 1879
Un viaje de novios, 1882 (*A Wedding Trip*, 1891)
La tribuna, 1883
El cisne de Vilamorta, 1885 (*The Swan of Vilamorta*, 1891; also known as *Shattered Hope: Or, The Swan of Vilamorta*, 1900)
Los pazos de Ulloa, 1886 (*The Son of the Bondwoman*, 1908)
La madre naturaleza, 1887
Insolación, 1889 (*Midsummer Madness*, 1907)
Morriña, 1889 (*Morriña: Homesickness*, 1891)
Una cristiana, 1890 (*A Christian Woman*, 1891)
La prueba, 1890
La piedra angular, 1891 (*The Angular Stone*, 1892)
Doña Milagros, 1894
Adán y Eva, 1896 (includes *Doña Milagros* and *Memorias de un solterón*)
Memorias de un solterón, 1896
El saludo de las brujas, 1897
El tesoro de Gastón, 1897
El niño de Guzman, 1898
Misterio, 1903 (*The Mystery of the Lost Dauphin: Louis XVII*, 1906)
La quimera, 1905
La sirena negra, 1908
Dulce dueño, 1911

OTHER LITERARY FORMS

In addition to her novels, the writings of Emilia Pardo Bazán (PAHR-doh bah-ZHAHN) include essays, criticism, autobiographical pieces, short stories, and plays. Some of her better-known nonfiction includes *La cuestión palpitante* (1883), *Apuntes autobiográficos* (1886), *La revolución y la novela en Rusia* (1887; *Russia: Its People and Its Literature*, 1890), *De mi tierra* (1888), *El nuevo teatro crítico* (1891-1893), *Polémicas y estudios literarios* (1892), *Los poetas épicos cristianos* (1895), *Lecciones de literatura* (1906), *Literatura francesca moderna* (1910-1914), and *Hernán Cortés y sus hazañas* (1914).

Pardo Bazán also is credited with having written approximately four hundred short stories, collected in numerous anthologies. Her plays, which are virtually unknown, are *Cuesta abajo* (pb. 1906) and *Verdad* (pb. 1906).

Emilia Pardo Bazán
(Library of Congress)

Achievements

Of all the major nineteenth century Spanish novelists, none has aroused as much contradictory and erroneous comment as Emilia Pardo Bazán. Emilio González López seeks to prove that she was first and foremost a regionalist writer of Galicia. José Balseiro misunderstands the evolving nature of her literary creed and ignores the positive contribution French naturalism made to her novels. Julio Cejador y Frauca fails to comprehend both the naturalistic movement itself and the extent of Pardo Bazán's understanding of the French techniques.

In fact, Pardo Bazán was, above all, an eclectic. The revolutionary period of 1870 to 1874 helped to shape her literary perspective, and the Restoration, years thereafter, caused her style to evolve and mature. These were years of social, political, and intellectual change, and Pardo Bazán, who studied and involved herself deeply in literary fashions and innovations, took part in the turmoil of this period. Perhaps to avoid monotony, perhaps to prove herself in literary circles dominated by men, perhaps because of her innate sense of curiosity, she moved among various literary schools, carefully avoiding extreme positions. Thus, there is a naturalistic emphasis in *La tribuna*, *The Son of the Bondwoman*, *La madre naturaleza*, *Midsummer Madness*, and *Morriña*; a mixture of naturalism and idealistic Romanticism dominates *A Wedding Trip* and *The Swan of Vilamorta*; a Christian idealism takes the form of increased optimism and abstract, religious thematic concerns in *A Christian Woman* and *La prueba*.

A symbolic emphasis is also evident in these two and in other later works. Yet one can apply no precise chronological divisions to Pardo Bazán's various literary phases. The Romantic appears, for example, in her use of historical allusion (as in the stories "En las cavernas" and "Belcebú"), her sentimentalism (*Morriña*), and her religious idealization (*Dulce dueño* or her other later novels). Romantic as well are her emotional characterizations, her dramatic effects, her occasional subjective authorial involvement, and her use of narrative crescendos and climaxes.

Although Pardo Bazán never developed a rigorous aesthetic system, she was an important literary critic. The prologue to *A Wedding Trip*, although relatively immature and lacking depth and completeness, came to be a milestone in the Spanish reaction to naturalism. Of even greater importance was *La cuestión palpitante*, which offered the most comprehensive and candid appraisal of naturalism in Spain during this period. In this treatise, the author rejected those facets of naturalism that substantially distinguished it from realism, as the latter term was then understood. She declared her objection to naturalism as practiced by Émile Zola, decrying its pessimism, utilitarianism, obscenity, positivism, determinism, apparent tastelessness, and truncated view of human existence, in which the author was obliged to omit much of what was beautiful. Nevertheless, she approved of naturalism's objectivity and relative impersonality, as well as its observational techniques and its penetrating study of life's problems. She agreed that a novel should be a relatively close copy of real life, as the writer sees it, and that, as a study of vital, contemporary issues, it must surpass the simple function of providing imaginative entertainment.

Pardo Bazán emphatically opposed the concept that the novelist should attempt to teach through scientific methods, however, believing that the search for truth is not the principal object of art, as it is in science; the artist should subordinate all other aims to the principal goal of attaining some measure of beauty. The real value of *La cuestión palpitante* lay in its stimulus to the ensuing polemics, for which service it retains a measure of historical significance.

Finally, *Russia* was the first treatise in Spanish dedicated to the study of the Russian novel. From the works of Leo Tolstoy and others, Pardo Bazán discovered how realism and Christian sentiment could be reconciled; this perspective coincided with her own deeply felt convictions.

In addition to her work as novelist and critic, Pardo Bazán was the outstanding short-story writer of her day. Only Pedro Antonio de Alarcón (before), Leopoldo Alas (Clarín), and Vicente Blasco Ibáñez (afterward) could rival her, but her hundreds of pieces attest the fact that no one could match the diversity, abundance, and high quality of her short fiction. Guy de Maupassant seems to have been her chief model.

Biography

Emilia Pardo Bazán's birthplace, La Coruña, in the Galician province, is in an area of conflicting cultures, in which modern, cosmopolitan influences blend or conflict with traditional, peasant ways of life. Similarly, her intellectual life was characterized by contradiction and ambivalence: Galician provincialism and traditionalism versus enthusiasm for the latest novelties of Madrid and Paris; social ambition and a desire for public attention versus a feminist emphasis on the importance of the individual in everyday life. A child of the rapidly changing times in which she lived—the age of positivism, scientific advance, and literary revolution—she was a person of somewhat conflicting beliefs. A vigorous, healthy, and ambitious woman, she was one of the most important and outspoken of Spain's early feminists, shocking the literary world with her promulgation of a mitigated form of French naturalism, attempting to teach at the University of Madrid, and fighting throughout her later years for membership in the Royal Spanish Academy.

A devout Roman Catholic, Pardo Bazán struggled vainly to reconcile her liberal feelings with her innate religious conservatism, her support for the Carlist cause, a distrust of democracy, and an intolerance of other forms of spiritual belief. She was an ardent expert on many facets of nature, and her happiest times were spent at her country manor in Meiras, near La Coruña.

Born and reared as the only child of well-to-do parents, Pardo Bazán had few childhood friends and associated mostly with older family acquaintances. Her father received the pontifical title of count in 1871, which she inherited in 1890, subsequently "legitimated" in 1908 by King Alfonso XIII's bequest of the comparable Spanish title of the realm.

As a child, Pardo Bazán was a voracious reader, a habit she continued when her family began to spend winters in Madrid in 1869, where she entered a French school. When she was eleven or twelve years old, her parents returned permanently to La Coruña, where she continued her education under private tutors. In 1868, she married a young lawyer named José Quiroga, and the following year the newlyweds accompanied her father back to the capital, since the latter had been elected to the congress that would write the new constitution. There she set aside her reading and plunged into Madrid society. The political disillusionment that followed upon the failure of Amadeo de Saboya as king and the dissolution of her father's new progressive party led the family to travel abroad, to France, Italy, Austria, and England. Pardo Bazán returned to her studies and, in 1874, visited Victor Hugo. A systematic absorption of reading material led to her first writings and, subsequently, to the publication of *La cuestión palpitante*. By 1881, a third child was born to Pardo Bazán and her husband, and by 1887 her trips to France had produced a close friendship with Edmond de Goncourt, a personal acquaintance with Zola, and her discovery of the Russian novel.

In 1887 and 1888, Pardo Bazán traveled to Rome for the magazine *El imparcial*. During those same years, she had an emotional audience with the pope and an introduction to Pretender Don Carlos in Venice. In 1889, she befriended the wealthy, young José Lázaro Galdiano, who was promoting cultural projects, including the literary journal *La España moderna*, to which Pardo Bazán contributed a number of articles. During that time, she had an affair with novelist Benito Pérez Galdós, which, because of the publication of their love letters, was widely discussed. The years following were ones of bitter literary and personal controversy, as she battled with writers Alas (Clarín) and José María de Pereda and initiated her fruitless campaign for a seat in the Royal Spanish Academy. Alas, for example, did not fail to mention Pardo Bazán's increasing corpulence. Also during these years, she single-handedly wrote and edited the monthly journal *El nuevo teatro crítico*, a Herculean task that serves as ample evidence of her energy and indomitable perseverance.

By the last years of the century, Pardo Bazán's novelistic powers began to wane, but during the last two decades of her life she was to encounter as many honors as disappointments. In 1906, she was elected as the first woman ever to chair the literary section of the Madrid Ateneo, and in 1916, she was appointed to the position of professor of contemporary literature at the University of Madrid. Since most students and faculty resented this action, attendance at her lectures fell until but a single auditor remained. When he, too, failed to appear, her career as a professor came to an end. A series of other events had deepened her pessimism and disillusionment: the defeat of Spain in the disaster of 1898, her failure to be accepted in Galician politics, the death of her husband in 1912, her continued rejection by the members of the Royal Spanish Academy, and the apparent indifference of Spanish women to their own emancipation. The sympathy of some of the young writers of the *generación del 1898*, or Generation of '98, did little to assuage her pessimism. Pardo Bazán died in Madrid, on May 12, 1921, after which hundreds of tributes were written, a statue of her was unveiled, and a number of people talked of the possibility of her posthumous election to the Royal Spanish Academy.

Analysis

In general, Emilia Pardo Bazán's works reveal a gradual passage from Romanticism to traditional realism to a modified naturalism and finally to a spiritual, symbolic approach. *Pascual López* is Pardo Bazán's only novel to bear clearly the sentimental, moralistic (in its condemnation of egotism), and unreal stamp of Romanticism, although a costumbristic atmosphere, also of Romantic origin, anticipates the realistic descriptions of later novels. *A Wedding Trip* introduces the physiological element and increased *detallismo*, but still reflects an aristocratic, conservative environment.

Pardo Bazán seems to have experienced a religious crisis in 1882—evident in her nonfiction work *San Francisco de Asís* (1882)—and this event may have been a factor in her subsequent shift of direction. The five novels that followed (and one in 1891) may be considered her most naturalistic works: *La tribuna*—"estudio de costumbres tomadas de la realidad"—contains a prologue in which the author renounces the idealism of Antonio de Trueba and Fernán Caballero. Reflecting thorough firsthand documentation, the work paints a naturalistic *tranche de vie* among tobacco-shop workers and includes detailed psychological descriptions and "crude" dialogue. In *The Swan of Vilamorta*, realistic elements are mixed with some Romantic sentiments. *The Son of the Bondwoman* and its sequel, *La madre naturaleza*, are both set in the author's native Galicia and are perhaps the most naturalistic of Pardo Bazán's novels. The second, particularly, demonstrates the force of environmental influence beyond the theoretical limits she had set in her treatises on realism and naturalism. *Midsummer Madness* is naturalistic in some of its details but seems far from Zola in its happy tone, its aristocratic milieu, and its general lack of detailed descriptions. *Morriña* contains "interior" symbolic and psychological elements that suggest the author's future direction. *The Angular Stone* recounts in naturalistic fashion the determining forces upon its characters, but has an inordinate amount of didactic content.

With *A Christian Woman* and its continuation, *La prueba*, Pardo Bazán's focus changes somewhat. Here and in two subsequent novels—*La quimera* and *La sirena negra*—a new spirituality, a stress on transcendent ideas and character introspection, and less exterior and regionalistic *detallismo* announce a new tendency. Her study of the Russian novel, along with a change in perspective linked with the approach of old age, led her to voice preoccupations that had never really been absent from her writing. In *La quimera*, modernistic and symbolic elements placed in an elegant, aristocratic social milieu indicate further shifts of viewpoint. *Dulce dueño*, which was inspired by the life and death of Santa Catalina de Alejandría, is equally alien to the author's earlier ventures into naturalism.

Pardo Bazán's native Galicia is the setting of her best novels; this region inspired her to an exact depiction of landscape, racial characters, customs, and local ways of thought. Nevertheless, she was able to give her settings and her plots an almost cosmopolitan breadth. Her regionalism was not the *huerto hermoso* of Pereda. Her characterizations went deep, generally avoiding rustic picturesqueness and *dialectismos* in re-creating local speech. Thus, she transcended the confines of strict regionalism.

Pardo Bazán's realism is a special, Spanish mixture of the real and the "ideal." Her eclectic variations in choosing points of emphasis, her psychological involvement with her characters, her avoidance of constant, local speech patterns or her use of linguistic *extranjerismos* and *arcaísmos*, her conscious attempt to create beauty—all of these elements demonstrate that she, too, found her own realistic approach. Indeed, her work is relatively free of two of the recurrent components of Spanish realistic writing: the middle-class backdrop and the consistent use of common, colloquial language.

Mary Giles has argued that an impressionistic bent for describing fleeting colors and the momentary effects of light, and for sketching changing images without a fixed "reality," appears in Pardo Bazán's novels that "represent her modified naturalism"; this impressionism is abandoned entirely in the novels between *La madre naturaleza* and *La quimera* and is resumed in her last three novels. An analysis of *The Son of the Bondwoman* will illustrate how, among other factors, new rich and coloristic linguistic effects are joined with a depth of psychological penetration to produce a realism that is uniquely Pardo Bazán's even while it remains utterly Spanish.

THE SON OF THE BONDWOMAN

Critics have long considered *The Son of the Bondwoman* Pardo Bazán's masterpiece. It was published in 1886, when the controversy over naturalism still raged in Spain. While some commentators have insisted that the story ultimately contradicts the deterministic philosophy of the naturalists, many have decided it is a truly naturalistic creation, both linguistically and thematically. It does seem to be one of the few major Spanish novels of the century that can in fact be termed naturalistic, even if not in the full sense of Zola's methodology.

The plot postulates nature as an uncompromising "mistress" who comes to dominate, almost totally, the lives of those human beings caught within her grasp. Julián, a refined and idealistic young priest, comes to live on an estate, Ulloa, situated deep in the interior of Galicia. His mission is to restore order to the household, since its degenerate owner, the "Marquis" Don Pedro Moscoso, has allowed it to deteriorate. Don Pedro himself keeps one of his servants, Sabel, as a concubine, with the blessing of her father, Primitivo, who wants to use the relationship as leverage to maintain control of the property.

In his desire to raise the manor to a level of moral and material respectability, Julián advises Don Pedro to marry not his beautiful, passionate cousin Rita, but rather Rita's delicate and religious sister Nucha. The priest hopes that this arrangement will rid Pedro of some of his animalistic inclinations. When Nucha gives birth to a girl, leaving her husband without a much-desired heir, Pedro returns to his former ways and becomes indifferent and cruel to his wife. Primitivo's detection of Julián's silent love for Nucha leads to the priest's dismissal from the house. After many years, he returns to the manor to find Nucha's grave neglected and her daughter in rags, while Primitivo's tomb is meticulously tended; his grandson, Perucho, the natural son of Pedro and Sabel, wears fine clothing. The essence of the plot, then, is, in Sherman Eoff's words, "a contest in which refinement and ideals prove to be helpless before their natural opponents," a struggle in which Julián is shown to be powerless in hostile surroundings.

Pardo Bazán's characterizations do occasionally probe deeply to produce some genuine impressions of human preoccupations and reactions. The major characters of the novel possess unique and distinguishing traits, despite their stereotyped roles and their "espíritu de clase." Although it is true that the author often interprets too much for the reader, some characters (such as Julián and Nucha) act out their roles convincingly.

Throughout the novel, human beings are exposed as *bestias*, blending in with the savagery of their surroundings. The scene in which the boy Perucho is forced to become drunk and the dogs receive more care than the people who are present is an early indication of the brutality to follow. Nevertheless, at least two characters—Julián and Nucha—escape such treatment.

The characterization of Julián is one of Pardo Bazán's most vivid and penetrating exercises in psychological realism. He is timid, idealistic, basically well-meaning, delicate, prudish, almost feminine in his outlook. Some noticeably unworthy traits also emerge: He suffers from the sin of pride (about his knowledge, his "victory" regarding Pedro's marriage); despite his active awareness of his Christian duties, he is occasionally cruel or lacking in charity (as in his pleasure in seeing the murder of Primitivo). His irresoluteness and procrastination suggest that Pardo Bazán wanted to convey a message about the need for initiative and fortitude to support good intentions. Finally, he is humanized in his physical attentions to Nucha's daughter, actions that represent a displacement of frustrated sexual aspirations.

One must note that all of these turns of character are made perfectly believable by the incidents or circumstances of Julián's background: He was an only child, perhaps of illegitimate birth; he lived under the domineering influence of a household *ama* of Pedro's uncle Don Manuel; he was not allowed to play with the daughters of Don Manuel and thus had no opportunity to develop normal social relationships; he had in his childhood no contact with the savagery and animal nature of the rural inhabitants; he was further influenced by Nucha, his substitute mother, with her prudishness and piety. Finally, Pardo Bazán uses the characterization of Julián as a medium for further experiments with literary portraiture: the use of dreams, fantasies, half-wakened states, and interior monologues.

The other figures in the novel do not display as much profundity or individuality as Julián. Nucha is a delicate, sensitive girl, an urban bourgeois given to gradually increasing hysteria and romantic, sentimental fantasies. Her nervous and mystical nature directly contrasts with that of Sabel. Primitivo, as his name suggests, symbolizes the forces of natural savagery and evil. Sly, self-serving, and taciturn, his excessive self-confidence hastens his own death. More important, his role furthers the plot, since it is he who dominates Pedro, who causes his "master" to lose the election and thus remain at the manor, and who leads him to suspect a love affair between Julián and Nucha.

Pedro himself is the degenerate, feudal aristocrat of Galicia, anticipating Ramón María del Valle-Inclán's Juan Manuel de Montenegro. His savage surroundings and the lack of an urban, civilized environment join with his increasing marital frustrations to make him progressively bestial. He is cruel, egotistical (he cannot pardon Nucha for her physical weakness), irresponsible, and indifferent, allowing himself to become a pawn of Primitivo's personal ambitions. He does, however, reveal some measure of individuality: He dares, for example, to challenge the political system in order to correct some of the social ills of his environment; his pride in the family line, along with his willingness to marry the submissive Nucha instead of her stronger sister, suggest that a certain inferiority complex operates beneath his facade of machismo.

Sabel likewise offers some semblance of individuality, although she seems to represent the pueblo. She is sensual and animalistic, calculating and provocative, and, in fact, the real señora of the mansion. Nevertheless, she is also humble and submissive; her relationship with Pedro stems only from obedience to her father's command, since she does not like the owner of the Manor and wants simply to marry el Gallo. Thus she, too, is a victim of the environment. The handsome child Perucho, whose devilish and egotistical traits seem to go along with his age, is, however, individualized somewhat by his surprisingly mature sexual instincts.

Pardo Bazán's thematic concerns in *The Son of the Bondwoman* include a condemnation of a number of social or psychological elements: the isolation that has allowed a decadent, feudal aristocracy to persist; political corruption; an exaggerated sense of class rank; pride and the lack of personal initiative. In this regard, however, the novel's naturalistic thrust is most significant. Eoff asserts that "the sinister force of nature which hovers over all the personages involved in the narrative action not only defeats outsiders who challenge it; it imposes itself destructively on those who are natives of its domains."

Further, the author explores in naturalistic fashion certain hereditary influences (for example, Señor de la Lage and his nephew, Pedro, demonstrate similar traits) and stresses other deterministic forces throughout the novel. It is wrong to say, however (as does Donald Brown), that the influence of heredity and environment "is the whole book." Without Primitivo's intercession, Pedro would have won the election and moved away; Julián will go on to live outside this savage region; and, most important, moments of light satire and interludes of comedy preclude any unrelieved, Zolaesque sense of inevitable doom and destruction. The novel, then, suggests a kind of regionalistic determinism. The characters seem doomed, less because of their mere existence as human beings than because of their remoteness from civilization and insufficient religious teaching.

Like all the major Spanish realists, Pardo Bazán assumes an authorial perspective that is only partially objective (that is, impersonal and neutral). While her frankness and boldness are very evident, in some ways she rejects a neutrality of values, Flaubertian *impassibilité*, completely impartial treatment of character, and authorial nonintervention. In *The Son of the Bondwoman* she takes part in her characters' thoughts and feelings by way of indirect free style and interior monologue. She is openly sympathetic toward many of her creations, her tone is often subtly ironic, and she contrives several incidents of comic relief. The last element, for example, is seen in four major passages: the celebration in Naya (the *guita* playing during the mass, the twenty-six courses of the banquet, and so on); Pedro and Nucha's social visits, during which, for example, the sister of the archpriest of Loiro had niches cut into her dining room table in order to "accommodate their stomachs"; the preparations for the hunting expedition and the merciless fun that the hunters make of the bungling Julián; and, finally, the satire of the corrupt elections and *caciquismo* of the area, in which voting urns are stolen or destroyed and the priests Tuerto and Limioso rout the drunken, rejoicing liberals. Julián's naïveté (as in his initial ignorance of the relationship among Pedro, Sabel, and Perucho and in his pious reluctance to touch the volumes of Voltaire and Jean-Jacques Rousseau) further exemplifies Pardo Bazán's subjective humor.

Finally, with respect to authorial perspective, one should note that, while the body of the narrative is presented from Julián's moralizing point of view, the perspective suddenly changes in chapter 28 to that of Perucho. In this chapter, the lad actually enacts Julián's fantasy: He escapes with the one he has "loved" (the daughter of Nucha, rather than Nucha herself). This change in perspective allows the author to avoid presenting directly the violence of Primitivo's assassination and the emotional confrontation of Pedro, Julián, and Nucha. In such ways Pardo Bazán escapes some of the brutal candor that often marks naturalistic novels.

Pardo Bazán's language is exact, rich, and permeated by *detallismo*. One is struck by the *solidez* of style, manifested in the frequent use of strong nouns, adjectives, and verbs. The vocabulary is remarkably varied and expressive; in the first few pages alone, Julián's horse is referred to as a *jinete, rocín, jaco, corcel, hípica, cuartago, cabalgadura, bestia, raza caballar,* and *caballo*. Although she apparently made no exhaustive effort to capture all the Galician speech patterns, Pardo Bazán did not shun representative bits of realistic colloquialism. Her sentences are often lengthy, yet they are direct and unencumbered by superfluous phrases. Often they consist of enumerations of nouns or phrases, at times without main verbs.

The imagery of the novel reflects the general rigor and sensuality of the style but is more moderate than many of Zola's figures of speech. Like the French author, Pardo Bazán frequently included analogies to animals or vegetation to stress the significance of natural forces in human conduct. Also adding to the expressiveness of the work is the rich *colorismo* of her language. One commentator has enumerated at least thirty-five different colors in the novel, of which twenty-seven are variations of hues and shades. Certainly in *The Son of the Bondwoman*, Pardo Bazán appeals to the visual sense more than to any other. "The vitalization of pictorial detail through color modifiers," says Giles, "is consonant with the theme and technique of the naturalist novel, with its strong emphasis on the sensual, superficial layer of reality." Another critic has studied the surprisingly frequent allusions to painting in the novel, as in the *sortilegio* scene, which alludes to Goya, or the many times Julián likens Nucha to portraits of the Virgin Mary.

Next to *La madre naturaleza*, *The Son of the Bondwoman* more completely captures the Galician landscape than any of Pardo Bazán's other works. The atmosphere, not unlike that evoked by Emily Brontë, is lush and primitive, constantly threatening to engulf man in its relentless encroachment upon civilization. These descriptions of a blind and brutal *naturaleza* are meant to reinforce the novel's vision of a spiritually barbaric caste. Thus, for example, details concerning the worms in the library symbolize the destruction of intelligence and spirit in a decadent family.

Certainly, the action of the novel is subordinate to the description of *ambiente*. "The author's attention," Eoff remarks, "is concentrated primarily on the creation of an atmosphere appropriate to the primitive lushness and unkemptness of a place far removed from the softening touch of civilization." At times these passages reveal a Romantic tone, which leads occasionally to extremely subjective "melodramatic swells of ebulliency." Usually the descriptions of landscape are meant to function in relation to the author's characterization. Thus the long opening picture of the forest at night helps enhance the reader's appreciation of Julián's fears. The vista of the countryside at the end of the book intensifies the reader's recognition, and Julián's, that he has failed to change the environment of the manor.

The Son of the Bondwoman, although Pardo Bazán's best work, cannot be compared with the few masterpieces of Spanish realism such as Alas's *La regenta* (1884) and Benito Pérez Galdós's *Fortunata y Jacinta* (1886-1887; *Fortunata and Jacinta*, 1973) and *Misericordia* (1897; *Compassion*, 1962). What is most striking in the novel, however, and what will most endure is Pardo Bazán's language; its richness, vividness, and exactness earns for her an indisputable place among the foremost writers of the late nineteenth and early twentieth centuries.

LA TRIBUNA

Among Pardo Bazán's other works, *La tribuna*, one of her early social novels, represents the first attempt in Spanish literature to reflect authentically and sympathetically the life of the urban working class. An experimental work that initiated her naturalistic phase, the story sprang from two months of intensive observation, notebook in hand, in a La Coruña tobacco factory. The naturalistic influence—then at its height in Spain—is explicit in the exact *detallismo* and pictures of industrial squalor, the use of heredity, the social criticism, the incorporation of popular speech, the appearance of a kind of collective protagonist (the factory), technical descriptions of cigarette making, and the utilization of real, albeit fictitiously named, locales. Zolaesque determinism and extreme pessimism, however, are not to be found. Against a background of the political uprising of 1868, the heroine, Amparo, goes to work in a tobacco shop, where she reads the political news aloud to the other workers and develops an enthusiasm for the republican cause. Instead of accepting an unromantic but stable country fellow for a husband, she allows herself to be seduced by an army captain. After giving birth to a son, she learns that her lover has fled to Madrid.

Luis Alfonso, a leading idealist critic of the times, condemned the novel for its use of crude language and its explicit description of proletarian life. He found the childbirth scene particularly offensive, even though the reader does not directly see it but merely hears Amparo's cries through the wall of an adjoining room.

In *La tribuna* one sees an excellent illustration of the author's mitigated naturalism and a noticeable advance over early works in which the themes are less naturally integrated into the narrative. The author set out to study the possibilities of happiness for a girl from the lower class. Amparo's downfall does not negate the validity of hope.

LA MADRE NATURALEZA

La madre naturaleza is the sequel to *The Son of the Bondwoman* and traces the love affair between Nucha's child, Manolita, and Perucho (who have the same father). Presented as a new Adam and Eve in a Galician version of Genesis (similar to Zola's *La Faute de l'abbé Mouret*, 1875; *The Sin of Father Mouret*, 1904, 1969), the two are invited by Nature's forces to indulge fully in their sexual instincts. Nature later proves impassive to their anguish when society imposes its incest taboo. After their "crime," Perucho goes off to Madrid in desperation and Manolita joins a convent, at least temporarily.

Besides the account of the protagonists' increasing affection for each other, there is little plot material in the novel. Pardo Bazán was more interested in demonstrating that humans' instinctive, animal side, nurtured by a powerful, inexorable, and indifferent Nature, will dominate over the force of social norms. Most important, *La madre naturaleza* was a magnificent vehicle for rich, sensuous descriptions of *paisaje* and extensive costumbristic delineation.

MIDSUMMER MADNESS

The sexual theme and a measure of environmental determinism continue in the short novel *Midsummer Madness* (and in its companion piece, *Morriña*), but the setting is Madrid. Asís de Taboada, a young Madrid socialite, accepts the invitation of Diego Pacheco, a charming Andalusian Don Juan, to visit the San Isidro Fair. There she becomes intoxicated and suffers a mild sunstroke. Later, after excursions into Madrid nightlife and a lovers' quarrel, the two agree to marry. Thus, even in the city, Nature (manifesting itself in the sun) is triumphant, but there is no social taboo to prevent their marriage.

Despite the accusation of pornography that accompanied the publication of *Midsummer Madness*, there is little explicitly naturalistic language, except perhaps in the frankness of a quarrel between two women or in a knife fight between men at the fair. The tone, certainly, is light and happy. The short novel is one of Pardo Bazán's best because of the vividness of its costumbristic description—lively, detailed pictures of the fair, the Roma who tell Asís's fortune, and carriage rides.

LA QUIMERA

Finally, Pardo Bazán's last phase (as well as her eclectic combination of realism and idealism) is well represented by *La quimera*, one of her finest novels. It concerns the search for success and immortality by a young painter named Silvio Lago (who himself symbolizes eternal aspiration). After he gains a reputation in Madrid with his portrait of a well-known woman composer, he encounters the influence of two other women: Clara Ayamonte, who wishes to marry him but whom he refuses because his artistic drive or chimera leaves no room for love, and Espina Porcel, who introduces him to Paris and then mistreats him with a mixture of sadism, jealousy, and deceit.

The protagonist gradually loses his confidence in objective depictions of reality and becomes enthused by Flemish painting. Standing before the van Eyck brother's *Divine Lamb*—a work that had deeply moved Pardo Bazán—he experiences a religious conversion similar in depth to his changes in artistic perspective. After contracting tuberculosis in Paris, he returns to Galicia, where he dies happy for having discovered the formula for the masterpiece he never achieves.

La quimera is a historically important novel for two reasons. First, it demonstrates the author's attempt to adapt to the sensitivities of a younger generation (that of 1898; Miguel de Unamuno y Jugo was fascinated by Pardo Bazán's study of the artist's search for immortality). Second, the conversion of the protagonist from an objective, naturalistic approach to one of symbolism and idealistic spirituality reflects Pardo Bazán's own artistic trajectory and represents the most effective statement of her mature literary formula.

Pardo Bazán was clearly one of Spain's finest nineteenth century writers. Her novels contain memorable pages of lush, natural description and distinctive character portraits. Equally as significant, however, was her own unique, aggressive personality—her fight for the dignity of women, her complex ambivalence with respect to opposing forces, ideologies, and aspirations, and her courage to speak out on the major literary and political issues of the day.

Jeremy T. Medina

OTHER MAJOR WORKS

SHORT FICTION: *La dama joven,* 1885; *Cuentos escogidos,* 1891; *Cuentos de Marineda,* 1892; *Cuentos nuevos,* 1894; *Circo iris, cuentos,* 1895; *Novelas cortas,* 1896; *Cuentos de amor,* 1898; *Cuentos sacro-profanos,* 1899; *Un destripador de antaño,* 1900; *A Galician Girl's Romance,* 1900; *En tranvía, cuentos dramáticos,* 1901; *Cuentos antiguos,* 1902; *Cuentos de la patria,* 1902; *Cuentos de Navidad y Reyes,* 1902; *Novelas ejemplares,* 1906; *El fondo del alma, cuentos,* 1907; *Cuentos actuales,* 1909; *Belcebú, novelas cortas,* 1912; *Cuentos trágicos,* 1912; *Cuentos de la tierra,* 1923; *Great Stories of All Nations,* 1927.

PLAYS: *Cuesta abajo,* pb. 1906; *Verdad,* pb. 1906.

POETRY: *Jáime,* 1881.

NONFICTION: *Ensayo crítico de las obras del Padre Feijóo,* 1876; *Reflexiones científicas contra el darwinismo,* 1878; *San Francisco de Asís,* 1882; *La cuestión palpitante,* 1883; *Apuntes autobiográficos,* 1886; *La revolución y la novela en Rusia,* 1887 (*Russia: Its People and Its Literature,* 1890); *De mi tierra,* 1888; *La romería,* 1888; *El Padre Luis Coloma,* 1890; *Al pie de la torre Eiffel,* 1890; *El nuevo teatro crítico,* 1891-1893; *Polémicas y estudios literarios,* 1892; *Por la España pintoresca,* 1895; *Los poetas épicos cristianos,* 1895; *Vida contemporánea,* c. 1896; *Cuarenta días en la exposición,* 1900; *Por la Europa católica,* 1902; *Lecciones de literatura,* 1906; *Retratos y apuntes literarios,* 1908; *Literatura francesca moderna,* 1910-1914; *La cocina española antigua,* 1913; *Hernán Cortés y sus hazañas,* 1914.

MISCELLANEOUS: *Obras completas,* 1891-1912 (41 volumes).

BIBLIOGRAPHY

Anderson, Lara. *Allegories of Decadence in Fin-de-Siècle Spain: The Female Consumer in the Novels of Emilia Pardo Bazán and Benito Pérez Galdós.* Lewiston, N.Y.: Edwin

Mellen Press, 2006. Anderson examines the connections between Spanish decadence and the character of the female spendthrift in seven novels by Pardo Bazán and Benito Pérez Galdós, describing how this character reflects late nineteenth century concerns about Spain's decline.

Brown, D. F. *The Catholic Naturalism of Pardo Bazán.* Chapel Hill: University of North Carolina Press, 1957. Brown situates Pardo Bazán within the literary movement of Catholic naturalism and discusses her connection with the theory and practice of French naturalist author Émile Zola. Emphasis is placed on Pardo Bazán's novels.

González-Arias, Francisca. *Portrait of a Woman as Artist: Emilia Pardo Bazán and the Modern Novel in France and Spain.* New York: Garland, 1992. González-Arias traces Pardo Bazán's intellectual and artist development during the course of her career by studying the intertextual relationships between her novels and novels by major French and Spanish authors of the same period.

Hemingway, Maurice. *Emilia Pardo Bazán: The Making of a Novelist.* New York: Cambridge University Press, 1983. Hemingway traces the literary development of Pardo Bazán, providing a detailed analysis of the novels written between 1890 and 1896, which have all but been forgotten by literary critics. Offers a limited biographical sketch.

Hilton, Ronald. "Pardo Bazán and the Literary Polemics About Feminism." *Romanic Review* 44 (1953): 40-46. Chronicles Pardo Bazán's strong feminist career and the resistance with which her stance was met.

Labanyi, Jo. "Problematizing the Natural: Pardo Bazán's *Los pazos de Ulloa* (1886) *and La madre naturaleza* (1887)." In *Gender and Modernization in the Spanish Realist Novel.* New York: Oxford University Press, 2000. This analysis of two of Pardo Bazán's novels is included in a study of the Spanish realist novel of the late nineteenth century. Labanyi argues that women characters in these novels reflect contemporary anxieties about modernization.

Pattison, Walter. *Emilia Pardo Bazán.* New York: Twayne, 1971. A good biography and examination of the intriguing personality and works of Pardo Bazán. Pattison discusses her most important naturalistic novels. Includes a bibliography.

Pereda, Tina. "Sniffing the Body Politic in Emilia Pardo Bazán's *Insolación.*" In *Unveiling the Body in Hispanic Women's Literature: From Nineteenth Century Spain to Twenty-First Century United States,* edited by Renée Sum Scott and Arleen Chiclana y González. Lewiston, N.Y.: Edwin Mellen Press, 2006. Pereda's analysis of *Midsummer Madness* is included in this study of how women authors from Spain, the United States, the Caribbean, and Latin America represent the human body in their work.

Scarlett, Elizabeth A. "The Body-as-Text in Emilia Pardo Bazán's *Insolación.*" In *Under Construction: The Body in Spanish Novels.* Charlottesville: University Press of Virginia, 1994. Pardo Bazán's *Midsummer Madness* is one of the novels analyzed in this feminist study of the representation of the human body, the dichotomy of mind and body, and gender issues in Spanish fiction.

RAMÓN PÉREZ DE AYALA

Born: Oviedo, Spain; August 9, 1880
Died: Madrid, Spain; August 5, 1962
Also known as: Ramón Pérez de Ayala y Fernández del Portal

PRINCIPAL LONG FICTION
Tinieblas en las cumbres, 1907
A.M.D.G., 1910
La pata de la raposa, 1912 (*The Fox's Paw*, 1924)
Troteras y danzaderas, 1913
"Prometeo," "Luz de domingo," "La caída de los Limones": Tres novelas poemáticas de la vida española, 1916 (*"Prometheus," "Sunday Sunlight," "The Fall of the House of Limón": Three Poematic Novels of Spanish Life*, 1920)
Belarmino y Apolonio, 1921 (*Belarmino and Apolonio*, 1931)
Luna de miel, luna de hiel and *Los trabajos de Urbano y Simona*, 1923 (combined in *Honeymoon, Bittermoon*, 1972)
Tigre Juan and *El curandero de su honra*, 1926 (combined in *Tiger Juan*, 1933)
Justicia, 1928

OTHER LITERARY FORMS

With the exception of the novel *A.M.D.G.*, the major writings of Ramón Pérez de Ayala (PAY-rayz day ah-YAH-lah) are compiled in the four volumes of his *Obras completas* (1964), edited by J. García Mercadel. Pérez de Ayala's canon shows that he was an author of varied talents and interests. Although he is best known for his novels, Pérez de Ayala began his career with the publication of a volume of poems, *La paz del sendero* (1904; the peace of the path). This was followed by two more poetry collections, *El sendero innumerable* (1916; the path of infinite variations) and *El sendero andante* (1921; the flowing path).

Pérez de Ayala was also a prolific essayist, contributing about one thousand articles to newspapers on topics ranging from literary criticism to politics and travel. Most of these essays were subsequently compiled and published.

ACHIEVEMENTS

Ramón Pérez de Ayala's accomplishments can best be summarized in terms of the attributes of the famed *generación del 1898*, or Generation of '98, of which he is generally considered a member. Like most of the leading writers of this generation, he was active in the political as well as the literary arenas of his time, seeking radical changes in both and hoping to effect a cultural and literary renaissance in Spain. Accordingly, he excelled in writing essays on current political and cultural topics together with novels that had no less a goal than the improvement of the world. In these novels, he was able both to express and to transcend the circumstances of his time and place. Combining an intensely regional viewpoint with universal human concerns, Pérez de Ayala fused invention and philosophy in an artful rendering of reality. His greatest achievements in the novel derive from the classical vision that informs his work, transforming individuals into archetypes, local politics into universal motifs.

It is undoubtedly as a result of this vision that Pérez de Ayala's novels have been translated into English, German, Japanese, Italian, French, Portuguese, and Swedish. Many of them have received a great deal of international critical attention and acclaim, particularly *Belarmino and Apolonio*, widely regarded as his best. Critics of Pérez de Ayala may note that he exposes the fictionality of his characters with the aplomb of Miguel de Unamuno y Jugo, ironically invites the reader to skip "superfluous" sections with no less technical dexterity than Julio Cortázar, and explores the boundary between dream and reality with the eloquence of Jorge Luis Borges. Pérez de Ayala received considerable recognition during his lifetime. He was awarded the Spanish National Prize for Literature for *Tiger Juan* in 1926, was elected to the Royal Spanish Academy in 1928, and was spoken of in that same year as a candidate for the Nobel Prize.

Biography

Ramón Pérez de Ayala y Fernández del Portal was born on August 9, 1880, in Oviedo, a major city of the mountainous Asturian region in the northwest of Spain—a region whose natural beauty would later find lyric expression in his novels. At the age of eight, he was sent to the Jesuit school of San Zoilo in nearby Carrión de los Condes. After studying there for two years, he went on to finish his baccalaureate at the Jesuit Colegio de la Inmaculada in Gijón, where he remained until the age of fourteen. His studies under the Jesuits, particularly in Greek, Latin, and the classics, gave him the basis of a sound humanistic education.

On the other hand, Pérez de Ayala would always consider the rigors of the Jesuit system of education to have done permanent damage to his sensitive nature. His second novel, *A.M.D.G.*, whose title is taken from the Jesuit motto, "ad majorem dei gloriam" (to the greater glory of God), is bitterly critical of that early educational experience. The author later described himself as having possessed an inquisitive and discontented nature—thus earning the nickname the Anarchist.

After four years at the Jesuit school in Gijón, Pérez de Ayala returned to Oviedo to study law at the university under what was at that time a highly distinguished faculty. After finishing his courses in law, he traveled to England, where he wrote, read, and dabbled in painting. His sojourn was interrupted by the suicide of his father following the collapse of the bank in which his money was invested. It may have been as a result of this family tragedy that Pérez de Ayala decided to become a professional writer. At any rate, he moved to

Madrid intending to study for a doctorate in law at the university, and there he became acquainted with the major literary figures of his time. In 1903, he helped found the journal *Helios* and went on to collaborate in many of the leading periodicals of the epoch. He published his first book of poetry, *La paz del sendero*, in 1904 and his first novel, *Tinieblas en las cumbres* (darkness on the heights), shortly thereafter. In 1911, he obtained a grant to study art in Germany and Italy. It was in Italy that he met the American Mabel Rick; in 1913, they were married in the United States. By this time, he had written his four autobiographical novels and was about to enter what he himself later called a "transitional phase" in his life and narrative.

During this transitional period, Pérez de Ayala replaced personal themes with political ones, prompted by the outbreak of World War I as well as by his increasing involvement in Spanish politics. He visited the Italian front as a war correspondent and in 1917 published a collection of essays, *Hermann, encadenado* (Hermann, enchained), based on those experiences. In general, the many essays Pérez de Ayala wrote between 1913 and 1919 represent an attempt to gain a philosophical perspective on human history. His novels *Prometheus*, *Sunday Sunlight*, and *The Fall of the House of Limón* belong to this phase of his career. Between 1919 and 1920, Pérez de Ayala again traveled in the United States, sending articles to newspapers in Madrid.

The third period of Pérez de Ayala's career as a novelist stretched from 1921 until 1926, and it was during those years that he wrote his three major novels. His last full-length novel, *Tiger Juan*, received the National Prize for Literature in 1926. In 1928, Pérez de Ayala published his last known work of fiction, the short novel *Justicia*; in the remaining thirty-four years of his life, he published no more fiction. This prolonged silence continues to puzzle critics and biographers, who attribute it in part to Pérez de Ayala's disillusionment over the Spanish Civil War and the fall of the Second Spanish Republic, an ideal for which he and many of his literary colleagues had worked. Pérez de Ayala served the Republic as ambassador to London from 1931 until his resignation in 1936, upon the outbreak of the civil war.

Pérez de Ayala then spent the war years, 1936 to 1939, abroad, and during the next fifteen years, he would return to Madrid only for brief visits, taking up residence in France, Lima, and Buenos Aires and continuing to publish newspaper articles on a variety of topics. After his final return to Madrid in 1954, he lived a quiet and private life, receiving a few friends, reading classical literature, and publishing occasional articles on cultural topics in a Madrid paper. By the time of his death on August 5, 1962, he had been virtually forgotten by the literary world.

Analysis

Ramón Pérez de Ayala's novels can be divided into three categories: the four interrelated autobiographical novels (*Tinieblas en las cumbres*, *A.M.D.G.*, *The Fox's Paw*, and *Troteras y danzaderas*), the transitional novels of Spanish life (*Prometheus*, *Sunday Sun-*

light, and *The Fall of the House of Limón*), and the mature works that focus on major themes (*Belarmino and Apolonio*, *Honeymoon*, *Bittermoon*, and *Tiger Juan*). Despite the author's development between the composition of his early novels and that of his later ones, several features remain constant: the tragic sense of life and the humanistic spirit that inform his work, the classical vision that conceives of the universe as an ultimately harmonious confluence of antitheses, and the narrative techniques that are necessary for expressing the complexity of such a worldview.

Pérez de Ayala's novels reflect the various influences that were brought to bear on them. At the basis of his vision is the excellent foundation he had in the classics of Greek and Latin literature. His novels abound in allusions to classical heroes and mythological figures, and he often gives their names ironically to rural characters singularly devoid of grace. More important, however, is his classical conception of the universe as an assemblage of warring elements. Individuals, from their limited perspectives, can discern only the discontinuity of the parts rather than the harmony of the whole. Because the perception of cosmic unity is beyond the grasp of the rational mind, the happy coexistence of contradictory truths may approach expression only in aesthetic orders. Thus, the task of the novelist is to challenge constantly the partial truths that constitute the individual perspective and open them up to new vistas.

Pérez de Ayala's technique is, on the whole, Jamesian. It serves his belief in a multifaceted reality and his advocacy for the virtue of tolerance. By providing multiple points of reference and juxtaposing conflicting opinions, Pérez de Ayala reminds readers of the inadequacy of the individual perspective and of the necessity to expand the mind to encompass alternative realities. In *Troteras y danzaderas* (mummers and dancers), a spokesman for the author insists that all so-called golden ages have been social states brought about by a few conspicuous thinkers who believed in the compatibility of intelligence and strength, art and money, science and religion, philosophy and arms. By way of encouraging such marriages, Pérez de Ayala constantly reminds his readers that what they perceive as truth is merely one side of a coin. For example, in the prologue to the stories of *El ombligo del mundo* (1924; the umbilical center of the world), the narrator explains that everything that happens in the world is equally a cause for laughter and tears. The comic and the dramatic, he asserts, depend on one's perspective. Pérez de Ayala's own worldview as presented in the novels is tragicomic.

Pérez de Ayala's literary friends and associates, among them many prominent members of the Generation of '98, had a hand in shaping his views on art and life. Among his acquaintances were Antonio Machado, Ramón María del Valle-Inclán, Miguel de Unamuno y Jugo, José Ortega y Gasset, and the Nicaraguan poet Rubén Darío. An outspoken admirer of Darío's poetry, Pérez de Ayala appears to have been affected by his sense of the burden of consciousness. Pérez de Ayala's early novels bring to mind lines from Darío's well-known poem "Lo fatal" ("Fatality"): "For there is no greater grief than the grief of being alive/ No greater affliction than conscious life."

Unamuno's basically existentialist philosophy and his "tragic sense of life" also exerted an undeniable influence on Pérez de Ayala, whose humanism, like Unamuno's, arose from his knowledge of pain and his sympathy for the suffering that is the lot of all people. These feelings were no doubt intensified by the historical events of the period: the two world wars, the Spanish Civil War, and the Spanish-American War. Particularly in his later works, Pérez de Ayala deplores the shortsightedness that makes adversaries of people. His response to the events of his time took the form of a comprehensive humanism and desire for social reform—much the same spirit expressed in Ortega y Gasset's famous statement in *Meditaciones del Quixote* (1942; *Meditations on Quixote*, 1961): "I am I and my circumstance, and if I do not save it, I do not save myself."

TINIEBLAS EN LAS CUMBRES

Pérez de Ayala's first novel, *Tinieblas en las cumbres*, is a fitting introduction to his canon. It is the story of a young artist, Alberto Díaz de Guzmán, resembling Pérez de Ayala himself, who makes a trip to a mountain summit with a group of friends and prostitutes to witness a solar eclipse. Nearing the summit, they are enveloped in a dense fog; this fog becomes a symbol for the crisis in consciousness that Alberto is about to experience and is thus a precursor of the mist of Unamuno's novel *Niebla* (1914; *Mist*, 1929). As Alberto approaches the peak, he engages in a colloquy with an intellectual friend, a discussion that leaves him questioning the meaning of existence. His friend, Yiddy, demolishes his romantic illusions concerning the transcendent value of the natural world and the immortality of art, and also informs him that consciousness is a nervous phenomenon.

This conversation is typical of Pérez de Ayala in its presentation of radically opposing viewpoints and metaphysical speculations that digress from the action of the novel. Also typical is the author's statement at the beginning of the "digression" that the reader may skip this "superfluous colloquy" if he or she desires. This section, rather than being expendable, contains the key to the novel. A person's unique ability to contemplate his or her own death forms the basis of the "tragic sense of life," as defined by Unamuno. A corresponding alienation from nature is a logical consequence of this awareness of impending death. Alberto's question at the end of *Tinieblas en las cumbres* is how one should live in the face of such understanding. He seems to decide in favor of hedonism, a decision that is followed by intimations of the Apocalypse. It has been suggested throughout the expedition that this solar phenomenon might signal the end of the world. Certainly, for Alberto it means the end of innocence as he feels a permanent darkness engulfing his soul. Deciding to embrace momentary pleasures, he proceeds to drink his way home and falls unconscious in his room as the novel closes.

Tinieblas en las cumbres is interesting as a first novel in that Pérez de Ayala begins his narrative career by exploring the existential void of a man overwhelmed by the reality of death. Unlike certain bildungsromans, such as D. H. Lawrence's *Sons and Lovers* (1913), in which the character is formed by his experiences of life and becomes the author of his own existence, this novel sees the character-artist stripped of his certainties and left half-dead. It was, for Pérez de Ayala, a fit beginning. In fact, his art—his humanism and his search for meaning—grew out of such an existential necessity, but before he was able to develop completely the comprehensive philosophy that shaped his later novels, he pursued the causes and effects of Alberto's mental state in the three autobiographical works that followed *Tinieblas en las cumbres*.

A.M.D.G.

Pérez de Ayala's second novel, *A.M.D.G.*, continues the story of Alberto Díaz de Guzmán by flashing back to his education (based on the author's own) in a Jesuit school, which is presumably at the root of his spiritual dilemma. The novel itself created a scandal upon its publication because of its shocking, and perhaps overstated, portrayal of the cruelty and hypocrisy of the Jesuits' methods of educating the young. Artistically, it is a failure, but it reveals both the best and the worst aspects of Pérez de Ayala's work.

Pérez de Ayala's novels being typically novels of ideas, the essayist is never far from the surface. Occasionally, the proper balance is not observed and the message becomes obtrusive. *A.M.D.G.* is an impassioned criticism somewhat lacking in the aesthetic detachment and spirit of tolerance that characterize Pérez de Ayala's best novels, yet the motivation behind it, to expose and thereby correct injustice, is also characteristic of his best work. Ortega y Gasset praised the novel for that very reason. Having had similar experiences with the Jesuits, he claimed that the novel transcended literature and was a valuable document for pedagogical reform. Pérez de Ayala never forgot his case against the Jesuits, but he did gain greater artistic control over it. Representatives of the order appear in unflattering contexts in his later fiction, and many of their basic principles, such as the separation of body and spirit, are severely criticized.

THE FOX'S PAW

The Fox's Paw resumes the story of Alberto Díaz de Guzmán at the point where *Tinieblas en las cumbres* concluded. The title is a reference to the fox's strategy of biting off its own paw when caught in a trap. Alberto wakes the morning after the eclipse feeling trapped by the conditions of life. Existence, he feels, is a flame between two shadows. Thus begins his search for meaning. Throughout the novel, Alberto vacillates between the desires of the flesh and the possibility of artistic commitment. Whenever he finds himself lured into demeaning emotional or physical involvements, he longs for the detachment from life that art affords. Life, he finds, enslaves the man, but the artist controls life. There is one possibility available to him for incorporating the real and the ideal, the flesh and the spirit. This is in the love offered him by his fiancé Fina—a love he has not the wisdom to accept nor the will to pursue.

Alberto, it is clear, has not made much progress since his setback on the mountaintop in *Tinieblas en las cumbres*. In fact, he seems to be moving in reverse. In the course of the novel, and in the process of trying to find himself, he joins a circus, travels to England, lives in Madrid writing books, and goes bankrupt. At his best moments, he is able to feel himself part of a cosmos that is harmonious and all-encompassing. He is never able to sustain that feeling; hence, he wanders. At the conclusion of the novel, he decides to return once again to Fina, but as a punishment for his moral failure, he is told by her furious old aunt that she is dead and that his desertion killed her. Pérez de Ayala's later novels show the main characters achieving the wholeness that eludes Alberto here. This novel, however, like *Tinieblas en las cumbres*, ends in a void. The last novel in the series, *Troteras y danzaderas*, fittingly descends with Alberto into the underworld of the Madrid literati and accounts for a gap in the chronology of *The Fox's Paw*.

TROTERAS Y DANZADERAS

Something of a departure from the other autobiographical novels, *Troteras y danzaderas* shifts its focus from Alberto in order to portray several of the literary figures with whom Pérez de Ayala associated in Madrid, among them Valle-Inclán and Ortega y Gasset. An involved, intelligent, ambitious, and finally an ungainly novel, it is interesting from the viewpoint of literary history and also for the insights into human nature and the lectures on art that the author delivers through Alberto, who in this work has become more of a mouthpiece than a character.

Nevertheless, the novel does not lack for characters; it contains innumerable starving artists, politicians, prostitutes, and related entertainers. Ultimately, it is a novel about people of mainly mediocre talents living a bohemian existence that has been divested of the innocence of Bohemia. The nadir of this Madrid underworld is an expedition Alberto and some friends make to the brothels, with each successive visit more horrifying than the last. The novel ends with the death of one tubercular artist, a discussion of politics, and Alberto's ironic response when asked what Spain has produced: "Mummers and dancers, my friend, mummers and dancers."

If, on the whole, this work appears to be a collection of loosely related episodes, many of its parts are excellent. One particularly noteworthy feature is the author's experimentation with multiple narrative perspectives. In one instance, Pérez de Ayala calls particular attention to his perspectivism: He describes a comic situation in which a "kept woman" is surprised by her keeper in a tête-à-tête with a poet, providing in separate paragraphs an account of the incident from the perspectives of the three principals in addition to that of a baby who happens to be in the room. He then laments the fact that no one knows the viewpoint of the pet turtle. More seriously, he later describes the dying poet from the perspectives of both sympathetic and unsympathetic observers. His mature works show a mastery of this technique and of the philosophy of tolerance and the necessary coexistence of opposites that underlies it.

Alberto's statement at the conclusion of *Troteras y danzaderas* provides an appropriate introduction to the novels belonging to this transitional phase of Pérez de Ayala's career. It concludes the autobiographical series with a shift of focus from individual concerns to national ones and indicates the overwhelming pessimism of Pérez de Ayala's political sentiments at that time.

PROMETHEUS

Strikingly unlike any of his other novels, the three-poematic novels of Spanish life are tales of failure and utter despair, related in a highly lyric style. *Prometheus*, the first of these short novels, begins with a humorous adaptation of Homer's *Odyssey* (c. 800 B.C.E.). Juan Pérez Setignano, who prefers to think of himself as Marco de Setiñano, is a modern-day Odysseus and a professor of Greek. A man of thought, like the author himself, he dreams of begetting a son who will be a man of action. He will call the son Prometheus, and Prometheus will redeem humankind. Juan sets out seeking a mother for Prometheus. He finds and marries his Nausicaa, who is called Perpetua Meana. The son is born precocious but deformed and malicious, and at the end of the novel, he hangs himself from a fig tree. The story appears to be an allegory of Pérez de Ayala's own desires—to engender from his art a corresponding action in the world—and a measure of his feelings of failure. A comment made by Juan's uncle confirms this reading. He wisely tells Juan that Prometheus is born of men yearning to soar and vanquished by their aspirations.

SUNDAY SUNLIGHT

Sunday Sunlight, despite its promising title, is a tale of injustice. It takes place in a town controlled by a large family of aristocratic bosses, the Becerriles, whose power comes from Madrid. The Chorizos, an opposing faction of workmen and merchants, are fighting for power in the town. The hero, Cástor, is caught in the middle. When he refuses to support the Becerriles, a group of them take turns raping his fiancé in what is probably the cruelest scene in any of Pérez de Ayala's novels. Cástor tells her she is still innocent and marries her, but the stigma remains. By this point, the fault is not only with the Becerriles but also with the society that punishes the victim rather than the perpetrator of the crime. Cástor, of course, represents the only humane attitude. Wherever the couple go, they are unable to escape the gossip that follows them. Even on a boat bound for the New World, they meet with people who know their story and tell them that the Chorizos, now in power, are even worse than the Becerriles. While in Pérez de Ayala's later fiction a merging of polarities will generally be cause for optimism, here it can only mean despair. Thus, when the ship sinks, Cástor and his wife are grateful to go to a land where there are neither Becerriles nor Chorizos.

THE FALL OF THE HOUSE OF LIMÓN

The third novel, *The Fall of the House of Limón*, combines the themes of defective offspring, political oppression, and human pettiness of the other two. It begins in a Spanish boardinghouse, a favorite setting and topic for Pérez de Ayala. Two sisters, Dominica and

Fernanda Limón, arrive and arrange to have mourning garments made for the following day. The narration then flashes back to the history of the family, their father's establishment of a political empire and his gradual transfer of power to Fernanda. The other daughter, Dominica, and the future heir, Arias, grow up in the rear of the family residence. They are left to themselves in this childhood kingdom. The boy, while not physically deformed, matures in a fantasy world that leaves him morally blemished and unable to distinguish fact from fiction. Neither Arias nor Dominica realizes that the town is beginning to rebel against the dominion of the Limóns. It is Arias who precipitates their downfall by raping and killing a young woman without quite grasping the reality of his act.

If justice is conspicuously absent in *Sunday Sunlight*, here the entire concept is called into question by Arias's execution, a punishment as cruel as the crime. Morever, the smug pronouncement of the boardinghouse residents that justice has been done is deeply disturbing. Prompted by their sense of moral superiority, they proceed to insist, within hearing of the sisters, that Fernanda should have been hanged as well. As with *Sunday Sunlight*, readers are initially convinced that the evil resides in the political bosses, but Pérez de Ayala's perspective is never that simple. Another framework reveals that the cruelty and pettiness so pervasive in these two stories are a function of human nature, a view that may have been the real reason the author felt the world was not ready for his Promethean redeemer.

In his three major novels, Pérez de Ayala uses the same themes and narrative techniques found in his previous fiction. Here, though, he puts aside disillusionment and existential anxiety to present a vision of wholeness at once optimistic and tenuous. In these works, he strikes what is for his purposes a perfect balance between fiction and essay. All three hinge upon a philosophical premise. At the same time, the author develops characters that are not mere vehicles of the novel's message but are uniquely believable and sympathetic. These novels, particularly *Belarmino and Apolonio*, show Pérez de Ayala to be in full control of his perspectivist technique and the accompanying philosophy of mutually beneficial oppositions. Even while urging his own humanistic position, he uses the novels as forums for antagonistic points of view, in keeping with his insistence that all beliefs are valid, although some are less informed than others.

HONEYMOON, BITTERMOON

Honeymoon, Bittermoon is primarily a novel about male-female relationships and human sexuality. It focuses on two characters, Urbano and Simona, who marry without any knowledge of sex, even the most basic. Urbano's mother, Doña Micaela, is a sterile, domineering, and rigidly spiritual woman; she recalls D. H. Lawrence's cerebral and castrating females who will not give themselves over to sensuality. In fact, Pérez de Ayala's novel, like those of Lawrence, his contemporary, has as its goal the exposure of the folly of the prevailing sexual attitudes of the time. Here, however, they are the unique product of Spanish Catholicism.

Doña Micaela has overseen her son's education, even in his law courses, to the point of making certain that questionable pages have been torn from his books. At the end of this education, he is totally ignorant of the world, and his mother engages him to a young lady who is equally innocent. Urbano's father does not agree with his wife's actions, and their dispute constitutes one of Pérez de Ayala's famous polemics. The ensuing events attest Doña Michaela's error. Urbano, not knowing what is expected of him, leaves his wife on their honeymoon without consummating the marriage. Yet, Simona believes she is pregnant. For either lack of information or extreme modesty, no one is able to acquaint the pair with the facts of life. They are left to weather a series of catastrophes and separations until they gain enough knowledge of the world to be reunited.

The novel also considers some peripheral sexual relationships and attitudes, all highly unusual. Urbano's tutor, for example, is redeemed from his sexual ignorance and lack of practical knowledge by a servant, one of the healthiest characters in the novel. Another character is not so lucky. He is in his fifties and has been engaged for thirty-five years because his mother thinks he is too young to marry. All in all, the novel is Pérez de Ayala's perceptive analysis of the sexual foibles of his society and an argument for a reasonable, and humane, sex education.

In *Honeymoon, Bittermoon*, harmony hinges on the successful reconciliation of female and male, mind and matter. Most of the novel's characters are grotesques, unable to fuse with their counterparts or join flesh to spirit.

TIGER JUAN

The union of male and female sensibilities also supplies the theme of *Tiger Juan*, which surveys the related topics of matrimonial honor and "Don Juanism" in the context of Spanish cultural history. Tiger Juan, the protagonist, is a misogynist. Females are altogether alien to his fiercely masculine, and egotistical, nature. Based on past experience, he links them with extramarital activities and the resulting dishonor to the unlucky husband. His perspective is, of course, limited, and the novel chronicles its growth. Initially, Juan esteems one woman only: Doña Iluminada, in whose widowhood he perceives complete faithfulness to her dead husband. He is unaware that she had, inexplicably and unwillingly, remained a virgin throughout her marriage.

Doña Iluminada is one of those bountiful virgins so prevalent in Pérez de Ayala's novels who, denied happiness for themselves, contrive to unite others. At the opposite extreme, Tiger Juan's male friend, Don Vespasiano, represents the Don Juan figure who, despite his apparent sexual activity, is barren. Tiger Juan's inordinate affection for this man derives from his notion that the Don Juan type is the scourge of womankind and an avenger of Eve's curse. Tiger Juan regularly argues with his son, Colás (a "child of air," as Tiger Juan is "salt of the earth"), about Don Juanism and about a husband's right to kill an unfaithful wife. Colás's ample and humane perspective is counterposed to Tiger Juan's selfishly narrow one. Tiger Juan receives an opportunity to broaden his views when he falls reluctantly in love with a young woman, Herminia. Repulsed by his bestial demeanor, Herminia is assured by Doña Iluminada that what she feels is the irresistible attraction of her opposite. When Herminia and Juan become engaged, without her ever having the opportunity to refuse, Juan anticipates marital disgrace. To ward it off, he gives Herminia a bracelet engraved with the words "I belong to Tiger Juan." For the occasion of their wedding, he buys her shoes several sizes too small—in emulation, the narrator explains, of the estimable Asian practice of footbinding. Pérez de Ayala is at his tragicomic best in his portrayal of Tiger Juan; the reader wishes at once to cry for Juan's ignorance and laugh at his folly.

Tiger Juan's expectation of dishonor is nearly self-fulfilling. Rebelling against Juan and the society that demands her domination by him, Herminia escapes with Vespasiano; she loses the desire to be unfaithful, however, when she realizes that she is pregnant by Tiger Juan, her ideal counterpart. She returns home, and Tiger Juan has a corresponding change of heart. Instead of killing her for the blemish to his honor her desertion has caused, he opens a vein in his own arm. As proof that he has incorporated the feminine principle into his fierce male nature, when the baby comes, Juan howls in pain while Herminia preserves stoic silence. Later, he takes on the mother's role by bottle-feeding the baby. As is so often the case in Pérez de Ayala's fiction, while the individual perspective has been amplified, the society remains small-minded. The end of *Tiger Juan* finds Juan and Herminia leaving their home to escape the censure of their neighbors.

Tiger Juan, like *Honeymoon, Bittermoon*, concludes with the merging of the antithetical qualities necessary to human happiness: spirit and flesh, femininity and masculinity, self and other. In order to show the confluence of these polarities, Pérez de Ayala expands upon his usual perspectivist technique and juxtaposes the radically different forms of consciousness represented by Herminia and Juan. When Herminia deserts Juan, the author records their separate thoughts and experiences in adjacent vertical columns. Trapped by their subjectivity, the characters do not have the perceptual advantage of the reader, who recognizes the harmony between the opposing columns even before they flow together in reconciliation.

A related innovation that Pérez de Ayala had gradually developed throughout his fiction reached fullness of expression here: his open declaration of the fiction of his constructs. This exposure of artifice serves his perspectivism by opening the hermetically sealed work into a larger context: the world. He admits his fabrication in the "Parergon," or accessory document, attached to the story's conclusion. Noting that the careful reader will have detected a gap in the narrative, the author explains that his "characters" were at that time discussing their warring emotions. Not wanting to distract the normal reader from the plot, he decided to append those dialogues. As usual, these "superfluous" debates present the philosophical basis of the novel, affirming as they do that truth is the sum of individual perspectives.

BELARMINO AND APOLONIO

Pérez de Ayala's perspectivism and his "diaphenomenal vision" reach a brilliant culmination in *Belarmino and Apolonio*. The novel has a bipolar structure and theme, as announced in the title, that derives from the conflict between two shoemakers: the dramatist Apolonio and the philosopher Belarmino. Their rivalry begins quite simply when Apolonio establishes his business on the same street as Belarmino's and they become competitors. Apolonio, although he quickly helps put Belarmino out of business, recognizes in his rival certain qualities that he does not possess, and he feels an instant antipathy that he assumes is mutual. There are many points of contrast between them, but the main conflict is that between philosophy and drama. As a philosopher, Belarmino invents his own language and eventually, when tragedy befalls him, lapses into silence. The ever-loquacious Apolonio borrows his language from tradition and is unable to refrain from speaking in verse. He converts tragedy to words, exploiting experience in the creation of dramas. Desiring fame, Apolonio produces a play that is a failure; Belarmino, without desiring it, becomes a prominent community figure because of his philosophizing. In fact, the town divides into two factions, Belarmines and anti-Belarmines, arguing whether he actually speaks a comprehensible language.

The dispute between Apolonio and Belarmino leads to a secondary bifurcation when Apolonio prevents the marriage of his son and Belarmino's daughter. The son then develops into a gregarious, hypocritical priest, while the disgraced daughter becomes an innocent, introspective prostitute—in yet another of the novel's unusual dichotomies. The narrator intercedes to reunite priest and prostitute, and when news of this event comes to Apolonio and Belarmino, now in a rest home, they embrace and speak to each other for the first time, admitting their mutual need.

These are but a few of the many schisms and reconciliations that make up the world of the novel. The conceptual and structural frame of the work is provided by two opposing points of view on the relationship between Belarmino and Apolonio, or drama and philosophy. The prologue records the musings of Don Amaranto, a boardinghouse philosopher, who believes that the dramatist immerses himself in experience while the philosopher removes himself to attain a better vantage point. The epilogue quotes from the notes of Froilán Escobar, who reverses these poles. He maintains that the dramatist acts out his life in borrowed gestures while the philosopher conceals his emotions with a cool exterior. Both opinions are correct, but in the context of the story, the latter is more informed. More important, these thinkers, like the narrator, affirm that philosopher and dramatist need each other.

On this level, the novel's theme and technique coalesce. While Pérez de Ayala generally combines philosophy and drama in his fiction, in *Belarmino and Apolonio*, he engages both with the object of illustrating their interdependence. At the same time, he juxtaposes conflicting opinions and perspectives on events to demonstrate the relativity of knowledge. The second chapter of the novel, another of those essential digressions that

Pérez de Ayala labels "superfluous," contains a discussion of perspective and artistic creation. It begins with Don Amaranto's ghost confronting the narrator with a disquisition on the limits of narration. The apparition insists that because the novel unfolds in time, it is unable to match the human visual apparatus, which sees in depth. The narrator responds with an exercise in point of view and narrative dexterity. He relates an anecdote about a poet, Lirio, and a positivist, Lario, viewing the street where Belarmino and Apolonio lived. In an involved dispute typical of Pérez de Ayala, Lirio insists on the absurd beauty of the street while Lario finds it ugly for its lack of symmetry. The debate concludes when Lirio shows Lario his painting of the street. Lario replies that the street is ugly but the painting is beautiful.

In *Belarmino and Apolonio*, Pérez de Ayala achieved an ideal balance between the fictional and empirical narrative modes that characterize his novels while making that balance the very subject of the work. As a measure of his success, when the narrator states in the epilogue that Belarmino and Apolonio have existed only as his creations but that he has loved them, the reader does not doubt it. Even as symbols of antithetical elements of artistic creation, they are uniquely real and lovable. Through their story, the author demonstrates once again that "there are as many irreducible truths as there are points of view."

Barbara L. Hussey

OTHER MAJOR WORKS

SHORT FICTION: *Bajo el signo de Artemisa*, 1924; *El ombligo del mundo*, 1924.

POETRY: *La paz del sendero*, 1904; *El sendero innumerable*, 1916; *El sendero andante*, 1921.

NONFICTION: *Hermann, encadenado*, 1917; *Las máscaras*, 1917-1919 (2 volumes); *Política y toros*, 1918; *Divagaciones literarias*, 1958; *El país del futuro: Mis viajes a los Estados Unidos*, 1959; *Más divagaciones literarias*, 1960; *Amistades y recuerdos*, 1961; *Pequeños ensayos*, 1963; *Tributo a Inglaterra*, 1963; *Escritos políticos*, 1967.

MISCELLANEOUS: *Obras completas*, 1964 (4 volumes; J. García Mercadel, editor).

BIBLIOGRAPHY

Best, Marigold. *Ramón Pérez de Ayala: An Annotated Bibliography of Criticism*. London: Grant & Cutler, 1980. A dated but useful resource for finding critical analyses of Pérez de Ayala's work. Includes indexes.

Johnson, Roberta. "From the Generation of 1898 to the Vanguard." In *The Cambridge Companion to the Spanish Novel: From 1600 to the Present*, edited by Harriet Turner and Adelaida López de Martínez. New York: Cambridge University Press, 2003. Johnson includes a discussion of several of Pérez de Ayala's novels in her analysis of Spanish literature in the early years of the twentieth century.

Longhurst, C. A. "Modernist Narrative in the 1920's." In *The Cambridge History of Spanish Literature*, edited by David T. Gies. New York: Cambridge University Press, 2004.

The novels of Pérez de Ayala are among the works examined in Longhurst's discussion of modernist literature; this article places Pérez de Ayala within the broader context of Spanish literary history.

Macklin, John. "Constructing the '98: Peréz de Ayala's 1942 Prologue to *Troteras y danzaderas*." In *Spain's 1898 Crisis: Regenerationism, Modernism, Post-Colonialism*, edited by Joseph Harrison and Alan Hoyle. New York: Manchester University Press, 2000. In 1898, Spain was defeated in the Spanish American War, a loss that marked the end of the Spanish Empire and led to a national identity crisis. Macklin's essay discusses Peréz de Ayala's fictional response to that crisis.

―――. *The Window and the Garden: The Modernist Fictions of Ramón Pérez de Ayala*. Boulder, Colo.: Society of Spanish and Spanish-American Studies, 1988. A thorough study of Pérez de Ayala's work, relating it to both realistic and modernistic fiction. The text is primarily in English, but some of the quotations are in Spanish. Includes a bibliography.

Rand, Marguerite C. *Ramón Pérez de Ayala*. New York: Twayne, 1971. One of the volumes in the Twayne World Authors series, this book provides a biography as well as analysis of Pérez de Ayala's fiction. Includes a bibliography.

Stock, Margaret Pol. *Dualism and Polarity in the Novels of Ramón Pérez de Ayala*. London: Tamesis Books, 1988. Stock focuses on the use of paired opposites in Pérez de Ayala's novels, such as spectator versus actor, ideal versus real, and male versus female, and discusses how his work seeks to unify these dualities.

Weber, Frances Wyers. *The Literary Perspectivism of Ramón Pérez de Ayala*. Chapel Hill: University of North Carolina Press, 1966. Weber provides an ideological portrait of Pérez de Ayala and a multifaceted analysis of his writings. Includes lists of his works and bibliographical footnotes.

BENITO PÉREZ GALDÓS

Born: Las Palmas, Canary Islands; May 10, 1843
Died: Madrid, Spain; January 4, 1920

PRINCIPAL LONG FICTION

La fontana de oro, 1868 (*The Golden Fountain Cafe*, 1989)
El audaz, 1871
La sombra, 1871 (*The Shadow*, 1980)
La corte de Carlos IV, 1873 (*The Court of Charles IV: A Romance of the Escorial*, 1888)
Trafalgar, 1873 (English translation, 1884)
Episodios nacionales, 1873-1912 (46 historical novellas written in 5 series, many of which were also published separately and are included in this list)
Gerona, 1874
Zaragoza, 1874 (*Saragossa: A Story of Spanish Valor*, 1899)
La batalla de los Arapiles, 1875 (*The Battle of Salamanca: A Tale of the Napoleonic War*, 1895)
Doña Perfecta, 1876 (English translation, 1880)
Gloria, 1876-1877 (English translation, 1879)
La familia de León Roch, 1878 (*The Family of León Roch*, 1888; also known as *León Roch: A Romance*, 1888)
Marianela, 1878 (English translation, 1883)
La desheredada, 1881 (*The Disinherited Lady*, 1957)
El amigo Manso, 1882 (*Our Friend Manso*, 1987)
El doctor Centeno, 1883
La de Bringas, 1884 (*The Spendthrifts*, 1951; also known as *That Bringas Woman*, 1996)
Tormento, 1884 (*Torment*, 1952)
Lo prohibido, 1884-1885 (*The Forbidden*, 2006)
Fortunata y Jacinta, 1886-1887 (*Fortunata and Jacinta: Two Stories of Married Women*, 1973)
Miau, 1888 (English translation, 1963)
La incógnita, 1889 (*The Unknown*, 1991)
Realidad, 1889 (*Reality*, 1992)
Torquemada en la hoguera, 1889 (*Torquemada in the Flames*, 1956; also known as *Torquemada at the Stake*, 1986)
Ángel Guerra, 1890-1891 (English translation, 1990)
La loca de la casa, 1892
Tristana, 1892 (English translation, 1961)

Torquemada en la cruz, 1893 (*Torquemada's Cross*, 1973; also known as *Torquemada on the Cross*, 1986)
Torquemada en el purgatorio, 1894 (*Torquemada in Purgatory*, 1986)
Halma, 1895
Nazarín, 1895 (English translation, 1993)
Torquemada y San Pedro, 1895 (*Torquemada and Saint Peter*, 1986)
El abuelo, 1897
Misericordia, 1897 (*Compassion*, 1962)
Casandra, 1905
Prim, 1906 (English translation, 1944)
El caballero encantado, 1909
La razón de la sinrazón, 1915
Torquemada, 1986 (collection contains *Torquemada at the Stake*, *Torquemada on the Cross*, *Torquemada in Purgatory*, and *Torquemada and Saint Peter*)

OTHER LITERARY FORMS

The work of Benito Pérez Galdós (PAY-rayz gahl-DOHS) in other literary forms can be divided into three groups: twenty-two plays, including six dramatizations of previous novels: *Realidad* (pr., pb. 1892), *La loca de la casa* (pr., pb. 1893), *Gerona* (pr. 1893), *Doña Perfecta* (pr., pb. 1896), *El abuelo* (pr., pb. 1904; *The Grandfather*, 1910), and *Casandra* (pr., pb. 1910); nonfiction works, such as *Discursos académicos* (1897), *Memoranda* (1906), *Fisonomías sociales* (1923), *Arte y crítica* (1923), *Política española* (1923), *Nuestro teatro* (1923), *Cronicón* (1924), *Toledo* (1924), *Viajes y fantasías* (1928), *Memorias* (1930), *Crónica de Madrid* (1933), *Cartas de Pérez Galdós a Mesonero Romanos* (1943), *Crónica de la Quincena* (1948), and *Madrid* (1956); and hundreds of newspaper articles, many unsigned.

ACHIEVEMENTS

The Spanish Romantics of the middle decades of the nineteenth century sought to re-create the local color of the past or the fantasy of exotic surroundings, while the *costumbristas* (regionalists) described the peculiar atmosphere of particular Spanish regions and customs. It remained for the realists of the last part of the century to transcend the picturesque sketches and emotional excesses of their predecessors. The realists directed their attention to the multiplicity and variety of observable reality in an attempt to enhance the verisimilitude of their productions. At first, they concentrated on the surface elements of this multiple panorama, while presenting psychological portraits that displayed only a few dominant and usually harmonious traits.

For more than half a century, the novel had viewed people as conforming to general social patterns, and individual character was seen as constant and without development. A descriptive delineation of a person's dominant motives or reactions to particular situations

Benito Pérez Galdós
(Library of Congress)

was the novelist's goal. The change from this strictly social viewpoint to a preoccupation with distinct individuals became possible when people were given the role of persistent striving, when personality itself was seen as subject to psychological and environmental influences. These new novelistic perspectives were partly the result of the rise of the theory of evolution.

Also contributing to the birth of the realistic novel was the development of new ideas concerning society (a rising middle class represented a new sector of reading public that looked for a literature depicting individual citizens amid a recognizable environment), history (seen now in relation to the ordinary person), and science (the growth of which stimulated the desire for more acute observation and documentation). Some critics view the rise of realism in the Spanish novel as a result of the intellectual ferment caused by the Revolution of 1868, which overthrew Queen Isabella II. During this period, writers began to place equal emphasis on plot and environment, with the two elements functioning within a unified, verisimilar whole.

Benito Pérez Galdós belonged to the mature stage of the realistic movement. He rejected the portrayal of static elements of human nature and turned instead to the description of the varying relationships between the individual personality and the environment. Next to Miguel de Cervantes, Pérez Galdós is perhaps the most important novelist that Spain has produced; he is the only Spaniard of his age who can be compared to Honoré de Balzac, Charles Dickens, Leo Tolstoy, or Fyodor Dostoevski. In the course of his long career, he alone succeeded in reconciling the traditional and the liberal ideological currents then prevalent in Spain, demonstrating the significance of both past events and recent developments. In spite of the fact that most of his works were set in Madrid, he alone was able to transcend the regionalism of the Spanish realistic novel. Although his works represent a historical, social, and literary synthesis of his era, he was able to penetrate and develop themes of truly universal significance—ideas concerning charity and spiritual values, problems of modern science and of materialism, the yearning for social justice, the necessity of tolerance and of personal liberty, and the notion of human equality achieved through love.

Pérez Galdós was clearly a realistic writer. His choice of verisimilar subject matter, his convincing psychological portraits, the minimization of overt didacticism (in later novels), his basically objective organizational techniques, and the naturalness, descriptive immediacy, and dialogic emphasis of his style all attest this fact. Yet there are other factors unique to Pérez Galdós that suggest a transcendence of mere nineteenth century realism: symbolic representations, the inclusion of seemingly fantastic elements, and impressionistic descriptions, among others.

This particular combination of realistic and "idealistic" elements was one of the traits that Pérez Galdós seems to have inherited from Cervantes. A basic goodness, a positive, conciliatory spirit, a special kind of ironic humor also came from the master. Like Cervantes, Pérez Galdós was able to penetrate beneath the psychological facades of his characters. He exposed the consistently contradictory nature of human reality, revealing wisdom in the insane, a sense of honor in the humble, charity among beggars, and the anguish for salvation in the person of a miserly moneylender.

Pérez Galdós was also one of the few Spanish writers of his time to recognize the importance and the greatness of contemporary literature of other countries. Indeed, the realistic movement can be said to have developed first and most completely in France with writers such as Balzac, Gustave Flaubert, and Émile Zola. It was Pérez Galdós who first incorporated these foreign elements into a truly Spanish creation.

Above all, Pérez Galdós's realism was a *social* one, centered not on the delineation of regionalistic characters and landscape, not on the psychological investigation of isolated personalities, but rather on the complicated interaction between individual perspectives and aspirations and the social, usually urban milieu within which these viewpoints and desires are expressed. In short, Pérez Galdós's realism was a *human* one, focusing on the physical, psychic, and emotional effects that people have on one another and showing how these elements function within, against, or in line with the pressures of society. With

The Disinherited Lady, Pérez Galdós recognized that an individual's personal characteristics are partly the result of social and cultural forces; conversely, societies and cultures gain a particular flavor from the individuals who constitute them. He was able to strengthen his picture of both levels (individual and social) by virtue of his perception of their interdependence and interplay.

Yet the individual-society conflict is not merely social or psychological. When the characters suffer from the extreme discrepancy between dream (illusions, romance) and reality, the conflict becomes a metaphysical one, reflecting the Hegelian dialectic implicit in the theories of realism proposed by such critics as Harry Levin, Arnold Hauser, José Ortega y Gasset, and György Lukács. In Pérez Galdós's mature novels, this dialectic operates in the individual's growth toward self-consciousness through his relationships with others, in the conflict between (and eventual integration of) social classes, and in the opposition and interplay of different elements within a character.

In part, the historical importance of Pérez Galdós's novels is that of having united and perfected the prevailing literary tendencies of the times: the interest in history and the past, initiated by the Romantics (whose sentimentality and imaginative excesses he avoided); the didactic or "thesis" approach, offered now without the sacrifice of psychological verisimilitude or artistic balance; and the emphasis on *costumbrismo*, extended from a local, regional level to a broader, national perspective in order to analyze and interpret the life and character of the entire Spanish community. For Pérez Galdós, these three aims were combined toward achieving a constant objective: to help his countryfolk become conscious of their reality as a people, searching in the recent past for the explanation of current conditions, for a sense of direction that would work toward a future ideal of *trabajo y educación* (work and education), an ideal that would encourage an atmosphere of tolerance instead of constant civil strife.

Biography

Benito Pérez Galdós was born in Las Palmas on May 10, 1843, the last of ten children. Some critics believe that his place of birth, geographically and socially separate from the mainstream of Spanish life, contributed to his subsequent ability to view national events with relative candor and objectivity. Benito's father, Sebastián Pérez, sixteen years older than his wife and more a grandfather than a father to his younger children, had inherited sufficient property to maintain his family in comfort and had ample leisure time to regale his youngest offspring with tales of his military exploits, events that were to become part of *Episodios nacionales* (national episodes). However, it was Benito's mother, Doña Dolores, who was to dominate the family. Her rigid, puritanical religiosity, intolerance, strength of will, and constant need for order were to be reflected in several of Pérez Galdós's characters, most particularly Doña Perfecta. From his mother, Pérez Galdós seems to have inherited a Basque physique, stubbornness, and the ability to adhere to an unswerving, ordered routine.

Although interested in painting and music, the young Pérez Galdós found little to enjoy in his childhood schooling, usually appearing bored and absentminded. In 1862, he was sent to Madrid by Doña Dolores to study law, a course that, despite poor grades, irregular class attendance, and extensive extracurricular writing, he finished in 1869. His real interest during these years was the Ateneo, a literary and artistic club in Madrid that housed a remarkably good library and sponsored lectures and discussion groups. Here, Pérez Galdós developed the progressive, liberal spirit that would dominate his first novels, became exposed to the Krausist perspective of tolerance toward opposing views, and discovered the works of such European writers as Balzac, whose eighty volumes he himself collected.

It was during these years that Pérez Galdós began to write for such newspapers as *La nación*, *Las cortes*, and *El debate*. Later, in 1872 and 1873, he himself was the general director of the prestigious *Revista de España*. He traveled widely and in 1866 witnessed the uprising of *los sargentos de San Gil*, a historical event that perhaps stimulated him to initiate the first series of *Episodios nacionales*. The composition of these works, which he undertook in 1873 and continued intermittently until his death, reflected a conception of history as a slow but inevitable development toward the establishment of a just and equitable society, one in which the growing bourgeoisie would absorb a decadent aristocracy and a well-meaning but ignorant lower class. The series was instantly popular, perhaps because of its stress on the importance of everyday events in the lives of common citizens. At first, the *Episodios nacionales* gave him the economic stability that he needed; later, however, even the resounding financial success of his play *Electra* (pr., pb. 1901; English translation, 1911) was not enough to liquidate the debts that were to plague him sporadically throughout his life.

In 1886, Pérez Galdós entered politics, and in 1889, he accepted the governmentally rigged election results that made him a deputy for Puerto Rico; he served in congress until 1890. While he did little to improve the well-being of his constituents across the ocean, he did subsequently devote considerable energy to liberal causes and eventually expended much of his meager financial resources on republican politics.

It was also in 1889 that Pérez Galdós traveled to the Rhine Valley, where he met and had a brief affair with the Galician novelist Emilia Pardo Bazán. Despite her wish to continue the relationship, however, Pérez Galdós soon broke it off when he became involved with Lorenza Cobián, the woman who was to be the mother of his daughter, María, born January 12, 1891. After Lorenza became insane and committed suicide in 1906, the novelist took charge of María's education and made her his legal beneficiary.

In 1889, Pérez Galdós was elected to the Royal Spanish Academy, but he did not take his seat until 1897. This, says Walter Pattison, was "owing in part to his timidity about making a public speech and perhaps partly to his resentment at having been passed over on the first vote."

In later years, Pérez Galdós served further republican terms in congress—in 1907 and

1910—but his health deteriorated rapidly. To the problem of arteriosclerosis was added a hemiplegic stroke in 1905. Several operations on his eyes were not enough to prevent blindness. These events, coupled with the disdain of the reactionaries and the indifference of the young *generación del 1898*, or Generation of '98, left him bitter and resentful. The failure of his proponents to gain for him the Nobel Prize and the continued financial insecurity that came from his mismanagement of money matters added to the aging novelist's despair. Pérez Galdós had outlived his literary career. When his statue in Madrid's Retiro Park was unveiled in 1919, few prominent figures were present. Death came from uremia on January 4, 1920.

In his prime, Pérez Galdós had been reported as

> tall and somewhat roughhewn in body and features, as if carved of stone. . . . His eyes were small and timid, his face not very expressive, his manner of speaking brief, fragmentary, and low-pitched; in short, he did not give . . . that impression of genius that we imagine in great men.

He was shy, withdrawn, given to stage fright (he refused once to come to a large banquet in his honor, until friends pursued him and brought him back from Toledo). He preferred to listen and observe, rather than talk. Yet on the printed page, he could fight stubbornly and valiantly for his ideals. His outward simplicity was so great, said one friend, "that at times it bordered on commonness." The *generación del 1898* called him *Don Benito el garbancero* (Mister Benito the grocer). Nevertheless, his remarkably exact and detailed descriptions attest his acute observational powers, and his fecundity and creativity amply demonstrate his remarkable imaginative capabilities.

Pérez Galdós was thought to have had few close personal relationships, even within his own family; but his letters have now revealed a profound involvement with his relatives and with a broad circle of intimate acquaintances, all of whom he treated with sensitivity and charity, and with whom he was an entertaining and witty conversationalist. The tender care he offered to Lorenza Cobián and their daughter—another reason for his later impoverishment—reveals that he was indeed a warm and loving person.

Also erroneous is the notion that Pérez Galdós was an obsessive womanizer. It is true that he had an affair with Pardo Bazán, produced an illegitimate daughter with Lorenza, and in his old age nurtured a close relationship with a refined lady named Teodosia Gandarias, but his interest in women was far from licentious or "pathological," as early critics have claimed. Perhaps a desire for individual freedom lay behind his reluctance to marry.

Despite his anticlerical activities and his hatred for the ritual and beliefs of the neo-Catholics, Pérez Galdós developed a deeply spiritual and religious orientation related to a profound love of nature and to a Krausist upbringing that stressed tolerance, everyday ethics, and the basic goodness and harmony of human faculties. This orientation was particularly pronounced during the third phase of his literary career.

Analysis

Through more than fifty years of literary creation, Benito Pérez Galdós's work underwent an evolution, a process of growth that both reflected and harmonized with broader European novelistic movements. In general, these shifts suggest a change from didacticism to more thorough, realistic documentary and later to a kind of symbolic spiritualism.

Pérez Galdós's initial orientation, however, was mostly historical. The Romantics had turned to the study of history in a desire to embrace the phenomenon of human temporality, but they had focused primarily on an atmosphere of the past—poetic, distant, and vague. Pérez Galdós and the realists inherited this historical sense, but utilized it primarily in an effort to understand the present. Pérez Galdós's first two novels, *The Golden Fountain Café* and *El audaz*, reflect such a historical orientation.

It was also during these early years that Pérez Galdós began the *Episodios nacionales*. These works, forty-six in all, were written throughout his long literary career. They narrate the then-recent history of Spain, from the Battle of Trafalgar (1805) against Napoleon Bonaparte through the Restoration in 1874. Again, the author's aim was to guide his fellow Spaniards toward a greater understanding of contemporary psychological and social circumstances. His artistic formula was that of combining novelistic fiction—the continuing story of certain literary characters, which gives a loose unity to each series—with the graphic presentation of historical events. Aside from their literary merits, these works represent in their totality the most vivid and most complete documentary of nineteenth century history that has yet been compiled.

Aside from Pérez Galdós's almost unbroken historical preoccupations, his novelistic output can be divided into four general periods. Between the years 1876 and 1879, many of Pérez Galdós's so-called *novelas de la primera época* (novels of the first epoch) appeared. Three *novelas de tesis* (thesis novels) represented a pronounced didactic intention, promulgating a liberal and *progresista* (progressive) spirit, opposed to religious and clerical intolerance and traditional absolutism. These novels expressed a youthful rebelliousness, a distinctly iconoclastic fervor. Indeed, the abstract, often symbolic level on which the young writer constructed such an ideological rebellion was in many respects distant from the objective immediacy of the contemporary European realists. *Doña Perfecta* describes the struggle of liberalism against outdated moral codes and religious bigotry, *Gloria* the mutual intolerance between Catholics and Jews, and *The Family of León Roch* a marriage that is the product of Catholic dogmatism.

In his second period, between 1881 and 1888, Pérez Galdós initiated the *novelas españolas contemporáneas* (contemporary Spanish novels). In these years, the author clearly settled into conformity with accepted European realistic techniques and attempted to offer something positive to replace those codes that he had tried to destroy during his early rebelliousness. *The Disinherited Lady* marks the change. A wholehearted adaptation of the use of background detail, a more complete treatment of central characters, increasing firsthand studies of his novels' milieus, a "biographical" method for exploring the interrelationships between the individual and society, and a constant attention to the ordinary circumstances of daily life—these factors suggest a stricter adherence to nineteenth century realistic practices and the influence of French naturalism. During these years also, a significant anomaly developed in Pérez Galdós's use of authorial perspective: Whereas the author appeared frequently as a minor character to enhance the effects of realism and autonomy, he allowed himself, at the same time, abundant revelations of a character's hidden thoughts, thus betraying authorial control.

Many of these novels attempted to depict Madrid society as representing a synthesis of national life. Among these works were some of Pérez Galdós's most important productions: *Our Friend Manso*, *The Spendthrifts*, *Miau*, the first of the Torquemada novels, and the four-volume masterpiece *Fortunata and Jacinta*.

If the novels of Pérez Galdós's second period placed greater emphasis on the individual and his complicated relationships with the broad scope of society, those written between 1889 and 1897 presented the spiritual and philosophical aspects of that individual's predicament. An increasing tendency toward the theme of tolerance and compromise, along with a stronger emphasis on the values of love, compassion, self-discipline, and individual creativity characterized this phase. Pérez Galdós's realistic techniques were continued and refined, while a more profound sense of universality was added to an already deep patriotic sentiment. The author no longer attempted to define morality in absolute terms; his spiritualist hero struggles to purify himself rather than to find the ultimate meaning of existence. He accepts the reality of the life around him, a reality marked by pain but suggesting an abiding hope in the future. The priest in *Nazarín* and the beggar woman of *Compassion* practice Christian charity and come to ennoble the miserable surroundings in which they live. This last novel in particular seems to represent a synthesis of Galdosian techniques: Its theme, realistic—even naturalistic—documentation, and spiritualistic emphasis are united in a harmonious whole. Here, Pérez Galdós demonstrated that, while fiction is an illusion created by the imagination, life itself is also unreal—an illusion created by the senses as one encounters the external world.

In the works of his fourth and final period, beginning in 1898, Pérez Galdós revealed a profound change in artistic perspective. His seminaturalistic objectivism gave way to a kind of subjective impressionism. The third series of *Episodios nacionales* and novels such as *Casandra* and *El caballero encantado* marked the mellowness of old age, an increase in fantasy and symbolism, and, to a certain extent, a diminishing of artistic excellence. It was during this period that Pérez Galdós turned to the theater, adapting some previous "dialogue novels" to the stage (novels such as *Reality* and *El abuelo*) and presenting such thesis plays as *Electra*, based on a condemnation of clerical intolerance and malpractice. Pérez Galdós, however, lacked true dramatic ability. Many of his plays were weighed down by psychological abstraction and slow-moving plots.

The first three stages of Pérez Galdós's literary production, then, reflect variations of general European realistic techniques of the nineteenth century. His youthful rebelliousness and abstractionism were an expression of the controversial atmosphere and ideological emphasis of the 1870's. Novels such as *The Disinherited Lady* and *The Forbidden* reflect the moderate propagation of naturalistic ideas in Spain during the 1880's, as the author attempted a more detailed study of the individual and his environment. Pérez Galdós's interest in transcending spiritual values in turn suggests a similar reaction throughout Europe during the 1890's.

To summarize those factors relating to the author's choice of subject matter, one may say that Pérez Galdós's realism grew out of the careful exercise of his powers of observation; it was supported by verisimilitude; its guiding concern was with society, and, more specifically, the individual's complex relationships with that society; it dwelt, in proportion to their numbers, on authentic treatment of the various social classes, breaking new ground in its inclusion of the middle class, and possibly showing some preference, in later years, for the humbler members of the social order. Pérez Galdós's version of realism reflected the organic, evolutionary quality of society. It incorporated, at least superficially, some vestiges of the costumbristic tradition, from which the author attempted to liberate himself during the latter part of his career. Finally, it assimilated historical materials, to the degree that they could shed light on contemporary social circumstances.

With respect to authorial point of view, Pérez Galdós was a realist in the humoristic tradition. He recognized that irony is implicit in realism because it exposes the often odious comparison between actuality and what one desires of life. A fundamentally comic vision came most clearly into play when he ironically deflated pretentious aspirations, or when he exposed human extravagance and self-deception. Another target of his humor was the delusion that the merely relative is the absolute. His novels offer a vast comic panorama in which moments of tragedy seem to eclipse the fundamental spiritual truth. Consonant with Cervantes' notions of the interplay of fiction and reality and of the ambiguity of truth, then, Pérez Galdós came to accept the view that finite truth changes. Any particular instance of human experience is only partially "true"; the total interrelation of these momentary revelations constitutes ultimate truth. Just as the multiplicity of realities remained a mystery to Pérez Galdós, so his characters fail to grasp absolute truth because they are permitted only glimpses of relative "realities."

Pérez Galdós's narrative point of view is a multiple one, suggesting the Cervantine idea that any person's view of reality is relative. These varied viewpoints include strictly impartial, omniscient commentary; total immersion within one character (made most striking by the use of *estilo indirecto libre* (free indirect style) and the *monólogo interior* (interior monologue); slanted (as opposed to neutral) omniscient perspectives; appearances of Pérez Galdós as omniscient author, speaking directly to his readers; moments in which Pérez Galdós appears as one of the characters, himself ignorant of facts and circumstances because of his limited personal vision (striking examples of this can be found in *The Spendthrifts* and *Our Friend Manso*); and total lack of direct authorial presence or intrusion, as manifested in the *novelas dialogadas*.

Thus, Pérez Galdós's attempts to describe all facets of contemporary Spanish society: his frequently lengthy, often unemotional descriptions, his basically impartial selectivity and means of organization, his shifting points of view—all of these contribute to a relative objectivity. At the same time, his didacticism or irony, his occasional failures to maintain authorial autonomy, and a strong, sympathetic identification with some of his characters serve to limit that very objective approach. His creations have life. They demonstrate verisimilitude, balance, and an almost infinite variety; but they come from the heart, and not the sociologist's notebook.

Pérez Galdós's characters are usually realistic in the sense that they are distinct individuals. At the same time, they are symbols: They are combinations of abstract types and concrete, humanized personalities. Torquemada, for example, symbolizes the coarse materialism of the rising Spanish middle class, but takes on a personal dimension in the emotionalism that erupts when his son dies, in his criticism at the banquet of businessmen like himself, his helplessness before the implacable Cruz, his comic attempts at verbal refinement, and his "transactions" with the Almighty. All of these factors particularize his predicament and suggest some measure of potential "roundness." Pérez Galdós's protagonists move within a double reality, reflecting the Cervantine notion that the human condition exists divided between secret, inner personality and acted, overt experience. Indeed, the constructs of the mind often seem more real than ordinary physical reality.

Despite Pérez Galdós's double emphasis upon social and individual characteristics, he does not attempt to explore the complexities and incongruities of personality in the manner of Dostoevski or some modern novelists. Often his characters are, by comparison, somewhat less complicated creatures, dominated generally by a limited number of motives (such as ambition, guilty conscience, charity, greed, and, above all, love).

With respect to style, Pérez Galdós was committed to painting even the smallest, seemingly least significant elements of reality. He was firmly convinced that the least noticeable facets of human existence and the least conspicuous details of a historical milieu are as important as the items that blaze from newspaper headlines. (Miguel de Unamuno y Jugo would later term this sphere of reality an *intra-historia*.) Quite often, these small details are worked into descriptions of surprising length, and the *generación del 1898* was quick to condemn the author's extraordinary descriptive elaboration. This trait is most noticeable in the novels of the 1880's, especially *Fortunata and Jacinta*. While it is true that this abundance occasionally tires the reader, one can still detect in it Pérez Galdós's larger motives: to picture the total sweep of contemporary Spanish life, to imply its actual magnitude and multiplicity.

The relative absence of natural settings is a well-known characteristic of Pérez Galdós's novels. The reason behind this is not hard to discern: Above all, Pérez Galdós was interested in people, and portraits of nature were subordinated to character treatment. Only rarely does one find lyric descriptions of landscape that are designed to capture the poetic nuances of the setting itself. As might be expected, such elaborations are important only for their symbolic or psychological enhancement of the people involved. Thus, the delightful description of an evening in the countryside in *Torquemada in Purgatory* is contrasted ironically with Torquemada's imperviousness to its beauty.

Other stylistic features of Pérez Galdós's novels are especially pertinent to a discussion of realistic technique. One such feature is the naturalness of his vocabulary and phrasing: Despite its remarkable richness and variety, Pérez Galdós's language is unaffected, often colloquial. His imagery, though based on ordinary, concrete, even prosaic elements, is remarkably rich and vivid. Similes appear frequently, since they are found so often in common speech. Frequent dialogue functions as a means of actualizing his material; in one way, it helps to typify characters (to identify them as representatives of a social or vocational class), and, on the other hand, it helps to individualize them (by the use of distinguishing speech "tags"). Finally, Pérez Galdós frequently employs interior monologues; although such passages differ from the arbitrary, "free-association" techniques of the twentieth century, the novelist certainly anticipated the formulation of the stream of consciousness method.

Doña Perfecta

Doña Perfecta best exemplifies Pérez Galdós's thesis novels, the type of writing produced during the more militant, aggressive years of his youth. It illustrates graphically Pérez Galdós's reaction to the intolerance expressed in the Constitution of 1876, which was widely discussed during the weeks when the work was appearing in installments in the *Revista de España*. The plot centers on Pepe Rey, a progressive, modern young engineer whose visit to the home of his aunt results in his sudden, tragic death. The author's main purpose is to depict the young man's struggle against the enemies of contemporary, liberal thought: bigotry, hypocrisy, reactionism, provincialism, and the weight of dead tradition.

At the suggestion of his father, Pepe goes to the remote cathedral town of Orbajosa (city of garlic), in order to survey the region for mining and irrigation projects, with the idea of meeting and possibly marrying his cousin Rosario. As the novel progresses, the conflict slowly develops between reactionary traditionalism (his aunt, Doña Perfecta, the priest Inocencio, and the latter's niece, María Remedios, who wants to marry her son, Jacinto, to Rosario) and modern thought (Pepe Rey, with the help of an army officer whose company is sent to Orbajosa to quell any possible uprisings of guerrilla bands). Finally, as Pepe tries to elope with Rosario, Doña Perfecta orders his execution. Afterward, Rosario becomes insane and is confined to an asylum, and Doña Perfecta continues her religious activities.

Thematically, then, Pérez Galdós condemns hypocrisy, fanatical religiosity, intolerance, and provincialism. On a slightly deeper level, however, he is also expressing his disdain for extremism of any kind, that passion that allows reason to be clouded by emotion. Spaniards, he says, must cast off a blind local patriotism rooted in ignorance, as well as the intolerance of many modern progressives (for Pepe's dogmatism and tactless inflexibility are also criticized). When violence engenders violence, when an oversimplified polarization of "them" and "us," of *moros* (Moors) and *cristianos* (Christians), takes place, there is no significant difference between the progressive and the reactionary perspectives. On the other hand, honesty, clearness of vision, restraint, charitable tolerance, and, above all, love are held up as factors that may unite the country and offer hope for the future. The lesson of the novel is ultimately a moral one that transcends the immediate political message about Spain of the 1870's.

Doña Perfecta, then, aptly demonstrates the Krausist justification of literature as an instrument of reform and education, as well as exemplifying the movement's belief that the moral and intellectual regeneration of the individual is the only path to the moral and intellectual reform of society. The Krausists' quest for "racial harmony," their recognition of the relationships between the whole and the part, relate directly to the technique in which biography and history are blended—the framework for this novel as well as for all the novellas in *Episodios nacionales*. Hence, Pepe's clash with his aunt, for example, is mirrored by the arrival of the troops from Madrid.

The artistic weakness of the novel lies primarily in its blatant didacticism and in the relative superficiality of its characterizations. Doña Perfecta, Pepe, Inocencio, Rosario, and María Remedios are what Stephen Gilman calls "rounded archetypes," symbolic representations of ideological viewpoints or human characteristics or passions (mostly negative).

Pepe himself is a kind of modern Don Quixote. His inevitable death, furthermore, is foreshadowed repeatedly by dramatic parallels and references to the Passion of Christ. He is individualized only by his flaws (inflexibility, tactlessness) and by his development from a straightforward, friendly, rational human being to a very intemperate, precipitous, even unethical conspirator. Generally, however, he remains a symbol.

Doña Perfecta, while more a symbolic type (almost a caricature) than a unique personality, is nevertheless also individualized somewhat and made understandable by aspects of her family background, her sincerity, and her own measure of development in the course of the novel. Rosario, whose main role is as a catalyst to the action, is nevertheless the most interesting of the characters, and Pérez Galdós's study of her conflicts, her dreams, and her neuroses is a superb precursor of the more profound pathological portraits that were to appear in later novels.

The author's style also points to later techniques. It is natural, direct, and at times even colloquial. A tone of irony predominates throughout the novel, usually expressed through dramatic contrast (Orbajosa's glorious past versus modern banditry; the symbolic dawn with which the novel opens versus the subsequent ineffectiveness of Pepe's actions; and so on). Theatrical elements abound, from the frequent use of dialogue to the descriptions of gestures and the author's "stage directions." Particular to this novel are the stress on animal imagery, classical references (as a means of revealing the ironic discrepancy between name and reality), and the symbolic use of sounds (such as the opening train whistle, the cockcrow, bugles, and the creaking of the cathedral weathercock).

The compact structure of the novel has been analyzed by two leading critics. Sherman H. Eoff has demonstrated that the movement of the plot is based on three decisive, progressively more intense moments of peripeteia: Pepe's "vehement defense of science at the end of chapter 8," his announcement of his intention to marry Rosario, and Doña Perfecta's ordering of his assassination. Stephen Gilman has suggested a number of parallels between the structure of the novel and that of neoclassical tragedy, in which "perfection" passes to "imperfection" through Pepe's tragic flaw and by way of a series of theatrically presented "acts." Indeed, the overt nature of the conflict (far different from the aim of synthesis and reconciliation evident in later works) made it an easy task to adapt the novel to the stage.

Doña Perfecta is far from a great work, and its tremendous popularity is probably undeserved. It is too schematized and melodramatic and lacks the warmth and humor, the feeling of movement, the depth of characterization, and the panorama of realistic detail that were to typify Pérez Galdós's best creations. Yet the skillful use of irony, the suggestion of pathological analysis (Rosario), and the start of a relativistic perspective in which a situation is viewed from several perspectives point to the more mature works that followed.

THE DISINHERITED LADY

The Disinherited Lady heralded a new phase in Pérez Galdós's career. The author no longer concentrated on examining merely the social implications of certain ideologies; rather, *The Disinherited Lady* reveals Pérez Galdós's forceful attempt to incorporate into the novel the world of external appearances, to accumulate innumerable, detailed images of outward, as well as inward, reality. Here, one finds the faithful representation of environment, daily customs, psychological motivation, and the formation of the new middle class—in short, the creation of an "accurate mirror of the society in which we live." This was now the author's central purpose, and the core of his subsequent realistic aspirations.

Pérez Galdós now went to work on a broader canvas, including naturalistic suggestions of hereditary and environmental influence; he introduced "collective" characters (*manicomio, fábrica, taller, asilo, barrio bajo*) and the theme that people must face reality; he initiated the idea that the real world and the world of fiction interact and are mutually dependent. Finally, *The Disinherited Lady* represents a closer joining of the two narrative paths expressed previously in a more separate form: the *episodio* of contemporary history (here the abdication of Amadeo, the floundering of the First Republic, and the advent of the Restoration) and the didactic representation of society seen in the early *novelas contemporáneas*.

The plot deals with the life of a woman, Isidora Rufete, who tries in vain to prove her claims of nobility. As Isidora clings to the illusion of noble birth, which is her major standard of personal worth, she comes to live with, first, a man of aristocratic family and, later, one whose money can satisfy her desire for luxury. Only two episodes suggest actual narrative "movement"—the heroine's visit to the Marquesa whose kinship she has claimed, and her eventual imprisonment for having supposedly falsified the documents that could prove her relation to the Marquesa's family. Isidora, says Eoff, thus

> subordinates her wholesome inclinations of friendliness, sympathy, and honesty as she tries to prove her nobility; . . . she is increasingly tyrannized by the love of wealth and luxury; and . . . her integrity dissolves completely after the final disillusionment following her imprisonment.

At the end, her illusions irreparably shattered, she descends to a life of prostitution.

Although Pérez Galdós's attitude and beliefs are less prominent here than in his earlier thesis novels, the tone of the work is far from objective. Most important is its pervasive air of indulgent, yet pointed, Cervantine irony; this is evident from the beginning, when Pérez Galdós draws a contrast between the beauty of nature and the frenzied self-occupation of the asylum inmates. It is seen also in the use of caricature (as in the descriptions of Isidora's friend Don José and of such minor characters as Tomás Rufete, Botín, and Juan Bou), in euphemism and in self-deception (in the moments of *estilo indirecto libre*, when self-deception is most conspicuous), and in the way in which the reader himself is deceived into identifying with the heroine.

Thematically, Pérez Galdós is saying that one must face reality as it is and reject false values and the worship of appearances; he condemns the attitude of "*quiero pero no puedo* (I want to but cannot)," supports the need for better educational facilities and opportunities (for the sake of children such as Pecado, Isidora's brother), and criticizes social parasites (such as her lover, Joaquín). There are specific commentaries about the Spanish propensity for civil war (symbolized in the children's battle), the Catholic Church ("Entreacto en la iglesia"), nepotism, *caciquismo*, politics, and mental institutions. Only in his more mature novels was Pérez Galdós able to incorporate his desire to teach into a more completely artistic framework.

Many critics who have dealt with *The Disinherited Lady* have been specifically interested in the novel's naturalistic content. Most of them have concluded that this is one of Pérez Galdós's most naturalistic novels (and one that probably demonstrates stronger naturalistic influence than any other Spanish novel of its time), but they agree that it still offers no evidence of Pérez Galdós's complete adherence to the philosophical and linguistic tenets of Zola. Elements that suggest naturalistic influence include the force of heredity, some measure of environmental determinism, the topic of the *bestia humana* (humans driven by their own mechanistic or animalistic impulses), and occasional frankness of language. Nowhere, however, does one find the morbidity of many of Zola's works. Despite Pérez Galdós's detail, he consciously avoided presenting the seamier aspects of Isidora's love affairs. There is no true fatalistic determinism. Above all, the novel is a moral work that acknowledges the power and possibilities open to the human will. Finally, Pérez Galdós avoided the cold, objective tone of the naturalists. Zola's rigor is neutralized here by *la risa cervantina* (Cervantine humor).

With respect to style, the growing force of realism in Pérez Galdós's new manner reveals itself most dramatically in the increased use of colloquial speech and in the descriptive atmosphere of the novel. The author "takes possession" of Madrid as the broad stage that was to form the background for so many of his works, leading the reader into all corners of the city and illuminating the contradictory, often oppressive aspects of the modern nineteenth century metropolis. Costumbristic scenes abound. Other linguistic techniques include theatrical elements, the fuller use of the *estilo indirecto libre*, the adaptation of language to circumstances and characters, and descriptions with an occasional impressionistic flavor. The last characteristic is evident, for example, at those moments when the author blurs the boundary between waking reality and reverie: "*insomnio número cinquenta y tantos*" and so on. The chapters titled "Beethoven" and "Sigue Beethoven" are deliberate linguistic tours de force; here Pérez Galdós uses the modernistic techniques of triple and quadruple adjectival construction, *sinestesia*, and musical elements to produce two moods analogous to major and minor keys.

In *The Disinherited Lady*, Pérez Galdós thus subordinated moralistic militancy to a relative stress on character delineation for its own sake. He continued to base his personages on one or two central attitudes or passions, but this focal impulse now became more personal. The real interest of the work lies in the evolution of the heroine. Only this progression gives the novel's structure continuity. The psychological movement of the story shows how Isidora subordinates her instincts of honesty, friendliness, and sympathy to her tyrannical obsession with her noble beginnings and her hunger for wealth and luxury. Ultimately, her integrity dissolves completely, in the final disillusionment that follows her imprisonment.

Through Isidora, one sees Pérez Galdós's first real venture into a further extension of "environment," what may be termed the world of "fiction," as opposed to that of immediate, physical circumstance. The intangible realm of the heroine's thoughts and beliefs is as real as the visible reality around her, although contrasting with it. The reader is left uncertain about the reality of Isidora's situation until her climactic conversation with the Marquesa de Aransis at the end of the first part. Pérez Galdós makes full use of the idea that men and women depend on their dreams. Isidora "dies" when her illusions are smashed, having declared that "*mejor es soñar que ver*" (it is better to dream than to see). The author demonstrates how critically trauma or psychic shock can function in the sphere of nominal sanity. As in Pérez Galdós's later novels, dreams serve two basic functions in *The Disinherited Lady*: as a means of characterization (Isidora's obsession, Don José's feelings toward the heroine) and as foreshadowing (Isidora's premonitions in jail concerning her lawyer's failure). The fact that almost all the major characters are prone to dreams and illusions echoes the Cervantine ambiguity of reality, with its intimation that "real" existence is a complicated blend of exterior and interior perceptions.

Certainly, Isidora is in part symbolic, representing aspects of the Spanish people as a whole. Yet, more important, she is a unique case of semi-insanity, individualized both by her faults (her aristocratic obsession, her fear of vulgarity, egotistical pride, financial ineptness, extreme nervousness) and by her virtues (in particular, her generosity).

Don José, probably one of Pérez Galdós's finest and most poignant psychological creations, serves primarily to dramatize the heroine's downfall with his own incidental destruction. Like Isidora, he is both a type-character (a kind of pathetic Don Quixote whose Dulcinea is the protagonist) and a peculiar blend of self-sacrificing, Platonic generosity and senile sexual illusions. The minor characters in the novel contribute in an essentially static fashion to Isidora's negative development.

The work's structure is not a tight one. In a way, the plot starts and ends in medias res. At times, one feels that Pérez Galdós is improvising, guided only by a plan to study the process of Isidora's psychological degeneration. Nevertheless, there is considerable evidence in the novel of careful structural techniques: the framework of two parts, each with its *suicidio*, each with a criminal act by Pecado, and so on (the first part contains the confirmation of Isidora's illusions and the second the gradual destruction of those hopes when the world of reality gains mastery); the careful social progression of the heroine's lovers in part 2; and finally, a series of parallels and correspondences: the two key events (the meeting with the Marquesa, Isidora's imprisonment), Pecado's world versus Isidora's interior world, the parallel scenes involving both Isidora and Joaquín, the two "Beethoven" chapters, the crimes of Pecado, the *cordelería* versus Bou's shop, the manner in which Pecado and his playmate Majito are eventually united after separate, but related descriptions, and so on.

The Disinherited Lady, then, was an experiment, and as such a turning point for Pérez Galdós. The novel retains at least something of the argumentative quality and abstractness of his thesis novels, yet points ahead to the greater psychological depth of such later characters as Fortunata and Benina. The work, viewed as a whole, adds in two ways to Pérez Galdós's maturing realistic technique: His details now fill in the canvas of external reality, and his insights take the reader deeper into the labyrinth of human psychology.

FORTUNATA AND JACINTA

Fortunata and Jacinta is Pérez Galdós's most complex creation and can be considered his masterpiece, probably one of the three greatest novels in Spanish literature. The framework for the action is a broad, detailed social record of Madrid life in the 1870's, with a veritable encyclopedia of customs, national types, and topographical minutiae. Above all, the work is an extraordinary study of the mutual influence of individual personalities and an exhibition of how one person's freedom can vanquish the potentially lethal effects of an immensely materialistic and erotic collectivity. The naturalistic semideterminism of *The*

Disinherited Lady has passed to a Cervantine open-ended quest for rehabilitating values.

In broadest outline, the story concerns the fortunes of two women, linked by Juanito Santa Cruz, an idle, pampered bourgeois. In the first half of the book, Juanito marries his cousin, Jacinta, a woman obsessed with the idea of bearing a child. Fortunata, a beautiful woman of the *pueblo* and Juanito's lover, marries the sickly Maximiliano Rubín. As the novel progresses, Juanito vacillates between the security and conformity of his upper-middle-class marriage to Jacinta and the spontaneous vitality of society's lower rank (Fortunata). Eventually, Fortunata, the real protagonist of the work, gravitates toward her refined rival, whom she comes to see as a victim of Juanito, as she is. In the end, Fortunata gives birth to Juanito's son and, in a final gesture of understanding and self-expression, gives the child over to Jacinta. Around these personalities, Pérez Galdós weaves a web of interrelating stories, events, and minor characters that is astounding in its richness and complexity.

Pérez Galdós's novelistic techniques had matured considerably since the publication of *The Disinherited Lady*, clearly visible in characterization, theme, and style. Although the two heroines are meant to symbolize the clash between natural and social law, they are above all extremely complex individuals. There are no exclusively malevolent or benevolent figures in the novel. Fortunata, purposely presented first without background description, makes a slow and intricate voyage through self-consciousness toward self-discovery. By the end, she has surpassed jealousy, emulation, and fear of inferiority. While maintaining her original straightforward sincerity, emotional temperament, compassion, and disregard for social convention, she undergoes the "civilizing" influence of Maxi's widowed aunt, Doña Lupe, the elderly bachelor, Evaristo Feijóo, the social conventionalism of the charity worker, Guillermina Pacheco, and, above all, the model of Jacinta. In comparison to the psychological penetration Pérez Galdós offered in *The Disinherited Lady* in his portrayal of the insomniac Isidora, whose consciousness is marked by the relentless ticking of the clock, the study of Fortunata allows for a kind of autonomous interior time in which development occurs more slowly, more hesitatingly, and more meaningfully. This psychological trajectory is the very essence of the novel and gives the work its structure.

Jacinta hides her feelings, at least most of the time, under a veneer of social propriety. She is dominated throughout the novel by her obsession with children. She is gentle and affectionate rather than passionate and volatile by nature. Her evolution is marked by a lessening of sentimentality, an increase in independence, and, later, by a deepening maturity as she clashes with and then is drawn to Fortunata. Juanito functions as a catalyst in the plot and is more a type-character: the idle, well-off, essentially superficial *señorito* (young master). The diminutive that is inevitably applied to his name suggests the apron strings to which he has been tied. While not a despicable Joaquín Pez (of *The Disinherited Lady*), he is frivolous, pedantic, selfishly unremorseful, and vain, calculating, and insatiable in his search for novelty. In general, his personality is too shallow to allow room for subtlety or surprise.

The character of Maximiliano is, in Geoffrey Ribbans's words, "second only to Don Quixote as a highly sympathetic study of madness in Spanish literature." One of Pérez Galdós's supreme examples of the dreamer given over to imagination, he conceives the romantic mission of redeeming Fortunata; Maxi's "madness" actually allows him to see her true worth. His development, marked by vacillations between outward anger and inward anguish, reveals the writer's most original techniques of characterization. The minor figures serve primarily as links between or foils for the major characters, but many of their own individualized personalities demonstrate a marked tendency to evolve.

Thematically, *Fortunata and Jacinta* is less a study of the evils of Madrileñan society (although ample evidence of injustice, immorality, and ignorance is presented) than a demonstration that good cannot be neatly separated from evil and that, within the shifting relationships between the individual and his community, one person's expression of freedom, one act of giving, can, in Gilman's words, "be considered a final, self-justifying epic deed, an autonomous affirmation of humanity in the very teeth of history." While not complacent or overly optimistic, the author is hopeful, calling on the untapped potential for human progress.

In *Fortunata and Jacinta*, Pérez Galdós achieves an almost obsessive probing of the limits of daily speech, staged within a specificity of setting and topographical detail never before seen in the Spanish novel. Nowhere, with the possible exception of Leopoldo Alas's *La regenta* (1884), could readers find such richness, such fullness of descriptive elaboration. Particularly original to this work is the consistent bird imagery (for the purposes of characterization and structural development of the plot), the remarkable proto-Freudian use of dreams, and the increasingly complicated manipulations of point of view: authorial narrative, dialogue, *estilo indirecto libre*, and direct interior monologue (the recording of unspoken dialogue). Pérez Galdós's more frequent use of the unreliable narrator and the omnipresence of situational and verbal irony add to the ambiguities of the major characterizations and of the theme.

Fortunata and Jacinta presents a world of profound, interacting psychological portraits amid an incredibly detailed material setting; in its denouement, it reveals the end of Pérez Galdós's naturalistic phase and the beginning of a spiritual emphasis that was to dominate many of his later works.

COMPASSION

Written during a time of great financial and legal difficulties for Pérez Galdós, *Compassion* nevertheless demonstrates a spirit of understanding, a philosophical serenity, and a proclamation of profound optimism for humankind. The novel represents the fullest and most artistic expression of Pérez Galdós's "spiritual" phase. The setting—the misery and poverty of the beggars' world in old Madrid—is portrayed with the same seminaturalistic verisimilitude seen in earlier works, but the unresolved struggle between good and evil seen in *Fortunata and Jacinta* gives way to a deeper humanization of outlook in which love, charity, and basic Christian values indicate the clear potential of final triumph for all human beings.

In contrast to *Fortunata and Jacinta*, *Compassion* presents a world of reduced dimensions. Although the technique of detailed examination is similar, the author has been more selective, more attuned to the proportion of microcosm, rather than macrocosm. Further, out of the process of increasing interiorization manifested in earlier works came a profound evolutionary step: the inclusion of fantasy and illusion as integral components in the creation of actual, physical, living entities.

Benina, the elderly protagonist, begs to provide the daily bread for her spendthrift mistress Doña Paca, telling her that this income is wages from work in the house of a fictitious priest, Don Romualdo. As the story develops, Benina's charity extends to Paca's daughter, Obdulia, the pretentious Frasquito Ponte, and an increasingly broad circle of dependents. When she and her blind companion Almudena are arrested for begging in a prohibited area, she is taken to the poorhouse of Misericordia (compassion). During her absence, Paca, Paca's children, and Ponte are redeemed from poverty by an inheritance delivered to them by a priest named Romualdo Cedrón, whom they take to be Benina's Don Romualdo. Paca's domineering daughter-in-law Juliana comes forward to manage the new wealth, and when Benina finally returns, she is turned away. Her devotion to Paca has spawned only ingratitude.

Ironically, the inheritance leads only to misery. The dismissal of Benina and the lack of energy needed to fulfill their own pretentious visions lead the family to a life of spiritual emptiness. Benina goes with Almudena to live in a hut near the outskirts of Madrid, where she is eventually visited by Juliana. Like Saint Paul, the latter has experienced a sudden conversion and begs Benina to bless her and assure her of her children's future well-being.

The novel is constructed on a series of thematic, structural, and psychological dualities. With respect to characterization, Benina (based perhaps on Pérez Galdós's family nurse in Las Palmas) is particularized by her *sisa* (pilfering from her "earnings"), her superstition, and occasional naïveté. Yet she stands as the personification of charity and is presented symbolically as a Christ figure who suffers and accepts sacrifice (parallels to the life and words of Jesus abound in the novel). In addition, she bears more than a little resemblance to traditional type figures of Spanish literature (Lazarillo, Don Quixote). Her development consists of an expansion and intensification of her charitable ways toward a point of increased confidence and adjustability, in which charity and self-sacrifice are actually essential to her being. Through contact with others, she evolves toward a conscious recognition of the morality inherent in what originally were purely spontaneous acts of compassion.

Ponte is likewise a "dual" character. Born of costumbristic satire, he is the *proto-cursi* who attempts to relive the past; yet, when a fall from a horse leads to madness, he (like Maxi Rubín) is able to perceive the more profound truths concerning others. Almudena, one of Pérez Galdós's unique and most memorable creations, symbolizes the Moors and

Jews who have been rejected and expelled from Spain and represents also the mystic exaltation of fantasy. His vices (egotism, jealousy, and so on) and his particular mixture of emotions toward Benina serve to individualize him. Paca embodies selfishness and irresponsibility, and the minor characters act as foils, parallels, or contrasts to Benina.

With respect to theme, the need to face reality is demonstrated, but (as the other side of the coin) certain kinds of fantasy or illusion (those with proper motives) are exalted as powerful, creative factors. The apparently "supernatural" appearance of Don Romualdo—which Benina herself feels may be the result of her own imagination—is the single most striking point of the novel and is meant to demonstrate this concept. A second general theme (the primary message) concerns the nature and importance of true charity. As a very significant link between the two main thematic statements, charity is seen to be the motive behind Benina's creature of fantasy, Don Romualdo. An additional bridge between the two messages lies in the thought that true charity provides a way of facing the hardships of reality.

Many elements of technique, tone, and style have been refined in *Compassion* but relate closely to those of Pérez Galdós's earlier works: expressive force, colloquial naturalness, frequent dialogue, naturalistic precision, costumbristic description, Cervantine irony, humor, the use of dreams. The gently ironic force of free indirect style is gradually abandoned in the later chapters, as Pérez Galdós identifies more closely with Benina, while allowing the heroine and others to testify more on their own behalf. The dualities of appearance and reality, seen throughout the author's career, are omnipresent here: Hunger becomes beneficial, blindness means vision, madness is wisdom, the servant is the leader, defeat equals victory.

The structure, based generally on Benina's development, reveals a dual or two-part organization. The first section (a week long, suggesting the Passion of Christ) is seen through Benina's eyes and presents the physical and temporal details of the beggars' lives and the heroine's expanding role; the second is a more generalized narration while Benina is in the poorhouse, leading to Paca's climactic rejection and the protagonist's final victory. Despite the relative haste with which Pérez Galdós composed the novel, the plot line is constructed with extraordinary care, exemplified by the steps leading to the meeting of Benina and the miserly Don Carlos at the start and by the careful stages in preparation for Don Romualdo's astonishing appearance with the news of the inheritance.

Compassion, then, is representative of Pérez Galdós's most mature creations. Within a framework of "spiritual" intentions, the work stands as the most artistic rendering of nineteenth century Cervantine dualities, seen from the two "faces" of the San Sebastián church, on the first page, through the seemingly contradictory reconciliations of charity and *la sisa* (Benina), Judaism/Mohammedanism and Christianity (Almudena), fantasy and truth (Don Romualdo), matter and spirit, naturalism and idealistic humanism. At the same time, one sees here the real culmination of Pérez Galdós's development as a novelist.

At this stage, Pérez Galdós was able to anticipate the twentieth century's expansion of the realistic approach; he recognized that one must go beyond the perceptible elements of physical surroundings to fill out a realistic perspective. The writer must also integrate into his or her picture qualities of transcendent, universal, or symbolic significance. The nineteenth century realistic novel did generally move in this direction; although it looked critically at the inclusion of imaginary events, it sometimes ended by absorbing the stuff of the imagination. A dose of "poetic substance" entered realistic transcription; myth was simultaneously destroyed and assimilated into the real. Influenced by the Cervantine interplay of diverse "fictions" and "realities," Pérez Galdós demonstrated that "fiction" and "reality" are not dichotomous; rather, they are interacting components of the substance of human existence.

Jeremy T. Medina

OTHER MAJOR WORKS

PLAYS: *Realidad*, pr., pb. 1892 (adaptation of his novel); *Gerona*, pr. 1893 (adaptation of his novel); *La loca de la casa*, pr., pb. 1893; *Los condenados*, pr. 1894; *La de San Quintín*, pr., pb. 1894 (*The Duchess of San Quintín*, 1917); *Voluntad*, pr. 1895; *Doña Perfecta*, pr., pb. 1896 (adaptation of his novel); *La fiera*, pr. 1896; *Electra*, pr., pb. 1901 (English translation, 1911); *Alma y vida*, pr., pb. 1902; *El hombre fuerte*, pb. 1902 (wr. 1864-1868); *Mariucha*, pr., pb. 1903; *El abuelo*, pr., pb. 1904 (adaptation of his novel; *The Grandfather*, 1910); *Amor y ciencia*, pr., pb. 1905; *Bárbara*, pr., pb. 1905; *Pedro Minio*, pr. 1908; *Zaragoza*, pr., pb. 1908 (music by Arturo Lapuerto; adaptation of his novel); *Casandra*, pr., pb. 1910 (adaptation of his novel); *Celia en los infiernos*, pr., pb. 1913; *Alceste*, pr., pb. 1914; *Sor Simona*, pr., pb. 1915; *El tacaño Salomón*, pr., pb. 1916; *Santa Juana de Castilla*, pr., pb. 1918; *Antón Caballero*, pr. 1921 (completed by Serafín and Joaquín Álvarez Quintero); *Un joven de provecho*, pb. 1935 (wr. 1867).

NONFICTION: *Discursos académicos*, 1897; *Memoranda*, 1906; *Arte y crítica*, 1923; *Fisonomías sociales*, 1923; *Nuestro teatro*, 1923; *Política española*, 1923; *Cronicón*, 1924; *Toledo*, 1924; *Viajes y fantasías*, 1928; *Memorias*, 1930; *Crónica de Madrid*, 1933; *Cartas de Pérez Galdós a Mesonero Romanos*, 1943; *Crónica de la Quincena*, 1948; *Madrid*, 1956.

BIBLIOGRAPHY

Anderson, Lara. *Allegories of Decadence in Fin-de-Siècle Spain: The Female Consumer in the Novels of Emila Pardo Bazán and Benito Pérez Galdós*. Lewiston, N.Y.: Edwin Mellen Press, 2006. Anderson examines seven novels by Pérez Galdós and Pardo Bazán, focusing on the connections between Spanish decadence and the character of the female spendthrift. Discusses how this character reflects late nineteenth century concerns about Spain's decline.

Fuentes Peris, Teresa. *Galdos's "Torquemada" Novels: Waste and Profit in Late Nineteenth-Century Spain*. Cardiff: University of Wales Press, 2007. A study of the character of Francisco Torquemada, a Madrid moneylender, analyzing how his ideas about waste and profit enhance an understanding of the novels in which he appears.

Gilman, Stephen. *Galdós and the Art of the European Novel, 1867-1887*. Princeton, N.J.: Princeton University Press, 1981. Divided into three sections, with one part on the historical novelist and the remainder on *Fortunata and Jacinta*. A perceptive work of scholarship that provides an important context for understanding the novels. Includes an appendix on classical references in *Doña Perfecta*.

Gold, Hazel. *The Reframing of Realism: Galdós and the Discourses of the Nineteenth-Century Spanish Novel*. Durham, N.C.: Duke University Press, 1993. Excellent discussions of individual novels as well as a concluding chapter on Pérez Galdós's place in his native tradition. Recommended for advanced students.

Larsen, Kevin. *Cervantes and Galdós in "Fortunata y Jacinta: Tales of Impertinent Curiosity."* Lewiston, N.Y.: Edwin Mellen Press, 1999. Examines the significance of Cervantes to Pérez Galdós's writing of the novel *Fortunata and Jacinta*.

McGovern, Timothy Michael. *Galdós Beyond Realism: Reading and the Creation of Magical Worlds*. Newark, Del.: Juan de la Cuesta, 2004. McGovern argues that Perez Galdós should not be defined solely as a realist writer, arguing that some of his works feature nonrational or magical events and other aspects of "nonrealism."

Pattison, Walter T. *Benito Pérez Galdós*. Boston: Twayne, 1975. A very helpful introduction, with a chapter on the novelist's life, his journalism and early novels, his first contemporary novels, his naturalistic style, and the end of his career. Includes a chronology, detailed notes, and a bibliography.

Percival, Anthony. *Galdós and His Critics*. Buffalo, N.Y.: University of Toronto Press, 1985. An analysis and interpretation of the works of Pérez Galdós, with emphasis on critical reaction to his work. Includes a bibliography and an index.

Turner, Harriet S. *Benito Pérez Galdós, "Fortunata and Jacinta."* New York: Cambridge University Press, 1992. A painstaking study of this masterpiece, with a chronology of the novel's main events; genealogical tables; a biographical introduction to the author; chapters on the social and historical contexts, the characters, and the novel's metaphors; and a guide to further reading.

Willem, Linda M. *Galdós's "Secunda Manera": Rhetorical Strategies and Affective Response*. Chapel Hill: University of North Carolina Press, 1999. Willem examines how Pérez Galdós's narrative style became more sophisticated and varied with the publication of *The Disinherited Lady*, his first contemporary novel.

_____, ed. *A Sesquicentennial Tribute to Galdós, 1843-1993*. Newark, Del.: Juan de la Cuesta, 1993. A collection of essays on various aspects of Pérez Galdós's life and works, including analyses of the novels *The Forbidden*, *Tristana*, and *Compassion*. Includes a bibliography.

RAMÓN JOSÉ SENDER

Born: Chalamera de Cinca, Spain; February 3, 1901
Died: San Diego, California; January 15, 1982
Also known as: Ramón José Sender Garcés; Ramon Sender

PRINCIPAL LONG FICTION
Imán, 1930 (*Earmarked for Hell*, 1934; better known as *Pro Patria*, 1935)
Siete domingos rojos, 1932, 1973 (*Seven Red Sundays*, 1936)
La noche de las cien cabezas, 1934
Mr. Witt en el cantón, 1936 (*Mr. Witt Among the Rebels*, 1937)
El lugar del hombre, 1939 (*A Man's Place*, 1940)
O. P.: Orden público, 1941
Epitalamio del prieto Trinidad, 1942 (*Dark Wedding*, 1943)
Crónica del alba, 1942-1966 (3 volumes, 9 parts; volume 1 translated as *Before Noon: A Novel in Three Parts*, 1957; includes *Crónica del alba*, 1942 [*Chronicle of Dawn*, 1944]; *Hipogrifo violenta*, 1954 [*Violent Griffin*, 1957]; *La quinta Julieta* [*The Villa Julieta*])
La esfera, 1947, 1969 (originally as *Proverbio de la muerte*, 1939; *The Sphere*, 1949)
El rey y la reina, 1949 (*The King and the Queen*, 1948)
El verdugo afable, 1952 (*The Affable Hangman*, 1954)
Mosén Millán, 1953 (also known as *Requiem por un campesino español*, 1960; *Requiem for a Spanish Peasant*, 1960)
Los cinco libros de Ariadna, 1957, 1977
Emen hetan, 1958
Los laureles de Anselmo, 1958
El mancebo y los heroes, 1960
En la vida de Ignacio Morel, 1969

OTHER LITERARY FORMS

By the end of 1981, first editions of Ramón José Sender's books, exclusive of an anthology of selections from his works, numbered ninety-six. At the time of his death early in 1982, Destino, the Barcelona publishing house, had scheduled for publication two new novels by Sender; an additional manuscript of a novel, appropriately titled "Toque de Queda" ("Taps"), was found among his papers, ready for publication.

Depending on one's criteria for the determination of literary genre (in Sender's case, a task made all but impossible by the author's disdain for such classifications and his deliberate attempts, at times, to blur traditional genre distinctions), Sender's total production of ninety-nine books (including the three unpublished novels) could be described as including sixty-four novels or novellas, seven collections of short stories, five works of drama, two volumes of poetry, and twenty-one books of essays, personal narratives, and journalistic articles. Almost all of this last category consists of material published earlier in newspaper articles or in Sender's literary column, "Los libros y los días" (books and days), which was syndicated in Spanish-language newspapers throughout Latin America from early in the 1950's until the author's death. More than eight hundred articles appeared in "Los libros y los días."

Achievements

Ramón José Sender surely ranks as one of the greatest Spanish novelists of the twentieth century. Marcelino Peñuelas, the Spanish critic, places him "at the head of the Spanish novelists of our time" and adds, in case there is any doubt, that he means by this to exalt Sender above Pío Baroja, generally held to be the preeminent Spanish novelist of the twentieth century. Few, if any, Spanish writers of all history, except for Miguel de Cervantes and Benito Pérez Galdós, have had their novels so widely translated as has Sender.

Sender's first novel, *Pro Patria*, was translated into ten major languages; by 1970, his novels had appeared in more than eighty foreign translations, according to Peñuelas. Thirteen of his novels have appeared in English, all in both British and American editions. In January, 1936, his first historical novel, *Mr. Witt Among the Rebels*, was awarded the National Prize for Literature, at that time regarded as Spain's highest literary award. In 1966, the first three-volume edition of his monumental autobiographical novel, *Crónica del alba* (chronicle of dawn), received the City of Barcelona Prize. In 1969, Sender won the lucrative Planeta Prize from the Planeta publishing house for his rather mediocre novel *En la vida de Ignacio Morel* (in the life of Ignacio Morel).

Biography

Ramón José Sender, whose full name is Ramón José Sender Garcés, was born in the village of Chalamera de Cinca, in the Aragonese province of Huesca, on February 3, 1901. His father was town clerk of both Chalamera and the nearby town of Alcolea de Cinca. Both his parents' families had long-standing roots in Alcolea, and the Sender family returned there in 1903, moving next to Tauste (Aragon) in 1908 or 1909. A composite of both Alcolea and Tauste can be recognized as the scene of three of the author's finest novels, *A Man's Place*, *Crónica del alba*, and *Requiem for a Spanish Peasant*. His deep attachment to his native region and pride in his Aragonese heritage never left him.

From his earliest years, Sender rebelled against the authoritarian attitude of his father, a strict Catholic whose efforts to force his views upon the future novelist seem to have been decisive in determining Sender's lifelong rebellion against the existing order of things, including his rejection of the Roman Catholic Church. Sender's attitude of rebellion and protest is evident in all of his writings, both journalistic and literary. His protests against the dictatorship of Primo de Rivera in 1927 led to his imprisonment for three months in Madrid, an experience that he novelized in *O. P.*

Difficulties with his father apparently led to Sender's being sent to a Catholic boarding school in Reus (Catalonia) for the academic year 1913-1914, a year that forms the basis for his novel *Violent Griffin*, which later became the second of the three parts of the first volume of his monumental three-volume autobiographical novel *Crónica del alba*. Only volume 1 of the series has appeared in English translation (as *Before Noon: A Novel in Three Parts*, 1957), and its first part initially appeared separately under the same title as the series—*Chronicle of Dawn*.

From 1914 to 1917, Sender attended the Institute of Zaragoza. During the next school year, he worked as a pharmacy clerk in Alcañiz while meeting, through special arrangements with the Institute of Teruel (in Teruel), the remaining requirements for his high school diploma. During the next three years, from 1918 to 1921, he worked on the editorial staff of *La tierra*, a small newspaper in Huesca published by the Association of Farmers and Ranchers of Upper Aragon.

Upon his return in 1924 from fourteen months of service in the Spanish army in the ill-fated Moroccan War, Sender joined the editorial staff of the prestigious liberal newspaper *El sol* in Madrid. Following the success of his first novel, *Pro Patria*, Sender left *El sol* to devote himself full-time to freelance journalistic writing and to writing novels. During the next six years, he published six novels in addition to nearly two hundred articles in the newspaper *La libertad* and numerous articles in *Solidaridad obrera*, the organ of the Confederación Nacional de Trabajo (National Labor Federation) in Barcelona.

During the Spanish Civil War, Sender served in the republican army, rising to the rank of *comandante* (major). His wife was executed by Nationalist forces in Zamora on October 10, 1936. Late in 1938, Sender, seeing that the republican cause was hopeless, fled to France and from there to Mexico City in March of 1939. From Mexico, he entered the United States on a Guggenheim Fellowship in 1942, becoming a naturalized U.S. citizen in 1946 and remaining in the United States until his death in 1982.

From 1947 until 1963, Sender was a professor of Spanish at the University of New Mexico in Albuquerque; from 1965 until 1971, he was a visiting professor of Spanish literature at the University of Southern California. Upon retirement in 1971, he moved to San Diego, California, where he lived until his death.

Sender remained an outspoken enemy of the Nationalist regime in Spain, and it was not until June of 1974 that he returned to his native land, his first visit since his self-imposed exile in 1938. During this three-week stay, he was warmly received and highly praised by the Spanish literary community.

Analysis

Though marked by great diversity, Ramón José Sender's vast novelistic production over five decades reveals a remarkable unity of vision. In substance, one finds that there are continuing, basic Senderian concepts and themes, found in large measure in his first novel, *Pro Patria*, as well as in his posthumously published works. In them all, one finds the author's deep concern with social justice, with the struggle of the individual for self-realization, for love, and for an ideal that gives transcendent value to life. Sender's writings serve as a vehicle for ceaselessly probing certain immutable problems of existence: the question of death or human mortality; the enigma of evil in the individual and in the world at large; the possibility of an ultimate basis for moral judgments; and the function of the mysterious and the nonrational in life. Ordinary realism is in a Senderian novel only the starting point or the springboard for reaching out for transcendent meaning, for discovery of the marvelous and the mysterious, for brief flights of poetic fantasy, and for a constant metaphysical-religious-lyric questioning of the ultimate nature of reality. Sender's novels usually move on three distinct levels: the realistic, the poetic, and the philosophical-religious.

Though neither an orthodox believer in God nor an atheist, Sender reveals in his novels a deep faith in and reverence toward humanity; in *The Sphere*, he elaborates his belief that the essential part of humanity is imperishable, believing (along with Benedict de Spinoza) that "man is an integral part of the infinite intellect of God." An offense to humanity thus becomes an offense to God. Humanity, both its individual persons and in the abstract, is squarely in the center of Sender's novelistic universe. Though his short stories, theatrical pieces, essays, and poetry have received very little critical attention, they all exhibit the same basic view of humans and explore the same fundamental questions to be found in his novels.

Sender's style is that of the author speaking directly and personally to the reader in simple, clear, unaffected language, even when passages of the harshest realism are interrupted with flights of lyric fantasy or dialectical probing of philosophical-religious problems (from which inconclusive and eclectic syntheses are derived; Sender is never dogmatic except to reiterate the impossibility of humanity arriving at absolute truth—at least in this life). In a taped interview at the University of Southern California on June 7, 1966, Sender named four Spanish authors as having greatly influenced him: Fernando de Rojas, Francisco de Quevedo y Villegas, Ramón María del Valle-Inclán, and Baroja. Sender, like Baroja, is a writer of substance, always with something worthwhile to say, and openly disdainful of mere style; he also is preoccupied with social, moral, and metaphysical problems.

The influence of Valle-Inclán can be seen in Sender's occasional juxtaposition of the grotesque and the lyrically innocent and in the use of tragicomedy. His bitter social satire, his tendency to caricature and his austere humor (never far removed from sadness) may owe something to Quevedo, the seventeenth century writer of *Los sueños* (1627; *The Visions*, 1640) and the celebrated picaresque novel, *Historia de la vida del buscón* (1626; *The Life and Adventures of Buscon*, 1657). Sender's peculiar fusion of realistic and nonrealistic elements (fantasy, dreams, hallucinations, the mysterious, the marvelous, the magical, and so on) recalls not only the two levels of realism and fantasy in *La Celestina*

(1499; *The Rogue*, 1634) of Rojas but also those in the greatest Spanish novel of all, Miguel de Cervantes' *Don Quixote de la Mancha* (1605, 1615).

Francisco Carrasquer calls Sender's first novel, *Pro Patria*, a "provisional anticipatory synthesis of all of Sender's work" and adds that it is such a great novel "that one cannot understand how a first work like it did not definitely consecrate its author." Peñuelas also calls it a "great novel," and he told Sender, "You have a few novels the equal of *Imán* [*Pro Patria*], but none better." Until recently, critics have tended to regard the work as simply a realistic account of the Moroccan War much in the style of Erich Maria Remarque's *Im Westen nichts Neues* (1929, 1968; *All Quiet on the Western Front*, 1929, 1969), published one year earlier in Germany. *Pro Patria*'s fantastic, poetic, philosophical, and symbolic dimensions were long overlooked, but masterful studies of the work by both Carrasquer and Peñuelas have helped to correct this misapprehension.

PRO PATRIA

Pro Patria tells the story of the Spanish military campaign to suppress the rebellion of the Moorish leader Abd-el-Krim in 1921 in Spanish Morocco. The story is told from the perspective of Viance, a Spanish private who attracts misfortune (hence the book's Spanish title, *Imán*, meaning "magnet"), alternating with that of a Spanish journalist, Antonio, and that of an omniscient narrator.

Harsh realism is especially evident in the first of the book's three major divisions, "The Camp—The Relief." In the tone and atmosphere set here for the rest of the narrative, there is an implied denunciation of the utter stupidity and uselessness of war, perhaps not only of the specific Spanish campaign but also of war in general—whether the novel is a pacifist work is subject to debate.

In the second division, "Annual—The Catastrophe," the suffering of Viance from hunger, thirst, and exhaustion reaches the limits of human endurance while the Spanish forces are routed. Through it all, however, Viance, though a common soldier (and symbolic of the Spanish masses), engages in some metaphysical-lyric probing of the meaning of his experience and of human life. Lying in the stinking belly of a horse, hiding from the Moors, he senses "that his own matter is alike to that which encircles him, that there is only one kind of matter, and that all of it is animated by the same blind impulses, obedient to the same law." One dark night inclines Viance "to believe in some kind of justice . . . [in] A kind of bright and translucent justice implicit in all things."

In the third and last division, "Escape—War—Discharge—The Peace of the Dead," Viance escapes from his Moorish captors and returns to the Spanish forces, only to receive inhuman treatment from them and finally to be discharged, a bitter, disillusioned man contemplating suicide. The book's social protest arises from the action itself; Viance's officers treat him as the upper classes have for centuries in Spain treated the lower classes. Because Sender's military service in Morocco occurred two years or more after the crushing defeat of the Spaniards at Annual, the events recorded are not autobiographical but are rather a composite of what the young author heard from others combined with his own vivid imagination.

MR. WITT AMONG THE REBELS

The first of several historical novels published by Sender over four decades, *Mr. Witt Among the Rebels* portrays an insurrection against the First Spanish Republic in the province of Cartagena in 1873; the action occurs in Murcia and, strangely enough, it seems to foreshadow the Civil War, which was to erupt July 18, 1936, almost immediately after the appearance of the novel. Fused with the outer events of the revolution is the private, inner story of Mr. Witt, a balding English engineer of fifty-three, stationed in Cartagena and married to Milagritos, a charming and vivacious Spaniard eighteen years younger than he; the two contrast sharply in temperament and character. Events from the outside world invade the calm and quiet of their domestic life; Milagritos, passionate and nonreflective, wholeheartedly abandons herself to the uprising, while Mr. Witt, logical, reflective, and timid, retreats further into his private world: His "world" and that of the revolution are the two main poles between which the novel is built.

The characterizations of both Mr. Witt and Milagritos are superb, an admirable study in contrasting human psychology. In the end, the uprising is utterly crushed; though Milagritos knows that during the insurrection her husband acted perfidiously, she suspects that his actions were motivated by jealousy, a jealousy that confirms his love for her. Accordingly, she pardons him, and the two resume normal relations. The objective and the subjective, the outer and the inner, are found here in delicate and subtle balance; a serene work, *Mr. Witt Among the Rebels* is probably Sender's best historical novel and surely one of his finest works.

CRÓNICA DEL ALBA

The monumental *Crónica del alba* narrates the author's life from the age of ten to his mid-thirties, the time of the Spanish Civil War. The first part, bearing the title of the novel as a whole—*Chronicle of Dawn*—appeared in 1942 and was well received; it and the second part, *Violent Griffin*, are regarded by Peñuelas as superior to the remaining parts.

The novel is essentially a study in idealism, a returning to one's origins to discover the sources of the idealism that led republican officers such as the protagonist José Garcés (obviously the author's alter ego) to risk their lives in defense of the Second Spanish Republic. José, nicknamed Pepe (Sender himself was called Pepe by members of his family), discovers love in the form of his sweetheart, Valentina, an embodiment of his idealistic values. Though Pepe's grandiose dreams as a ten-year-old boy in the "dawn" of life contrast sharply with the cruel realities of defeat that José the mature man suffers at the end of the series (the "noon" of life), his devotion to Valentina remains firm. Lying ill in a concentration camp in Algiers as the Civil War ends, José writes his autobiography in a desperate attempt to remain a man "of substance." "In a man," he explains, "substance is faith." Purportedly, he gives the three notebooks in which he has written his autobiography to Sender the author, then dies.

Following a chronological order, the series follows José's life from childhood through adolescence, young manhood, and into maturity; through it all, he seeks to live up to the grandiose ideals he had conceived as a child, especially as Valentina's sweetheart. An ancient document found in a castle by the young José declared that the men most needed to ensure the greatness of Spain were saints, poets, and heroes, though "there can be no true saint without a touch of the poet, nor, finally, any of the three without some of the virtues of the others."

In the last volume, Valentina assumes in memory the force of a pure ideal, no longer an entity of flesh and blood but a mysterious influence, a dream, a secret nostalgia for some "lost paradise." It is a longing made all the more poignant by the harsh realities of civil war.

THE SPHERE

A revision and considerable augmentation of an earlier novel, *Proverbio de la muerte*, *The Sphere* could properly be called a new novel; its first Spanish edition appeared in 1947; its definitive edition, slightly augmented and retouched from the first edition, was published in 1969. Sender regarded it as his most serious work; in it, he presents his lifelong belief in the spheroidal nature of all reality. The title of the novel is itself a metaphor of the author's monistic conception of total reality.

While crossing the Atlantic on the way to the Western Hemisphere after having escaped from Spain at the end of the Civil War, Saila, Sender's alter ego, observes that nature is composed of an infinite number of spheres or spheroids. This is true in the infinitely small (atoms), and in the infinitely large (planets, suns, the entire universe). By analogy with observable physical phenomena, Saila imagines that moral life is likewise "spherical," unified but showing two sides or two faces. As day is the other side of night and sound the other side of silence, so hate is the other side of the hate-love sphere, good the other side of evil; even death is only the complementary side of life. Thus, Saila reasons, death does not exist, and this idea becomes the fundamental thesis of the book.

To support his thesis of the nonexistence of death, Sender elaborated in *The Sphere*—and in other works as early as *La noche de las cien cabezas* (the night of one hundred heads), for example—his theory of *hombría* and the "persona." The "persona" is the human mask, the individualization of one's personality, which begins at birth, or soon thereafter, and grows throughout life—human self-consciousness. It is temporal and fears death. On the other hand, *hombría*, or "man-ness," is a mystical essence that endows humans with eternal worth; it is a person's essential self and lives in the unconscious. Upon the death of the individual, it joyfully returns to its source, the Great All or the Great Nothing.

Overladen with metaphysical musings and poetic and symbolic meaning, *The Sphere* loses the reader in a labyrinth of levels, dimensions, and meanings to the detriment of narrative force and direction. As a novel, it fails if a novel is to be judged by traditional criteria—narrative interest, character creation, sense of place, and so on. Perhaps such criteria should not be applied; nevertheless, *The Sphere* is notable for its originality and density of ideas, and it is a key work in understanding Sender's self-made philosophy or what, in all seriousness, amounted to his private religion.

REQUIEM FOR A SPANISH PEASANT

Requiem for a Spanish Peasant (originally titled *Mosén Millán*) is perhaps the most widely read of Sender's novels, at least in the Spanish-speaking world, where it has undergone numerous reprintings in Mexico, Argentina, and Spain; an English-Spanish bilingual edition was issued by Las Americas in New York in 1960. A short novel, it is probably Sender's most perfectly constructed work.

In an unnamed Aragonese village, Mosén Millán, a priest, waits in the sacristy to perform a requiem Mass for Paco, a peasant unjustly executed one year earlier by Nationalist forces in the early days of the Spanish Civil War. This period of waiting while the church bell tolls, calling the villagers to the Mass, lasts about twenty minutes and constitutes the novel's primary plane of action. On this plane, nothing happens except for the arrival of the three men most responsible for Paco's execution, the coming and going of the acolyte (who occasionally recites fragments of a ballad recounting Paco's life and death), the discovery of Paco's colt in the sanctuary and its subsequent ejection, and in the end the priest's moving to the chancel and beginning the Mass—with no one except the acolyte and the dead man's chief enemies (all wealthy) present, while the villagers absent themselves in mute protest against the priest's role, ambiguous and unintentional as it may have been, in the events that led to Paco's execution.

While waiting in vain for people to come to the Mass, the priest in a series of flashbacks reconstructs the story of Paco—the second plane of action—his baptism, childhood, adolescence, marriage, protest against an unjust feudal landholding system, capture, and execution. Past and present are thus skillfully woven together while the ballad recited by the acolyte and interspersed throughout the narrative comes to create what Peñuelas calls a third plane, a legendary one beyond the confines of time.

The structure of *Requiem for a Spanish Peasant*, with the priest and his memories as the focal point, provides it with remarkable unity and compactness; past and present are tightly but unobtrusively interwoven; the classical unities of time, place, and action are almost totally observed; social protest is implicit in the events themselves, related in a sober and objective tone, making such protest all the more effective. Here the author's realism is at its best, and Paco emerges as both an individual and a symbol of the Spanish masses; what happened to him in essence happened throughout Spain during the Civil War. At the same time, Mosén Millán, for whom the events of the narrative constitute a deep personal tragedy, likewise comes to embody the inertia of the Spanish Church and its tragically misguided intervention in secular affairs and lack of social conscience. The ballad, composed anonymously by the villagers, is a projection of the author's idealistic faith in the cause of a just social order. Noble also is the book's vivid and memorable portrayal of the life and customs in a Spanish village early in the twentieth century, its humor—the rough humor of country folk—and its psychological realism in the characterization of Mosén Millán.

Sender was a highly individualistic author who never adhered to any literary movement (nor to any political movement or party, despite some flirtation with the communists in the early 1930's) but who did not hesitate to take whatever seemed useful to him from any and all literary and philosophical movements (existentialism, for example), absorbing and adapting them to his own peculiar mode of expression. The voluminous totality of his production surprises and impresses not only by its great diversity but also by its amazing consistency and unity in outlook and vision as well as its unmistakable style and manner. In a sense to be taken with adequate caution, Sender, like other great writers, wrote only one novel, though he wrote it in more than sixty versions, each revealing a different angle or perspective on that reality called life, the enigma of human existence.

Charles L. King

OTHER MAJOR WORKS

SHORT FICTION: *Novelas ejemplares de Cíbola*, 1961 (*Tales of Cibola*, 1964); *Cabrerizas Altas*, 1965; *Las gallinas de Cervantes, y otras narraciones parabólicas*, 1967.

POETRY: *Las imagenes migratorias*, 1960; *Libro armilar de poesía y memorias bisiestas*, 1974.

NONFICTION: *Viaje a la aldea del crimen*, 1934; *Counter-attack in Spain*, 1937; *Hernán Cortés*, 1940; *Mexicayotl*, 1940; *Examen de ingenios: Los noventayochos*, 1961; *Valle-Inclán y la dificultad de la tragedia*, 1965; *Ensayos sobre el infringimiento cristiano*, 1967; *Tres ejemplos de amor y una teoria*, 1969; *Ensayos del otro mundo*, 1970; *El futuro comenzó ayer*, 1975.

BIBLIOGRAPHY

Devlin, John. *Spanish Anticlericalism: A Study in Modern Alienation*. New York: Las Americas, 1966. Sender is included in this study of anticlerical Spanish literature from the nineteenth and twentieth centuries. Includes a bibliography.

Eoff, Sherman Hinkle. "Ramón J. Sender: *The Sphere* (1949) and *El lugar del hombre* (1939)." In *The Modern Spanish Novel: Comparative Essays Examining the Philosophical Impact of Science on Fiction*. New York: New York University Press, 1961. An analysis of two of Sender's novels, *The Sphere* and *A Man's Place*, is included in this study of Spanish literature.

Hart, Stephen M. *Sender: "Réquiem por un campesino español."* Reprint. 1990. London: Grant & Cutler, 1996. A brief guide to *Requiem for a Spanish Peasant* designed to introduce the novel to graduate and undergraduate students. Includes a revised bibliography.

King, Charles L. *Ramón J. Sender.* New York: Twayne, 1974. An introductory overview to Sender's life, with analysis of his writings. One of the volumes in the Twayne World Authors series. Includes a bibliography.

Lough, Francis. *Politics and Philosophy in the Early Novels of Ramón J. Sender, 1930-1936: The Impossible Revolution.* Lewiston, N.Y.: Edwin Mellen Press, 1996. An analysis of novels published in the early to mid-1930's, in which Sender expressed his concern with the historical background of Spain's social and political problems and with the morality of the anarchists, communists, and other revolutionaries.

Perriam, Chris, et al., eds. *A New History of Spanish Writing, 1939 to the 1990's.* New York: Oxford University Press, 2000. This history of almost sixty years of Spanish writing includes a chapter, "Representing Ordinary Histories: Ramón José Sender and Ignacio Aldecoa," in which Sender's work is discussed.

Trippett, Anthony M. *Adjusting to Reality: Philosophical and Psychological Ideas in the Post-Civil War Novels of Ramon J. Sender.* London: Tamesis Books, 1986. Trippett's analysis of Sender's work focuses on three novels: *The Affable Hangman, Emen hetan,* and *Crónica del alba.* Includes a bibliography.

MIGUEL DE UNAMUNO Y JUGO

Born: Bilbao, Spain; September 29, 1864
Died: Salamanca, Spain; December 31, 1936

PRINCIPAL LONG FICTION
 Paz en la guerra, 1897 (*Peace in War*, 1983)
 Amor y pedagogía, 1902
 Niebla, 1914 (*Mist: A Tragicomic Novel*, 1928)
 Abel Sánchez: Una historia de pasión, 1917 (*Abel Sánchez*, 1947)
 Tres novelas ejemplares y un prólogo, 1920 (*Three Exemplary Novels and a Prologue*, 1930)
 La tía Tula, 1921 (*Tía Tula*, 1976)
 San Manuel Bueno, mártir, 1931 (*Saint Manuel Bueno, Martyr*, 1954)
 Dos novelas cortas, 1961 (James Russell Stamm and Herbert Eugene Isar, editors)

OTHER LITERARY FORMS

Miguel de Unamuno y Jugo (ew-nah-MEW-noh-ee-KEW-goh) wrote extensively in all genres. Manuel García Blanco has compiled Unamuno's works under the title of *Obras completas* (1959-1964), a collection numbering sixteen volumes, edited with prologues and notes. Only a few articles are missing from this collection, published in Madrid by Vergara Editorial, by special concession of Afrodisio Aguado. A later edition, in ten volumes, has appeared since, but neither edition is definitive.

ACHIEVEMENTS

Miguel de Unamuno y Jugo achieved distinction as a philosopher, a novelist, a poet, and a scholar. Fluent in many languages, active in public life, he was indeed a protean figure, and his achievements are still being assimilated. Unamuno had important and influential admirers, particularly among French scholars and writers, such as Jean Cassou, Marcel Bataillon, and Pierre Emmanuel. Martin Heidegger read and admired him. Though studies of existentialism done in English have largely neglected him, Unamuno was among the first to recognize the greatness of Søren Kierkegaard and to adapt his ideas to his own philosophy.

For Hispanists, Unamuno stands among the greatest of Spanish writers. That does not mean that he is without detractors. Pío Baroja, a famous contemporary of Unamuno, predicted that Unamuno's works would not endure. Ramón José Sender, a generation removed from Unamuno, made a similar prediction, and José Ortega y Gasset later added that if Unamuno's virtues are gigantic, so are his defects. Nevertheless, more than a century after Unamuno's birth, scholars are still filling volumes in homage to his works, with a circumspect nod at his idiosyncracies.

Biography

Miguel de Unamuno y Jugo was born in Bilbao, Spain, an important industrial center of the Basque province, on September 29, 1864, the third of six children. His father died when he was six years old. Womanhood exerted a great influence on his work. His early religious training shaped his mind toward a career as a priest, but other influences won out, not the least of which was his childhood sweetheart, Concepción Lizárraga (Concha), who seems never to have had a rival, before or after matrimony, for Unamuno's loyalty.

In *Recuerdos de niñez y de mocedad* (1908; memories of childhood and adolescence), Unamuno recalls highlights of his early years, especially the bombardment of Bilbao in 1874 during the Carlist War. These memories find further development in his first novel, *Peace in War*, and provide a great deal of insight into young Unamuno's state of mind during the four years he spent at the University of Madrid, beginning in 1880. Francisco (Pachico) Zabalbide, a youthful character in the novel, parallels that of Unamuno in his intellectual appetites, his shyness, dreaminess, and the decay in his religious resolve.

Unamuno received his licentiate degree in 1883, and one year later he was awarded the doctorate. That same year (1884), he returned to Bilbao, taught part time, and began publishing in regional newspapers. Following several unsuccessful attempts to obtain posts at the Instituto Viscaíno (Basque Institute), he was appointed the chair of Greek at the University of Salamanca in 1891. In that same year, he married Concha.

Whether writing of current political problems, religion, or professional issues at the university, Unamuno was always outspoken. Yet in 1900, he was named rector of the University of Salamanca. His writing always reflected the agony of the loss of his childhood faith and the struggle to find solutions to the insoluble problems of identity and immortality. A short story, "Ver con los ojos" (using the eyes to see), was published in *El noticiero bilbaíno* in 1886, wherein the introspective young protagonist reflects Unamuno's own questioning of the value of life and his antagonism toward prevailing beliefs.

In 1897, one of Unamuno's children, a son born the previous year, contracted meningitis, which resulted in a terminal hydrocephalic condition. This precipitated a spiritual crisis in Unamuno, and the experience rooted itself so deeply in his thoughts and feelings that it surfaced repeatedly in scenes throughout his works. Following this crisis, Unamuno attempted a return to the religious pursuits of his childhood, but he found that he could not shake himself free of his uncertainties. His life and his works thereafter reflect in varying degrees the agony of tension between his nostalgic attachment to traditional faith and the rending doubts that would not die.

In 1914, for no formally explained reason, Unamuno was relieved of the rectorship at Salamanca. In 1920, he accepted the appointment of vice rector, which he held until 1924, when his open criticism of Primo de Rivera resulted in the loss of his post and his subsequent exile. He went to Fuerteventura, in the Canary Islands, then fled to Paris, then later to Hendaye, France, where he settled for the rest of his exile. Primo de Rivera's dictator-

Miguel de Unamuno y Jugo
(Library of Congress)

ship fell in 1930, and Unamuno returned triumphantly to Spain in February of that year. In 1931, he was reappointed rector at Salamanca.

In May, 1934, death claimed the quiet, unpretentious Concha, his "habit," who had represented the spiritual strength and stability of motherhood for Unamuno and his nine children. In July of that same year, a married daughter, Salomé, also died. A few months later, Unamuno retired from his teaching duties at the university, but he was named lifetime rector, an appointment far more temporary than it promised, notwithstanding the little time left to him. His criticism of Francisco Franco prompted his dismissal, and he was confined to his home, where he died on December 31, 1936.

Analysis

Miguel de Unamuno y Jugo described himself as a man of contradiction and struggle. The intensity of his pursuit of autonomy against a doubtful backdrop of twentieth century dehumanization amounts almost to monomania. The quantity of his output betrays his comfortless conviction that the only immortality he could expect would come from his legacy to the world, either his physical offspring, the children of his body, or his spiritual offspring, the children of his mind. Scholarly attention to his works and personal idiosyncracies thus at least fulfills his hope that his works would keep his name alive.

Unamuno's consciousness is structured by the inevitable life-death cycle and the problem of immortality. He often portrays motherhood as a symbol of immortality and uses, conversely, the barrenness of the womb as a representation of the futility of a life without meaning. His men are reminiscent of Adam in a nonparadisiacal wilderness or of a modern Ishmael in an existential desert. Unamuno constantly wraps the vast limits of his universe about himself like a security blanket, making existence his hobby, profession, and obsession.

In Unamuno's characters, the differentiation between the opposites of good and evil is rarely, if ever, clear-cut. The Good Mother or Earth Mother possesses some of the qualities of the Terrible Mother; the Soul Mate reveals also the aspects of the femme fatale; the hero is also in some respects the antihero.

MIST

Unamuno's *Mist* is the story of Augusto Pérez, an individual whose spirit has never matured and whose personality consequently remains unaffirmed. In his struggle to establish his identity, Augusto feels drawn toward Eugenia, a piano teacher, and he seeks to assert his existence by establishing a vital relationship with her. She, in turn, agrees to marry him but immediately elopes with her former lover. She further plays Augusto for a fool by taking advantage of his willingness to pull her out of economic straits and even to arrange for a comfortable position for her lover in a distant province. On the verge of suicide, Augusto seeks the advice of a certain Miguel de Unamuno, who informs him that he is but a fictitious entity and cannot of his own will work out his own destruction. At this point, Augusto's resolution to kill himself completely dissolves; face-to-face with his creator, he asserts that his existence is as real as Unamuno's own, whereupon Unamuno irascibly retorts that Augusto will die, not because Augusto wills it, but because he, the author, so wills.

In keeping with this typically Unamunian inversion is the fact that Augusto's mother, genuinely concerned with Augusto's welfare, has so smothered him with solicitude that she has absorbed his will, his power to assert himself—his identity. At the moment of her death, her advice to Augusto to look for a wife who will mother him is a recognition of the fact that he is still unable to take care of himself. In her genuine concern, she deprives him of real existence, while Eugenia in her indifference is the agent who brings about the one great assertion in his otherwise meaningless life. Thus, the mother figure is in a sense the femme fatale, while the fatal woman gives him life.

ABEL SÁNCHEZ

The love of paradox evident in *Mist*, characteristic of Unamuno's philosophy as well as of his fiction, animates the novel that many critics regard as his greatest, *Abel Sánchez*. This novel also offers Unamuno's most striking treatment of one of his favorite motifs: the double. In Unamuno's treatment of the archetypal Cain-Abel relationship, "the other one" represents a second self that reminds the Unamunian man of his finiteness. Unamuno sees the sibling rivalry as the battle of man with his alter ego. The "hero" of the novel is not Abel Sánchez but Joaquín Monegro. He is the point-of-view character, but the title gives the story to Abel. Joaquín, it seems, must yield everything to his alter ego, Abel.

Abel's death is the culmination of many events. Abel and Joaquín have known each other since infancy; Abel, an artist, has been the more popular of the two, Joaquín, a doctor, the more intellectual. Joaquín has long been jealous of Abel's attainments, but the jealousy begins to turn to a bitter hatred when Abel steals the affection of Joaquín's sweetheart, Helena. Abel is complacent and easygoing; Heaven seems to smile on him. He paints a portrait of Helena that becomes famous, thus immortalizing her. Joaquín's envy consumes him. With all of his medical training and intellect, Joaquín can only temporarily preserve life; he cannot immortalize it. This idea is shown clearly when one of Joaquín's matronly patients dies, despite his efforts to save her life. Hanging in her living room is a large, stunning portrait: She has been immortalized by Abel.

Fostering his intense hatred for Abel, Joaquín marries Antonia, a motherly woman who pities him. His envy of Abel reaches new proportions when he learns that Helena has given birth to Abel's son, Abelín. When his own wife, Antonia, conceives, she bears a daughter, whom they name Joaquina.

Abel and Joaquín discuss a picture Abel plans to paint—a representation of the Old Testament version of the first murder. The subject tantalizes Joaquín. In addition to the Bible, he reads Lord Byron's *Cain* (1821) and finds himself inexorably identifying with Cain. Abel completes the painting and triumphs again. Joaquín swallows his bitterness and gives a banquet in Abel's honor, making a speech so eloquent that he increases Abel's fame considerably.

As Abelín and Joaquina grow up, the young Abelín decides to study medicine and eventually joins Joaquín as an assistant in his medical office. Joaquín takes heart when he learns that Abelín has little love for his father, whom he regards as a self-contained, rather selfish person. Eventually, Abelín and Joaquina marry. Their first child is a son, whom they name Joaquín. Joaquín tries incessantly to win the affections of his grandson, but as the child grows older, he seems to prefer Abel. Finally, Joaquín, desperately longing for the love of his grandson, approaches his old friend and begs him not to take the boy's love from him, as he has taken everything else during their lifetime. At Abel's cold response, Joaquín angrily grips him by the throat to choke him, but he does not kill him. In that instant, Abel suffers a heart attack. The horror of the moment is intensified as Joaquín realizes that his grandson, too young to comprehend fully the situation, has watched the "murder" from the doorway. The child flees, as if from a madman.

Joaquín is a reflection of the first rebel, the first to fall from grace—Satan himself. His surname, Monegro, insinuates into the reader's consciousness the suggestion of "Monseigneur de Negro"—the Prince of Darkness. This parallel is established in a conversation between Joaquín and Helena. Joaquín confesses to her that he plans to find a mate and get married, but he fears his inability to love. "That's what Don Mateo, the priest, says of the devil—that he can't love," observes Helena.

The devil, then, is the antithesis of God. If God is love, the devil is the negation of love; hence, Joaquín speaks bitterly of the "eternal hatred" that freezes his breast (his reference to the "dragón de hielo," or "ice dragon," recalls Dante's ninth circle of Hell, reserved for those who had committed some act of treachery against love). On his deathbed, Joaquín's last confession consists of an open admission to his wife, Antonia, that he has never loved her; love, he grants, would have saved him, but he has been incapable of loving. Joaquín's life is cankered by envy, the vice that caused the devil's downfall.

SAINT MANUEL BUENO, MARTYR

If Joaquín is a devil figure, Don Manuel in *Saint Manuel Bueno, Martyr* is diametrically opposite. Manuel Bueno, the priest of the village of Valverde de Lucerna, with tremendous personal magnetism, draws the entire village into a faith in life and Christ while he himself agonizes in the conviction that there is nothing after death: no life, no hope, nothing.

The archetype for this work, especially the life-death cycle, is first established in the author's choice of proper names. Manuel (from Immanuel, meaning "God with us") is clearly a Christ figure, his name identifying his function from the outset. Angela Carballino's name betokens at once her angelic tenderness and the fact that she, as the narrator, brings the story to the reader (*Angel*, from the Greek meaning "messenger"). Moreover, she represents the Good Mother or Soul Mate, for she is a life-giver. The reader knows of Manuel only through her; hence, his achievements live on through her instrumentality. Lázaro becomes a foil for Manuel's power for creating "new life" in the irony of the Unamunian way. Manuel raises Lázaro from the deathbed of skepticism to the "new life" of awareness—the awareness of utter death.

The source for the name Blasillo is less readily apparent. Antonio Sánchez Barbudo (in *Estudios sobre Unamuno y Machado*, 1959) sees in the name a reflection of Unamuno's opinion regarding one of Blaise Pascal's *Pensées* (1670). Blasillo (Blas being the equivalent of Blaise), the simple believer, reflects a simple philosophy: "Drink holy water, and it will make you a believer." More plausible, perhaps, is the theory advanced by James Russell Stamm and Herbert Eugene Isar, editors of two short novels by Unamuno, who hold that Blas is typically the name of the credulous rustic, the "rube" of Spanish tradition. He is referred to, they indicate, as a *pobre idiota* (poor idiot) in the novel. Unamuno has pointed out that the word "idiot" in its original Greek means simply a common or ignorant person, or, by extension, a villager. Thus, in the largest sense, Blasillo, with pitiful limitations on his awareness, symbolizes the abandonment from which all the characters suffer. Finally, with greatly compressed irony, Unamuno sets the story in a village named Valverde de Lucerna, which suggests "green valley of eternal light" (*valle verde de luz eterna*)—a paradise that is paradisiacal only through the villagers' ignorance of the dark truth that Manuel hides in his bosom.

The archetypal intent of the novel is further evident in Unamuno's treatment of the setting. Valverde de Lucerna lies "like a brooch" between the lake and the lofty mountain reflected in it. Angela continually links Manuel with the countryside, the mountain, and the lake. To her, "everything revolved around Don Manuel: Don Manuel, the lake and the mountain." Later, alluding to the climactic moment when Lázaro receives Holy Communion, she describes Don Manuel as "white as January snow on the mountain, and moving like the surface of the lake when it is stirred by the northeasterly wind." Water (the lake) is a symbol of the mystery of creation, as well as the source of life, the element of the security of prenatal confinement. It is also, according to Carl Jung, the most common symbol of the unconscious. Earth (the mountain) symbolizes the harvest, productivity, and—by contrast to the water symbol—consciousness. Reflecting on life, Don Manuel observes, "Have you seen, Lázaro, a greater mystery than the snow falling on the lake, and dying there, while it covers the mountain with a hood?" Snow represents death, enshrouding everything except the lake. Beneath this shroud, conscious life and achievements disappear, yet death itself disappears in the mystery of creation. Moreover, Don Manuel is torn between his conscious desire to act and the agonizing urge to return to the source of creation.

The setting provides still another symbol for the life-death cycle in the magnificent walnut tree that, even after it has dried up, continues to give life to the village—in the form of toys for the children and wood for the poor. Manuel calls the tree a matriarchal tree and fashions his coffin out of the wood of its trunk, for in his suffering, he longs to return to the primordial womb, or the origin of creation. The tree is a symbol of the Earth Mother, who gives life, harbors and protects her "children." Manuel's longing is repeated in his attraction for the lake, toward which he is drawn irresistibly. The lake here represents the peace of prenativity, the urge to return to the womb, the source of life.

Don Manuel seems to find in the lake the secret of his spiritual agony. Village tradition has it that after death, fortunate souls go to dwell in a city at the bottom of the lake—a city identical to their own. Part of Manuel's "sacrificial punishment" (he suffers so that his village may be free from suffering) is that he must carry inside himself the knowledge that the heaven the people see for themselves is but a reflection of their own lives. The only life after death, as Manuel envisions it, is the essence created by the individual—that pitiful portion of one's identity that he leaves behind in others. His mission is to keep this awful secret to himself and let the villagers dream their lives as the lake dreams the heavens.

Manuel's yearning for the maternal confines of prenativity, reflected in both his attraction for the lake and his fascination with the walnut tree, suggests the motherhood motif, a motif elaborated more fully and literally in the two principal female figures, Don Manuel's mother and Angela, both of whom function as Christian symbols of the life-giving, almost divine Mother. They provide an absorbing influence for Manuel's overriding anguish. When he reaches the climactic moment of his Good Friday High Mass, his personal suffering overflows in his cry, "My God, My God, why hast thou forsaken me?" At that moment, the people believe they are hearing the Lord Jesus Christ himself, his voice springing from the ancient Crucifix. On one such occasion, Manuel's mother, hearing his words and sensing his anguish, cries out to him, "My son," and it is as if her cry has issued from the lips of the Mater Dolorosa, "her heart transfixed by seven swords."

Don Manuel, with the power and trust to absolve the town's citizens of their sins, is the spiritual father of them all, but Angela, even from the beginning, senses a deeper participation in Manuel's life and struggles than is typical of the generic body of his "flock." She yearns for his personal protection and feels the need of his personal influence. Her opening words:

> I want to leave in writing my testimony . . . of all that I remember of that matriarchal man who pervaded the most secret life of my soul, who was my true father, the father of my spirit, the spirit of myself, Angela Carballino.

Then, following her first confession with Don Manuel, an inversion begins to take place in their relationship. Her original feelings of awe become compassion and intuitive understanding. She has already begun to fill the need for him that she originally felt was her own. She observes that, even though only a girl, she has felt the flow and stirrings of maternity, and finding herself in the confessional next to the priest, she senses his own quiet confession in the submissive murmur of his voice. As her feelings deepen, she sees herself with qualities that the reader can identify with the Good Mother, for she longs to absorb Don Manuel's sorrow, sensing his need for solace and refuge. She says:

> I missed my Don Manuel, as if his absence called to me, as if he were endangered by my being so far away, as if he were in need of me. I began to feel a kind of maternal affection for my spiritual father; I longed to help him bear the cross of birth.

Finally, in her ultimate role as the redeeming Good Mother, she hears the echo of Manuel's own mother's voice within her, crying, "My son!" He, at last, is unable to withhold from her his awful secret, and he begs her to absolve him from blame for his pious deceit. She assumes a matriarchal priesthood that invests her with the voice of the whole village, and she absolves her confessor "in the name of the Father, the Son, and the Holy Ghost." As they leave the church, she again feels the tremblings of maternity within her.

It is in her role as both spiritual daughter and mother that she reflects the angelic qualities that her name suggests. In her relationship with Don Manuel there are also clear resonances of the Virgin Mary. Angela, who remains a virgin all of her life, becomes the immaculate spiritual mother to the Savior of Valverde de Lucerna, Don Manuel, thus assuming the same ironic qualities of deification that Unamuno vouchsafes to Manuel. She fills the function reserved in more orthodox theology for the Holy Ghost. As Manuel administers his last Communion, he whispers to Angela while giving her the Host, "Pray, my child, pray for us . . . and pray also for Our Lord Jesus Christ." Angela is the earthly version of the Virgin Mother, a Mother of Sorrows, to whom the tormented priest turns in his need.

Unamuno calls his hero a martyr, and so he is. A martyr gives his life for what he believes. Manuel believes in his mission: to give solace, consolation, and faith to others. He does not believe in the Resurrection or in life everlasting. On the traditional expectation that a priest should be personally engaged in that faith, a champion of his own convictions, rests the Unamunian irony: Manuel gives his life for what he does not believe. Martyrs create faith, says Unamuno; faith does not create martyrs.

Unamuno styled himself a man of contradiction and struggle, and so he proved to be. The struggle that characterized his own life finds reflections in the lives of all of his fictional offspring. Absolutes, like mirages, disappear as one draws close enough to them to feel that they are within one's grasp. Unamuno's characters reflect the lonely condition of humankind without God, and in this respect, Unamuno's message has never ceased to be timely.

Harold K. Moon

OTHER MAJOR WORKS

SHORT FICTION: *El espejo de la muerte*, 1913; *Soledad y otros cuentos*, 1937; *Abel Sánchez, and Other Stories*, 1956.

PLAYS: *La esfinge*, pr. 1909 (wr. 1898); *La difunta*, pr. 1910; *La princesa doña Lambra*, pb. 1913; *La venda*, pb. 1913 (wr. 1899); *Fedra*, pr. 1918 (wr. 1910; *Phaedra*, 1959); *El pasado que vuelve*, pr. 1923 (wr. 1910); *Raquel encadenada*, pr. 1926 (wr. 1921); *Sombras de sueño*, pr., pb. 1930; *El otro*, pr., pb. 1932 (wr. 1926; *The Other*, 1947); *El hermano Juan: O, El mundo es teatro*, pb. 1934 (wr. 1927); *Soledad*, pr. 1953 (wr. 1921); *Teatro completo*, pb. 1959.

POETRY: *Poesías*, 1907; *Rosario de sonetos líricos*, 1911; *El Cristo de Velázquez*, 1920 (*The Christ of Velázquez*, 1951); *Rimas de dentro*, 1923; *Teresa*, 1924; *Romancero del destierro*, 1928; *Poems*, 1952; *Cancionero: Diario poético*, 1953 (partial translation as *The Last Poems of Miguel de Unamuno*, 1974).

NONFICTION: *Nicodemo el fariseo*, 1899; *De la enseñanza superior en España*, 1899; *Tres ensayos*, 1900; *En torno al casticismo*, 1902; *De mi país*, 1903; *Vida de Don Quijote y Sancho según Miguel de Cervantes Saavedra, explicada y comentada por Miguel de Unamuno*, 1905 (*The Life of Don Quixote and Sancho According to Miguel de Cervantes Saavedra Expounded with Comment by Miguel de Unamuno*, 1927); *Recuerdos de niñez y de mocedad*, 1908; *Mi religión, y otros ensayos breves*, 1910; *Soliloquios y conversaciones*, 1911 (*Essays and Soliloquies*, 1925); *Contra esto y aquello*, 1912; *Del sentimiento trágico de la vida en los hombres y en los pueblos*, 1913 (*The Tragic Sense of Life in Men and in Peoples*, 1921); *La agonía del Cristianismo*, 1925 (in French as *L'Agonie du Christianisme*; in Spanish 1931; *The Agony of Christianity*, 1928, 1960); *Cómo se hace una novela*, 1927 (*How to Make a Novel*, 1976); *La ciudad de Henoc*, 1941; *Cuenca* ibérica, 1943; *Paisajes del alma*, 1944; *La enormidad de España*, 1945; *Visiones y commentarios*, 1949; *Tratado del amor de Dios*, 2005 (wr. 1905-1908; *Treatise on Love of God*, 2007).

MISCELLANEOUS: *De Fuerteventura a París*, 1925; *Obras completas*, 1959-1964 (16 volumes).

BIBLIOGRAPHY

Ellis, Robert Richmond. *The Tragic Pursuit of Being: Unamuno and Sartre*. Tuscaloosa: University of Alabama Press, 1988. Ellis compares and contrasts the existential ideas revealed in the works of Unamuno and Jean-Paul Sartre. Includes a bibliography and an index.

Evans, Jan E. *Unamuno and Kierkegaard: Paths to Selfhood in Fiction*. Lanham, Md.: Lexington Books, 2005. Evans examines how Unamuno was influenced by the ideas of Danish philosopher Søren Kierkegaard. Analyzes three of Unamuno's novels— *Mist*, *Saint Manuel Bueno, Martyr*, and *Abel Sánchez*—from a Kierkegaardian perspective.

Franz, Thomas R. *Unamuno's Paratexts: Twisted Guides to Contorted Narratives*. Newark, Del.: Juan de la Cuesta, 2006. Focuses on paratextual material, such as epigraphs, prefaces, postlogues, epilogues, and notes, in Unamuno's novels and novellas. Franz argues these materials are an integral part of the narratives and describes how Unamuno makes use of these devices.

Hansen, Keith W. *Tragic Lucidity: Discourse of Recuperation in Unamuno and Camus*. New York: Peter Lang, 1993. Hansen examines the political and social views of Unamuno and Albert Camus, as evidenced in their literary works, to arrive at a twentieth century definition of tragedy. Includes a bibliography.

Jurkevich, Gayana. *The Elusive Self: Archetypal Approaches to the Novels of Miguel de Unamuno*. Columbia: University of Missouri Press, 1991. Jurkevich examines Unamuno's work from the perspective of Jungian analytical psychology and discusses the writer's psychological portrayal of his characters. Includes bibliographical references and an index.

Nozick, Martin. *Miguel de Unamuno*. New York: Twayne, 1971. An introductory overview, featuring a biography and discussion of Unamuno's works. Includes a bibliography. One of the volumes in the Twain World Authors series.

Olson, Paul R. *The Great Chiasmus: Word and Flesh in the Novels of Unamuno*. West Lafayette, Ind.: Purdue University Press, 2003. Examines Unamuno's use of chiasmus— parallel phrases in which there is a reversal in the order of words or parts of speech. Olson demonstrates how this word order transforms things that appear to be contrary by making them easily reversible and therefore identical.

Rubia Barcia, José, and M. A. Zeitlin, eds. *Unamuno: Creator and Creation*. Berkeley: University of California Press, 1967. A collection of transcripts of lectures from a program commemorating the centennial of the birth of Unamuno. Contains valuable biographical material and critical studies. Includes bibliographical references.

Sinclair, Alison. *Uncovering the Mind: Unamuno, the Unknown, and the Vicissitudes of Self.* New York: Manchester University Press, 2002. An examination of the fictional works of Unamuno, including the novels *Mist* and *Tía Tula*, that focuses on his portrayal of the self. Includes a bibliography and an index.

JUAN VALERA

Born: Cabra, Spain; October 18, 1824
Died: Madrid, Spain; April 18, 1905
Also known as: Juan Valera y Alcalá Galiano

PRINCIPAL LONG FICTION
Mariquita y Antonio, 1861
Pepita Jiménez, 1874 (*Pepita Ximenez*, 1886)
Las ilusiones del doctor Faustino, 1875
El comendador Mendoza, 1877 (*Commander Mendoza*, 1893)
Pasarse de listo, 1878 (*Don Braulio*, 1892)
Doña Luz, 1879 (English translation, 1891)
Juanita la larga, 1896
Genio y figura, 1897
Morsamor, 1899

OTHER LITERARY FORMS

The first edition of the collected works (*Obras completas*, 1905-1935) of Juan Valera (vah-LEHR-ah) came to fifty-three volumes. In addition to his nine novels, he published poetry, drama, and short stories. He composed short stories early in his career, worked again in the genre in midcareer, and returned to the form more assiduously during the last decade of his life.

Valera also was a notable literary critic, with a number of volumes to his credit, among them *Disertaciones y juicios literarios* (1878; literary discourses and judgments), *Apuntes sobre el nuevo arte de escribir novelas* (1887; notes on the new art of writing novels), *Nuevos estudios críticos* (1883; new critical studies), and *Cartas americanas* (1889; American letters). If his criticism were to be faulted, it would be on the grounds of unwarranted benevolence toward some of his less gifted contemporaries and occasionally hastily conceived, shallow reviews; if it is to be especially praised, it is for opening the public's eyes to the then largely unknown field of Latin American literature. In general, his point of view was classically conservative.

Finally, there is Valera's five-volume edition of the *Florilegio de poesías castellanas del siglo XIX* (1902-1903; anthology of nineteenth century Spanish poetry) and his translation into Spanish of Adolf F. Schack's *Poesie und Kunst der Araber in Spanien und Sicilien* (1865) as *Poesía y arte en los árabes en España y Sicilia* (1867, 1868, 1871). In addition to almost every form of literature, critical and creative alike, Valera wrote on matters political and social and left a large body of well-crafted letters, of which more than a thousand have already turned up, addressed to his many friends in Spain and abroad.

Achievements

Although today Juan Valera is remembered mainly for the ever-popular *Pepita Ximenez* (and perhaps to a lesser extent for *Juanita la larga*), during the latter part of the nineteenth and into the twentieth century, he ranked high among the great Spanish novelists and even among the better Spanish critics of his day. His complete works in fifty-three volumes appeared in Madrid from 1905 to 1935, and the widely disseminated Aguilar compact series devoted to him a three-volume set of virtually the same material. Only Benito Pérez Galdós, the dominant Spanish novelist of that time, stood preeminently above him. Because Pérez Galdós himself and other potential rivals, such as Emilia Pardo Bazán, Leopoldo Alas (Clarín), and José María de Pereda, wrote in the realistic or naturalistic vein, the one serious competitor in Valera's chosen field was probably Armando Palacio Valdés, whose *La hermana San Sulpicio* (1889; *Sister San Sulpicio*, 1890), in subject, treatment, and acclaim, bears favorable comparison to the best of Valera's work.

Valera was also an excellent critic of the literature of his day and was largely responsible for popularizing with the Spanish public the works of the then quite ignored Latin American writers from across the sea, especially the Nicaraguan poet Rubén Darío. Indeed, Valera's early election into the Spanish Academy was principally the result of his criticism rather than of his (rather slim) accomplishments as a poet. His career as a novelist was still in the future. It might be added that his short stories and plays come to no more than should be expected from any major writer in a related genre.

Valera's long diplomatic career did not prevent an impressively large literary output: Forty works bear his name, including works he not only wrote but also edited and translated. Only in a country such as Spain, proverbial for the abundant output of its writers (Lope de Vega y Carpio reputedly penned more than two thousand plays, of which more than four hundred are indisputably his; Pérez Galdós wrote some one hundred novels and dramas), could Valera be considered slothful. By any other national standard, his production is impressive.

Biography

Juan Valera, whose full name is Juan Valera y Alcalá Galiano, was born on October 18, 1824, in Cabra, a hill town some thirty-five miles southeast of Córdoba, Spain. His parents were distinguished if not affluent, his mother of the Spanish nobility, his father a naval officer, and his maternal uncle the famous orator and politician Antonio Alcalá Galiano. Valera attended a good secondary school in Málaga from 1837 to 1840, studied law in Granada's Colegio del Sacro Monte and in Madrid, and—back in Granada—graduated in 1844. Though an avid reader of literary classics, he was not a diligent student. It might be noted that many nineteenth century Spanish undergraduate law majors never intended a career in jurisprudence. Such degrees were closer to what would be considered today as the bachelor of arts. Valera, however, despite predictable excursions into the field of literature (a few poems in magazines and a volume of verses whose publication was subsidized by his father as a graduation present), actually attempted to practice law in Madrid.

Valera's family connections gave him entrée into high society. It was a pleasant but unremunerative existence; he soon had to think of correcting his course. Diplomacy appeared a more likely choice, and, after a slow start, it proved a good one. He obtained an unofficial post in Naples, working for his friend the great Romantic author the Duque de Rivas, at the time Spanish Ambassador, from 1847 to 1849. Valera was sent to Lisbon in 1850 and to Rio de Janeiro in 1851. There followed a post in Dresden (1855) and a visit to Russia (1856).

Returning to Spain, Valera ran for the office of deputy (similar to the position of congressman) in 1858, an office he held during two not very outstanding terms. In 1865, he received his first really important diplomatic appointment as minister in Frankfurt. In 1868, Isabel II lost her throne; Valera became undersecretary of state for most of one year. He even helped choose Amadeo of Savoy as the new king of Spain in 1870 and was made director of public instruction, if only for a very short time. The king soon abdicated, leaving Valera out of political favor. For seven years, Valera devoted himself to writing.

During previous lulls in his public career, Valera had already managed to produce a volume of poetry in 1858, helped found two satiric literary magazines in the two succeeding years, and was editor in chief for the middle-of-the-road *El contemporáneo* (where his first, unfinished, novel *Mariquita y Antonio* appeared in 1861). Although he had only one book to his credit, the 1858 volume of poetry (an earlier one in 1844 had sold so poorly that he had had it withdrawn from the market), he was elected in 1861 into the Spanish Academy, whose standards, it must be admitted, were somewhat less strict than those of its sister institution in France.

Valera's first collection of essays—*Estudios críticos sobre literatura, política, y costumbres de nuestros días* (critical studies on contemporary literature, politics, and customs)—appeared in 1864. In 1867, by then in his early forties, he married Dolores Delavat, a daughter of a career diplomat, whom he had first known in Rio de Janeiro in 1851. She was half his age, stubborn, and extravagant; he was usually strapped for funds, given to sarcasm, and notably fond of affairs of the heart (an early addiction still catered to long after his marriage). It was not an especially happy union, although they never separated, and the last few years proved somewhat calmer.

From 1881 to 1883, needing funds to support a growing family along with his extravagant wife, Valera accepted a post as minister in Lisbon, where the accusation of certain financial and political improprieties almost led to a duel. He resigned the position, supposing that his career was ruined but, on the contrary, the next year he was appointed minister to the United States in Washington, D.C. His wife stayed in Spain with the children.

Washington, D.C., like almost all of his appointments, seemed a mixed blessing. He was forever impugning the climate, the manners, the dress, or the tastes of the places—European or American—where he served his country. American men he termed dull money-grubbers; as always, however, he enjoyed the women. One of them, Katherine Lee

Bayard, the twenty-eight-year-old daughter of the U.S. secretary of state, loved him deeply enough to commit suicide in 1886, on hearing that he was to return to Spain. Despite her death and that of his eldest son from typhoid, he seems to have enjoyed his transatlantic stay. Besides his usual active social life, he found time to read generously from American literature, even translating a few poems by James Russell Lowell and John Greenleaf Whittier with an eye to adding fifty or so more to make up a whole book, a project that died aborning.

Valera's last two diplomatic posts were as minister in Brussels, from 1886 to 1887, and, after a six-year lapse, in Vienna, from 1893 to 1895. There ended his diplomatic career, rendered untenable by questionable health and increasing blindness. Returning to Madrid, he resumed his pursuit of literature. Even in government harness, he had produced *Cartas americanas* and *Nuevas cartas americanas* (1890; new American letters), discussing Latin American writers such as the Nicaraguan *Modernismo* poet Rubén Darío. Full-time commitment allowed for three more novels—*Juanita la larga* (shrewd Juanita), usually considered his best after *Pepita Ximenez*; *Genio y figura* (the title a shortened version of "genio y figura hasta la sepultura," an expression signifying "what's bred in the bone will be with you until you die"); and his historical novel, *Morsamor*—as well as short stories, essays, polemics, and an extensively annotated five-volume anthology of nineteenth century Spanish poetry. Valera died peacefully on April 18, 1905, while composing a discourse to be delivered before his beloved Spanish Academy.

The author-cum-diplomat was a proud man, at times even haughty, a chronic complainer, occasionally belligerent. He was often guilty of provincialism, not above denigrating foreign writers who dared pass judgment on things Spanish. He could be superficial and flighty, traits he exhibited all of his adult years. That he utilized some dozen publishers during his writing career is somewhat unusual, though the large body of his oeuvre may to some extent justify what seems to indicate a difficult personality. He was quite outspoken, a characteristic not always found among professional diplomats. Yet, despite his thorniness, he was normally kind to writers of his own generation in Spain (even too kind, some critics have objected), and he encouraged young writers and scholars. The public tends to expect social and moral perfection in its famous men. Valera might fail his critics, but he remains basically someone to honor and respect.

ANALYSIS

Juan Valera's constant preoccupation with language and form (not merely in a restricted but also in a spiritual sense); his knowledge of and deep respect for the classics, which he doubted modern authors could surpass; his demand for balance and moderation; his belief in absolute ideals; his rejection of Romantic excesses and imperfections—all bespeak a latter-day classicist. Where he diverges somewhat from classicism is in what could be called the pleasure principle. The aim of art is to please; it has no intrinsic end, moral or instructive. Its goal is beauty alone. Valera derided the ancient Roman Horace's famous precept that art should be at once useful and delightful. Valera's demand, so often heard from nineteenth century writers, was "art for art's sake," a phrase capable of various interpretations and inevitably given them, as often occurs with aesthetic theories.

Valera's most famous pronouncement on his concept of the ideal novel is to be found in the preface to *Pepita Ximenez*:

> A pretty novel cannot be a servile, prosaic, common representation of life; a pretty novel should be poetry, not history; it should depict things, not as they are, but more beautiful than they are, casting upon them a light with a certain magical charm.

He disliked the prevailing doctrine of naturalism, enunciated by Émile Zola in France and taken up in Spain by Pardo Bazán and Clarín, which to Valera justified wallowing in things filthy and unpleasant, sexually degraded, morbid, and diseased, in an attempt to show what life was really like, especially for the great masses of the poor.

Valera's word *bonita* (pretty), as opposed to the naturalists' seeming preference for the ugly, must not, however, be understood to justify insipidity or smothering the reader in sweetness and light. Even the rather idyllic *Pepita Ximenez* hints strongly at seduction and presents a sixteen-year-old heroine forced to marry an unlovable old man in his eighties, as well as a bastard hero who breaks his religious vows to marry her. Furthermore, Valera confessed that this early novel echoed his benevolent view of life at the time. His later novels often describe more unpleasant events, tragic failures, broken loves—one novel even features a prostitute as protagonist. Valera knew the seamier side of life and could on occasion depict it. Some of his uncharacteristic short stories (in the 1898 collection *Cuentos y chascarrillos andaluces*) are actually pornographic, but normally, with good classicist reticence, he chose to select aspects of life refined through the sieve of artistry. If the expression "pretty novel" must be taken with a grain of salt, Valera still remains far from Zolaesque naturalism.

Finally, Valera's psychological acumen warrants mention. More than his rather conventional, occasionally clumsy plots and as much as his fine eye for the accurate physical detail, it is his knowledge of the human psyche that lends depth and credibility to his fiction. His characters convince because their creator accurately sounds the wellsprings of their actions. His long life and his experiences around the world served him well.

What term, then, best fits his literary theory and practice? "Neoclassicism" as well as any, yet his predilection for heroes that mirror, if imperfectly, his own character and events from his own life, heroines who embody his ideals of womanhood, his love of outer nature, his sensuous side—all indicate Romanticist. His mocking, detached, worldly, rational attitude toward life suggests eighteenth century rationalism. He can reflect paganism and Christianity in turn. He really is not like any other Spanish writer of his day: a genius unto himself. Many critics have foundered trying to categorize the elusive quality of his literary production.

Valera, who was seemingly born to write, who took up the career of diplomacy as a livelihood rather than as a vocation, who published a volume of poetry at age twenty, who, in high school, read extensively from such literary masters as Voltaire, William Shakespeare, and Sir Walter Scott, still failed to compose anything in the field of the novel—his one real claim to greatness—until well into maturity. He had written criticism since 1853 and a second volume of poetry in 1858, helped found two literary reviews, and edited a newspaper between 1859 and 1863, but his first novel began to appear in 1861 in the literary section of his own newspaper. Even then, he abandoned it in midstream. Its main importance lies in its foreshadowing of many of the characteristics of his later fiction, from 1874 on.

To understand what Valera was offering his public, it is necessary to say a word about the status of the nineteenth century Spanish novel. In the 1830's and 1840's, Spain was copying the Romantic novel of the school of Scott, but not the social novels of Charles Dickens or William Makepeace Thackeray. Eighteenth century Spanish literature had not enjoyed the richness of French and English literature of the period, particularly in the field of the novel. Miguel de Cervantes' *Don Quixote de la Mancha* (1605, 1615), often termed the first modern novel and a unique masterpiece, had had no worthy offspring. Hence, Spain's reentry into the mainstream of the European novel came about by a different route.

In the 1830's, a popular literary form was a little local-color sketch describing regional customs—a country fair, peasant dances, a religious holiday, and the like—which in Spain is called *costumbrismo* (*costumbres* meaning "customs" in Spanish). The *costumbrista* format permitted realism but downplayed reality's drab side. In 1849, the writer Fernán Caballero was the first to combine a group of related *costumbrista* sketches with a story line into a novel, *La gaviota* (1856; *The Seagull*, 1864). From this badly flawed effort, the Spanish regional novel of the second half of the nineteenth century was born, destined to produce a distinguished group of practitioners: Pereda, Pérez Galdós, Pedro Antonio, and Valera himself, among others.

Mariquita y Antonio

Mariquita y Antonio is such a regional novel, a genre to which Valera was to turn again and again. The beautiful, capable heroine Mariquita is the niece of the keeper of the pension (depicted realistically, even humorously) where the law student, Antonio, is staying. The latter is hardly the serious type. He gambles, indulges in love affairs, composes poetry. He is, in short, the amorous Valera as young law student (1840-1844), in the same city (autobiographical elements do not prove uncommon in Valera's later work). Improbably, Mariquita is kidnapped, and the story breaks off before one learns whether Antonio, for all of his taking her disappearances to heart, really loved her. Originally, his aim simply had been to seduce this woman whom he considered beneath him socially.

Valera lost interest in or could not find time to continue the work. The reader cannot feel any deep sense of loss: The novel, at least in the chapters at hand, is not well developed; the heroine, who is, as usual with Valera, the principal character, is not clearly defined; there is on the face of it no good reason for the melodramatic kidnapping. It would not have been easy to rectify these flaws in the unfinished section, as perhaps Valera realized in abandoning his project.

PEPITA XIMENEZ

Valera's next attempt at full-length fiction, *Pepita Ximenez*, almost certainly his finest work, became an immediate success and has remained a staple of Spanish literature ever since. The author was almost fifty; he had spent more than thirty years polishing his craft when he sent his first completed novel to press. He had lived in Madrid, Lisbon, Rio de Janeiro, Dresden, St. Petersburg, and Frankfurt; he was an experienced diplomat; he had had several love affairs and had already been married for six years. This novel was hardly the first fruit of an apprentice in literature or in the business of life itself.

The setting is once again Andalusia. The structure is classically tight, almost too intricate. Section 1 is titled "Letters from My Nephew," given the reader by the dean of a religious seminary, the uncle of the protagonist, Luis. Section 2, "Paralipómenos" ("Supplementary Revelations"), is followed by the coda "Letters from My Brother." The Greek title for section 2, many occasional phrases in the text itself, references in the preface and elsewhere in his writings approving of an idealized depiction of reality, and his meticulous attention to form and style all hint at Valera's leanings toward classicism. He shows an equal love and appreciation for and knowledge of the sixteenth century Spanish mystics, such as Saint Teresa de Ávila and Saint John of the Cross. Robert Lott, in his *Language and Psychology in "Pepita Jiménez"* (1970), has revealed the extent of Valera's debt to both of these mystics, from whom he borrowed many ideas and much religious terminology (here sometimes used profanely). Lott has also analyzed Valera's style, a carefully balanced mixture of Spanish Golden Age turns of phrase, archaisms, and grammar with nineteenth century refinements.

Luis de Vargas, twenty-two years of age, reared by his uncle in the relative seclusion of a religious seminary, returns to visit his worldly-wise father, a local political power and small-town leader, before taking his final vows as a priest. He happens to be illegitimate and as a result experiences a sense of guilt mixed with pride in the brilliant future he envisages for himself, converting heathens in faraway lands. Valera suggests that Luis is only falsely devout; he intends to achieve union with God through effecting salvation for others, not by mortifying himself before Him. In short, he is a dubious candidate for the rigors of missionary life.

This proud, naïve young man meets the irresistible Pepita Ximenez, one in a long line of Valera's vivacious Andalusian heroines, beautiful, charming, clever, an idealized version of most men's concept of the perfect wife. The formula may vary on occasion: mistress, not wife, her perfection perhaps flawed, not merely clever but scheming. Rarely, however, are these women actually antipathetic, Pepita least of all. She had already been married at the age of sixteen to a very elderly, unprepossessing moneylender and is now a widow of only twenty. Luis, as is clearly shown in letters to his uncle, gradually becomes infatuated with her. The uncle warns him to break short his visit. Obviously, Luis will not. His attempts to explain away his newfound attraction for Pepita are scarcely convincing (nor are they meant to be), and his naïveté in failing to diagnose his love borders on the incredible, but he is such a likable chap, she so desirable, that from the very start the reader wants him to abandon his priestly vocation and opt for marriage. Thus, his growing worldliness, his pleasure in the sensual beauty of the Andalusian countryside, his pride in finding that he can ride a horse well, his gradual if reluctant feeling of congeniality with his father, and his final spiritual downfall (which outraged certain Spanish religious conservatives) are all quite palatable.

This downfall, fittingly occurring on Saint John's Eve—that is, Midsummer's Eve, from time immemorial devoted to merrymaking and amorous escapades the world over—is spectacular. Luis announces to Pepita his decision to give her up and return to the seminary. There is a tearful scene in her parlor; she runs into her bedroom; he follows her; and when he emerges some time later, he has obviously succumbed. The language—Valera is rarely crude, and certainly not in this novel—is oblique but realistic, the whole scene effective, even somewhat humorous. Neither author nor reader thinks Heaven has lost a sinner. Rather, an innocent young man has grown up. Now considering himself in a position to retaliate more properly, he returns to the casino where he had earlier been forced to endure insults to Pepita's morals uttered by a rejected suitor, challenges him to a duel, and nearly kills him. The former seminarian's transformation is now complete. He becomes his father's son and marries Pepita. The obligatory *costumbrista* village wedding scene concludes the novel.

This bare outline cannot do more than hint at the felicities of style, the charm of the local color (if not as pronounced here as in some of Valera's later novels, still quite in evidence), the author's psychological perspicacity, and his feeling for the beauty of outer nature used to symbolize Luis's increasingly secular love. There may be countless novels more powerful than this one, but few more captivating or better crafted. The reader's joy echoes the writer's own; as Valera said, it came when he felt most healthy, optimistic, and warm toward the whole world. He added, "Unfortunately, it will not happen again."

LAS ILUSIONES DEL DOCTOR FAUSTINO

No sooner had Valera published *Pepita Ximenez* serially in the distinguished *Revista de España* than the first installments of his next novel, *Las ilusiones del doctor Faustino*, started to appear in the same magazine, in October, 1874. Much longer than any of his other novels, it is at the same time philosophically his most ambitious. Valera fully intended the allusive name he bestowed on his protagonist. "Although," he wrote,

> I am not very fond of symbols or allegories . . . Dr. Faustino has something of the symbolic or allegorical about him . . . a man for a whole contemporary generation . . . Dr. Faust in miniature, without magic, without a devil . . . a composite of the vices, ambitions, dreams, scepticism, disbelief, and longings that afflicted the youth of my day.

In a word, Faustino is a Romantic, one of those who embodies "useless knowledge, political ambitions, aristocratic prejudices," according to Valera, who considered his creation his most real literary achievement. It is nevertheless debatable whether this petty Faust is strong enough to support so lofty a philosophical superstructure, even if Christopher Marlowe's original was equally lightweight. It is Johann Wolfgang von Goethe's later incarnation that possesses the grandeur more naturally inviting comparison.

Clarín, Valera's fellow novelist and a percipient critic as well, considering the novel one of the most important in nineteenth century Spanish literature, compared it to Gustave Flaubert's *L'Éducation sentimentale* (1869; *A Sentimental Education*, 1898). Frédéric, like Faustino, is indeed a Romantic weakling, buffeted by the fates of his time, but Flaubert did not ask him to stand for a Romantic Everyman as Valera expected of Faustino. Few critics today would rank Valera's novel very high, much less in a class with Flaubert's counterpart.

The plot involves most of Faustino's life. It begins with his days as a young law student at the University of Granada (another of the autobiographical details so numerous in Valera's fiction), from which he is graduated without having burned much midnight oil.

He hopes for an important career in Madrid in law, the government, or perhaps journalism, but realizes that his talents are not matched by the necessary wealth. Marriage with his rather well-to-do cousin, Costanza, fails to materialize. Back in his small hometown, he takes up with Rosita, though considering her beneath him. They spend a night together, but he abandons her for María, who turns out to be the illegitimate daughter of a bandit by whom Faustino is later kidnapped. In all fairness to Valera, it should be noted that this bit of melodrama is to an extent necessary for the plot, and capture by highwaymen was a recurrent nightmare for Spanish travelers at the time, but the author is never especially felicitous in his handling of action scenes. They rarely ring true or seem well motivated. This one at least keeps the hero out of town long enough to let Rosita, the woman scorned, have her father foreclose on the property of Faustino's mother, who dies from worry and sorrow.

Faustino moves to Madrid and, by now middle-aged, is eking out a living as a subordinate government bureaucrat. María arrives in the city with a sixteen-year-old daughter; María and Faustino marry. He should at last find success and happiness with the only woman who really loves him, but he dissipates his opportunities and, worse, resumes his old affair with cousin Costanza. Rosita, ever vindictive, avenges herself on the man who jilted her by telling his wife. María dies of sorrow; Faustino kills himself. This weak Romantic, suffering from what a later generation of Spanish writers at the turn of the twentieth century came to call *abulia* ("lack of willpower," "apathy," after the psychological term "aboulia"), a disease afflicting the whole country in their eyes, falls victim to his own flawed character and the faults of his day: bad education, political chaos, aristocratic social climbing.

Is Faustino really Valera's alter ego? They had the same education, the same trouble in deciding on a career. Valera eventually became internationally famous, but in 1874 he was only beginning to find himself as a writer, and successes in his diplomatic career were balanced by some notable failures. He quite likely saw himself in many ways as another Romantic Faustino. At the least, his is a cautionary tale, with himself an example for those who could read between the lines.

Some of the early parts of the story recall the unfinished *Mariquita y Antonio*, while Cyrus C. DeCoster, in *Bibliografía crítica de Juan Valera* (1970), notes a similarity between the theme and the character of Faustino and those of a projected novel Valera titled "Currito the Optimist," about a spendthrift who tried to make a pact with the Devil. DeCoster dates the few extant pages of the manuscript as probably early 1850's. Valera's plots tend toward repetition; his male characters are often himself as a youth or idealized, while his women are cast much in the same mold. His early creation, Pepita, for example, is replicated in *Juanita la larga* near the very end of his career. Regardless of its originality, the novel is at best only moderately successful. The plot suffers from imbalance: Most of the book deals with a very few months; the next twenty years are merely summarized; then the story again slows to set the stage for Faustino's suicide. Finally, the philosophical contents do not fit comfortably into the dimensions of the plot, and Faustino seems ill at ease carrying them.

COMMANDER MENDOZA

Commander Mendoza started to appear serially in 1876. Unlike Valera's other long fiction, with the exception of his one historical novel, it lacks a contemporary setting. The novel is set in the eighteenth century; Mendoza is a sort of French philosophe; a rationalistic Deist; a skeptic; a believer in the infinite perfectibility of humans, in freedom and justice; a sensualist with Condillac; and perforce, another persona of his author. Middle-aged, now wealthy, and disgusted with Spanish atrocities that he has seen committed against the Indians in Peru, where he has made his fortune, he goes to Paris but runs into the French Revolution, equally marred by inhuman excesses. He returns to his native Andalusia, to Villabermeja, the same small fictional town in which Valera had located some of the action of *Las ilusiones del doctor Faustino*. This place, under one name or another, turns up in most of Valera's novels, being an idealization of Doña Mencía, a hilltown where the author had spent a good part of his early life.

An equally strong role in the novel is played by the formidable Doña Blanca, seduced many years before in Peru by Mendoza himself. Soon after this affair, she married; with her husband, she has also returned to Villabermeja, leading a life of exemplary expiation in a world she views as cursed with moral evil, a cross to be borne on the road to eventual salvation. She has reared her daughter, Clara, strictly, in an effort to shelter her from a mistake like her own. The daughter is Mendoza's, though the husband does not suspect.

Insistent that Clara should not unjustly inherit her husband's estate, Doña Blanca plans to marry her off to his rightful heir, an elderly, undesirable cousin. Mendoza sees through her plan and, though admitting that Clara should not inherit unjustly, still cannot bear to see her married to the old cousin (compare Pepita's old husband in Valera's earlier novel). Clara meanwhile decides to enter a convent, because she cannot have the man whom she really loves. Mendoza solves the dilemma by posing as the father of the woman whom the cousin is currently courting, giving her a generous dowry that the cousin will receive in lieu of Clara's inheritance. Before these improbable subterfuges can be effected, Mendoza must soften Doña Blanca's indomitable will, for she remains adamant, at first that Clara and her cousin wed, then—when that solution proves untenable—that she enter the convent. Doña Blanca suffers a stroke; on her deathbed, she forgives Mendoza and releases Clara from her vows so that she can marry Carlos, the young man whom she has loved all along.

Doña Blanca, though absent in person from most of the story, remains a spiritual force throughout, and when she does appear, she easily bests her antagonists. The only likely solution was to have her removed from the stage, as Valera did. The story ends with the marriage of Clara and Carlos and, less credibly, with Mendoza, who has been having many long discussions of family problems with his young niece, Lucía, finding that they share a mutual affection. The concept of the union of old age with youth, already found in *Pepita Ximenez* and in the aborted marriage of Clara and her cousin, reappears in Valera's next novel, *Don Braulio*, and in *Juanita la larga* almost twenty years later.

The plot complications in *Commander Mendoza* are badly contrived, the happy ending is barely convincing, and the long contest of wills between a stubborn, overly possessive, dominant woman and a tolerant yet persistent male adversary is the sort of thing that Spaniards perhaps even more than other European readers of that day accepted but that today seems childish at best and at worst risible. It must be remembered, however, that those drawn battles between moral imperatives were a commonplace of Victorian fiction.

If the plot is handled somewhat clumsily, the characters come off better. Mendoza is attractive and credible. Doña Blanca, though shown to be harsh and domineering, is treated nobly. Mendoza's friend, the village priest, Jacinto, is admirably humanistic, acting as a worthy foil for the skeptical protagonist. Lucía represents Valera's usual vivacious and charming young female lead. The story possesses a tragic undertone that lends depth, although the contrived happy ending mitigates it, as do the obligatory bits of local color that Valera almost always inserts. The considered judgment of most of the modern critics gives *Commander Mendoza* qualified approval as a good novel but certainly not a great one.

Don Braulio

The following season, Valera produced another novel, *Don Braulio*. The original title, *Pasarse de listo*, is a colloquial Spanish idiom meaning something like "to be too clever for one's own good." The protagonist, Braulio, another study in frustration, has indeed outsmarted himself. Talented, bright, and lazy (compare *Las illusiones del doctor Faustino* only three years before), Braulio remains in his mediocre position with the Department of the Treasury. Valera, as the omniscient narrator, observes that his hero is mistaken: Brains are not enough to ensure success in government positions; it takes drive and character as well. Braulio unjustly suspects his beautiful young wife (not half his age—a recurring theme with Valera) of having an affair with a nobleman and commits suicide. Actually, the Count is courting Braulio's sister-in-law, whom he later weds. Braulio's widow remarries, to a childhood friend. Though all the principal characters act irresponsibly, all but Braulio achieve a measure of happiness.

Although this is Valera's shortest novel, it is still fleshed out with authorial digressions. There are also *costumbrismo* sketches (the bullfight, for example, a common set piece with many Spanish novelists). Andalusian country life is compared with the mores of Madrid, to the detriment of the latter. Valera paints a black picture of the capital, the idle-rich Count, and his coterie of friends.

Doña Luz

In the late 1870's, Valera was averaging a novel a year, and *Doña Luz* appeared on schedule. The author complained that serial publication had hurt his previous work, *Don Braulio*, a fact that writers as great as Dickens and Honoré de Balzac had already learned. The demands of story segments that can stand on their own, with enough excitement to hold reader interest and satisfy magazine editors bent on increasing circulation, force compromises, pander to lowered standards of taste, and control the flow of the story line, often to its disadvantage. Valera had expensive tastes, however, as well as family obligations: *Doña Luz* began in *Revista contemporánea*, in the fall of 1878.

With this story, Valera returns to the problem of secular versus religious love. Doña Luz, the proud but illegitimate daughter of a Madrid nobleman, elects to remain a spinster and live as her poverty prescribes. She strikes up a warm Platonic friendship with Enrique, an older priest, who has come back to Andalusia to regain his health, shattered while he was a missionary in the Philippines. Late in the story, her mother dies, and she is suddenly rich. She is courted by a local politician, marries him only to find that he was after her money, and leaves him. The priest, meanwhile, realizes that he actually loves Doña Luz. His health further undermined by the ravages of his concealed passion, he takes to his bed, finally in a coma. Sitting beside him, Doña Luz bestows a kiss. He dies soon after. As one of his heirs, she is privileged to read his private diary, in which he confesses his criminal love. Remorseful for having unintentionally aroused his passion, yet flattered, she will name her unborn child after him.

In his preface, Valera claimed that the novel teaches a lesson: to guard against the possibility of erotic sin. Was he serious, or was he merely attempting to avoid the kind of criticism that Roman Catholic conservatives heaped on *Pepita Ximenez* four years earlier? His sympathies undeniably lay with Doña Luz and her priest, facing a love whose only solution was the latter's death, but in none of his books did he ever go so far as to depict a priest actually succumbing to sexual temptation, as Anatole France was to do in *Thaïs* (some ten years later and as Zola had already done in 1875 with *La Faute de l'abbé Mouret* (*Albine: Or, The Abbé's Temptation*, 1882; better known as *The Sin of Father Mouret*, 1904, 1969). If Luis opted for the secular life in *Pepita Ximenez*, he had not taken his final vows. Conscience permitting, he was free to break them and marry. Enrique was not. Nevertheless, Valera consistently preached the basic rightness of earthly love.

A larger point involves the matter of "preaching" in the first place. Like many European novelists of his day, Valera professed avoidance of didacticism, yet *Doña Luz* comes rather close to preaching. To be sure, the many nineteenth century novelists who abjured preachments in favor of art for art's sake did not always follow their own advice strictly. Indeed, their favorite technique of the omniscient narrator favors commentary and judgment. Valera is really following a tradition at least as ancient as Vergil: the writer as seer, bringer of light to the public. The particular subject he chooses, priestly versus secular love, has long been a mainstay of Catholic Spanish fiction and drama, from the seventeenth century plays of Pedro Calderón de la Barca and Tirso de Molina to the twentieth century existentialist novels of Miguel de Unamuno y Jugo. The reading public was conditioned to expect it, whatever stand Valera might choose to take.

Luckily, the heavy religious moral tone of the book is leavened with greater than usual attention paid by Valera to descriptions of village life. Next to *Juanita la larga*, not destined to appear until seventeen years later, *Doña Luz* is Valera's most strongly costumbristic novel, with its detailed scenes of the life, dwellings, customs, and character of the villagers. The town is here named Villafría, but as always, it remains a composite of the places where Valera lived out his younger years.

In the doomed priest Enrique, Valera created one of his few really fine male protagonists, a truly tragic figure deeply appealing to the reader; his Doña Luz is an interesting, well-rounded portrait as well. Among secondary characters, her father's former overseer and Enrique's uncle, the unscrupulous Don Acisclo, is a minor masterpiece, a picturesque old scoundrel whose clever financial schemes have drained Luz's father dry and filled his own coffers. Any artistic problems with the novel involve Valera's usual shortcomings. He narrates and describes well, his style is admirable, his characters incisively drawn, his psychology penetrating, but his plots are artificial and contrived. Events occur because the plots demand them.

JUANITA LA LARGA

Improbably, *Juanita la larga* (the word *larga* also suggesting something of the Amazon), which appeared serially, like his earlier novels, had the verve and charm of Valera's youthful period. Indeed, the novel is almost as fine a production as *Pepita Ximenez*, though Valera was in his early seventies at the time of its publication. It is another idyll of life in his beloved small-town Andalusia. His earlier depictions of this milieu are often darkened by thematic profundities—religious, economic, and social clouds on the horizon. It is a simple love story, grinding no ideological axes. In outlook, intent, tone, and conclusion, it compares with *Pepita Ximenez*, his first great work, dating back twenty years. It might seem to differ in one substantial respect in that Pepita and Luis face the formidable barrier of the latter's priestly vocation. Actually, the reader knows very well that the barrier is paper-thin. No one really expects Luis to withstand for long Pepita's charms or to be shorn of his prize. The novels that follow, however, turn more somber. Their problems of religion and social ambition and their character flaws raise truly resistant walls. Happy outcomes are no longer certain. With *Juanita la larga*, once again, and for one last time, the weather turns fair.

Juana and her daughter, Juanita, live in the little southern town of Villalegre. Significantly, the name Valera has coined for it means "Happytown" (in contrast to Villafría, "Coldtown," his name for the locale of the more somber *Doña Luz*). Like the Villabermeja ("Redtown") of several of his other stories, it is modeled on the Doña Mencía of his earliest days. There is something of the Edenic myth, the withdrawal from Paradise into the evil big city and the return, sometimes unrealizable, sometimes fatally too late, in Valera's longing, not only novelistically but in real life as well, for the simple country life of his youth. The old Valera manages to return home through the persona of Paco López, fifty-three years old and in love with Juanita, thirty-six years his junior.

Juanita, as is so common with Valera's characters, is illegitimate. She and her mother, Juana, are of the less favored class, the latter earning a good living as cook, seamstress, and midwife. Juanita is proud for all of her lowly birth, beautiful, energetic, sturdy, and sufficiently strong-willed that when she realizes her love for the older Paco, nothing will prevent her getting him, even if she has to knock another suitor down, kneel on him, and choke him until he agrees to support her own suit. Nor is she above using the same suitor to make Paco jealous. There are complications, however spurious. Paco's daughter, Inés, a snob married into one of the town's upper-crust families, opposes her father's wedding out of his own class. She is domineering, a meddler into the affairs of the whole town, miserly, and speciously mystical. This unsympathetic woman is in league with a narrowly orthodox priest (the first time Valera has presented a basically unlikable man of the cloth). Another repugnant character is Inés's immoral, profligate nobleman husband, given his just deserts at the story's end when he becomes senile. No force, no characters, however evil or mean, will prevail against the marriage. Juanita and Paco are happily wed at the conclusion of the book.

No more than in his other novels is Valera's success in this one primarily the result of a strong story line. The plot is reasonably credible, simple enough not to detract from the reader's joy in cheering for the protagonists. Inés's opposition is determined but destined for failure. The plot is adequate, no more, but things work out satisfactorily. Valera himself, in the dedicatory preface, writes of his concept of the novel in general and of *Juanita la larga* as well, "I do not know whether this book is a novel or not. I have written it very artlessly, combining recollections of my earliest youth." In all fairness, his novel is not merely a series of costumbristic sketches or youthful personal reminiscences held together by a narrative thread, for all of its heavy burden of *costumbrismo*.

Even more oddly, in the selfsame preface, Valera characterizes his novel, which most would call something close to a pastoral idyll, as a true copy of reality. He even goes on to speak of it as a photographic reproduction and calls himself more historian than novelist. He would seem to be breaking bread with the naturalistic school of Zola, who called himself a literary scientist and recorder of truths, or at least to be enlisting in the ranks of realists such as Flaubert and Balzac. Could Valera be saying that reality and the realists' method need not be applied exclusively to scenes of brutality, unpleasantness, stark passion, and the like, or is he simply using the term "reality" in a different sense? *Juanita la larga* contains more *costumbrismo* than any of his other novels. Country life, the many local dishes, lovingly and accurately described, local deformations of the Spanish language, the wines, legends, festivals, the Holy Week procession—all of these and more take up a good part of the novel. This attention to the details of regional peculiarities and distinctions necessarily helps bind the characters and their actions to their environment, a fact in keeping with the general tenets of realism and naturalism. Nevertheless, the tone of the book remains determinedly antirealist.

A word, too, must be said about the author's charmingly light, humorous touch. Valera always displays an ironic temper, a distancing of writer from the problems of his own characters, the double vision that allows the creator, even one given, like Valera, to autobiographical incidents and to characters who to some extent represent himself, to mock, however gently, their trials, tribulations, and shortcomings. It is what keeps him from falling into the Romantics' solipsistic trap. Never is his touch lighter than in this novel of his late years. He can let Juanita make fun of the very relationship he has made possible: her youth and Paco's middle age. He can write a wonderful scene in which the despondent lover escapes to the hills and contemplates suicide but fills his knapsack with meat and bread to avoid starving. Valera's customary mockery has become true humor.

Juanita la larga and *Pepita Ximenez* are the works on which Valera's reputation will continue to rest—his contribution to the impressive reemergence of the novel in Spain in the later years of the nineteenth century.

Armand E. Singer

Other major works

SHORT FICTION: *Cuentos y diálogos*, 1882; *Algo de todo*, 1883; *Cuentos, diálogos y fantasías*, 1887; *Cuentos y chascarrillos andaluces*, 1898 (with Narciso Campillo, Conde de las Navas, and Doctor Thebussem); *De varios colores*, 1898.

PLAYS: *Tentativas dramáticas*, pb. 1879; *Teatro*, pb. 1908.

POETRY: *Ensayos poéticas*, 1844; *Poesías*, 1858; *Canciones, romances, y poemas*, 1885.

NONFICTION: *De la naturaleza y carácter de la novela*, 1860; *Estudios críticos sobre literatura, política, y costumbres de nuestros días*, 1864; *Crítica literaria*, 1864-1871;

Disertaciones y juicios literarios, 1878; *Nuevos estudios críticos*, 1883; *Apuntes sobre el nuevo arte de escribir novelas*, 1887; *Carta al señor don Juan Valera*, 1888; *Cartas americanas*, 1889; *Nuevas cartas americanas*, 1890; *Las mujeres y las academias*, 1891; *Ventura de la Vega: Estudio biográfico crítico*, 1891; *Ecos argentinos*, 1901.

TRANSLATION: *Poesía y arte en los árabes en España y Sicilia*, 1867, 1868, 1871 (of Adolf F. Schack's nonfiction study *Poesie und Kunst der Araber in Spanien und Sicilien*).

EDITED TEXTS: *Florilegio de cuentos, leyendas y tradiciones vulgares*, 1860; *Florilegio de poesías castellanas del siglo XIX*, 1902-1903 (5 volumes).

MISCELLANEOUS: *Obras completas*, 1905-1935 (53 volumes); *Obras completas*, 1947-1958 (3 volumes).

BIBLIOGRAPHY

DeCoster, Cyrus Cole. *Juan Valera*. New York: Twayne, 1974. An informative biography. Contains an overview of Valera's life and literary career and analyzes the literary characters and themes of his fiction. Includes a bibliography.

Ford, J. D. M. *Main Currents of Spanish Literature*. 1919. Reprint. New York: Biblio and Tannen, 1968. In these critical lectures delivered at the Lowell Institute in Boston, Valera's novels are considered high points of Spanish American literature. Includes a bibliographical note.

Franz, Thomas R. *Valera in Dialogue = In Dialogue with Valera: A Novelist's Work in Conversation with That of His Contemporaries and Successors*. New York: Peter Lang, 2000. Chronicles the debate between Valera and his contemporaries and chief rivals, Benito Pérez Galdós and Leopoldo Alas, over the aesthetics of Spanish realist fiction, and how this debate influenced the later writing of Miguel de Unamuno y Jugo and Ramón María del Valle-Inclán.

Lott, Robert E. *Language and Psychology in "Pepita Jimenez."* Urbana: University of Illinois Press, 1970. A well-regarded study of language and psychology in the novel *Pepita Ximenez*. The first part is an analysis of language, style, and rhetorical devices. The second section is a psychological examination of characters.

Taylor, Teresia Langford. *The Representation of Women in the Novels of Juan Valera: A Feminist Critique*. New York: Peter Lang, 1997. Taylor's feminist literary critique of Valera's novels focuses on his representation of women and the underlying patriarchal ideology of his works. Includes bibliographical references and an index.

Trimble, Robert. *Chaos Burning on My Brow: Don Juan Valera in His Novels*. San Bernardino, Calif.: Borgo Press, 1995. A critical study of Valera's novels. Includes an index and a bibliography.

Turner, Harriet, and Adelaida López de Martínez, eds. *The Cambridge Companion to the Spanish Novel: From 1600 to the Present*. New York: Cambridge University Press, 2003. Numerous references to Valera in this historical survey of the Spanish novel, but the most extensive consideration of his work is found in two chapters: "The Regional

Novel: Evolution and Consolation" by Alison Sinclair and "The Realist Novel" by Harriet Turner.

Valle, José del. "Historical Linguistics and Cultural History: The Polemic Between Rufino José Cuervo and Juan Valera." In *The Battle over Spanish Between 1800 and 2000: Language Ideologies and Hispanic Intellectuals*, edited by Valle and Luis Gabriel-Stheeman. New York: Routledge, 2002. Valle's essay recounts the debate between Valera and Rufino José Cuervo, a nineteenth century Colombian writer and linguist, over issues pertaining to the Spanish language. The debate among intellectuals of the time shaped national identity and Hispanic culture.

RAMÓN MARÍA DEL VALLE-INCLÁN

Born: Villanueva de Arosa, Spain; October 28, 1866
Died: Santiago de Compostela, Spain; January 5, 1936
Also known as: Ramón José Simón Valle Peña

PRINCIPAL LONG FICTION
Cara de Dios, 1899
Sonatas, 1902-1905 (*The Pleasant Memoirs of the Marquis de Bradomín: Four Sonatas*, 1924; includes *Sonata de otoño*, 1902 [*Autumn Sonata*]; *Sonata de estío*, 1903 [*Summer Sonata*]; *Sonata de primavera*, 1904 [*Spring Sonata*]; *Sonata de invierno*, 1905 [*Winter Sonata*])
Flor de santidad, 1904
La guerra carlista, 1908-1909 (includes *Los cruzados de la causa*, 1908; *El resplandor de la hoguera*, 1909; and *Gerifaltes de antaño*, 1909)
Tirano Banderas: Novela de tierra caliente, 1926 (*The Tyrant: A Novel of Warm Lands*, 1929)
El ruedo ibérico, 1927-1958 (includes *La corte de los milagros*, 1927; *Viva mi dueño*, 1928; and *Baza de espadas*, 1958 [serialized 1932])

OTHER LITERARY FORMS

Ramón María del Valle-Inclán (BAHL-yay-eeng-KLAHN) was a highly innovative dramatist as well as an accomplished novelist. His best-known and most influential plays include the three *comedias bárbaras*—*Águila de blasón* (pb. 1907), *Divinas palabras* (pb. 1920; *Divine Words*, 1968), and *Luces de Bohemia* (pb. 1924; *Bohemian Lights*, 1967)—and the three plays that are included in *Martes de carnaval* (1930; Shrove Tuesday carnival). He also published several collections of short stories, among them *Femeninas* (1895; feminine vignettes), *Corte de amor* (1903; court of love), *Jardín umbrío* (1914; garden of shadows), and three volumes of poetry that were collected and republished in 1930 as *Claves líricas* (lyrical clues).

Other work includes *La lámpara maravillosa* (1916; *The Lamp of Marvels*, 1986), an aesthetic statement written in poetic prose; translations from the Portuguese and Italian; and numerous critical essays and prologues. Many of these short pieces have been collected and republished by individual scholars, but there is not yet a complete edition of Valle-Inclán's writing, one that would contain all of his essays, letters, and interviews, as well as the variants of the many works that were serialized in contemporary newspapers and magazines before their publication as books. The series of his collected works that Valle-Inclán initiated in 1913 (*Opera omnia*, 1913-1930) is not complete, nor is the two-volume edition *Obras completas*, which was first published posthumously in 1944. Espasa Calpe in Madrid has begun to publish critical editions of Valle-Inclán's major plays and novels in the Cla icos Castellanos series; *Bohemian Lights*, *The Tyrant*, and *La guerra carlista* have appeared.

Achievements

Ramón María del Valle-Inclán's life and work have occasioned considerable controversy, much of it provoked by his eccentric personal manner, but there is no doubt about his reputation as one of Spain's greatest authors: He is highly respected as a brilliant, versatile writer who was able simultaneously to ridicule and renovate Spanish prose, thereby linking an acute awareness of Spain's diminished historical position with the quality of its language and literature.

Especially at the beginning of his career, his careful attention to form and style led many critics to place Valle-Inclán's work with that of the Spanish-American *Modernismo* poets rather than with that of his Spanish contemporaries. These Spanish writers (including Miguel de Unamuno y Jugo, Pío Baroja, Azorín, Jacinto Benavente y Martínez, and Antonio Machado), who are usually referred to as the *generación del 1898*, or Generation of '98, seemed more explicitly concerned with revitalizing Spain's literature and self-esteem. The richness of Valle-Inclán's early stories and novels was recognized and praised, but he was reprimanded by critics such as José Ortega y Gasset, who found the work overly precious and wished that it were less mannered and more concerned with human, down-to-earth themes.

As Valle-Inclán matured as a writer, his work did, in fact, change considerably. The primacy of his aesthetic considerations never lessened, but his use of irony intensified and redirected itself; in the *esperpentos*, his moral, social, political, and historical preoccupations became increasingly explicit. After World War I, he was recognized as a highly committed writer, and he has come to be considered one of the most significant writers of the Generation of '98. This recognition did not, however, mean that his work was fully comprehended and accepted during his lifetime. On the contrary, for both political and aesthetic reasons, much of it was not accessible to the general public. His theater, for example, was not widely represented; some of his plays were banned for their satiric content, and others were thought to be unpresentable because of their experimental, avant-garde nature. For the most part, this inaccessibility continued through the Spanish Civil War and the Francisco Franco years until 1966, when, with Valle-Inclán's centennial, a serious reevaluation of his work began in Europe and the United States as well as in Spain. There remains a great deal of editorial and interpretive work awaiting Valle-Inclán scholars.

Valle-Inclán's plays have been edited and performed in Spain and abroad, his presence in contemporary Spanish literature is increasingly evident, and the overall unity of his work is becoming more and more apparent. Because only a few of his books have been translated into English, his North American reputation is limited, but his influence on modern Spanish American literature, especially on the novel, is considerable.

Biography

Ramón María del Valle-Inclán was born Ramón José Simón Valle Peña in Villanueva de Arosa, Pontevedra, Galicia, Spain, on October 28, 1866. His father, Ramón Valle Bermúdez, was an amateur writer and a seaman. Both of his parents belonged to distinguished families; it was from their names that he created his authorial name and the aristocratic titles he bestowed on himself: Ramón María del Valle-Inclán y Montenegro, Marqués del Valle, Vixconde de Viexín, and Señor del Caramiñal. These were names that also reflected his ties to Galicia, a region that is still known for its myths and legends, for the survival of its Celtic, pagan substratum, and for the rural, medieval ambience that characterizes both the many tiny farms of its mountainous interior and the small ports—such as Villanueva de Arosa—that dot its rocky coast. The landscape and the culture are often likened to those of Ireland and northern England, and their stamp on Valle-Inclán's work was strong and lasting. From his earliest writing, he seemed to identify both with Galicia's rural, oral tradition and with that of its declining aristocracy.

The Galician language also survives in Valle-Inclán's work, for although he wrote only a few poems in his regional tongue, he infused Spanish with the Galician vocabulary, syntax, and tone. Like other writers of his generation who were not born in central Spain, he brought a critical vision to bear on the crisis confronting the nation; unlike most of his contemporaries, however, his harshness toward Castile never softened. He lived a large part of his life outside Galicia but continued to return and to stay for varying lengths of time.

Valle-Inclán first left Galicia in 1890, when he went to Madrid. He had studied law for two years in Santiago de Compostela, but he left the university after the death of his father. Although he had published a few short stories as a student, and he published a few others while he was in Madrid, it was during a trip to Mexico in 1892 that his career as a writer truly began, with the stories and newspaper articles that he wrote and published there. In 1895, after a period of several years in Pontevedra, where the library of one of his father's friends enabled him to read widely in contemporary European literature, he published his first book, *Femeninas*. The following year, he went back to Madrid, where he began to establish himself as a writer. He frequented artists' cafés; made friends with artists, critics, and writers (including the Nicaraguan poet Rubén Darío); and soon acquired a singular reputation for his extravagant bohemian appearance; his highly articulate, witty, and forthright opinions; and his famous lisp.

Because there is no definitive biography of Valle-Inclán and because he deliberately elaborated a complicated and at times contradictory series of anecdotes about his experiences, it is difficult to speak with certainty about many of the details of his life. It is certain, however, that he lived in Madrid from 1896 until 1912. During those years, he lost his right arm after a skirmish with another writer, Manuel Bueno. He published extensively, both fiction and drama, and was active in the theater. There he met the actor Josefina Blanco, whom he married in 1907. In 1910, he accompanied his wife's theater company to South America and in Buenos Aires delivered a series of lectures about aesthetics.

In 1912, Valle-Inclán decided to move his family to Galicia; the first two of his six children had been born, and despite his publications and growing literary reputation, his financial situation was precarious. He continued to live in the north until 1924, although on many occasions he left to travel. In 1916, for example, as a correspondent for the Madrid newspaper *El imparcial*, he journeyed to France and the Allied war fronts. In 1921, at the invitation of the Mexican government, he made his second trip to Mexico, to participate in the centennial celebration of Mexican independence. While he was there, he created no small consternation among the representatives of "Official Spain" by publicly supporting a popular land reform designed to break up large estates, many of which were held by wealthy Spaniards. This outspokenness was consistent with Valle-Inclán's lifelong articulation of his convictions, which were often both controversial and apparently contradictory. His opinions, which would be echoed directly in *The Tyrant*, reflect the increasingly social and political nature of his writing in the years following the trip to France. These were years of intense creative work; in 1920 alone he published four plays, two of which, *Divine Words* and *Bohemian Lights*, are among his finest.

In 1924, Valle-Inclán returned once again to Madrid, where for nearly all the next decade he continued to write prolifically and develop as a writer. Although he was never wealthy, for a time his writing brought economic security as well as considerable esteem. His outspoken comments continued, in particular his opposition to the military dictatorship of General Miguel Primo de Rivera; three of Valle-Inclán's plays were banned by the censors, and in 1929 he spent several days in a Madrid jail. After the dictatorship ended, Valle-Inclán tried unsuccessfully for a seat in the constituent Cortes, representing one of Galicia's districts as a member of one of the newly founded republican parties. The republican government, however, was to honor him with an appointment as director of the Spanish Academy of Fine Arts in Rome, a position he held for almost two years, between 1933 and 1935. During this time, both his financial position and his personal life were difficult; he had divorced his wife, and he was quite ill with health problems that had plagued him for many years. In 1935, he returned to Galicia, where he continued to work on *El ruedo ibérico* and to receive friends at the sanatorium where he was hospitalized until his death from cancer on January 5, 1936.

Analysis

"We are no longer a race of conquerors and theologians, and that fiction always breathes in our ballads and our popular speech." This statement, from *The Lamp of Marvels*, is central to an understanding of Ramón María del Valle-Inclán's novels, for it suggests and synthesizes his most important ideas about the potential of fiction and its position in contemporary Spanish literature and culture. In the first place, there is an unmasking of Spain's self-image, which is described as a false expression frozen in the pretense that Spain is still the imperialist world power it was at the time of the Catholic kings. Such self-deception is dangerous, according to the wise old poet who narrates *The*

Lamp of Marvels, particularly because of its effect on Spanish sensibility, which—because of its egotism and lack of perspective—refuses to grapple with significant spiritual and historical issues.

In the second place, the fiction of Spain's importance is shown to be closely linked to its language and literature; instead of expanding to include the linguistic changes it has undergone in the New World, Spanish is rigid and brittle. It insists on the fiction of its own purity, which implies an inappropriate, warped perception of integrity. Furthermore, the literature that could work to renovate language and open perspective is also locked in a dead rhetoric that maintains the lie of Spanish sovereignty: Both popular speech and the ballads, the traditional repositories of spontaneous popular expression, reveal the deterioration of language and an obsessive national pride.

For Valle-Inclán, then, the writer of fiction is linked to the poet as a "visionary" who can break the limits of his or her own sensory perceptions. Although this vision, as it is presented in *The Lamp of Marvels*, does not unlock the secrets of the future, it is able to recognize the complexity of the present, to perceive and present an incident—or an instant—from multiple points of view. It is clearly linked to the irony that characterizes Valle-Inclán's work from his earliest stories, as well as to the aesthetic and artistic perspectives that he enumerated in the three *esperpentos* of *Martes de carnaval*.

The world, Valle-Inclán explained, can be witnessed with reverence, on one's knees, as if events and characters were larger than life; it can also be seen eye-to-eye; and it can be watched from above, with distance and even with disdain. Although each of these attitudes can be said to predominate at one time or another in Valle-Inclán's work, the aesthetics presented in *The Lamp of Marvels* suggest that the ideal fiction has something of each: A certain distancing is necessary to break free of traditional perspective, but in the same way that an excess of awe leads one to "wallow" in emotions, extreme distancing can lead to overabstraction and a lack of feeling. The nature of language, which is always rooted in the "earth" of human feelings, is, when perfected by poetry, a link between the two extremes that hold them both in a kind of dynamic stillness or insight, which the poet calls "aesthetic quietism."

This aesthetic experience or principle is valid for both Valle-Inclán's fiction and his theater, for even though he was well aware of their differences and distinct possibilities, he continually explored the boundaries and relations between them. In his early work, this exploration includes the use of dramatic settings in his novels whereby characters and situations are presented in a series of tableaux, as if they were on stage. Ambience, gesture, and the spoken word are always important, and even in the first-person narrative of *The Pleasant Memoirs of the Marquis de Bradomín*, the reader becomes acquainted with the narrator through his poses and highly selected "confessions," not through the "inner workings" of his thoughts. This absence of psychological development remains constant in Valle-Inclán's fiction; in fact, individual characters became less important as Valle-Inclán strove to encompass Spanish society and create a collective protagonist.

As the novels and plays developed, the perfected vision he described for Spanish fiction in *The Lamp of Marvels* became increasingly linked, for both forms, with the absence of any true Spanish collectivity and with the distortion and deformation Valle-Inclán perceived around him. As Max Estrella, the blind poet-protagonist of *Bohemian Lights*, explains, old literary forms are inappropriate for contemporary Spain; a new aesthetic genre is necessary, one that—like the distorting mirrors found in a fun house—will mathematically distort an already deformed society and sensibility. Estrella names this genre the *esperpento* (literally, "absurdity" or "nonsense"), a term that Valle-Inclán used to label some of his own plays. Hence, to capture the distortions of reality, Valle-Inclán peopled his dramatic works with unheroic, grotesque characters presaging the Theater of the Absurd. Although Valle-Inclán does not label his novels *esperpentos*, he does discuss them in terms of the *esperpentos* and indicates ways in which their fragmented structure is "almost theater."

This deliberate fusion of genres mirrors the careful way in which Valle-Inclán controlled the story of his own life, intentionally mixing fact and artifice and elaborating a fiction that welded those two ingredients. His "real" life was not a particularly exciting one: He frequently lived in poverty, he was often ill, and he had few adventures. He nevertheless was able to declare himself "an aesthetic adventurer": He knew how to make his own life a supple fiction by continually experimenting and taking risks as a writer, by rethinking and restating his opinions, by publishing fictional autobiographies and giving conflicting interviews, and by encouraging multiple versions of the events of interest that did happen to him (among them, the loss of his arm and his trips to South America). In other words, in the same way that his fiction and drama were developed as interlocking forms, fiction and history were seen and lived as interchangeable rather than mutually exclusive.

Thus it was especially appropriate when in June of 1981, Spain's king Juan Carlos created the marquisate of Bradomín, a hereditary title that he bestowed on Carlos Luis del Valle-Inclán, the writer's eldest living son. During his lifetime, Valle-Inclán had petitioned to have the nobility of his self-defined titles recognized. That petition was denied, but after his death, in recognition of his contribution to Spain's fiction, his heirs were awarded the title he had created for his best-known fictional character, a most controversial being who appeared in both plays and novels, who both does and does not resemble his creator.

The Marquis de Bradomín made his definitive appearance in 1902 as the narrator of *Autumn Sonata*, Valle-Inclán's first major work of fiction, but he had been prefigured earlier in some short stories and articles. There is also a hint of him in *Cara de Dios* (the face of God), a long novel that, although it was published in 1899, is generally considered Valle-Inclán's first because it was a serialized adaptation of a play by the Madrid dramatist Carlos Arniches. Although Valle-Inclán never hid the fact that he began his novelistic career by writing fiction in installments, he did not include *Cara de Dios* in his *Opera omnia*, and for a long time it remained out of print and virtually forgotten. All of this early work was important to the development of Valle-Inclán's later novels, for in it he experimented with different styles and themes, and much of it he reworked for incorporation into his later books. It was, however, the publication of *Autumn Sonata* that established him as one of Spain's most talented and promising writers, at the same time that influential and innovative novels were also published by Azorín, Baroja, and Unamuno.

THE PLEASANT MEMOIRS OF THE MARQUIS DE BRADOMÍN

Autumn Sonata is the first of four novels of *The Pleasant Memoirs of the Marquis de Bradomín*. The title character is an aging dandy who defines himself as "ugly, Catholic and sentimental." He begins his narrative in the autumn of his life and moves "backward" to summer, spring, and, finally, winter. The novels can also be read according to the calendar, for in *Spring Sonata*, the marquis is a young man who proceeds to age as the seasons progress. Each novel has a different setting and, to some extent, a different tone: *Autumn Sonata* is set in Galicia; *Summer Sonata*, in Mexico; *Spring Sonata*, in Italy; and *Winter Sonata*, in Navarre.

The four novels are unified, however, by the personality and the prose of the marquis and by the fictional purpose that Valle-Inclán had in mind for them as a whole. As he explained himself, in these novels he wanted to work with an "eternal" Spanish theme, the legend of Don Juan. For Valle-Inclán, Don Juan was a complex figure, and in addition to presenting him as a great seducer of women, Valle-Inclán believed that it was necessary to examine Don Juan's lack of respect for religion and the dead, along with his willingness to satisfy his own desires by trampling on the rights of others. Valle-Inclán's "Don Juan," the marquis, defines himself in terms of those three themes—the trinity of the World, the Flesh, and the Devil—presenting his exploits and conquests in a tongue-in-cheek manner that is at once sentimental and stoic. As if fully aware of the ironic self-portrait he is drawing, the marquis speaks proudly of his aristocratic lineage, his participation in the Carlist War, his ability to resist pain, and the great attraction he has for women. At the same time, he is conscious of the various elements of decadence that characterize his life: the excessive sentimentality of his writing; the morbid, even macabre nature of some of his experiences; the fact that Carlism has become a lost cause.

The irony and ambiguity is what makes *The Pleasant Memoirs of the Marquis de Bradomín* fascinating; thanks to the richness and precision of "his" writing, the Marquis de Bradomín seems to breathe life into the decadent figure whose death he exemplifies. His prose is elegant and highly refined; its musicality and suggestiveness reveal Valle-Inclán's reading of fin de siècle writers from Spanish America, France, and Italy. His sensuous descriptions are highly visual, and each sonata evokes its different setting. On the other hand, there is something too precious about the writing, the descriptions are complex but static, the Marquis repeats his images of regret, and his laments of lost youth and the absence of further adventures grow tiring. His reader is likely to recognize long before the Marquis does that he is—as he fears—like a god whose cult has died out and that the greatest loves of his life have not led to enduring relationships but to melancholy, resentment, and even death.

Although Valle-Inclán eventually referred to the *Sonatas* as "trivial tunes for the violin," the Marquis de Bradomín continued to appear throughout his work (in *La guerra carlista*, *Bohemian Lights*, and *El ruedo ibérico*). This reappearance and the many similarities between novelist and character (for example, a noble Galician birth, journeys to Mexico, the loss of an arm) have prompted much speculation about the extent to which Valle-Inclán's stories about the Marquis and his adventures are autobiographical. It is clear that the *Sonatas* are, in many ways, "writer's novels" (for example, the Marquis is a highly self-conscious narrator who continually refers to himself as a confessional writer, constantly examines the possibilities and power of language, and alludes frequently to other autobiographical works), which suggests that Valle-Inclán was using the Marquis to write about his own aesthetic development. The links between them are, however, highly fictionalized: Valle-Inclán was interested not in telling his own personal "story" but in personifying his thoughts about fiction and legend in such a way that the reader could also experience, simultaneously, decadence and virtuosity—the end of a legend and the process of its re-creation. That he succeeded is proved by the popularity of the *Sonatas*, which continue to prompt new critical studies and are perhaps his most widely read novels.

THE TYRANT

In 1926, fifteen years after his previous novel, Valle-Inclán published *The Tyrant*. This first novel after a long break was an immediate success, and it has continued to be one of Valle-Inclán's most influential and popular books; indeed, many critics consider it his masterpiece. Although he was sixty years old when this novel was published, Valle-Inclán himself called it his "first" work and said that his labor as a writer was only beginning.

The Tyrant does signal the ambitious and innovative novelistic undertaking that would occupy the final decade of Valle-Inclán's life. It incorporates in a work of fiction the perspective and techniques that Valle-Inclán had recently perfected and exemplified in the *esperpentos*. *The Tyrant* also brought to fruition the theme of Spain in the New World, which had been present in Valle-Inclán's work since his first trip to Mexico. It was in Mexico, he believed, that the truest or purest essence of Spain could be found, although—as he shows in *The Tyrant*—that essence was not so much a living influence as a deathly presence. It was apparently this deathly presence that he wanted to explore, for, as he wrote to Alfonse Reyes in 1920, the *gachupines* (or Spaniards) in Mexico owned seventy percent of the land and were the "quintessence of Iberian barbarity." True revolution, he said, would involve a change in the position of the Indian, not merely "a shuffling of viceroys."

The Tyrant is set in Santa Fe de Tierra Firme, the capital of an imaginary republic on the eve of a revolutionary uprising. Death is indeed a central presence in the novel; the action spans three days during the feasts of All Saints and All Souls, and the uprising is responsible for the demise of the tyrant Santos Banderas and the end of his dictatorship. The plot of *The Tyrant* can be stated briefly: Valle-Inclán was not concerned with chronicling the entire history of an attempted revolution but in presenting—from many perspectives—the instant of its explosion: On the eve of the rebellion, the interests and aspirations of the republic's three racial groups (Indians, Creoles, and *gachupines*) are detailed, and the links and antagonisms among them are revealed or suggested. Santos Banderas is first seen after he has impassively squelched an insurrection in another town; at the end of the novel, he just as impassively kills his own daughter to protect her from the revolutionaries, before he himself is riddled with bullets.

The victorious uprising, which is only one of several quite disparate revolutionary efforts, is led by Filomeno Cuevas, a Creole rancher, and Domiciano de la Gándara, a former military officer who has his own ambitions for power. The participation and motivation of their Indian troops is pivotal to their success, just as the Indians' role in New World society is pivotal to most of the novel's discussions of social change. This role is examined from various points of view by politicians who hope to inspire revolution, by the Diplomatic Community, and by the Spanish Colony, whose economic ties to the dictatorship make any genuine sympathy for the Indians virtually impossible. Many aspects of the novel's historical and political situation, its landscape, and its characters are reminiscent of Mexico and the revolution that overthrew Porfirio Díaz, but there are also suggestions of other Central and South American nations, and the novel is clearly not confined within the boundaries of any one country.

The structure of *The Tyrant* has been studied in detail and praised for the exemplary manner in which it fuses Valle-Inclán's constant attention to form and his thoughts about society and change in Spanish America. As in the trilogy *La guerra carlista*, *The Tyrant* is composed of short (often very short) fragments. In this later work, however, their ordering conforms to a stricter and more meaningful pattern. The novel itself is framed by a brief prologue and a brief epilogue; the prologue presents Filomeno Cuevas, Domiciano de la Gándara, and their rebel Indians as they prepare to march on the former convent where the Tyrant has his headquarters; the epilogue takes place within the Tyrant's headquarters as the uprising succeeds.

Suspended between the prologue and epilogue, the novel's plot unfolds not as a linear series of events but as three concentric circles. The central part, which is also the longest, contains the most developed story in the novel, that of the Indian Zacarías San José, who joins Filomeno Cuevas's insurgents in order to wreak vengeance on the *gachupín* Quintín Pereda, a miserly pawnbroker who was responsible for the imprisonment of Zacarías's wife and, indirectly, for the fact that their young son was killed by pigs. This circular structure is closely related to the ideas about Gnostic and Christian time, history, and poetic vision that are presented in *The Lamp of Marvels*; it also reflects Valle-Inclán's interest in theosophy and the occult, which is linked to his aesthetics. The recurrence of the numbers three and seven in the novel's structure and action, for example, is not coincidental but highly symbolic, as is the fact that Santa Fe's three social "circles" revolve around a center of mutual responsibility that may explode but will not change.

Although this artificial structure and, in particular, the compactness of the short chapters or fragments—the events of which often occur simultaneously—link *The Tyrant* to Valle-Inclán's dramatic work of the years immediately preceding, it is in the development and description of the novel's characters that the aesthetics perfected in his plays become most evident. Like the characters of the *esperpentos*, many of the inhabitants of Santa Fe are puppet figures who are not described psychologically but are presented externally, by means of their gestures and grotesque appearance and through their dialogue. Aside from the Tyrant, who is often referred to as a mummy or skull and identified by his dark glasses and his grimace (which is green because his saliva is discolored from chewing coca leaves), the most grotesque characters are the *gachupines*.

Their most extreme representative is the Spanish minister, a gay drug addict who is shunned by other foreign ministers and referred to alternately as the Plenipotentiary Minister of His Catholic Majesty and as Isabelita, the name given him by his lover, a former bullfighter. As puppets of their own maliciousness and hypocrisy, these characters are thoroughly dehumanized. Described with reference to masks, animals, parts of the body, or articles of clothing, they become objects; at times, some of the objects and animals in the novel take on more life than its characters. That is not to say, however, that all of the characters are deformed or distorted. Some of them, such as the Indian Zacarías, are presented as dignified, almost epic figures. Filomeno Cuevas and Roque Cepeda—the latter a popular apostle of the Revolution, a spiritual figure who offers a striking contrast to the Tyrant and in many ways resembles the precipitator of the Mexican Revolution, Francisco Madero—are presented as noble men, even though, for different reasons, their efforts to alter society will not be effective in a lasting way. Like Cepeda, many of the characters are based to varying degrees on historical personages, a resemblance that reveals Valle-Inclán's careful documentation and great familiarity with Mexican history; even so, like the situation itself, which seems to take place simultaneously in 1873 and during the Mexican Revolution, the characters differ significantly from the models they synthesize and re-create.

Although it is difficult to say which aspect of *The Tyrant* has proved to be most innovative and influential, certainly one of the more admirable elements of the novel is its language. In the same way that the landscape suggests various South American countries and the characters are both historical and fictional, the language of *The Tyrant* is created from a highly artificial vocabulary that draws on Spanish as it is spoken in all parts of the New World. This synthesis makes for difficult reading for Spanish speakers unfamiliar with the dialects of their Hispanic counterparts, but it creates a fascinating phenomenon that is almost an antidote to the death of Spanish that the novel chronicles in so many other ways. As the narrator presents the brief, condensed, allusive descriptions (which are more like the stage directions of the *esperpentos* than like traditional novelistic passages) and as the characters strut grotesquely, uttering their short, telegraphic outbursts, a rebirth of the Spanish language does, indeed, occur. As the boundaries of strict discourse are broken down, the possibility of a new language is suggested; the message is one of discouragement and death, but in the words that convey that message there are signs of life.

El ruedo ibérico

At the time of his death, Valle-Inclán was working on an ambitious project, which he hoped would "bring to the novel Spanish sensibility as presented in its reaction to events of importance." He believed that "a nation's sensibility is reflected in and can be measured by the way it reacts to those events." The historical period that he chose for his "measurement" was much the same one that had interested him in *La guerra carlista* and *The Tyrant*; this time, however, he would focus on the entire Spanish nation. There were to be nine novels, which would span the years 1868 to 1885 in three cycles of three novels each; only the first three were written.

Collectively titled *El ruedo ibérico*, Valle-Inclán presents in them the multiplicity of revolutionary schemes, monarchical abuses, and social injustices that filled the seven months immediately preceding the "Glorious" Revolution of September, 1868, and Isabel II's flight into exile. Later novels were to include the period of the first Spanish Republic and the Bourbon Restoration, and they were to end with the death of Alfonso XII. Valle-Inclán knew that he would not be able to complete the entire project, but he worked on it steadily during the last decade of his life, writing and rewriting the novels that were to make up the first cycle.

The first novel, *La corte de los milagros* (the court of miracles), appeared in 1927; the second, *Viva mi dueño* (hurrah for my master), in 1928. In 1931 and 1932, these two novels were republished in serial form, with alterations, in the Madrid newspaper *El sol*. In the spring of 1932, the same newspaper published five sections of *Baza de espadas* (military tricks), a novel that was never completed but was published posthumously in book form in 1958. Since Valle-Inclán's death, several additional fragments of *El ruedo ibérico* have been published, and scholars have linked other fragments published during his lifetime to its theme and plots; at least one of its characters appeared in some of his early articles.

Although the novels of *El ruedo ibérico* are much more extensive than *The Tyrant* (as Valle-Inclán indicated himself), his novelistic techniques, his perspective on Spain, and his use of historical documentation were established with that earlier novel. Like *The Tyrant*, the first cycle of *El ruedo ibérico* studies the end or death of an era; as *The Tyrant* explores the fiction of Spain's heroic posture in the New World, the first novels of *El ruedo ibérico* expose the "eternal duality" of its "soul" and its "deceptive national unity." This notion is explained quite clearly in *Viva mi dueño*:

> In those amens, once the bonfires of the Holy Office had been extinguished, the unity of a religious creed, which for three dark centuries managed to serve as a political bond, began to slacken, for it could no longer sustain its fiction.

Once again, as he had done before in *La guerra carlista* and *The Tyrant*, Valle-Inclán documented his novels by reading voluminously in nineteenth century history. He also studied exhaustively the popular press and popular literature; as a result, *El ruedo ibérico* reiterates the link between popular songs, language, and Spain's "finest hours" that was suggested in *The Lamp of Marvels*. As in his earlier works, however, Valle-Inclán's use of his historical material is highly original; his intention was not to recount history but to reorder it by altering Spain's traditional historical perspective. To do so, he employed (as he had in *The Tyrant*) a highly artificial structure and language, as well as new renditions of many well-known historical figures. The result is a rich but highly demanding narrative, for in order to appreciate fully Valle-Inclán's new focus on Spanish sensibility the reader must be thoroughly familiar with Spain's history.

The work's title illustrates the integral way in which Valle-Inclán's vision of history was related to the actual form of the novels, for in addition to "arena" or "bullring," the word *ruedo* means "rotation." Although the events in the three novels move forward chronologically, each book is structured circularly, with a long, pivotal section at its center. The narrative is broken into sections, which are further divided into chapters of varied lengths. To some of Valle-Inclán's early critics, the arrangement of the chapters appeared arbitrary, but recent scholars have discovered a careful patterning in each of the novels.

The first impression is indeed one of confusion and fragmentation, but attentive readers learn that this fragmentation coherently suggests hidden links between characters and intrigues. It also clearly suggests that in the jumble of revolutionary schemes and plots that existed throughout Spain in 1868, those at the top (the upper or outer circles) were the least revolutionary—that in order for lasting social change to occur, it would be necessary to focus on the nation's true center, the peasants and workers, who are at the center of *El ruedo ibérico*. The message inherent in this concentric structure could not help but remind Spanish readers of the conflicts of their own era.

In much the same way that *El ruedo ibérico*'s relatively short time span is crowded with events and intrigues, those events and intrigues are peopled with a large cast of characters; as Valle-Inclán himself said, the cycle of novels was not to have a traditional protagonist, because "its major protagonist is its social milieu, its ambience." Within this milieu, some characters are more prominent than others, but the effect is one of a complex world of interwoven stories in which the characters move into the spotlight for varying lengths of time but none dominates it. This complexity can be confusing, for at times a subtle allusion or small detail is the only clue provided to a character's motive or identity. Readers are, moreover, expected to be familiar with Valle-Inclán's earlier novels, some of whose characters (such as the Marquis de Bradomín) reappear.

In addition, the novels of *El ruedo ibérico* are peopled with many historical figures, whose significance depends to a large degree on the reader's recognition of them. These historical characters include the inept and scandalous Queen Isabel II and her weak and effeminate husband; Sor Patrocinio, a nun on whom the queen relied almost fanatically; Father Claret, the Royal Confessor; General Juan Prim, one of the revolution's leading figures; the anarchist Michael Bakunin; and numerous military officers, revolutionaries, ministers, advisers, and aristocrats. Many of these figures are presented as ridiculous, grotesque, and culpable; as in *The Tyrant*, Valle-Inclán's descriptions are at times scathing. Not all of the characters are reflected in the distorting lens of *esperpento*, but those who are—particularly the figures of "official" Spanish history—are shown to be egotistical, deceitful, and corrupt.

Given Valle-Inclán's intention to make an entire society the protagonist of these novels, it was necessary that the language of this collective character contain the speech patterns of the whole nation. *El ruedo ibérico* presents exactly this kind of spectrum, and the language of the novels is one of Valle-Inclán's greatest accomplishments. His own vocabulary is a synthesis of Spanish as spoken throughout the Iberian Peninsula, and as his many characters speak (which they do continually—there is a great deal of dialogue in these novels), they exemplify Spanish as spoken, from that of the queen's bed-chamber to the slang of workers and peasants.

To render some of this jargon, particularly the speech of the Andalusian bandits and gypsies, Valle-Inclán consulted cultural studies and reference works, encrusting the dialogue with authentic vocabulary. These passages are highly artificial, but they do accomplish an important goal, one that is closely linked to the purpose of *El ruedo ibérico*. The fiction of a pure and elegant Spanish language is destroyed, but the language itself expands to include the speech of all of Spain's inhabitants. In *El ruedo ibérico*, Valle-Inclán realized his most complete simultaneity of language destruction and re-creation. His achievement, however, surpasses the boundaries of a single genre: *El ruedo ibérico* is a culmination of his work in all genres, a synthesis of narrative, poetry, and theater confirming Valle-Inclán's lifelong preoccupation with the fictions of Spain.

Carol S. Maier

OTHER MAJOR WORKS

SHORT FICTION: *Femeninas*, 1895; *Corte de amor*, 1903; *Jardín umbrío*, 1914.

PLAYS: *Cenizas*, pr., pb. 1899; *El marqués de Bradomín*, pr. 1906; *Águila de blasón*, pb. 1907; *Romance de lobos*, pb. 1908 (*Wolves! Wolves!*, 1957); *El yermo de las almas*, pb. 1908; *La cabeza del dragón*, pr. 1910 (*The Dragon's Head*, 1918); *Cuento de abril*, pr., pb. 1910; *Voces de gesta: Tragedia pastoríl*, pb. 1911; *La marquesa Rosalinda*, pr. 1912; *El embrujado*, pb. 1913; *Divinas palabras*, pb. 1920 (*Divine Words*, 1968); *Farsa de la enamorada del rey*, pb. 1920; *Luces de Bohemia*, pb. 1920 (in French), pr. 1971 (in Spanish; *Bohemian Lights*, 1967); *Los cuernos de don Friolera*, pb. 1921 (in Italian), pr. 1936 (in Spanish; *The Grotesque Farce of Mr. Punch the Cuckold*, 1991); *Cara de Plata*, pb. 1922; *Farsa y licencia de la reina castiza*, pb. 1922; *Las galas de difunto*, pb. 1926; *La hija del capitán*, pb. 1927; *Retablo de la avaricia, la lujuria, y la muerte*, pb. 1927; *Obras completas de don Ramón del Valle-Inclán*, 1944 (2 volumes); *Las "comedias bárbaras":*

Historicismo y expresionismo dramático, 1972 (includes *Águila de blasón, Wolves! Wolves!*, and *Cara de Plata*); *Plays*, 1993; *Savage Acts: Four Plays*, 1993.

POETRY: *Aromas de leyenda*, 1907; *La pipa de kif*, 1919; *El pasajero*, 1920; *Claves líracas*, 1930 (includes the three earlier collections).

NONFICTION: *La lámpara maravillosa*, 1916 (*The Lamp of Marvels*, 1986); *La media noche*, 1917.

MISCELLANEOUS: *Opera omnia*, 1913-1930; *Obras completas*, 1944.

BIBLIOGRAPHY

Almeida, Diane M. *The Esperpento Tradition in the Works of Ramón del Valle-Inclán and Luis Buñuel*. Lewiston, N.Y.: Edwin Mellen Press, 2000. Almeida takes a close look at *esperpento*—a Spanish style of black comedy—in the novels of Valle-Inclán and in the films of Luis Buñuel. Includes a bibliography and an index.

Andrews, Jean. *Spanish Reactions to the Anglo-Irish Literary Revival in the Early Twentieth Century: The Stone by the Elixir*. Lewiston, N.Y.: Edwin Mellen Press, 1991. Andrews examines the search for spiritual and aesthetic fulfillment in the works of Valle-Inclán and Juan Ramón Jiménez and contrasts them to contemporary Anglo-Irish works. Includes a bibliography and an index.

Flynn, Gerard C. *The Aesthetic Code of Don Ramón del Valle-Inclán*. Huntington, W.Va.: University Editions, 1994. An extensive analysis of the aesthetics of Valle-Inclán's works. Includes a bibliography and an index.

Lima, Robert. *Valle-Inclán: The Theater of His Life*. Columbia: University of Missouri Press, 1988. A full-length biography of Valle-Inclán, covering his life and works. Includes a bibliography and an index.

LoDato, Rosemary C. *Beyond the Glitter: The Language of Gems in Modernista Writers Rubén Darío, Ramón del Valle-Inclán, and José Asunción Silva*. Lewisburg, Pa.: Bucknell University Press, 1999. LoDato examines the use of gems and jewelry as symbols in the works of Modernista writers Valle-Inclán, Rubén Darío, and José Asunción Silva. Includes a bibliography and an index.

Longhurst, Alex. "The Survival of Genre: Cervantine Paradigms in Unamuno, Valle-Inclán, and Pérez de Ayala." In *"Never-Ending Adventure": Studies in Medieval and Early Modern Spanish Literature in Honor of Peter N. Dunn*, edited by Edward H. Friedman and Harlan Sturm. Newark, Del.: Juan de la Cuesta, 2002. This collection of essays about medieval and early modern Spanish literature includes Longhurst's examination of the influence of Miguel de Cervantes on the work of Valle-Inclán and two other Spanish writers.

Schoolfield, George C. "Spain: Ramón María del Valle-Inclán." In *A Baedeker of Decadence: Charting a Literary Fashion, 1884-1927*. New Haven, Conn.: Yale University Press, 2003. Schoolfield's study of thirty-two Decadent writers devotes a chapter to the works of Valle-Inclán, which includes an examination of the Sonatas.

Bibliography

Every effort has been made to include studies published in 2000 and later. Most items in this bibliography contain a listing of secondary sources, making it easier to identify other critical commentary on novelists, movements, and themes.

Theoretical, Thematic, and Historical Studies

Altman, Janet Gurkin. *Epistolarity: Approaches to a Form*. Columbus: Ohio State University Press, 1982. Examines the epistolary novel, explaining how novelists use the letter form to develop characterization, further their plots, and develop meaning.

Beaumont, Matthew, ed. *Adventures in Realism*. Malden, Mass.: Blackwell, 2007. Fifteen essays explore facets of realism, which was critical to the development of the novel. Provides a theoretical framework for understanding how novelists attempt to represent the real and the common in fiction.

Brink, André. *The Novel: Language and Narrative from Cervantes to Calvino*. New York: New York University Press, 1998. Uses contemporary theories of semiotics and narratology to establish a continuum between early novelists and those of the postmodern era in their conscious use of language to achieve certain effects. Ranges across national boundaries to illustrate the theory of the development of the novel since the seventeenth century.

Brownstein, Rachel. *Becoming a Heroine: Reading About Women in Novels*. New York: Viking Press, 1982. Feminist survey of novels from the eighteenth century through the latter half of the twentieth century. Examines how "becoming a heroine" defines for women a sense of value in their lives. Considers novels by both men and women, and discusses the importance of the traditional marriage plot.

Bruzelius, Margaret. *Romancing the Novel: Adventure from Scott to Sebald*. Lewisburg, Pa.: Bucknell University Press, 2007. Examines the development of the adventure novel, linking it with the medieval romance tradition and exploring readers' continuing fascination with the genre.

Cavallaro, Dani. *The Gothic Vision: Three Centuries of Horror, Terror, and Fear*. New York: Continuum, 2005. Study of the gothic novel from its earliest manifestations in the eighteenth century to the early twenty-first century. Through the lenses of contemporary cultural theories, examines readers' fascination with novels that invoke horror, terror, and fright.

Doody, Margaret Anne. *The True Story of the Novel*. New Brunswick, N.J.: Rutgers University Press, 1996. Traces the roots of the novel, traditionally thought to have been developed in the seventeenth century, to classical Greek and Latin texts that exhibit characteristics of modern fiction.

Hale, Dorothy J., ed. *The Novel: An Anthology of Criticism and Theory, 1900-2000*. Malden, Mass.: Blackwell, 2006. Collection of essays by theorists and novelists. Includes commentary on the novel form from the perspective of formalism, structuralism, poststructuralism, Marxism, and reader response theory. Essays also address the novel through the lenses of sociology, gender studies, and feminist theory.

_____. *Social Formalism: The Novel in Theory from Henry James to the Present*. Stanford, Calif.: Stanford University Press, 1998. Emphasizes the novel's special ability to define a social world for readers. Relies heavily on the works of contemporary literary and cultural theorists. Provides a summary of twentieth century efforts to identify a theory of fiction that encompasses novels of many kinds.

Hart, Stephen M., and Wen-chin Ouyang, eds. *A Companion to Magical Realism*. London: Tamesis, 2005. Essays outlining the development of Magical Realism, tracing its roots from Europe through Latin America to other regions of the world. Explores the political dimensions of the genre.

Hoffman, Michael J., and Patrick D. Murphy, eds. *Essentials of the Theory of Fiction*. 2d ed. Durham, N.C.: Duke University Press, 1996. Collection of essays by influential critics from the late nineteenth century through the twentieth century. Focuses on the essential elements of fiction and the novel's relationship to the world it depicts.

Lodge, David. *The Art of Fiction: Illustrated from Classic and Modern Texts*. New York: Viking Press, 1993. Short commentaries on the technical aspects of fiction. Examples from important and minor novelists illustrate literary principles and techniques such as point of view, suspense, character introduction, irony, motivation, and ending.

Lynch, Deirdre, and William B. Walker, eds. *Cultural Institutions of the Novel*. Durham, N.C.: Duke University Press, 1996. Fifteen essays examine aspects of long fiction produced around the world. Encourages a redefinition of the genre and argues for inclusion of texts not historically considered novels.

Moretti, Franco, ed. *The Novel*. 2 vols. Princeton, N.J.: Princeton University Press, 2006. Compendium exploring the novel from multiple perspectives, including as an anthropological, historical, and sociological document; a function of the national tradition from which it emerges; and a work of art subject to examination using various critical approaches.

Priestman, Martin, ed. *The Cambridge Companion to Crime Fiction*. New York: Cambridge University Press, 2003. Essays examine the nature and development of the genre, explore works by writers (including women and ethnic minorities) from several countries, and establish links between crime fiction and other literary genres. Includes a chronology.

Scaggs, John. *Crime Fiction*. New York: Routledge, 2005. Provides a history of crime fiction, explores key subgenres, and identifies recurring themes that suggest the wider social and historical context in which these works are written. Suggests critical approaches that open crime fiction to serious study.

Shiach, Morag, ed. *The Cambridge Companion to the Modernist Novel*. New York: Cambridge University Press, 2007. Essays explaining the concept of modernism and its influence on the novel. Detailed examination of works by writers from various countries, all influenced by the modernist movement. Includes a detailed chronology.

Vice, Sue. *Holocaust Fiction*. New York: Routledge, 2000. Examines controversies generated by novels about the Holocaust. Focuses on eight important works, but also offers observations on the polemics surrounding publication of books on this topic.

Zunshine, Lisa. *Why We Read Fiction: Theory of Mind and the Novel*. Columbus: Ohio State University Press, 2006. Applies theories of cognitive psychology to novel reading, explaining how experience and human nature lead readers to constrain their interpretations of a given text. Provides numerous examples from well-known novels to illustrate how and why readers find pleasure in fiction.

THE SPANISH NOVEL

Landeira, Ricardo. *The Modern Spanish Novel, 1898-1936*. Boston: Twayne, 1985. Surveys works by authors writing between the Spanish American War and the Spanish Civil War. Analyzes themes and techniques that make these works modern.

Ter Horst, Robert. *The Fortunes of the Novel: A Study in the Transposition of a Genre*. New York: Peter Lang, 2003. Reviews the rise of the English novel from its roots in early Spanish prose fiction, especially the work of Miguel de Cervantes, through the novels of Daniel Defoe, Sir Walter Scott, and Charles Dickens. Focuses on the preoccupation of novelists with economic issues, broadly defined.

Turner, Harriet, and Adelaida López de Martínez, eds. *The Cambridge Companion to the Spanish Novel from 1600 to the Present*. New York: Cambridge University Press, 2003. Explores the development of the Spanish novel since the early seventeenth century. Focus on the characteristics of the novel's evolving form. Includes discussion of the regional novel, women writers, and the relationship between film and literature.

Laurence W. Mazzeno

Glossary of Literary Terms

absurdism: A philosophical attitude, pervading much of modern drama and fiction, that underlines the isolation and alienation that humans experience, having been thrown into what absurdists see as a godless universe devoid of religious, spiritual, or metaphysical meaning. Conspicuous in its lack of logic, consistency, coherence, intelligibility, and realism, the literature of the absurd depicts the anguish, forlornness, and despair inherent in the human condition. Counter to the rationalist assumptions of traditional humanism, absurdism denies the existence of universal truth or value.

allegory: A literary mode in which a second level of meaning, wherein characters, events, and settings represent abstractions, is encoded within the surface narrative. The allegorical mode may dominate an entire work, in which case the encoded message is the work's primary reason for being, or it may be an element in a work otherwise interesting and meaningful for its surface story alone. Elements of allegory may be found in Jonathan Swift's *Gulliver's Travels* (1726) and Thomas Mann's *Der Zauberberg* (1924; *The Magic Mountain*, 1927).

anatomy: Literally the term means the "cutting up" or "dissection" of a subject into its constituent parts for closer examination. Northrop Frye, in his *Anatomy of Criticism* (1957), uses the term to refer to a narrative that deals with mental attitudes rather than people. As opposed to the novel, the anatomy features stylized figures who are mouthpieces for the ideas they represent.

antagonist: The character in fiction who stands as a rival or opponent to the *protagonist*.

antihero: Defined by Seán O'Faoláin as a fictional figure who, deprived of social sanctions and definitions, is always trying to define himself and to establish his own codes. Ahab may be seen as the antihero of Herman Melville's *Moby Dick* (1851).

archetype: The term "archetype" entered literary criticism from the psychology of Carl Jung, who defined archetypes as "primordial images" from the "collective unconscious" of humankind. Jung believed that works of art derive much of their power from the unconscious appeal of these images to ancestral memories. In his extremely influential *Anatomy of Criticism* (1957), Northrop Frye gave another sense of the term wide currency, defining the archetype as "a symbol, usually an image, which recurs often enough in literature to be recognizable as an element of one's literary experience as a whole."

atmosphere: The general mood or tone of a work; atmosphere is often associated with setting but can also be established by action or dialogue. A classic example of atmosphere is the primitive, fatalistic tone created in the opening description of Egdon Heath in Thomas Hardy's *The Return of the Native* (1878).

bildungsroman: Sometimes called the "novel of education," the bildungsroman focuses on the growth of a young *protagonist* who is learning about the world and finding his or her place in life; typical examples are James Joyce's *A Portrait of the Artist as a*

Young Man (1914-1915, serial; 1916, book) and Thomas Wolfe's *Look Homeward, Angel* (1929).

biographical criticism: Criticism that attempts to determine how the events and experiences of an author's life influence his or her work.

bourgeois novel: A novel in which the values, preoccupations, and accoutrements of middle-class or bourgeois life are given particular prominence. The heyday of the bourgeois novel was the nineteenth century, when novelists as varied as Jane Austen, Honoré de Balzac, and Anthony Trollope both criticized and unreflectingly transmitted the assumptions of the rising middle class.

canon: An authorized or accepted list of books. In modern parlance, the literary canon comprehends the privileged texts, classics, or great books that are thought to belong permanently on university reading lists. Recent theory—especially feminist, Marxist, and poststructuralist—critically examines the process of canon formation and questions the hegemony of white male writers. Such theory sees canon formation as the ideological act of a dominant institution and seeks to undermine the notion of canonicity itself, thereby preventing the exclusion of works by women, minorities, and oppressed peoples.

character: Characters in fiction can be presented as if they were real people or as stylized functions of the plot. Usually characters are a combination of both factors.

classicism: A literary stance or value system consciously based on the example of classical Greek and Roman literature. While the term is applied to an enormous diversity of artists in many different periods and in many different national literatures, "classicism" generally denotes a cluster of values including formal discipline, restrained expression, reverence for tradition, and an objective rather than a subjective orientation. As a literary tendency, classicism is often opposed to *Romanticism*, although many writers combine classical and romantic elements.

climax/crisis: The term "climax" refers to the moment of the reader's highest emotional response, whereas "crisis" refers to a structural element of plot, a turning point at which a resolution must take place.

complication: The point in a novel when the *conflict* is developed or when the already existing conflict is further intensified.

conflict: The struggle that develops as a result of the opposition between the *protagonist* and another person, the natural world, society, or some force within the self.

contextualist criticism: A further extension of *formalist criticism*, which assumes that the language of art is constitutive. Rather than referring to preexistent values, the artwork creates values only inchoately realized before. The most important advocates of this position are Eliseo Vivas (*The Artistic Transaction*, 1963) and Murray Krieger (*The Play and Place of Criticism*, 1967).

conventions: All those devices of stylization, compression, and selection that constitute the necessary differences between art and life. According to the Russian Formalists, these conventions constitute the "literariness" of literature and are the only proper concern of the literary critic.

deconstruction: An extremely influential contemporary school of criticism based on the works of the French philosopher Jacques Derrida. Deconstruction treats literary works as unconscious reflections of the reigning myths of Western culture. The primary myth is that there is a meaningful world that language signifies or represents. The deconstructionist critic is most often concerned with showing how a literary text tacitly subverts the very assumptions or myths on which it ostensibly rests.

defamiliarization: Coined by Viktor Shklovsky in 1917, this term denotes a basic principle of Russian Formalism. Poetic language (by which the Formalists meant artful language, in prose as well as in poetry) defamiliarizes or "makes strange" familiar experiences. The technique of art, says Shklovsky, is to "make objects unfamiliar, to make forms difficult, to increase the difficulty and length of perception. . . . Art is a way of experiencing the artfulness of an object; the object is not important."

detective story: The so-called classic detective story (or mystery) is a highly formalized and logically structured mode of fiction in which the focus is on a crime solved by a detective through interpretation of evidence and ratiocination; the most famous detective in this mode is Arthur Conan Doyle's Sherlock Holmes. Many modern practitioners of the genre, however, such as Dashiell Hammett, Raymond Chandler, and Ross Macdonald, have de-emphasized the puzzlelike qualities of the detective story, stressing instead characterization, theme, and other elements of mainstream fiction.

determinism: The belief that an individual's actions are essentially determined by biological and environmental factors, with free will playing a negligible role. (See *naturalism*.)

dialogue: The similitude of conversation in fiction, dialogue serves to characterize, to further the *plot*, to establish *conflict*, and to express thematic ideas.

displacement: Popularized in criticism by Northrop Frye, this term refers to the author's attempt to make his or her story psychologically motivated and realistic, even as the latent structure of the mythical motivation moves relentlessly forward.

dominant: A term coined by Roman Jakobson to refer to that which "rules, determines, and transforms the remaining components in the work of a single artist, in a poetic canon, or in the work of an epoch." The shifting of the dominant in a *genre* accounts for the creation of new generic forms and new poetic epochs. For example, the rise of *realism* in the mid-nineteenth century indicates realistic conventions becoming dominant and *romance* or fantasy conventions becoming secondary.

doppelgänger: A double or counterpart of a person, sometimes endowed with ghostly qualities. A fictional character's doppelgänger often reflects a suppressed side of his or her personality. One of the classic examples of the doppelgänger motif is found in

Fyodor Dostoevski's novella *Dvoynik* (1846; *The Double*, 1917); Isaac Bashevis Singer and Jorge Luis Borges, among others, offer striking modern treatments of the doppelgänger.

epic: Although this term usually refers to a long narrative poem that presents the exploits of a central figure of high position, the term is also used to designate a long novel that has the style or structure usually associated with an epic. In this sense, for example, Herman Melville's *Moby Dick* (1851) and James Joyce's *Ulysses* (1922) may be called epics.

episodic narrative: A work that is held together primarily by a loose connection of self-sufficient episodes. *Picaresque novels* often have episodic structure.

epistolary novel: A novel made up of letters by one or more fictional characters. Samuel Richardson's *Pamela: Or, Virtue Rewarded* (1740-1741) is a well-known eighteenth century example. In the nineteenth century, Bram Stoker's *Dracula* (1897) is largely epistolary. The technique allows for several different points of view to be presented.

euphuism: A style of writing characterized by ornate language that is highly contrived, alliterative, and repetitious. Euphuism was developed by John Lyly in his *Euphues, the Anatomy of Wit* (1578) and was emulated frequently by writers of the Elizabethan Age.

existentialism: A philosophical, religious, and literary term, emerging from World War II, for a group of attitudes surrounding the pivotal notion that existence precedes essence. According to Jean-Paul Sartre, "Man is nothing else but what he makes himself." Forlornness arises from the death of God and the concomitant death of universal values, of any source of ultimate or a priori standards. Despair arises from the fact that an individual can reckon only with what depends on his or her will, and the sphere of that will is severely limited; the number of things on which he or she can have an impact is pathetically small. Existentialist literature is antideterministic in the extreme and rejects the idea that heredity and environment shape and determine human motivation and behavior.

exposition: The part or parts of a fiction that provide necessary background information. Exposition not only provides the time and place of the action but also introduces readers to the fictive world of the story, acquainting them with the ground rules of the work.

fantastic: In his study *The Fantastic* (1970), Tzvetan Todorov defines the fantastic as a *genre* that lies between the "uncanny" and the "marvelous." All three genres embody the familiar world but present an event that cannot be explained by the laws of the familiar world. Todorov says that the fantastic occupies a twilight zone between the uncanny (when the reader knows that the peculiar event is merely the result of an illusion) and the marvelous (when the reader understands that the event is supposed to take place in a realm controlled by laws unknown to humankind). The fantastic is thus essentially unsettling, provocative, even subversive.

feminist criticism: A criticism advocating equal rights for women in political, economic, social, psychological, personal, and aesthetic senses. On the thematic level, the feminist reader should identify with female characters and their concerns. The object is to provide a critique of phallocentric assumptions and an analysis of patriarchal ideologies inscribed in a literature that is male-centered and male-dominated. On the ideological level, feminist critics see gender, as well as the stereotypes that go along with it, as a cultural construct. They strive to define a particularly feminine content and to extend the *canon* so that it might include works by lesbians, feminists, and women writers in general.

flashback: A scene in a fiction that depicts an earlier event; it may be presented as a reminiscence by a character in the story or may simply be inserted into the narrative.

foreshadowing: A device to create suspense or dramatic irony in fiction by indicating through suggestion what will take place in the future.

formalist criticism: Two particularly influential formalist schools of criticism arose in the twentieth century: the Russian Formalists and the American New Critics. The Russian Formalists were concerned with the conventional devices used in literature to defamiliarize that which habit has made familiar. The New Critics believed that literary criticism is a description and evaluation of its object and that the primary concern of the critic is with the work's unity. Both schools of criticism, at their most extreme, treated literary works as artifacts or constructs divorced from their biographical and social contexts.

genre: In its most general sense, this term refers to a group of literary works defined by a common form, style, or purpose. In practice, the term is used in a wide variety of overlapping and, to a degree, contradictory senses. Tragedy and comedy are thus described as distinct genres; the novel (a form that includes both tragic and comic works) is a genre; and various subspecies of the novel, such as the *gothic* and the *picaresque*, are themselves frequently treated as distinct genres. Finally, the term "genre fiction" refers to forms of popular fiction in which the writer is bound by more or less rigid conventions. Indeed, all these diverse usages have in common an emphasis on the manner in which individual literary works are shaped by particular expectations and conventions; this is the subject of genre criticism.

genre fiction: Categories of popular fiction in which the writers are bound by more or less rigid conventions, such as in the *detective story*, the *romance*, and the *Western*. Although the term can be used in a neutral sense, it is often used dismissively.

gothic novel: A form of fiction developed in the eighteenth century that focuses on horror and the supernatural. In his preface to *The Castle of Otranto* (1765), the first gothic novel in English, Horace Walpole claimed that he was trying to combine two kinds of fiction, with events and story typical of the medieval romance and character delineation typical of the realistic novel. Other examples of the form are Matthew Gregory

Lewis's *The Monk: A Romance* (1796; also known as *Ambrosio: Or, The Monk*) and Mary Wollstonecraft Shelley's *Frankenstein: Or, The Modern Prometheus* (1818).

grotesque: According to Wolfgang Kayser (*The Grotesque in Art and Literature*, 1963), the grotesque is an embodiment in literature of the estranged world. Characterized by a breakup of the everyday world by mysterious forces, the form differs from fantasy in that the reader is not sure whether to react with humor or with horror and in that the exaggeration manifested exists in the familiar world rather than in a purely imaginative world.

Hebraic/Homeric styles: Terms coined by Erich Auerbach in *Mimesis: The Representation of Reality in Western Literature* (1953) to designate two basic fictional styles. The Hebraic style focuses only on the decisive points of narrative and leaves all else obscure, mysterious, and "fraught with background"; the Homeric style places the narrative in a definite time and place and externalizes everything in a perpetual foreground.

historical criticism: In contrast to *formalist criticism*, which treats literary works to a great extent as self-contained artifacts, historical criticism emphasizes the historical context of literature; the two approaches, however, need not be mutually exclusive. Ernst Robert Curtius's *European Literature and the Latin Middle Ages* (1940) is a prominent example of historical criticism.

historical novel: A novel that depicts past historical events, usually public in nature, and features real as well as fictional people. Sir Walter Scott's Waverley novels established the basic type, but the relationship between fiction and history in the form varies greatly depending on the practitioner.

implied author: According to Wayne Booth (*The Rhetoric of Fiction*, 1961), the novel often creates a kind of second self who tells the story—a self who is wiser, more sensitive, and more perceptive than any real person could be.

interior monologue: Defined by Édouard Dujardin as the speech of a character designed to introduce the reader directly to the character's internal life, the form differs from other kinds of monologue in that it attempts to reproduce thought before any logical organization is imposed on it. See, for example, Molly Bloom's long interior monologue at the conclusion of James Joyce's *Ulysses* (1922).

irrealism: A term often used to refer to modern or postmodern fiction that is presented self-consciously as a fiction or a fabulation rather than a mimesis of external reality. The best-known practitioners of irrealism are John Barth, Robert Coover, and Donald Barthelme.

local colorists: A loose movement of late nineteenth century American writers whose fiction emphasizes the distinctive folkways, landscapes, and dialects of various regions. Important local colorists include Bret Harte, Mark Twain, George Washington Cable, Kate Chopin, and Sarah Orne Jewett. (See *regional novel*.)

Marxist criticism: Based on the nineteenth century writings of Karl Marx and Friedrich Engels, Marxist criticism views literature as a product of ideological forces determined by the dominant class. However, many Marxists believe that literature operates according to its own autonomous standards of production and reception: It is both a product of ideology and able to determine ideology. As such, literature may overcome the dominant paradigms of its age and play a revolutionary role in society.

metafiction: This term refers to fiction that manifests a reflexive tendency, such as Vladimir Nabokov's *Pale Fire* (1962) and John Fowles's *The French Lieutenant's Woman* (1969). The emphasis is on the loosening of the work's illusion of reality to expose the reality of its illusion. Other terms used to refer to this type of fiction include "irrealism," "postmodernist fiction," "antifiction," and "surfiction."

modernism: An international movement in the arts that began in the early years of the twentieth century. Although the term is used to describe artists of widely varying persuasions, modernism in general was characterized by its international idiom, by its interest in cultures distant in space or time, by its emphasis on formal experimentation, and by its sense of dislocation and radical change.

motif: A conventional incident or situation in a fiction that may serve as the basis for the structure of the narrative itself. The Russian Formalist critic Boris Tomashevsky uses the term to refer to the smallest particle of thematic material in a work.

motivation: Although this term is usually used in reference to the convention of justifying the action of a character from his or her psychological makeup, the Russian Formalists use the term to refer to the network of devices that justify the introduction of individual *motifs* or groups of motifs in a work. For example, "compositional motivation" refers to the principle that every single property in a work contributes to its overall effect; "realistic motivation" refers to the realistic devices used to make a work plausible and lifelike.

multiculturalism: The tendency to recognize the perspectives of those traditionally excluded from the canon of Western art and literature. In order to promote multiculturalism, publishers and educators have revised textbooks and school curricula to incorporate material by and about women, members of minority groups, persons from non-Western cultures, and homosexuals.

myth: Anonymous traditional stories dealing with basic human concepts and antinomies. According to Claude Lévi-Strauss, myth is that part of language where the "formula *tradutore, tradittore* reaches its lowest truth value.... Its substance does not lie in its style, its original music, or its syntax, but in the story which it tells."

myth criticism: Northrop Frye says that in myth "we see the structural principles of literature isolated." Myth criticism is concerned with these basic principles of literature; it is not to be confused with mythological criticism, which is primarily concerned with finding mythological parallels in the surface action of the *narrative.*

narrative: Robert Scholes and Robert Kellogg, in *The Nature of Narrative* (1966), say that by "narrative" they mean literary works that include both a story and a storyteller. The term "narrative" usually implies a contrast to "enacted" fiction such as drama.

narratology: The study of the form and functioning of *narratives*; it attempts to examine what all narratives have in common and what makes individual narratives different from one another.

narrator: The *character* who recounts the *narrative*, or story. Wayne Booth describes various dramatized narrators in *The Rhetoric of Fiction* (1961): unacknowledged centers of consciousness, observers, narrator-agents, and self-conscious narrators. Booth suggests that the important elements to consider in narration are the relationships among the narrator, the author, the characters, and the reader.

naturalism: As developed by Émile Zola in the late nineteenth century, naturalism is the application of the principles of scientific *determinism* to fiction. Although it usually refers more to the choice of subject matter than to technical conventions, those conventions associated with the movement center on the author's attempt to be precise and scientifically objective in description and detail, regardless of whether the events described are sordid or shocking.

New Criticism: See *formalist criticism*.

novel: Perhaps the most difficult of all fictional forms to define because of its multiplicity of modes. Edouard, in André Gide's *Les Faux-monnayeurs* (1925; *The Counterfeiters*, 1927), says the novel is the freest and most lawless of all *genres*; he wonders if fear of that liberty is the reason the novel has so timidly clung to reality. Most critics seem to agree that the novel's primary area of concern is the social world. Ian Watt (*The Rise of the Novel*, 2001) says that the novel can be distinguished from other fictional forms by the attention it pays to individual characterization and detailed presentation of the environment. Moreover, says Watt, the novel, more than any other fictional form, is interested in the "development of its characters in the course of time."

novel of manners: The classic examples of this form might be the novels of Jane Austen, wherein the customs and conventions of a social group of a particular time and place are realistically, and often satirically, portrayed.

novella, novelle, nouvelle, novelette, novela: Although these terms often refer to the short European tale, especially the Renaissance form employed by Giovanni Boccaccio, the terms often refer to that form of fiction that is said to be longer than a short story and shorter than a novel. "Novelette" is the term usually preferred by the British, whereas "novella" is the term usually used to refer to American works in this *genre*. Henry James claimed that the main merit of the form is the "effort to do the complicated thing with a strong brevity and lucidity."

phenomenological criticism: Although best known as a European school of criticism practiced by Georges Poulet and others, this so-called criticism of consciousness is also propounded in the United States by such critics as J. Hillis Miller. The focus is less on individual works and *genres* than it is on literature as an act; the work is not seen as an object but rather as part of a strand of latent impulses in the work of a single author or an epoch.

picaresque novel: A form of fiction that centers on a central rogue figure, or picaro, who usually tells his or her own story. The plot structure is normally *episodic*, and the episodes usually focus on how the picaro lives by his or her wits. Classic examples of the mode are Henry Fielding's *The History of Tom Jones, a Foundling* (1749; commonly known as *Tom Jones*) and Mark Twain's *Adventures of Huckleberry Finn* (1884).

plot/story: "Story" refers to the full *narrative* of *character* and action, whereas "plot" generally refers to action with little reference to character. A more precise and helpful distinction is made by the Russian Formalists, who suggest that "plot" refers to the events of a narrative as they have been artfully arranged in the literary work, subject to chronological displacement, ellipses, and other devices, while "story" refers to the sum of the same events arranged in simple, causal-chronological order. Thus story is the raw material for plot. By comparing the two in a given work, the reader is encouraged to see the narrative as an artifact.

point of view: The means by which the story is presented to the reader, or, as Percy Lubbock says in *The Craft of Fiction* (1921), "the relation in which the narrator stands to the story"—a relation that Lubbock claims governs the craft of fiction. Some of the questions the critical reader should ask concerning point of view are the following: Who talks to the reader? From what position does the narrator tell the story? At what distance does he or she place the reader from the story? What kind of person is he or she? How fully is he or she characterized? How reliable is he or she? For further discussion, see Wayne Booth, *The Rhetoric of Fiction* (1961).

postcolonialism: Postcolonial literature emerged in the mid-twentieth century when colonies in Asia, Africa, and the Caribbean began gaining their independence from the European nations that had long controlled them. Postcolonial authors, such as Salman Rushdie and V. S. Naipaul, tend to focus on both the freedom and the conflict inherent in living in a postcolonial state.

postmodernism: A ubiquitous but elusive term in contemporary criticism, "postmodernism" is loosely applied to the various artistic movements that followed the era of so-called high modernism, represented by such giants as James Joyce and Pablo Picasso. In critical discussions of contemporary fiction, the term "postmodernism" is frequently applied to the works of writers such as Thomas Pynchon, John Barth, and Donald Barthelme, who exhibit a self-conscious awareness of their modernist predecessors as well as a reflexive treatment of fictional form.

protagonist: The central *character* in a fiction, the character whose fortunes most concern the reader.

psychological criticism: While much modern literary criticism reflects to some degree the impacts of Sigmund Freud, Carl Jung, Jacques Lacan, and other psychological theorists, the term "psychological criticism" suggests a strong emphasis on a causal relation between the writer's psychological state, variously interpreted, and his or her works. A notable example of psychological criticism is Norman Fruman's *Coleridge, the Damaged Archangel* (1971).

psychological novel: A form of fiction in which *character*, especially the inner lives of characters, is the primary focus. This form, which has been of primary importance at least since Henry James, characterizes much of the work of James Joyce, Virginia Woolf, and William Faulkner. For a detailed discussion, see *The Modern Psychological Novel* (1955) by Leon Edel.

realism: A literary technique in which the primary convention is to render an illusion of fidelity to external reality. Realism is often identified as the primary method of the novel form: It focuses on surface details, maintains a fidelity to the everyday experiences of middle-class society, and strives for a one-to-one relationship between the fiction and the action imitated. The realist movement in the late nineteenth century coincides with the full development of the novel form.

reception aesthetics: The best-known American practitioner of reception aesthetics is Stanley Fish. For the reception critic, meaning is an event or process; rather than being embedded in the work, it is created through particular acts of reading. The best-known European practitioner of this criticism, Wolfgang Iser, argues that indeterminacy is the basic characteristic of literary texts; the reader must "normalize" the text either by projecting his or her standards into it or by revising his or her standards to "fit" the text.

regional novel: Any novel in which the character of a given geographical region plays a decisive role. Although regional differences persist across the United States, a considerable leveling in speech and customs has taken place, so that the sharp regional distinctions evident in nineteenth century American fiction have all but disappeared. Only in the South has a strong regional tradition persisted to the present. (See *local colorists*.)

rhetorical criticism: The rhetorical critic is concerned with the literary work as a means of communicating ideas and the means by which the work affects or controls the reader. Such criticism seems best suited to didactic works such as satire.

roman à clef: A fiction wherein actual people, often celebrities of some sort, are thinly disguised.

romance: The romance usually differs from the novel form in that the focus is on symbolic events and representational characters rather than on "as-if-real" characters and events. Richard Chase says that in the romance, character is depicted as highly stylized, a function of the plot rather than as someone complexly related to society. The romancer is more likely to be concerned with dreamworlds than with the familiar world, believing that reality cannot be grasped by the traditional novel.

Romanticism: A widespread cultural movement in the late eighteenth and early nineteenth centuries, the influence of which is still felt. As a general literary tendency, Romanticism is frequently contrasted with *classicism*. Although many varieties of Romanticism are indigenous to various national literatures, the term generally suggests an assertion of the preeminence of the imagination. Other values associated with various schools of Romanticism include primitivism, an interest in folklore, a reverence for nature, and a fascination with the demoniac and the macabre.

scene: The central element of *narration*; specific actions are narrated or depicted that make the reader feel he or she is participating directly in the action.

science fiction: Fiction in which certain givens (physical laws, psychological principles, social conditions—any one or all of these) form the basis of an imaginative projection into the future or, less commonly, an extrapolation in the present or even into the past.

semiotics: The science of signs and sign systems in communication. According to Roman Jakobson, semiotics deals with the principles that underlie the structure of signs, their use in language of all kinds, and the specific nature of various sign systems.

sentimental novel: A form of fiction popular in the eighteenth century in which emotionalism and optimism are the primary characteristics. The best-known examples are Samuel Richardson's *Pamela: Or, Virtue Rewarded* (1740-1741) and Oliver Goldsmith's *The Vicar of Wakefield* (1766).

setting: The circumstances and environment, both temporal and spatial, of a *narrative*.

spatial form: An author's attempt to make the reader apprehend a work spatially in a moment of time rather than sequentially. To achieve this effect, the author breaks up the *narrative* into interspersed fragments. Beginning with James Joyce, Marcel Proust, and Djuna Barnes, the movement toward spatial form is concomitant with the *modernist* effort to supplant historical time in fiction with mythic time. For the seminal discussion of this technique, see Joseph Frank, *The Widening Gyre* (1963).

stream of consciousness: The depiction of the thought processes of a *character*, insofar as this is possible, without any mediating structures. The metaphor of consciousness as a "stream" suggests a rush of thoughts and images governed by free association rather than by strictly rational development. The term "stream of consciousness" is often used loosely as a synonym for *interior monologue*. The most celebrated example of stream of consciousness in fiction is the monologue of Molly Bloom in James Joyce's *Ulysses* (1922); other notable practitioners of the stream-of-consciousness technique include Dorothy Richardson, Virginia Woolf, and William Faulkner.

structuralism: As a movement of thought, structuralism is based on the idea of intrinsic, self-sufficient structures that do not require reference to external elements. A structure is a system of transformations that involves the interplay of laws inherent in the system itself. The study of language is the primary model for contemporary structuralism. The structuralist literary critic attempts to define structural principles that operate intertextually throughout the whole of literature as well as principles that operate in *genres* and in individual works. One of the most accessible surveys of structuralism and literature available is Jonathan Culler's *Structuralist Poetics* (1975).

summary: Those parts of a fiction that do not need to be detailed. In *Tom Jones* (1749), Henry Fielding says, "If whole years should pass without producing anything worthy of... notice... we shall hasten on to matters of consequence."

thematics: According to Northrop Frye, when a work of fiction is written or interpreted thematically, it becomes an illustrative fable. Murray Krieger defines thematics as "the study of the experiential tensions which, dramatically entangled in the literary work, become an existential reflection of that work's aesthetic complexity."

tone: The dominant mood of a work of fiction. (See *atmosphere*.)

unreliable narrator: A narrator whose account of the events of the story cannot be trusted, obliging readers to reconstruct—if possible—the true state of affairs themselves. Once an innovative technique, the use of the unreliable narrator has become commonplace among contemporary writers who wish to suggest the impossibility of a truly "reliable" account of any event. Notable examples of the unreliable narrator can be found in Ford Madox Ford's *The Good Soldier* (1915) and Vladimir Nabokov's *Lolita* (1955).

Victorian novel: Although the Victorian period extended from 1837 to 1901, the term "Victorian novel" does not include the later decades of Queen Victoria's reign. The term loosely refers to the sprawling works of novelists such as Charles Dickens and William Makepeace Thackeray—works that frequently appeared first in serial form and are characterized by a broad social canvas.

vraisemblance/verisimilitude: Tzvetan Todorov defines vraisemblance as "the mask which conceals the text's own laws, but which we are supposed to take for a relation to reality." Verisimilitude refers to a work's attempts to make the reader believe that it conforms to reality rather than to its own laws.

Western novel: Like all varieties of *genre fiction*, the Western novel—generally known simply as the Western—is defined by a relatively predictable combination of *conventions*, *motifs*, and recurring themes. These predictable elements, familiar from many Western films and television series, differentiate the Western from *historical novels* and idiosyncratic works such as Thomas Berger's *Little Big Man* (1964) that are also set in the Old West. Conversely, some novels set in the contemporary West are regarded as Westerns because they deal with modern cowboys and with the land itself in the manner characteristic of the *genre*.

Charles E. May

Guide to Online Resources

Web Sites

The following sites were visited by the editors of Salem Press in 2009. Because URLs frequently change, the accuracy of these addresses cannot be guaranteed; however, long-standing sites, such as those of colleges and universities, national organizations, and government agencies, generally maintain links when sites are moved or updated.

American Literature on the Web
http://www.nagasaki-gaigo.ac.jp/ishikawa/amlit

Among this site's features are several pages providing links to Web sites about specific genres and literary movements, southern and southwestern American literature, minority literature, literary theory, and women writers, as well as an extensive index of links to electronic text collections and archives. Users also can access information for five specific time periods: 1620-1820, 1820-1865, 1865-1914, 1914-1945, and since 1945. A range of information is available for each period, including alphabetical lists of authors that link to more specific information about each writer, time lines of historical and literary events, and links to related additional Web sites.

Books and Writers
http://www.kirjasto.sci.fi/indeksi.htm

This broad, comprehensive, and easy-to-use resource provides access to information about hundreds of authors throughout the world, extending from 70 B.C.E to the twenty-first century. Links take users from an alphabetical list of authors to pages featuring biographical material, lists of works, and recommendations for further reading about individual authors; each writer's page also includes links to related pages on the site. Although brief, the biographical essays provide solid overviews of the authors' careers, their contributions to literature, and their literary influences.

The Canadian Literature Archive
http://www.umanitoba.ca/canlit

Created and maintained by the English Department at the University of Manitoba, this site is a comprehensive collection of materials for and about Canadian writers. It includes an alphabetical listing of authors with links to additional Web-based information. Users also can retrieve electronic texts, announcements of literary events, and videocasts of author interviews and readings.

A Celebration of Women Writers
http://digital.library.upenn.edu/women

This site presents an extensive compendium of information about the contributions of women writers throughout history. The "Local Editions by Authors" and "Local Editions by Category" pages include access to electronic texts of the works of numerous writers, including Louisa May Alcott, Djuna Barnes, Grazia Deledda, Edith Wharton, and Virginia Woolf. Users can also access biographical and bibliographical information by browsing lists arranged by writers' names, countries of origin, ethnicities, and the centuries in which they lived.

Contemporary Writers
http://www.contemporarywriters.com/authors

Created by the British Council, this site offers "up-to-date profiles of some of the U.K. and Commonwealth's most important living writers (plus writers from the Republic of Ireland that we've worked with)." The available information includes biographies, bibliographies, critical reviews, news about literary prizes, and photographs. Users can search the site by author, genre, nationality, gender, publisher, book title, date of publication, and prize name and date.

Internet Public Library: Native American Authors
http://www.ipl.org/div/natam

Internet Public Library, a Web-based collection of materials, includes this index to resources about writers of Native American heritage. An alphabetical list of authors enables users to link to biographies, lists of works, electronic texts, tribal Web sites, and other online resources. The majority of the writers covered are contemporary Indian authors, but some historical authors also are featured. Users also can retrieve information by browsing lists of titles and tribes. In addition, the site contains a bibliography of print and online materials about Native American literature.

LiteraryHistory.com
http://www.literaryhistory.com

This site is an excellent source of academic, scholarly, and critical literature about eighteenth, nineteenth, and twentieth century American and English writers. It provides numerous pages about specific eras and genres, including individual pages for eighteenth, nineteenth, and twentieth century literature and for African American and postcolonial literature. These pages contain alphabetical lists of authors that link to articles, reviews, overviews, excerpts of works, teaching guides, podcast interviews, and other materials. The eighteenth century literature page also provides access to information about the eighteenth century novel.

Literary Resources on the Net
http://andromeda.rutgers.edu/~jlynch/Lit

Jack Lynch of Rutgers University maintains this extensive collection of links to Internet sites that are useful to academics, including numerous Web sites about American and English literature. This collection is a good place to begin online research about the novel, as it links to hundreds of other sites with broad ranges of literary topics. The site is organized chronically, with separate pages for information about the Middle Ages, the Renaissance, the eighteenth century, the Romantic and Victorian eras, and twentieth century British and Irish literature. It also has separate pages providing links to Web sites about American literature and to women's literature and feminism.

LitWeb
http://litweb.net

LitWeb provides biographies of more than five hundred world authors throughout history that can be accessed through an alphabetical listing. The pages about each writer contain a list of his or her works, suggestions for further reading, and illustrations. The site also offers information about past and present winners of major literary prizes.

The Modern Word: Authors of the Libyrinth
http://www.themodernword.com/authors.html

The Modern Word site, although somewhat haphazard in its organization, provides a great deal of critical information about writers. The "Authors of the Libyrinth" page is very useful, linking author names to essays about them and other resources. The section of the page headed "The Scriptorium" presents "an index of pages featuring writers who have pushed the edges of their medium, combining literary talent with a sense of experimentation to produce some remarkable works of modern literature." The site also includes sections devoted to Samuel Beckett, Umberto Eco, Gabriel García Márquez, James Joyce, Franz Kafka, and Thomas Pynchon.

Novels
http://www.nvcc.edu/home/ataormina/novels/default.htm

This overview of American and English novels was prepared by Agatha Taormina, a professor at Northern Virginia Community College. It contains three sections: "History" provides a definition of the novel genre, a discussion of its origins in eighteenth century England, and separate pages with information about genres and authors of nineteenth century, twentieth century, and postmodern novels. "Approaches" suggests how to read a novel critically for greater appreciation, and "Resources" provides a list of books about the novel.

Outline of American Literature
http://www.america.gov/publications/books/outline-of-american-literature.html

This page of the America.gov site provides access to an electronic version of the ten-chapter volume *Outline of American Literature*, a historical overview of prose and poetry from colonial times to the present published by the U.S. Department of State. The work's author is Kathryn VanSpanckeren, professor of English at the University of Tampa. The site offers links to abbreviated versions of each chapter as well as access to the entire publication in PDF format.

Voice of the Shuttle
http://vos.ucsb.edu

One of the most complete and authoritative places for online information about literature, Voice of the Shuttle is maintained by professors and students in the English Department at the University of California, Santa Barbara. The site provides thousands of links to electronic books, academic journals, association Web sites, sites created by university professors, and many, many other resources about the humanities. Its "Literature in English" page provides links to separate pages about the literature of the Anglo-Saxon era, the Middle Ages, the Renaissance and seventeenth century, the Restoration and eighteenth century, the Romantic age, the Victorian age, and modern and contemporary periods in Britain and the United States, as well as a page focused on minority literature. Another page on the site, "Literatures Other than English," offers a gateway to information about the literature of numerous countries and world regions.

Electronic Databases

Electronic databases usually do not have their own URLs. Instead, public, college, and university libraries subscribe to these databases, provide links to them on their Web sites, and make them available to library card holders or other specified patrons. Readers can visit library Web sites or ask reference librarians to check on availability.

Canadian Literary Centre

Produced by EBSCO, the Canadian Literary Centre database contains full-text content from ECW Press, a Toronto-based publisher, including the titles in the publisher's Canadian fiction studies, Canadian biography, and Canadian writers and their works series, *ECW's Biographical Guide to Canadian Novelists*, and *George Woodcock's Introduction to Canadian Fiction*. Author biographies, essays and literary criticism, and book reviews are among the database's offerings.

Literary Reference Center

EBSCO's Literary Reference Center (LRC) is a comprehensive full-text database designed primarily to help high school and undergraduate students in English and the humanities with homework and research assignments about literature. The database contains massive amounts of information from reference works, books, literary journals, and other materials, including more than 31,000 plot summaries, synopses, and overviews of literary works; almost 100,000 essays and articles of literary criticism; about 140,000 author biographies; more than 605,000 book reviews; and more than 5,200 author interviews. It also contains the entire contents of Salem Press's MagillOnLiterature Plus. Users can retrieve information by browsing a list of authors' names or titles of literary works; they can also use an advanced search engine to access information by numerous categories, including author name, gender, cultural identity, national identity, and the years in which he or she lived, or by literary title, character, locale, genre, and publication date. The Literary Reference Center also features a literary-historical time line, an encyclopedia of literature, and a glossary of literary terms.

MagillOnLiterature Plus

MagillOnLiterature Plus is a comprehensive, integrated literature database produced by Salem Press and available on the EBSCO*host* platform. The database contains the full text of essays in Salem's many literature-related reference works, including *Masterplots, Cyclopedia of World Authors, Cyclopedia of Literary Characters, Cyclopedia of Literary Places, Critical Survey of Long Fiction, Critical Survey of Short Fiction, World Philosophers and Their Works, Magill's Literary Annual,* and *Magill's Book Reviews.* Among its contents are articles on more than 35,000 literary works and more than 8,500 writers, poets, dramatists, essays, and philosophers, more than 1,000 images, and a glossary of more than 1,300 literary terms. The biographical essays include lists of authors' works and secondary bibliographies, and almost four hundred overview essays offer information about literary genres, time periods, and national literatures.

NoveList

NoveList is a readers' advisory service produced by EBSCO. The database provides access to 155,000 titles of both adult and juvenile fiction as well information about literary awards, book discussion guides, feature articles about a range of literary genres, and "recommended reads." Users can search by author name, book title, or series title or can describe the plot to retrieve the name of a book, information about the author, and book reviews; another search engine enables users to find titles similar to books they have enjoyed reading.

Rebecca Kuzins

CATEGORY INDEX

ADVENTURE NOVEL
    Baroja, Pío, 39
    Cervantes, Miguel de, 87

CHRISTIANITY
    Unamuno y Jugo, Miguel de, 175

DIDACTIC NOVEL
    Pérez Galdós, Benito, 142

EXISTENTIALISM
    Cela, Camilo José, 73
    Unamuno y Jugo, Miguel de, 175
EXPRESSIONISM
    Cela, Camilo José, 73

FANTASY
    Sender, Ramón José, 165

HISTORICAL NOVEL
    Blasco Ibáñez, Vicente, 60
    Gironella, José María, 107
    Pérez Galdós, Benito, 142
    Sender, Ramón José, 165
    Valera, Juan, 186

LATINO CULTURE
    Valera, Juan, 186
LOCAL COLOR AND REGIONALISM
    Blasco Ibáñez, Vicente, 60
    Delibes, Miguel, 98
    Valera, Juan, 186
    Valle-Inclán, Ramón María del, 203

MODERNISM
    Benet, Juan, 49
    Pérez Galdós, Benito, 142

NATURALISM
    Alas, Leopoldo, 27
    Cela, Camilo José, 73
    Pardo Bazán, Emilia, 114
    Pérez Galdós, Benito, 142
NOBEL PRIZE WINNERS
    Cela, Camilo José, 73

PHILOSOPHICAL NOVEL
    Baroja, Pío, 39
    Sender, Ramón José, 165
PICARESQUE NOVEL
    Cervantes, Miguel de, 87
POLITICAL NOVEL
    Blasco Ibáñez, Vicente, 60
    Gironella, José María, 107
    Valle-Inclán, Ramón María del, 203
PSYCHOLOGICAL NOVEL
    Blasco Ibáñez, Vicente, 60
PSYCHOLOGICAL REALISM
    Alas, Leopoldo, 27
    Pardo Bazán, Emilia, 114

REALISM
    Alas, Leopoldo, 27
    Blasco Ibáñez, Vicente, 60
    Delibes, Miguel, 98
    Gironella, José María, 107
    Pardo Bazán, Emilia, 114
    Pérez Galdós, Benito, 142
    Sender, Ramón José, 165
RELIGIOUS NOVEL
    Unamuno y Jugo, Miguel de, 175
ROMANTIC NOVEL
    Valera, Juan, 186

SATIRE AND BLACK HUMOR
    Baroja, Pío, 39
    Sender, Ramón José, 165
SOCIAL REALISM
    Pérez Galdós, Benito, 142
SYMBOLISM
    Alas, Leopoldo, 27

TRAGICOMEDY
    Pérez de Ayala, Ramón, 128
    Sender, Ramón José, 165

WOMEN AUTHORS
    Pardo Bazán, Emilia, 114

SUBJECT INDEX

Abel Sánchez (Unamuno y Jugo), 178
Adventure novels
  Pío Baroja, 44
  Miguel de Cervantes, 91
Aestheticism, 15
Alarcón, Pedro Antonio de, 10, 116
Alas, Leopoldo, 12, 27-38, 116, 187
Alemán, Mateo, 5
Allegory, 135
A.M.D.G. (Pérez de Ayala), 133
Antagonists
  Leopoldo Alas, 32
  Juan Valera, 196
Antiheroes
  Camilo José Cela, 79
  Miguel de Unamuno y Jugo, 178
Archetypes
  Ramón Pérez de Ayala, 129
  Miguel de Unamuno y Jugo, 180
Art for art's sake, 190
Asesinato del perdedor, El (Cela), 84
Atmosphere
  Juan Benet, 53
  Vicente Blasco Ibáñez, 69
  Camilo José Cela, 76
  Miguel Delibes, 103
  Ramón José Sender, 169
Aub, Max, 21

Baroja, Pío, 16, 39-48, 50, 101, 166, 168, 175, 204
Belarmino and Apolonio (Pérez de Ayala), 139
Benavente y Martínez, Jacinto, 204
Benet, Juan, 49-59
Bildungsromans, 132
Blasco Ibáñez, Vicente, 15, 42, 60-72, 116
Borges, Jorge Luis, 94, 129

Brontë, Emily, 123
Byron, Lord, 179

Cabin, The (Blasco Ibáñez), 67
Calderón de la Barca, Pedro, 198
Camus, Albert, 79
Catholic themes
  Miguel Delibes, 101
  Benito Pérez Galdós, 149
  Ramón Pérez de Ayala, 136
  Juan Valera, 197
  Ramón María del Valle-Inclán, 212
Cela, Camilo José, 19, 73-86, 101
Celestina, La (Rojas), 4
Cervantes, Miguel de, 6, 27, 61, 87-97, 145, 166, 169
Christ Versus Arizona (Cela), 84
Classicism, 189
Commander Mendoza (Valera), 195
Compassion (Pérez Galdós), 160
Cortázar, Julio, 129
Costumbrista, 10
Crónica del alba (Sender), 170
Cypresses Believe in God, The (Gironella), 109

Dante, 180
Darío, Rubén, 131, 187
Decadence, 209
Delibes, Miguel, 20, 41, 98-106
Detective novels, 23
Didactic novels, 149
Disinherited Lady, The (Pérez Galdós), 155
Don Braulio (Valera), 196
Don Quixote de la Mancha (Cervantes), 6, 91
Doña Luz (Valera), 197
Doña Perfecta (Pérez Galdós), 153

Existentialism
    Camilo José Cela, 76
    Ramón José Sender, 173
    Miguel de Unamuno y Jugo, 175
Expressionism, 76

Faber, Cecilia Böhl von, 10
Fall of the House of Limón, The (Pérez de Ayala), 135
Family of Pascual Duarte, The (Cela), 76
Fantastic
    Benito Pérez Galdós, 145
    Ramón José Sender, 169
Faulkner, William, 50
Feminist fiction, 12, 24
Five Hours with Mario (Delibes), 102
Flashbacks
    Leopoldo Alas, 33
    Miguel Delibes, 101
    Ramón José Sender, 172
Foreshadowing
    Vicente Blasco Ibáñez, 68
    Benito Pérez Galdós, 157
    Juan Valera, 191
Fortunata and Jacinta (Pérez Galdós), 158
Four Horsemen of the Apocalypse, The (Blasco Ibáñez), 71
Fox's Paw, The (Pérez de Ayala), 133
France, Anatole, 197

Gasset, José Ortega y, 42, 131, 175, 204
Gay and lesbian novels, 24
Generation of '36, 108
Generation of '50, 51
Generation of '98, 15, 42, 128, 204
Gironella, José María, 20, 41, 107-113
Goncourt, Edmond de, 117
Goytisolo, Juan, 19

Grotesque
    Leopoldo Alas, 30
    Ramón Pérez de Ayala, 137
    Ramón José Sender, 168
    Ramón María del Valle-Inclán, 208
Grotesque novels, 18
Guzmán de Alfarache (Alemán, Mateo), 5

Hedge, The (Delibes), 103
Hemingway, Ernest, 41
His Only Son (Alas), 34
Historical novels, 3
    Vicente Blasco Ibáñez, 64
    José María Gironella, 108
    Ramón José Sender, 166
    Juan Valera, 189
Hive, The (Cela), 79
Honeymoon, Bittermoon (Pérez de Ayala), 136
Howells, William Dean, 61
Huxley, Aldous, 103
Illusions of Doctor Faustino, The (Valera), 12

Impressionism
    Emilia Pardo Bazán, 119
    Benito Pérez Galdós, 150
Interior monologues, 21
    Vicente Blasco Ibáñez, 67
    Miguel Delibes, 103
    Emilia Pardo Bazán, 121
    Benito Pérez Galdós, 151
Ionesco, Eugène, 103

Juanita la larga (Valera), 198

Kafka, Franz, 103
Kierkegaard, Søren, 175

Subject Index

Laforet, Carmen, 22
Las ilusiones del doctor Faustino (Valera), 193
Lazarillo de Tormes (1554), 4
Local color
    Pío Baroja, 43
    Benito Pérez Galdós, 143
    Juan Valera, 193
Lope de Vega y Carpio, 3, 87, 187
Lowell, James Russell, 189

Machado, Antonio, 131, 204
Madre naturaleza, La (Pardo Bazán), 124
Manuscript of Ashes, A (Muñoz Molina), 24
Mariquita y Antonio (Valera), 191
Marsé, Juan, 22
Martín Gaite, Carmen, 22
Matute, Ana María, 22
Maupassant, Guy de, 116
Mayflower, The (Blasco Ibáñez), 65
Mazurka for Two Dead Men (Cela), 84
Medio, Dolores, 22
Meditation, A (Benet), 54
Mendoza, Eduardo, 23
Midsummer Madness (Pardo Bazán), 125
Mist (Unamuno y Jugo), 178
Modernismo, 15
Moix, Terenci, 23
Molina, Tirso de, 198
Montalbán, Manuel Vázquez, 23
Montero, Rosa, 23
Motifs
    Juan Benet, 51
    Camilo José Cela, 80
    Miguel Delibes, 101
    Ramón Pérez de Ayala, 129
    Miguel de Unamuno y Jugo, 178
Motivation, 56
Mr. Witt Among the Rebels (Sender), 170
Mrs. Caldwell Speaks to Her Son (Cela), 82
Muñoz Molina, Antonio, 23

Nabokov, Vladimir, 94
Naturalism, 12
    Leopoldo Alas, 29
    Vicente Blasco Ibáñez, 65
    Camilo José Cela, 76
    Emilia Pardo Bazán, 115
    Benito Pérez Galdós, 150
    Juan Valera, 190
Neorealism, 21

Oficio de tinieblas, 5 (Cela), 83
One Million Dead (Gironella), 111
Ortiz, Lourdes, 23

Palacio Valdés, Armando, 12
Paradox, King (Baroja), 45
Pardo Bazán, Emilia, 12, 27, 114-127, 147, 187
Pascal, Blaise, 180
Passos, John Dos, 41, 79
Path, The (Delibes), 101
Peace After War (Gironella), 112
Pepita Ximenez (Valera), 192
Pérez de Ayala, Ramón, 15, 128-141
Pérez Galdós, Benito, 11, 13, 27, 64, 118, 124, 142-164, 166, 187
Philosophical novels
    Pío Baroja, 45
    Ramón José Sender, 168
Picaresque novel, 4
    Pío Baroja, 43
    Camilo José Cela, 74
    Ramón José Sender, 168
Pleasant Memoirs of the Marquis de Bradomín, The (Valle-Inclán), 209
Point of view
    Leopoldo Alas, 29
    Vicente Blasco Ibáñez, 70
    Miguel Delibes, 101
    José María Gironella, 111

Emilia Pardo Bazán, 122
Ramón Pérez de Ayala, 140
Benito Pérez Galdós, 151
Juan Valera, 186
Political novels
   Vicente Blasco Ibáñez, 67
   José María Gironella, 109
   Ramón María del Valle-Inclán, 210
Pro Patria (Sender), 169
Prometheus (Pérez de Ayala), 135
Proust, Marcel, 55
Psychological novel
   Vicente Blasco Ibáñez, 64
   Gabriel Miró, 19

Quimera, La (Pardo Bazán), 125

Realism
   Leopoldo Alas, 27
   Vicente Blasco Ibáñez, 64
   Miguel Delibes, 99
   Emilia Pardo Bazán, 116
   Benito Pérez Galdós, 144
   Ramón José Sender, 168
   Juan Valera, 191
Reeds and Mud (Blasco Ibáñez), 69
Regenta, La (Alas), 30
Regional novel, 11
   Leopoldo Alas, 30
   Juan Valera, 191
Remarque, Erich Maria, 169
Requiem for a Spanish Peasant (Sender), 172
Restlessness of Shanti Andía (Baroja), 46
Return to Región (Benet), 52
Rodriguez de Montalvo, Garci, 2
Rojas, Fernando de, 4
Romance novels, 2
Romanticism, 9
   Leopoldo Alas, 29
   Emilia Pardo Bazán, 115

Ruedo ibérico, El (Valle-Inclán), 213
Ruiz, José Martínez, 15

Saint Manuel Bueno, Martyr (Unamuno y Jugo), 180
Same Sea as Every Summer, The (Tusquets), 24
San Camilo, 1936 (Cela), 82
San Pedro, Diego de, 2
Satire, 7
   Pío Baroja, 45
   Ramón José Sender, 168
Sender, Ramón José, 21, 104, 165-175
Sentimental novel, 2
Serna, Concha Espina de la, 15
Social realism, 4, 158
Son of the Bondwoman, The (Pardo Bazán), 120
Spanish long fiction, 1-26
Sphere, The (Sender), 171
Stream of consciousness
   Juan Benet, 54
   Benito Pérez Galdós, 153
Sue, Eugène, 10
Sunday Sunlight (Pérez de Ayala), 135
Surrealism, 82
Symbolism, 33

Thesis novel, 11, 149
Tiger Juan (Pérez de Ayala), 137
Tinieblas en las cumbres (Pérez de Ayala), 132
Toledo, Alfonso Martínez de, 2
Tolstoy, Leo, 30, 116
Tragicomedy, 168
Tree of Knowledge, The (Baroja), 45
Tribuna, La (Pardo Bazán), 124
Troteras y danzaderas (Pérez de Ayala), 134
Tusquets, Esther, 23
Tyrant, The (Valle-Inclán), 210

Subject Index

Unamuno y Jugo, Miguel de, 15, 42, 67, 126, 129, 131, 152, 175-185, 198, 204
Unreliable narrator, 160

Valera, Juan, 12, 27, 186-202
Valle-Inclán, Ramón María del, 16, 36, 42, 121, 131, 168, 203-216
Vergil, 198
Verisimilitude
    Leopoldo Alas, 32
    Miguel Delibes, 102

José María Gironella, 111
Benito Pérez Galdós, 143
Viaje de invierno, Un (Benet), 56

War novels, 21, 64
Wars of Our Ancestors, The (Delibes), 104
Whittier, John Greenleaf, 189
Williams, Tennessee, 40
Zalacaín el aventurero (Baroja), 45
Zola, Émile, 116, 145